The Wallace Collection
for
Casual Reading

FROM
MANY LANDS

Other Books by Louis Adamic

FROM MANY LANDS

By
LOUIS ADAMIC

HARPER & BROTHERS *Publishers*
New York and London

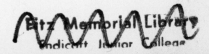

This publication was made possible by funds granted by Carnegie Corporation of New York. That Corporation is not, however, the author, owner, publisher, or proprietor of this publication, and is not to be understood as approving by virtue of its grant any of the statements made or views expressed therein.

Contents

FROM
MANY LANDS

From six continents, seven seas, and several archipelagos
From points of land moved to wind and water
Out of where they used to be to where they are,
The people of the earth marched and travelled
To gather on a great plain.

—CARL SANDBURG, in *The People Yes*

OFFICIAL UNITED STATES STATISTICS OF IMMIGRANTS ADMITTED FROM ALL COUNTRIES—BY FISCAL YEARS

Year	Number	Year	Number	Year	Number
1820..........	8,385	1861..........	91,918	1902..........	648,743
1821..........	9,127	1862..........	91,985	1903..........	857,046
1822..........	6,911	1863..........	176,282	1904..........	812,870
1823..........	6,354	1864..........	193,418	1905..........	1,026,499
1824..........	7,912	1865..........	248,120	1906..........	1,100,735
1825..........	10,199	1866..........	318,568	1907..........	1,285,349
1826..........	10,837	1867..........	315,722	1908..........	782,870
1827..........	18,875	1868..........	138,840	1909..........	751,786
1828..........	27,382	1869..........	352,768	1910..........	1,041,570
1829..........	22,520	1870..........	387,203	1911..........	878,587
1830..........	23,322	1871..........	321,350	1912..........	838,172
1831..........	22,633	1872..........	404,806	1913..........	1,197,892
1832..........	60,482	1873..........	459,803	1914..........	1,218,480
1833..........	58,640	1874..........	313,339	1915..........	326,700
1834..........	65,365	1875..........	227,498	1916..........	298,826
1835..........	45,374	1876..........	169,986	1917..........	295,403
1836..........	76,242	1877..........	141,857	1918..........	110,618
1837..........	79,340	1878..........	138,469	1919..........	141,132
1838..........	38,914	1879..........	177,826	1920..........	430,001
1839..........	68,069	1880..........	457,257	1921..........	805,228
1840..........	84,066	1881..........	669,431	1922..........	309,556
1841..........	80,289	1882..........	788,992	1923..........	522,919
1842..........	104,565	1883..........	603,322	1924..........	706,896
1843..........	52,496	1884..........	518,592	1925..........	294,314
1844..........	78,615	1885..........	395,346	1926..........	304,488
1845..........	114,371	1886..........	334,203	1927..........	335,175
1846..........	154,416	1887..........	490,109	1928..........	307,255
1847..........	234,968	1888..........	446,889	1929..........	279,678
1848..........	226,527	1889..........	444,427	1930..........	241,700
1849..........	297,024	1890..........	455,302	1931..........	97,139
1850..........	369,980	1891.	560,319	1932..........	35,576
1851..........	379,466	1892..........	579,663	1933..........	23,068
1852..........	371,603	1893..........	439,730	1934..........	29,470
1853..........	368,645	1894..........	285,631	1935..........	34,956
1854..........	427,833	1895..........	258,536	1936..........	36,329
1855..........	200,877	1896..........	343,267	1937..........	50,244
1856..........	200,436	1897..........	230,832	1938..........	67,895
1857..........	251,306	1898..........	229,299	1939..........	82,998
1858..........	123,126	1899..........	311,715	Tot. 1820–1939.	38,219,687
1859..........	121,282	1900..........	448,572		
1860..........	153,640	1901..........	487,918		

IMMIGRANTS BY DECADES OR PERIODS

Period	Number	Period	Number	Period	Number
1820–1830.......	151,824	1861–1870.......	2,314,824	1901–1910......	8,795,386
1831–1840.......	599,125	1871–1880.......	2,812,191	1911–1920......	5,735,811
1841–1850.......	1,713,251	1881–1890.......	5,246,613	1921–1930......	4,107,209
1851–1860.......	2,598,214	1891–1900.......	3,687,564	1931–1939......	457,675

Photo by Lewis W. Hine

ELLIS ISLAND MADONNA

AMERICA BOUND

1908: A GERMAN IMMIGRANT LIFTED A LITTLE FRENCH GIRL
TO HELP HER SEE THE STATUE OF LIBERTY

1,285,349 CAME IN 1907

ON THE BARGE LEAVING ELLIS ISLAND

FROM ALBANIA

FROM POLAND

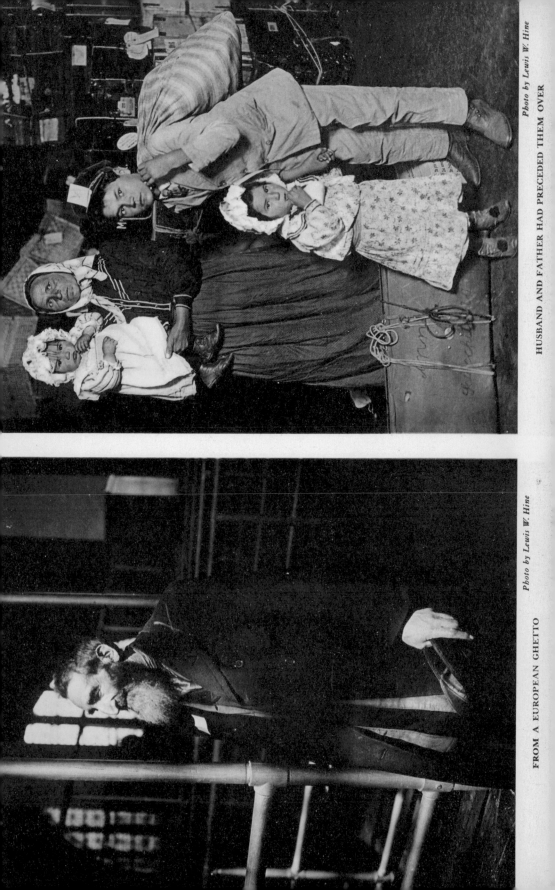

Photo by Lewis W. Hine

HUSBAND AND FATHER HAD PRECEDED THEM OVER

Photo by Lewis W. Hine

FROM A EUROPEAN GHETTO

FROM THE BALKANS

Photo by Lewis W. Hine

FROM ITALY

Photo by Lewis W. Hine

GUESTS OF UNCLE SAM AT ELLIS ISLAND *Brown Brothers*

JAPANESE PICTURE BRIDES ARRIVING AT SAN FRANCISCO

ELLIS ISLAND

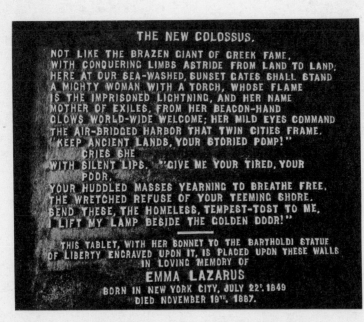

INSCRIPTION ON THE STATUE OF LIBERTY

To

DeWITT ("PASHA") and ALICE STETTEN

Dear Alice & Pasha:

Twice within the memory of men now living dreams have had a force strong enough to reshape the world. At this moment it is the dream of personal power on the part of "men of destiny" that is dominant, that tumbles the Old World and its culture into ruin and sends men scurrying in fear before it. This dream is a nightmare.

Only yesterday it was another dream, a dream which set in motion the greatest migration in history. Then men did not scurry in fear; they were led by hope. The broad Atlantic became a common highway to the Land of Promise, where people were needed and wanted. And they came from many lands, a little lost, a little frightened, but eager-eyed, possessed of high belief, the belief in the possibility of function, of self-realization, of creativeness, of growth, of human worth.

But somewhere in the roar of our industrialism, somewhere in the tension of our commercialism, that dream was all but lost, or confused well-nigh beyond recognition. While at first the rich soil of the new continent and the wealth beneath it were magic and yielded us a flashy surface growth and an oversupply of material power, we have never yet flowered all-inclusively as a country and a culture. To a large degree we are a rootless, bewildered, uncertain people. Life on a mere economic plane, we have come to realize, has proved as impermanent, shallow, and sterile as the lands of the Dust Bowl, and we fume and blow fruitlessly in the winds of Depression. We have no deep tap roots in a cultural past to give us continuity, stability.

Now here we are, in this fateful year of 1940, still a groping people, splashed by the backwash of events in the Old World, our thoughts and actions touched by hysteria; the strands of our complicated ethnic past not yet interlaced into anything that gives pattern and texture to our life as individuals and as a people. Here and there the stuff in the "Melting Pot" has melted the pot. We eye one another uneasily. We are on the defensive against ourselves. Here is a danger of our own—perhaps unavoidable—making.

In the lands whence we come or stem civilization crashes into ruin, and, watching from our ringside seats, we are appalled. But to be appalled is no answer to anything. Within our American borders are tens of millions of people who carry within them, whether they know it or not, many of the things we bemoan losing—many of the things that were lost in Europe long before the Second World War began—began, in part, because they were lost in Europe.

We need not lose them. They were brought here by the waves of our immigration. They are still here. We need to cease eyeing one another uneasily and take a positive approach to meeting on common ground. We need to take stock of our resources, embark upon self-discovery, self-appraisal and *self-criticism*, and come into our rich and varied cultural heritage of democracy and the arts, of courageous and co-operative living.

Awareness is the first step in making these firmly our own. We shall need them. Before us is the necessity of a tremendous effort. If we do not exert ourselves now, the old dream that brought us here is apt to be swallowed by the furious nightmare of the Old World.

Is it too late to recapture the magic of that dream? Many people of the second and third and later generations, to whom America is a platitude, have never glimpsed its power. They are the majority of the youth of today. What if we could revive it, lift to bewildered and cynical eyes the vision of new frontiers, rich in culture and spirit, wide and deep as the best in man—an America with a sweep to which a continent's breadth is narrow—a democracy not only of political inheritance but of the heart and the handclasp?

You and I and some of our friends have talked of this for a number of years, especially since 1938, when I first began the task of which this book is one of the early tangible results. We thought then, in '38 and '39, it was not too late. You were always interested in this job of mine, and more helpful with friendliness and encouragement than you are aware. So I want *From Many Lands* to be your book.

My purpose, as you know, is to begin exploring our American cultural past and to urge the cultivation of its many common fields, not nostalgically, or historically or academically, but imaginatively and creatively, with eyes to the future, until as a people we find and dare to sink our roots into our common American subsoil, rich, sun-warmed and well watered, from which we still may grow and flower. The failure of America to harness the dreams and motives of its past to the processes of its life is one of the greatest wastes of human resources this age has known. For there was power there, power to make miracles commonplace. Into no other country, ever, was so much of the best of human yearning poured.

It is still not too late. On the contrary, this is our moment. Now we can do things. This period is in a way a testing time for us. An opportunity. Now, in crisis and tension, the situation and its problems in which we are interested will be clearer than ever before. Our national weaknesses will become obvious and we will want to remove them. Our awareness will be intensified, our emotional quality heightened. As a people, we will be eager for orientation—for integration and unity under the sway of an affirmative concept of liberty.

We will realize that democracy even as we have it in the United States is far,

far from what it should and could be; that the evil that seems to have engulfed Europe is not so much the creation of those who believe in lies and slavery as of those who believing in truth and liberty do not practice their beliefs, either not at all or with insufficient consistency, intelligence, passion and energy. We—many of us—will want to correct this fault in ourselves and others, and become geared to the real motives and propulsions of our country—the same motives and propulsions, essentially, that were behind the successive waves of our immigration.

Here in America, if anywhere, man can achieve an all-dimensional quality: strong, rich and secure in his appreciations, sane in his values, intelligent in his knowledge, firm in his morality, just and generous in his freedom, cool and deliberate in combat with the enemies of his ideals and principles, and great in the enduring hunger and the epic reach of his spirit.

These are not the exact words of our talks during the past few years, but they are their substance, which I wanted to put into this book. If we are right, and I believe we are, America is just beginning.

Yours,

LOUIS

Milford, New Jersey
August 1, 1940

THE MAN
IN A QUANDARY

It should be our pride to exhibit an example of one nation, at least, destitute of national antipathies, and exercising, not merely the overt acts of hospitality, but those more rare and noble courtesies which spring from liberality of opinion.

What have we to do with national prejudices? They are the inveterate diseases of old countries, contracted in rude and ignorant ages, when nations knew but little of each other, and looked beyond their own boundaries with distrust and hostility. We, on the contrary, have sprung into national existence in an enlightened and philosophical age, when the different parts of the habitable world, and the various branches of the human family, have been indefatigably studied and made known to each other; and we forego the advantages of our birth if we do not shake off the national prejudices as we would the local superstitions of the old world.

WASHINGTON IRVING, in *Sketch Book*

Our debt to the foreign born and their sons and grandsons will never be paid by any patronizing kind of mere sufferance. Why should a man pat himself on the back simply because he says, "I have nothing against the Germans, or the Irish, or the Italians"? Why should he have anything against any of them? What have they done to him? The point is, "What has he got for them?"

If we would take the time to understand the various peoples of the world we would come to realize that every nation has made great contributions to the sum of truth and beauty and happiness. The America which we know and for which we are prepared to live and die simply would not exist if it were not for the immigrant. The roads beneath our feet, the tower over head are part of their handiwork. You cannot build a city of brick and mortar and lime. It requires the sweat and the soul and the dream of a multitude.

The aspirations of the men and women from the far corners of the earth have given the breath of life to America. Of course, we should have nothing against them. But let us go much further. Let us be alert to realize that whoever raises the knife of prejudice against any group whatsoever stabs with his dagger the flesh and honor and, indeed, the heart of America.

HEYWOOD BROUN, in *The New York World Telegram*

Doctor
Eliot Steinberger

IN THE spring of 1938 a bad case of poison ivy—contracted in the course
of an overambitious campaign to liquidate the objectionable shrub along
the roadside and fields' edges of the little farm I had acquired in the Delaware
Valley—compelled me to seek the services of a dermatologist. Desperate for
relief, I asked my friend Dr. DeWitt Stetten, in New York, to send me to a
good one who could see me immediately . . . and so I found myself in the
office of Dr. Eliot Steinberger, who regarded my affliction as the least alarming
of all matters. Not appearing to hurry, he disposed of me in five or six minutes,
suggesting I return in a week, when I saw him as briefly as on the first occasion.

Doctor Steinberger was then forty-three, but seemed younger in spite of his
baldness; a lean man of medium height, with good posture and easy movements. Although far from handsome in the more conventional sense, he impressed one as being very attractive. His white smock and calm, matter-of-
fact manner had an immediate cooling effect upon the inflamed surface of
my body, and something about his mien suggested he was immensely competent not only in his profession but in nearly anything he might essay. His
personality, though finely restrained, was independent, vivid, open, capable
of varied expression. But there was a subtlety in its independence and openness,
as there is in strong, clear colors. Between the rather prominent ears, his
clean-shaven, small face, with its lively brown eyes, held firmly a delicate
balance between sardonic amusement and an uncertain, palpitating sadness,
apt to merge at any moment with amusement or turn into near-despair.

The Stettens were close personal friends of Eliot Steinberger and his wife,
Peggy, but their replies to my questions about him were only meagerly in-
formative. He was "very interesting . . . one of the Steinbergers"—implying
I ought to know who the Steinbergers were; I did not, although I had heard
and seen the name here and there. In a remarkably short time, I was told,
he had developed into a leader in his field of medicine. Two or three of his
books and many of his papers on skin diseases in the American and European
medical journals were distinct contributions, and had helped to win him international recognition. The influence of Hitler's race ideas on contemporary
thought caused my informants to add that Mrs. Steinberger was Gentile; and
Alice Stetten said both Peggy and Eliot were "simply tops."

During the next two and a half years I met the Steinbergers socially, mostly
at the Stettens'. Tall, slim, good-looking, some years younger than her husband, Peggy Steinberger was, like her husband, direct, unpretentious, a good

3

talker, always pleasant company; but also very different from him. His easy manner, quick intelligence and humor, great fund of information, objectivity, deep and continual concern over developments in America and Europe, and far-ranging sensitiveness appeared to find full release and scope among congenial friends in the sitting-room and at the dinner table.

Eliot Steinberger continued to interest me, as a man and successful physician, and as a figure in the American maze; but also because I was trying to dig into the Jewish Question, so called, which, largely as a backwash of events in Europe, had lifted sharply to the surface in the United States during the late 1930's. Like many Jews, he did not "look Jewish"; indeed, his physiognomy could have been attributed to any of a dozen or more elements included in the American population. He was not Jewish in religion; and I discovered that I was familiar with items of Jewish history and lore he did not know, and that he was a Jew—intensely, self-consciously, with a peculiar interlacement of pride and discomfort—for the same reasons most other Jews I knew were Jews.

One evening, curious what he would say, I asked him, "Why are you a Jew?"

He looked at me quizzically for a moment without replying.

"I mean: what makes you a Jew?"

"Well," he smiled, "I know I am a Jew, I just am; and—to put it awkwardly—I know that, because I just am and because, therefore, in one way or another, nearly every non-Jew draws a superficially or deeply cut line between himself and me, which underscores the fact that I am a Jew." He told me that when he entered a room in which there were Gentiles he knew with a basic, inevitable awareness that everybody there thought or soon would think of him as a Jew, and that—somehow—was important.

He and I had occasional discussions about this, and related questions. At such times, listening, he seemed to be standing on his toes even when he sat in a comfortable divan. I told him that, although by origin I was a Slovenian and my parents had made attempts to raise me as a Catholic, when I entered a room I did not care if anyone present thought of me as a man whose original nationality was Slovenian or as a Catholic; or, rather, that I did not think of myself as this or that, or of what the other fellow was thinking of me in terms of national origin or religion.

"You're not a Jew!" said Eliot Steinberger with an uncertain smile.

II

Then, after dinner at the Stettens' one evening, the whole company (there were about a half-dozen of us) suddenly turned attentive to Eliot Steinberger, who—on an impulse he could not explain later—began to talk about his father, the rest of his family, and himself. Perhaps the impulse had something to do with his being a Jew in the late 1930's, and was linked to the widespread contemporary tendency of many Americans, especially those of recent-immigrant strains, to examine their backgrounds. Puzzled at himself for having started the narration, and a little self-conscious, he tried to stop or cut it short at several points, but our urging—almost to the point of insistence—that he continue held him to the story for several hours.

At first the frankness with which he spoke about his family and himself was a bit startling; by-and-by, however, as I listened to him, it began to appear perfectly natural. The calm, objective recounting simply documented his being the sort of individual he was.

That evening I came to like him very much. The expression of his face fascinated me. It was like a sensitive instrument throbbing to a deep urgency over and above the humor, grace, and factual totality of his words. It summed him up. Also, to slip into a seeming contradiction of terms, it was a neat diagram of a deep incongruity in the man, of which I became more and more clearly aware; of a quandary, which—personal, but also more than personal; Jewish, but also more than Jewish—underlay his life.

Later I went a few times to the Steinbergers' apartment, the living-room of which struck me as a setting peculiarly fitting for the lovely white-marble piece of Rodin sculpture, *The Convalescent Girl,* placed on a pedestal in a carefully lighted corner . . . and I gradually learned the whole Steinberger* saga, which Eliot had barely sketched at the Stettens'.

* Nearly all the personal and some of the place names, as well as a number of facts, incidents and situations in this essentially and otherwise factually true narrative are disguised in order to prevent widespread or popular identification of "Doctor Steinberger," and at his request. The ethics of the medical profession frowns on publicizing its members.

The names in a few other narratives in this book are disguised, for other reasons. All are true, dealing with actual people.

The Family
and the Company

THE Steinbergers are a numerous and impressive family in the United States. Their European background can be traced to the early seventeenth century in the Bavarian Palatinate. The name derives from the town of Steinberg, where the clan apparently gained its initial foothold in Germany. In the eighteenth century the Steinbergers were prominent in many towns in Baden; in the middle nineteenth century they started to emigrate to America, and in the last eighty or ninety years produced interesting and outstanding individuals in New York, Philadelphia, Cincinnati, Chicago, and elsewhere. Even a partial list of them would require pages; they range from a scholarly and pious character in Philadelphia in the 1850's to one of the most important contemporary publishers. The family is divided into a half-dozen or so branches which had their origin with the early emigrants.

Of the latter probably the most noteworthy was Eliot Steinberger's father, Heinrich (or Henry) Steinberger. A son of a small merchant in a little town near Karlsruhe, he was born in 1843. His education in the old country was the equivalent of two years in high school. While not lacking in charm and other compensations, life in Baden was even then set and channelized and marked by special restrictions for the Jews; so at twenty, in 1863, Henry—who, as he soon amply demonstrated, had within him the makings of an empire builder—left for America.

He immediately found employment in a kosher butcher shop located near the present site of the Woolworth Building in New York, owned by Isaac Silbermann, also an emigrant from Germany and then the leading Jewish butcher in Manhattan. Ambitious, capable, and very energetic, the young man performed three jobs: slaughtering, selling, and delivering. He worked sixteen hours a day, receiving at first two dollars a week, out of which he saved seventy-five cents. Every third day he bought a foot-and-a-half-long loaf of bread and marked it off into three parts. Possessing a powerful will which he enjoyed testing, he never ate more than the day's portion of the loaf. He bought no other food, but swallowed an occasional scrap of cured beef or sausage in the shop which would otherwise have been thrown away. Eventually his pay advanced to four dollars, and he put two dollars and a quarter in the bank.

Toward the end of the sixties, impressed by the young man's ability, stamina, and business imagination, Isaac Silbermann made him a partner and called the firm Silbermann and Steinberger Company; whereupon, as general manager,

Henry so developed the business that in a few years they were slaughtering thirty, forty, fifty head of cattle a day—practically big business in the early and middle seventies. The S. & S. meats, now no longer solely kosher, became favorably known not only in Manhattan but beyond both the rivers flowing by it, and before long in Philadelphia and even in Washington, Baltimore and Boston.

A go-getter in the strongest, most exciting American sense of that period, and adhering strictly to good business principles and practices, with emphasis on honesty and quality, Henry Steinberger—now in his early thirties—began to perceive vast potentialities in the butcher business. His Bavarian background with its devotion to *Gruendlichkeit*, or thoroughness, helped him to see that slaughtering as practiced in the United States was an enormously wasteful process, and that its future was in the advantageous handling and utilizing of by-products, particularly the fats, which had been almost ignored even by such shrewd old-timers in the business as Isaac Silbermann. With this realization, Henry Steinberger set about making his ideas tangible, and took the lead in developing and installing the new machinery and methods which led to the eventually world-famous packed products, including oleo-margarine. Many of them were quickly and profitably copied by other packers, and the butcher trade became the packing industry. Five years after he became a partner, the S. & S. was doing an international business. Its new stockyard and slaughter-house was near the junction of First Avenue and Forty-fifth Street.

II

In the mid-seventies refrigeration was in its infancy, but Henry Steinberger already seemed to envision the time when the cheap Western beef would be brought to Eastern markets in pieces neatly stacked or hung in sanitary ice-boxes on wheels and rails rather than in livestock cars. The latter method of transportation was expensive, the low freight rates notwithstanding, because it involved shipping valueless pounds (viscera, etc.), loss of weight while the animals were enroute, feeding them, and the stockman's wages.

Early in his career he made his contacts in Chicago and Kansas City. By 1890, when he was forty-seven, with business continually expanding, he foresaw that the S. & S. must extend its organization or risk going under, either *via* sudden bankruptcy or slow degeneration. There was no standing still. Petty business enterprises of any kind had no strong future in this country. In back of his mind was the epic thought of becoming the greatest butcher in the world, supplying meats and fats to great sections of the human race. So, in 1892, he acquired the Mid-Western Packing Company, which had a small plant in Kansas City, a few distributing branches in the East, and an inadequate refrigerator-car line called the Arctic Transportation Company. He quickly enlarged and thoroughly modernized the slaughtering facilities, and took over direction of improving refrigeration, both at the plants and especially in freight cars. The S. & S. continued in the kosher business, which increased by leaps and bounds with the large influx of Jewish immigration beginning in the nineties; however, the non-kosher business grew so rapidly that the kosher was soon a trifle alongside the total. Branch houses were established the country over, and the export business took a sharp upswing. The S. & S. built an immense plant in Chicago, which caused internal upsets in Swift and Armour; and the Steinberger firm—a veritable empire by 1900—became one of the three most important packing outfits in the world. New plants were started also in New York, Oklahoma City, Los Angeles, and Sioux Falls, and distributing agencies all over the East and in Europe.

Henry Steinberger was president and actual directing head of the S. & S. itself, and also president of the Arctic Transportation Company, the West-East Live-Stock Transport Company, and a half-dozen other large enterprises. He was financially interested in several steamship companies which had installed refrigeration systems in their vessels on his urging. In the late 1900's and early 1910's, soon after it became known as Steinberger and Sons, the company grossed more than $100,000,000 annually.

III

At the apex of his amazing career—or, say, between 1895 (the year Eliot was born) and 1912, when he was in his fifties and sixties—Henry Steinberger was a heavy-set man of medium height. He had a ponderous head and a round, fleshy face, rather dull-seeming at times, but capable of a diversity of expression, from deep unhappiness to high jollity. He became bald in his twenties and wore a wig which was always very obviously a wig.

He was a man of simple tastes, with no even faintly extravagant personal requirements. The stench of the stockyards was his favorite atmosphere. His general offices in New York were practically in the slaughterhouse, within sound of dying cattle and hogs.

Henry Steinberger had no social ambitions, and regarded with disfavor those immigrant and second-generation Jews who, upon acquiring wealth, turned into what he called "climbers." He had no use for people of pretensions of any sort, Jewish or Gentile.

He spoke simple English with an accent, and copies of his dictated correspondence testify to his imperfect command of the language. He was a citizen of the United States, with a passionate regard for the country of his adoption. Speaking from inner conviction, he often referred to it as "the best place under the sun," but was not reticent about voicing his disapproval of those phases of American life which went against his grain—notably wastefulness. He frequently declared there was little basis for the American boast of efficiency. It was mostly an illusion, a matter of the fact that Americans had, or thought they had, nearly limitless resources to "play with." Politically, he was an indifferent Republican, with a blunt contempt for politicians as a class.

His original nationality, he held, was German; and his picture and biography appear in an awkward (now rare) volume printed in New York in 1908 and entitled *A History of German Immigration in the United States and Successful German Americans and Their Descendants.* At infrequent moments of relaxation he liked to read Goethe and Schiller in the original, and often broke into German speech, especially to quote lines of wisdom from his favorite authors.

Of course he was also a Jew; not a very religious but a very conscious one who made liberal donations to Jewish charities. He was the financial mainstay of a large hospital in New York and of a number of other institutions. Twice widowed, he married three times, each time a girl of German-Jewish stock. Friday evenings candles were lit in his home. On Saturdays he refrained from smoking; this, not only because he was a Jew who wanted to observe the Sabbath, but to test and exercise his will.

The acquisition and accumulation of money, apparently, was not the chief motivating force in Henry Steinberger's life. He derived his keenest thrill out of creating and running a vast concern. It satisfied his ambition, and served as a release of the powerful force that churned within him. It was "something," he thought, to supply meat to a good part of the world. A responsibility. Money was important, to be sure, but mostly as an element, a necessary means, in his tremendous function. In the late 1900's and early 1910's, he was worth tens of millions of dollars, perhaps close to a hundred million, but he never knew, nor cared, just how much. He never thought of his money as intimately his own. All of it was always tied up with the concern, a stormy, ultra-dynamic organism, uncertainly geared to the wild process of the country's economic and industrial life, the soul of which was cutthroat competition. Business was war.

Scorning the clock, he worked fourteen to eighteen hours a day, and harder than anyone in his employ. But of his immediate assistants he demanded they work hard and long, too, and give themselves totally to their jobs. He was regarded a taskmaster, a "slave driver," who sometimes gave the impression of manipulating his executive and minor chiefs as though they were push buttons on the control board of his great machine, the S. & S.

At the peak of his career he employed between ten and fifteen thousand men. Occasionally he brooded over the labor question; and on the whole he treated his workers a trifle, but not much, better than did the other big packers, who provoked Upton Sinclair to write *The Jungle*. By and large, labor, too, was only an element, a necessary means, in his enterprise. He was too far above the workers in the yards and slaughterhouse, and there were too many of them, to feel about them continually as people. He tended to lump them in a mass when away from them, although when he went on his tours through the plants he knew and recognized them as individuals. But he felt a deep responsibility toward the employees who performed their tasks closer to him. He saw himself as their commander-in-chief and protector, and thought—like the general of an army corps in relation to his officers—that their welfare and happiness depended upon his ability and "success."

Financially, he strove always to be an independent, having nothing to do with Wall Street and stock speculation. Therein was at once his great strength and weakness as an industrialist, one continually working against the other.

He knew some of the people in the other big packing concerns were referring to him as "that Jew," "that Dutchman" and "that foreigner." These derogations influenced his business mentality, temperament and procedure. A few times, irritated, he privately exclaimed in German or English, "They think they're so much better, those *goys!*" This resentment was part of the force driving him to further conquests, expansions, and successes.

But underneath and above all were Henry Steinberger's creative-progressive business impulses and instincts, his European passion against waste, his attachment to systematic efficiency, and his American boldness. Even in his sixties, his primary interest was continually to better the mathematical business formulas to which he had reduced the hog, the steer, and the sheep; and to so improve the packing methods that eventually everything in the slaughtered animal might be utilized. In his rare joking moods he confessed to having designs on the hog's last squeal, the cow's final low, the sheep's ultimate bleat.

Henry Steinberger was a schemer; he had to be in his business, and was that naturally. His was a suspicious nature. There were few people outside his immediate family whom he consistently trusted. At times he mistrusted even members of his own family, at least in the matter of their ability to stand on their own feet, both as persons and in reference to his company. With all the power and money at his command, his life was shot through with a feeling of insecurity. The Jew in him? Perhaps. Most of the time he seemed to feel threatened. He inclined to expect the worst, and much of his thought and general energy went toward establishing a continuous series of systematic precautions. He traveled a lot, and would frequently call his home long-distance from Chicago or Kansas City in the middle of the night to inquire if everything was all right, or to ask his wife to hasten to the basement and make sure nothing had caught fire there. A foreboding of doom gripped him every once in a while.

He was really interested only in his family and his business—which of the two came first would be difficult to say. His entire life revolved around them. He could not endure the idea of being "honored" by anybody. Deep in him he was a humble man, an immigrant; a self-made giant a little scared of himself, of what he had become and of the enormous outfit he had created.

IV

In a way, Henry Steinberger's family was as large and complicated as his business. He was the father of three series of children which, in relation to one another and to the entire family, had some of the aspects of three competing corporations within a holding company whose head is equally interested in them all.

He first married in the late 1860's, immediately on becoming a partner in his former boss' firm. A native of New York, his wife was the daughter of an immigrant family who were close friends of the Isaac Silbermanns. In three years she gave birth to as many children, a boy and a pair of female twins. The girls died in early infancy, and their mother soon after them, of sudden illness. The boy, Adolph, was exceptionally endowed and, in part because of that, did not get along with his half brothers and sisters of the subsequent marriages (most of whom also were exceptionally endowed individuals), and in consequence turned into a black sheep of the family. Reaching adulthood, he commenced to roam the world, mostly the Orient. His father supplied him with money. He has never met his second stepmother, six years his junior; nor most of his half brothers and sisters of the second and third series. Now in his seventies, Adolph Steinberger lives in Hawaii.

Henry Steinberger remarried a year after the death of his first wife, and the second Mrs. Steinberger had five sons and three daughters: Henry, Jr., Charles, Max, Ferdinand, Louis, Sylvia, Esther, and Julie. Beginning in the mid-nineties, four sons of the second series went into their father's business, and three stayed in it till its end. Two of the eight children are dead; the rest—now in their late middle age—are leading unique lives in the United States and various parts of the world. All were educated in private schools and foremost universities in America and Europe: Yale, Harvard, Vassar, Heidelberg, Sorbonne, Vienna.

While he was a student in Germany, Ferdinand Steinberger decided to stay there and eventually became a successful German dramatist, writing under a nom de plume a score of "hits," two of which were translated into English and presented on Broadway in 1911 and in the late 1920's. He married a German Gentile woman. In 1936 he and his family fled to Vienna, in 1937 to Prague; as I write this, in June, 1940, they are in a little town in Switzerland—refugees.

The most interesting person in this group is Louis, an eccentric now in his late fifties. He is a graduate of Yale and the inventor of a number of gadgets, timesavers, pills, etceteras, the patents on which have brought him about ten million dollars in twenty-five years. One day he asked himself: what do Americans do most? He supplied the answer: chew gum and take laxatives; then invented a combination of chewing gum and laxative which is now sold in every drugstore in the United States and in many other countries. But on seeing him in the streets of New York, where he "batches" in a forty-dollar-a-month two-room flat in an old brownstone house, the generous person might have difficulty in suppressing an impulse to stop him and proffer him a dime. He procures his food in the cheapest stores and from pushcart peddlers, buying partly decayed fifteen-cent melons for a nickel. His fortune, however, is sensibly invested; and if one takes a close look at him, one cannot help recognizing a superior person who has somehow become overindividualized. Often he crosses Fifth Avenue holding aloft a white handkerchief, his fierce glare commanding traffic to stop or slow down till he reaches the sidewalk. He is his half brother Eliot's favorite character. They meet several times a year, and Eliot relishes telling anecdotes about Louis.

The other children of the second marriage, though not rich, are well-to-do. Some live in considerable style, tastefully and with grace. Two or three are very civic-minded, responsible and positive citizens. But nearly all are out-of-the-ordinary, either in talents or in the turns their lives have taken. One paints, another is an unusually gifted musician. One has become a devout Catholic and almost entered the orders; his closest friend now is the priest in a little town in eastern Connecticut. Another is a Christian Scientist. . . . Except for Louis, they are all married; some to Jews, others to Gentiles. For years one of the daughters has been on the verge of Anglicizing her name; she is intensely and miserably anti-Semitic. . . .

v

Their mother died in the early 1890's. One day about a year later Henry Steinberger, Sr., just fifty and rapidly looming up as one of the best-known Jewish Americans and big industrialists in the country, happened to be in Norfolk, Virginia, and met a young lady, Bella Friedman, who was not yet twenty, the daughter of a local German-Jewish American merchant. The packer had seen her years before as a little girl; now, fully developed, she pleased him, and he asked for her hand. She was not only younger than his son by his first wife but younger than were two children of the second series.

They were married, and he brought her to his large but unpretentious new residence in the Sixties near Fifth Avenue. Then trouble began. Loyal to their late mother, several of the older children objected to the bride and considered ridiculous the suggestion that they accept her as their new mother. There were scenes.

Practical man that he was, Henry Steinberger reorganized the household into two sections. The two upper storeys, fully staffed with servants, were given to the eight children by his second wife, while the two lower floors, with another set of servants, became the home of the new family. For years the only contact between the two households was the old man, who often visited his older children upstairs, but spent most of his non-business moments downstairs.

In six years Bella gave birth to four children: Eliot, Marshall, Ann, and Harold. Marshall fell off a horse at the age of twenty-five and was killed; the other three are as unique and remarkable in their different ways as are the sons and daughters of the second marriage.

The reaction of the older children to his third marriage saddened the big industrialist considerably. As hard as he was on himself and his important employees, he inclined to be all tenderness toward his children and to give them almost anything they desired. He had high ambitions for them, which ran generally toward making them competent, useful, and cultured men and women. He held to the idea that the future would belong to the highly educated ("education is everything"), to those acutely aware of the world and their place in it, and the most highly regarded institutions were not too good for his boys and girls. But, although he tried not to show it, the sons disappointed him one by one. When he began to draw those by his second wife into the packing business, he discovered, to his growing dismay, that sending them to Yale and Harvard and Europe had been a mistake. They were all right for routine administrative work, but seemed unable to develop a passion, a "feel," for the meat industry; the passion that, in spite of occasional doubts and fears about himself and his function in life, gave a positive, single-minded quality to everything he himself did in a business way. He found out they—particularly his namesake, Henry, Junior—were interested in S. & S. not so much as a meat-packing industry with world-wide markets, an instrument on which they might practice their talents and abilities, and an opportunity to develop as men, but as a basis and source of their prestige, and as a tremendous, though cumbersome, money-making machine designed to serve them specially in order they might follow their own personal propensities, which were sports, travel, the arts. He felt that eventually, after he died, they might be overdisposed to leave the business in the hands of others; this he knew would be dangerous, for his competitors were obviously doing their utmost to rub the S. & S. out of existence.

These thoughts depressed Henry Steinberger, Sr., increasingly as he grew older. They brought on insomnia. He worried, even during the period when all the signs about him should have contributed to his assurance; on his desk in New York were five telephones at the end of as many direct wires connecting him with his interests in Chicago, Kansas City, Oklahoma City, Sioux Falls, and Boston, and he received daily reports. S. & S. was at its height, doing an annual gross business of more than a hundred million. The fact of the matter was that his *"goy"* competitors maneuvered endlessly to embroil him in difficulties. They conducted intensive sales campaigns in his territories. They called them "invasions." Some were taking advantage of latent anti-Semitism here and there to take customers away from S. & S.

The size and the far-flung markets of the company involved enormous financial problems, which the least dislocation in production or sales aggravated urgently. This obliged him to keep his personal fortune, or what could have been his personal fortune, constantly tied up; and every now and then, often in consequence of some unfriendly maneuver, he found himself in sudden need of a half-million or a million dollars in cash for a few weeks or months, and he had to borrow from the banks, some of whose officers he more than suspected were "in" with his competitors.

Early in 1913, when he was seventy, the S. & S. had to borrow two million. The old man worried day and night. He had been in ill-health for months before. Now the strain of his years and the financial situation, which he magnified, abruptly brought on a near-collapse. There was more than a touch of heart trouble.

Bella Steinberger had not loved Henry Steinberger when she married him; in the twenty years since then, however, she had perceived his stature and quality, and developed a profound affection for the man. Now, on the advice of the family doctor, she took him off to Europe and put him in a famous sanitarium in Switzerland. He did not improve. He fretted about his business, then about the war, and went slowly from bad to worse . . . and died in the summer of 1915, with the knowledge that the S. & S., in charge of his sons, was in a bad way, heavily indebted to banks, and doomed.

VI

The National Provisioner wrote: ". . . The news of his demise brought sorrow to the entire meat-packing trade, for his ability and personality had united to win him the respect and admiration of all who were connected with the trade to which his life was devoted. His death removes the last of that wonderful group of business men who built up the meat-packing trade and made America the leader in meat and meat products. All are gone, but the industry they founded and built still profits by their organizing ability, and ever will."

These sentiments, while sincerely held by many in the packing field, did not restrain the schemes of those who meant to get hold of the S. & S.

The beginning of the company's internal crisis came with the World War, when its business neared an annual gross of two hundred million dollars. Immediately, in 1914, along with the other big packers, the S. & S. began to ship immense cargoes of meat and other products not only to the Allies, but also to neutral Dutch and Scandinavian ports, whence the greater portion of them were then quickly transshipped to Germany . . . till the British woke up to this latter fact and took to stopping American and other neutral vessels carrying such supplies, and confiscating them as prize cargoes when the captains could not prove the meat and fats and casings (which could be used not only in sausage-making but also in Zeppelins) would not eventually reach their enemy.

In 1915, this caused serious diplomatic complications between the United States and Britain, with Britain getting the better end of the situation. The American packers lost tens of millions of dollars, although the business in which they had engaged was technically within the provisions of international law. The confiscations, however, were hardest on the Steinbergers, amounting to something like twenty millions. The S. & S. joined the other packers in a concerted attempt to fight the British government in the British courts, but when the other packers discovered that the British thought of the Steinbergers not as Americans but as Germans and, as such, special culprits in this trade, they got clear of them and left them to certain and complete defeat. They knew this would further weaken the financial structure of the company, already shaky, and put it into the hands of the banks, giving them a chance to seize its vast resources, plants and markets, and either to destroy or re-form it as an organization. They felt the young Steinbergers did not have it in them to fight and preserve the S. & S. They were correct. And to shorten a long and nasty tale, the company which Henry Steinberger had created ceased to exist under its old name a few years after the Armistice.

Out of the wreckage, the Steinbergers salvaged about three millions. A half-million went to the widow; the rest was divided in quarter million lots among the children.

Eliot's
Early Years

ELIOT was the oldest of the third group of children. A tiny, unimportant figure in the big Steinberger story, he came to boyhood in the years immediately preceding the peak of his father's success as an industrialist.

His young mother bore her three other children in the four years immediately after his birth. His two brothers and one sister were all so handsome as youngsters that nearly everyone who visited the house exclaimed over them, while no one ever enthused about him, who was somewhat of an ugly duckling, with a small, puckish face and large, fanlike ears. His half brothers and sisters upstairs referred to him as "that little monkey downstairs." His mother tried constantly to improve his looks. She dressed him variously, experimenting with collars of different shapes which might set off his face and head to better advantage, and she combed his hair this way and that way . . . all to scant avail.

His father sometimes looked at him a long while with an uneasy expression on his face, and was always gentle toward him on those rare occasions when they came into close personal contact. Sometimes, with an awkward kind of humor, he called him "Starving Cuban," for the boy was thin, all his ribs showing, like the Cuban children whose pictures were then—during and after the Spanish-American War—current in the newspapers. Absorbed in his business, however, perennially waiting for an "important phone call," the old man was usually remote and dull-faced, and at about the age of four Eliot became afraid of him.

Eliot was fear-ridden generally. He had frequent feelings of imminent disaster and death. These fears probably crept into him from the strained atmosphere his father created in the home with his telephoning to ask whether or not everything was all right, and with his manner, which seemed to imply that this was a hostile, complicated world.

Also, Eliot learned early that he was a Jew. This was all right in a way, something mysterious and wonderful, in fact, to be proud of at home, but something, too, for which the world unaccountably made you suffer.

Those People Upstairs were simultaneously part of the family and apart from it. They were rather superior persons, to whom, apparently, even his mother was inferior. Eliot resented Them and was awed by and afraid of Them. At the same time he also aspired to go Upstairs some day and see Them in Their rooms, which he assumed must be very elegant.

One day his father absent-mindedly took him by the hand and led him upstairs on one of his periodic calls, and Eliot was, in confusing succession, terrified, thrilled and disappointed. The rooms on the upper storeys were very much like those downstairs, and the boy was interested to note that the people living in them, who were also his father's children (this seemed very strange), were not superior to the old man. He talked to them much as he talked to his mother and everybody else below. They thereupon ceased to be They with a capital T, and Upstairs became just the floors above.

The world in which Eliot lived was strange, and he grew into a rather strange boy. He was intensely conscious of himself and perpetually on his toes, for he never could know when or whence a blow might fall. At night he awakened in the grip of the thought he was about to die. The ceiling would crash on him and sever him from existence. When it didn't, sometimes he wondered why.

Filled with questions and ever alert, the boy's mind worked all the time, trying to understand situations, people and things, and partly in consequence of this he developed into something like a prodigy. At five and six, he would say things which indicated penetrating insight, careful thought and precocious objectivity, and caused adults to glance at one another. The long, concernful looks which his father directed at him lengthened. Off and on, when the two of them happened to meet in the hallway or on the staircase, the old man put his hand on the boy's head or pinched his cheek. These encounters and contacts with his parent filled Eliot with mixed feelings of panic, pain, and bliss.

He liked his governess Hedwig, who was a young blond German girl with a pretty round face, large wide-apart blue eyes, and a lovely voice. She spoke a little English, and taught him German and French. She was full of fun, and laughed a lot, especially when she took him out for walks in Central Park. His "fonny" face, as she called it, delighted her, and often she pressed him to herself in spontaneous affection.

When Eliot was six, Hedwig abruptly left the Steinberger employ. The reason was that one of his half brothers upstairs had fallen in love with her, and she, engaged to another man, could not reciprocate. Her departure upset Eliot a great deal, and he turned sullen and rebellious. He hated "the bunch upstairs" and tried to perpetrate bits of mischief that would annoy them, such as ringing their doorbell and running away, calling them on the phone and then hanging up.

He was sent to a private school, where he got into a succession of petty difficulties. But his father never reprimanded him, even when Eliot, uneasy in the old man's presence, dared verge on being discourteous to him. He just studied him for minutes at a spell, wondering what was the matter, and granted almost his every request and demand.

The elder Steinberger decided in his troubled mind that the boy was unsuited for the packing business, and thinking he might fit into some profession, perhaps law, asked him when he was about thirteen, and then again a year or so later, what college he wanted to enter. Eliot responded that he did not want to go to college: why should he?

The last year in private school he kept mainly to himself, joining no clubs, taking part in no group activities. He wanted to be different, aloof from the disquieting normality of the others. At fifteen, when he discovered his father did not think he belonged in the meat industry, he asked, then demanded, he be allowed to learn "the business from the ground up." This was in 1910.

Surprised and pleased, Henry Steinberger, Sr.—now in his late sixties—let Eliot come into the plant. After all, he might have been mistaken in thinking the boy unsuitable; he was strange, unpredictable, and might yet be a potential packing genius. Who could say what was stewing behind that abrupt manner? His teachers, whom he frequently exasperated, described him as brilliant. In the days to come there might be a place for that quality in the packing industry.

II

Eliot plunged into learning the packing business with great determination. He was at the huge First Avenue plant every morning at five, and quit at five in the afternoon. Slaughtering at first horrified him, while the stench of the place nauseated him; he felt himself fainting and evenings he bathed long and thoroughly. By-and-by, however, he got used to the place, and within a few months, although yet no more than a boy, developed into a most competent worker. As soon as he mastered the various jobs and functions in one department, he was moved on to the next. The superintendents and foremen were delighted with him, and sought and made opportunities to tell the Big Boss how well his son was getting along. Eliot sharply resented any effort to favor him because his father was the president of the company.

The boy caught glimpses of his father in his element. The old man's personality, with its old-country *Gruendlichkeit*, permeated the place. The men respected him, were geared to his will and plans, and usually knew what he wanted before he told them. He was natural with them; natural and matter-of-fact with the whole process. Almost in spite of himself Eliot developed a profound regard for his father; which, however, he could not show for some time. His heart jumped proudly when he overheard snatches of the men's conversations about the Big Boss or the Old Boy, as some of them called him.

At sixteen, from the slaughterhouse, Eliot advanced to the office, where he went swiftly through the various departments—stock inventory, sales and orders, bookkeeping and billing, and research. He liked the office much less than the slaughter plant. Here he came into frequent contact and near-conflict with his half brothers, who were heads or assistant heads of departments. They did not like him, and he did not like them.

Eliot finally decided that the scientific end of the business interested him most. He began to spend nearly all of his time in the research department, of which the Old Boy was himself the directing head. The production formulas, to which the slaughtered animals were reduced, fascinated the young man, and, to the Old Boy's intense delight, he even worked out a few improvements. Gradually, the father and son became good friends. For his birthday in 1911, the elder Steinberger bought the boy a new roadster he had observed him admire.

Meantime, a number of things in Eliot's life were converging on a common point from which he flew off on a tangent directly opposite to the tendencies he had begun to reveal in the plant and the office. Overdeveloped mentally for his sixteen years, emotionally unstable, and turning gradually into an attractive male despite his lack of what usually passes for good looks, he fell in and out of love a few times, mostly with women twice his age. This brought on sharp ups and downs in mood, and he became acutely dissatisfied with himself; with being a rich man's son and a Jew (for he bumped into mild forms of anti-Semitism every once in a while); with the packing business; with life at home; with things in general. He took to writing poetry, to contemplating human existence cynically. Despite his stature, the Old Boy began to strike him as a little ridiculous. This importance attached to meat and fats, to refrigeration! This endless worrying and scheming! Whether or not those trainloads of cattle would arrive in time for the morning shift on Tuesday of next week! This fear of what Armour and Swift might do! His half brothers in the office were ridiculous, too. They held their jobs because they were Steinbergers, not because of any real capacity. Crown princes! They really did not belong in the business, knew very little about it, and were afraid of him mostly because of that. He might beat them at the game. What did he care for the business! They could have it and be damned with it!

Eliot did not like any of the "upstairs bunch" . . . except Louis, who was beginning to tinker with his inventions, and who now was no longer upstairs, but in Chicago, taking charge of some aspects of the Steinberger interests in the Middle West; and to whom the packing business was interesting, but also a bit of a malodorous joke. He had a suite at the Palmer House for business reasons and also a little twenty-dollar-a-month flat in the German-Bohemian section on the east side, where he cooked his own meals, washed his socks and handkerchiefs, and worked on the gadgets and concoctions he had set his mind to invent or perfect. Late in 1911, Louis came on a visit to New York, and he and Eliot had a talk. Eliot told him how he felt about things. Louis said, "Why don't you quit?"

Reluctant to hurt the Old Boy, however, and thereby upset his mother, Eliot did not know for a while how to go about quitting. He began stepping out with some of the clerks in the office, and drinking. Finally, during an encounter with one of the half brothers he spoke his mind. After that there was no retreating. He was through with the packing business. The Old Boy was on a trip West, and knew nothing of what had transpired in the home office till he returned. Meantime, Eliot, not yet seventeen, ran around and drank in earnest; and when he next met his father, he was drunk and bruised. He had engaged in a café brawl with a fellow who had called him "a dirty-rich Jew"; however, he declined now to explain the bruises to his parents.

Eliot's step was a blow to the Old Boy. But he continued to be gentle to him and tried vainly to understand him.

III

Two or three months in the summer of 1911 Eliot devoted solely to wild doings, some of which brought him into intimate contact with the police. One night, at a police station, he heard an officer describe him to the sergeant at the desk as "just another damn-fool kid, a rich man's son." Drunk, Eliot tried to take a swing at the policeman, which made matters more difficult the next morning for the Steinberger lawyer, whose task it was to get him out of the jug.

When sober, Eliot did not seem to understand himself, and felt extremely foolish, his self-respect all the way down. And the only way out of this dilemma seemed to be to get drunk again.

Finally his father succeeded in catching him in a sober moment, and asked him to accompany him on a trip to Sioux Falls, where he was going on business. Eliot went along, and the two had a talk. The Old Boy apologized for his older sons' attitude and behavior toward him, and said that as the father of them all he naturally found himself in a difficult position. This remark cut Eliot to the quick, and he blurted in a half-sullen tone he was sorry for his part in the mess, but— He was inarticulate and could not make clear what was in his mind and what he felt. But gradually he brought out that he was very discontented with himself and the whole setup in which he found himself. He disliked being a rich man's son. He did not want his (the old man's) position in the world to regulate the course of his own life. He advanced this—probably as an afterthought, but not unrelated to truth—as the real reason for his leaving the packing business.

The elder Steinberger understood and nodded sympathetically, recalling that he himself had come to America, in part, because he did not want his life to become a mere extension of his father's, hemmed in by the tight rules and customs of European existence.

Eliot said, too, that "this fact of being a Jew" bothered him a great deal. His father did not reply for a long moment, and his face looked very heavy. Then he remarked slowly, as though it pained him to speak, that being a Jew was "a complicated business," hard to understand and harder to explain, but that maybe things would gradually improve, at least in the United States, with its democracy and attachment to fair play. The only thing Jews could do about it, he said, was to strive toward being the best sort of people, decent and progressive, in whatever field they might develop their activities. Some of the Jews were not trying any too hard, and one could not blame them (the worst of them were no worse than the worst of the Gentiles); however, they did make it hard on Jewry as a whole, for the Jews, as a group and as individuals, were watched by the rest of the human race—the poor conduct of one reflected on them as a group.

"But *why* are we watched?" demanded Eliot, angrily.

The expression of his father's face became even heavier. He seemed unable to answer in a way that could satisfy the boy, the intensity of whose gaze cut into him. He said it all seemed a matter of history, tradition, and the ways of the world.

"What makes us Jews?" asked the young man.

"We just *are* Jews, that's all," returned the old man, unsatisfactorily. "I can't tell you why."

They fell silent.

"But this is neither here nor there," the Old Boy said, wanting to change the subject. He asked Eliot what he thought he wanted to do now. Eliot did not know. The old man suggested he go on with his schooling. How about Harvard? Of course they might not take him. Why not? Because Harvard's requirements were very stiff, especially for Jewish boys; the number of Jews they took in was limited. Involuntarily, the elder Steinberger had returned to the Jewish question, which Eliot promptly took up. *Why* did Harvard limit the number of Jewish students? The Old Boy replied, "It's part of the same thing you asked me about awhile ago. I can't explain it, son; I'm sorry."

Eliot felt challenged; and by the time they returned from Sioux Falls, they decided—holding one another in mutual respect again—that he would "try" Harvard.

IV

Eliot applied for entrance to a small, exclusive preparatory school in Boston which annually "prepared" for Harvard from ten to a dozen sons of prominent, well-to-do families who lacked the necessary entrance credits. Eliot declared he wanted to enter the college in the fall of 1912. The headmaster exclaimed that, in view of his slender scholastic record, that was practically an impossibility. But Eliot was determined to get into Harvard the following year or abandon the idea of further education.

He gave up drinking, and for a year seldom went out. He studied most of the time. There were no other Jewish boys in the school then. Most of the students were old-stock New Englanders, and disposed to be friendly toward Eliot. But he made no close friendships. Something in the atmosphere of the place inhibited his impulses for comradeship.

One day he overheard a couple of boys talk about him. They said they liked him, he was a nice fellow, and all that; but wasn't it too bad, remarked one, that he was a Jew. Why? asked the other. Because it was difficult, said the first boy, for Jews to get into Harvard; and if Eliot did get in, they would be unable to associate with him on close terms. He would not be "available" for membership in this and that. Why? asked the second boy. Because he was a Jew, said the first; his father was a Jew; his name was Jewish. . . .

This conversation pierced Eliot like a rusty dagger. But after the first over-whelming feeling of anger and pain it acted as a further stimulus for his determination. He became even more aloof and studied still harder. Harvard Yard was a citadel to be taken.

He took it . . . and enjoyed his victory awhile. Then the thrill wore off, and he decided he did not like Harvard. He could not bring himself to study. His father was giving him a generous allowance, he had a car, and he resumed drinking and carousing. He went out with a small group of students, the majority of them Gentiles, who were regular (or, rather, *ir*regular) fellows and regarded themselves as "bums," scorning the general social life of the students.

There was a Jewish group or clique, but Eliot steered clear of it, with this thought in his head: why should he become part of the Jewish group simply because he was Jewish (whatever being Jewish was supposed to mean)? He was thinking over the conversation of the two boys in the "prep" school and what his father had said to him on the subject of being a Jew. It was all a great puzzle; where could one begin to unravel it? Some Jews "looked Jewish"; others did not. He, himself, for one, did not. So what made him a Jew? His name? The accident of being the son of a man named Steinberger? He was an American; no? Was he or wasn't he? He was born here. He was a citizen. In a few years he would be able to vote. His father was a citizen. The Old Boy's function reached deep into the existence of the country. If all this didn't make him an American, what could? What made anybody else an American? Assuming he was a Jew, why should that interfere with his being an American? Why should *he* get it in the neck because some Jews were not what some of the Gentiles thought they should be, while individual Gentiles (which apparently meant simply being non-Jewish) and Gentiles as a whole did not suffer the consequences of the misdeeds, crimes, and bad manners of Gentiles who were not everything they should be according to the standards which the Gentiles applied to Jews? . . . Eliot's head whirled. He thought his father's ideas on these questions were most unsatisfactory. "History," "tradition." Why should he have to try to be "the best sort of person" because he was a Jew? He resented that requirement and every impulse in him went against any effort toward meeting it; and, trying to puzzle things out, he felt his brain reeling in confusion. He was at once intensely and vaguely uncomfortable.

This discomfort increased. While there was no open, active anti-Jewish sentiment at Harvard, Jews were merely (but very definitely) not accepted, not really taken in, particularly by the New Englanders, who seemed to be the majority and the dominant element in the student body. They were unfailingly polite to him (as they were to all other Jews), but he was essentially "out," not of them, and there seemed to be an unwritten law that he never could be. He noticed that when he or some other Jewish student approached a group of old-stock Americans, they fell silent or abruptly changed the subject to some innocuous topic. Jews could occasionally go out drinking with them, but not appear where they might meet their girls, families and close friends.

Eliot perceived that Jews were virtually forced (quite apart from their own impulses in that direction) to congregate in a clique of their own; but he would be damned, he said to himself, if these perfect-mannered New England snobs would drive *him* into it! He continued to go out with the "bums," drinking with them, taking part in their escapades. After the first two or three weeks, he attended no classes and did no work whatever, sleeping till two or three in the afternoon. He wanted to leave Harvard, but delayed taking this step because he heard his father was not well. He did not want to upset him.

Then he learned that, on account of his unsatisfactory behavior and utter indifference to what the college had to offer him, he would be asked to leave, or be dropped or expelled; and so—sick not only of Harvard, but everything, including himself—he just left his dormitory room one afternoon, carrying only a little bag into which he had thrown some of his belongings, and never went back. To the devil with Harvard.

He had twelve dollars and went to New York, intending to see his family for a few minutes or hours, possibly have a talk with the Old Boy if he was not too sick or too busy, then take a ship, any ship, somewhere, anywhere. He wanted to get the hell away from all this being a rich man's son who as such should go to Harvard, away from being a Jew and the importance of being one, and all the other aspects of his plight which could hardly be put into coherent thoughts.

v

Reaching the family house in New York, Eliot learned from the housekeeper that his father was very ill and on the way to a sanitarium in Europe with his mother and the younger children. This upset him badly. His mother had written him a letter just before their departure, but in the excitement had neglected to post it. Not knowing this, however, Eliot resented furiously their failure to inform him. A few of his half brothers and sisters were upstairs, but he did not want to see them. The housekeeper gave him his family's address in Europe, and he walked out of the house with this thought trembling in his brain, "I don't want anything more from the family till I find out if I can stand on my own . . . till I see if I can make something of myself, not because I am my old man's son or this mysterious thing called a Jew, but just on general principles, because I am what I am. If I cannot stand on my own and make something of myself with the resources within me (if any), rather than with my father's money or under the stimulus of the fact that I am a Jew, then I am no damn good and should not live."

The Test
and a Book

ELIOT pawned his expensive watch, then bought a steerage passage on a ship sailing for Hamburg the next day. In those days no passports were necessary.

America-bound the ship was usually jammed with emigrants; now it had but a few hundred passengers in the steerage, mostly men who had spent two or three years in the United States and were returning home for a visit or to stay: peasants and workingmen from the Polish, Slovak, and Ukrainian regions and cities of Germany and Austria and Russia, from Hungary and the Balkans. Eliot liked their looks. They had craggy, toil-etched faces. Some sported derbies, gold watches and heavy watch chains, and a few had gold teeth—symbols of their success as miners and steel and stockyard workers in America.

Eliot tried to think—a difficult matter, not only because of himself, but on account of his surroundings. His bed was a piece of canvas, two-by-six feet, soiled and stretched taut between two iron rails in a four-tiered row, but he spent very little time in it, even at night. The place was close, ill-ventilated; it stank. The air in it had passed through thousands of lungs of various nationalities. The iron-plate floors were covered with a much-stepped-on mixture of dirt, grease and spittle. Enormous roaches darted about. Fat, button-eyed rats peered from behind pipes and life preservers. In the galley, at one end of the steerage quarters, a number of individuals whose very appearance would discourage any appetite were dishing out inedible food three times a day to passengers who filed by them with tin plates and cups.

But the passage cost only twelve dollars; one could not expect luxury. In moments of revulsion and weakness, Eliot thought of trying to transfer himself to second class, but managed not to yield to the temptation; also, he had very little money. He spent most of the voyage, even when it rained, amid the booms and winches on the section of the lower deck allowed to steerage passengers. He lay on a canvas hatch cover, or sat with his back against a pile of rope, looking at the sky and the sea, or writing poetry, which came to him easily, but was only ordinary.

II

Eliot had scarcely eaten aboard the ship; and, on reaching Hamburg with ten dollars, he first treated himself to a tasty, abundant meal and a room for a night in a good hotel. He took a bath lasting two hours, soaping and scrubbing himself over and over again.

He spoke fluent German and found a job in a café kitchen, where for a month he peeled great quantities of potatoes and onions, washed dishes, and scrubbed the floor. He shared a cheap little room with another young man employed in the same place, who at first seemed to be a German but eventually turned out to be a Polish fugitive from justice in Prussian Poland, where he had attempted to assassinate an official. He was saving the little money he earned to make his way to America.

Eliot, too, saved as much of his small wage as possible, and worried about his father: he could not disassociate himself from his family. He wrote to his mother in Switzerland, who replied first by telegram, then by letter, explaining why he had not heard from her at Harvard, expressing concern over his quitting college, and saying she would not tell Father of his being in Europe. Father, she emphasized, was *very* sick. The doctors' orders were he must not be disturbed.

After the month in the café kitchen, Eliot visited his mother in Switzerland. She was frantic over the Old Boy's condition, and listened with only a distant anxiety to Eliot's stumbling, uncertain answer to her question as to what he meant to do with himself. He said he planned to "move around awhile and see what I am made of." He might go to England for a time; after that, he did not know.

The doctors would not let him see his father.

His mother offered him a large roll of bank notes, but he declined it. He stayed at her fine hotel near the sanitarium for a few days (his brothers and sister were in school at Lausanne), then left.

III

Eliot arrived in London with a few shillings and, in a couple of days, started to work on the docks. This was back-breaking toil for a slight youth of eighteen who had spent his recent months chasing around and drinking, but, following the first excruciating week, during which he put in seventy-eight hours handling a cargo of iron rails, he managed to stand it.

He lived in the rat- and vermin-infested slums, jammed with poverty- and ignorance-oppressed, drinking, diseased, and yet humorous people, full of a curious friendliness, buoyancy, and spunk. They appealed to Eliot exceedingly. For days at a time, he felt deeply at home among them and in the stench of their streets and tenements, as he did on the docks and in the water-front pubs among the cursing stevedores with their twisted mouths, cockney dialects and voices, bad teeth, and foul breath. They called him "the bloody Yank."

He fell in love with a ragged guttersnipe with a lovely, shameless body and a pair of squinty, sneering eyes, who had never had a bath in the seventeen years of her life.

At the same time, however, something in his make-up pulled him away from the docks and the slums. Having lived his childhood and early boyhood in the strange two-in-one family, aspiring to get Upstairs, feeling the antagonism of his half brothers, simultaneously working in the slaughterhouse and enjoying the comforts of wealth, he had been conditioned for the profound quandary which was ever to cut the rhythm of his life. He was (and is) at once an upperdog and an underdog, and could not (and cannot) decide definitely to be only the one and cease being the other. Not improbably, his being a Jew had (and has) no insignificant role in this inner drama; especially his being a Jew who was also the son of Henry Steinberger, the great tycoon who deep inside of him was a threatened, scared man.

IV

When Eliot had lived in the Lower Depths for about two months, his mother wrote him that his father was "a little better, thank God"; and into the large linen envelope containing this welcome message she had stuffed a wad of thousand-franc notes. So now, with the autumn coming on, he abruptly bought himself a wardrobe, including silk shirts, and moved into the Savoy Hotel, feeling an irresolute weakling, a backslider for using the family money and violating the resolution he had made before leaving New York, while in the same flow of thought he told himself that the sordidness of the slums had become intolerable, and he needed a taste of this other life, lest he go crazy.

The second day at the Savoy, slumped in a deep, too-comfortable armchair in the vast, ornate lobby, Eliot found himself engaged in a conversation with a youngish man, who introduced himself as William Bond ("call me Bill"), an American, a New Yorker, who said he represented the Boston Garters firm in Great Britain and on the continent, and asked Eliot if he was one of *the* Steinbergers of the S. & S. Eliot admitted he was "in a way" and, in reply to the man's further casual-like interrogations, gave him a partial explanation of his sojourn in London; whereupon Bill suggested that, since he was footloose and out to see the world, he go with him to Paris next week. He had some business to attend to there. Then they would go to Brussels, Rotterdam, and so on.

Eliot went to Paris, where, during the next several days, his new friend, pleading he was impossibly busy, asked him to deliver little boxes marked "Boston Garters—*Sample*" all over the city. He paid for his cab and offered him a salary. After the first few days, however, Eliot began to think it a little queer that most of the deliveries should be to private homes and hotel rooms, rather than to haberdasheries. Finally, he opened a package and under the garters found a tiny vial, which mystified him till his innocence was pierced by the sudden realization that this fellow Bill was a dope peddler.

Shaken by this, and assuming on the basis of his mother's last letter that his father was recovering, Eliot decided to drop out of Bill Bond's life and made for Marseilles, where he took ship for Australia—a long, pleasant trip by way of Suez and India. He chose Australia because he wanted to put distance between his family and himself.

At Ceylon the vessel stopped for three days, and, as a last fling in the upperdog world, Eliot put up at a luxury hotel for the period. He got drunk and pulled a rickshaw coolie all over the city in his vehicle. Finally he wanted to have a map of the world tattooed on his body, but there wasn't sufficient time or money for so ambitious a project.

v

Landing in Adelaide penniless, he starved for a week . . . till he landed a job with a large British sheep and wool firm, which had stations and vast herds throughout the interior of South Australia and also in Queensland, New South Wales, and Western Australia.

Claiming to be a good horseman (on the basis of a half-dozen rides in Central Park in New York City a few years before), Eliot was hired as a boundary rider, and was sent to a station "up beyond Innamincka," wherever that was. The place had no name, only a number—No. 9. His pay was to be a pound a week in cash and food supplies, and he was given a small advance to enable him to put a few meals under his belt before he set out for his post, and to purchase some toilet articles which were not procurable "in the Bush."

Eliot then traveled several hundred miles by rail and coach and on horseback, taking nearly a week, along the Darling River, then toward the Stanley Range, and through the Sturt Desert, to Innamincka. The town consisted of a group of corrugated-iron bunkhouses, shearing sheds and miscellaneous shacks strung around "The Office," a clay-and-wood building; and a sun-baked, profane polyglot population of two hundred, preponderantly male. It was the company's sheep station in that region.

Here Eliot was equipped for his job. The equipment included a scrawny but tough little native horse, two pack mules, a tomahawk, a revolver and a rifle, ammunition for these arms, several knives, two large canteens, a tent, a first-aid kit, yards of mosquito netting, cooking utensils, a tiny thermometer, a carton of matches, twenty pounds of flour, two cans of baking powder, two bottles of ketchup, two jars of jam, six pounds of sugar, three of salt, two of raisins, and three of tea. This food supply was for two weeks.

At Innamincka Eliot became promptly known again as "the bloody Yank" or "the Yank kid." One of the old-timers in the territory, whom everybody called Tim and who was an Oxford man in revolt against civilized life, was assigned to accompany him to No. 9, which now seemed to be up "toward the Arunta Desert," a region described by those who knew it in unquotable terms. They rode two days, till they came to a barbed-wire fence, which was part of an inclosure called a paddock forty-odd miles in circumference, containing about six thousand sheep grazing on sparse grass that grew over stony ground. The next day, giving him a few final bits of instruction and advice, Tim the Oxonian left him, and Eliot was on his own.

The paddock was really a system of paddocks with a common outer fence; the inner fences converged onto a great pond or waterhole. Eliot's duties consisted of riding along the several hundred miles of fences, of seeing that they (especially the outer one) were in good repair, of rescuing the sheep which might have caught or hung themselves on the wire, and of keeping himself alive in the face of considerable odds.

The most important rule, which Tim had impressed upon Eliot by repeating it a dozen times, was that he must take no risk of letting the animals, especially the horse, get away from him. The loss of the horse and mules was invariably fatal to fence riders at stations as remote and difficult as No. 9.

Eliot had a rough map of the paddock, giving the distance around each sub-inclosure, and showing the approximate location of water holes and shady spots where he might rest himself and his animals and cook his noontime meal. At nightfall he was always to return to the waterhole, where he had his camp and a small corral for the horse and mules. He must never get out of sight of the outer fence. The territory was a gently rolling plateau two thousand feet above sea level, virtually a desert, all but treeless and without other identifying landmarks. The scrub growth, mostly salt bush, was inadequate even for cooking his meals; firewood was brought to him by pack train from Innamincka. There were a few eucalypti near his night camp.

The water was stagnant, warm, and green with slime. He boiled it before drinking, but even then, during the first few days, he got it down only when made into tea, heavily sweetened, its color and odor disguised.

He got to the location a few days before Christmas, when the average heat was 125° in the shade, of which there was next to none. In the ensuing three months the place cooled down to between ninety and a hundred.

His biggest enemies were mosquitoes, which were known to have killed men who found themselves in that country without netting between dusk and dawn; ants, which lived in enormous mounds all over the region, and had about them a vile odor, and found their way to nearly everything edible; a great variety of snakes, most of them deadly; and flies, which daily accompanied him on his ride in cloudlike swarms. Almost perennially black with them, as was he himself, his animals were inured to the flies, daring creatures so intent on the pursuit of food that, to keep them out of his mouth as he ate, Eliot was obliged to shake his left hand over his mouth as though he were playing tremolo on a mouth organ.

For two weeks at a spell he saw no other human being, except an occasional aborigine in the distance, beyond the outer fence. These bushmen were tame, but an unhandsome, uncommunicative lot. They ignored Eliot and his herds. The soles of their feet from an inch to two inches thick, they walked barefoot over the hot stone and sand.

There was a species of wild coyote-like dogs called dingos, bent on getting within the inclosure to kill the sheep. Eliot was instructed to trap and skin them; there was a reward of one pound for each pelt.

The place was maddening at first, and there were moments when he thought he would be unable to endure it. Then he would say to himself—sometimes aloud—that these difficult circumstances would prove whether he was good for anything or not. If they destroyed him, he probably ought to be destroyed. He knew that many men had lived through worse experiences.

He was instructed to slaughter a ewe, past lambing, every two weeks, eat of it what he could the first day, and salt and pack the rest of the meat in a sack with which the Innamincka station superintendent had provided him. He had also been given written directions on how to salt the meat, which, with his background in the meat industry, he scarcely needed.

At the beginning, however, he had some difficulty cooking food so it was edible. The first week he all but starved. The vile-smelling ants attacked his meat sack, which he had hung by a rope on a limb of one of the few trees near the waterhole. He drank the filthy liquid which was supposed to be water or tea only when thirst became intolerable. This, on top of the long and strenuous trip to reach No. 9, reduced him to skin and bone.

The second week, however, Eliot bounced into a new attitude. He re-read the meat-salting instructions and learned that he should have hung the sack by a hobble chain generally used to "hobble" the front legs of the horses and mules to prevent their straying too far at night; then the ants, smelling the meat, would crawl up the tree and to the spot on the limb from which it depended, but would almost never get past the first link or ring. The leaders would circle around it madly, till they were stopped by exhaustion and would then be followed by other ants on the limb immediately behind them, and so on. The frustration of the ants furnished Eliot with one of the first thrills at No. 9. He watched their mad circling for hours with self-forgetting absorption.

He discovered, too, a few tricks of cooking, and began to eat. His bread, called "damper," was made of flour, baking powder and water, which always gave it a greenish-brown tinge. He baked it in a flat, covered iron stove among the coals of the wood fire, and most of the time it turned out so he was able to get it down. He also learned to make "puffaloons"—holeless doughnuts fried in sheep fat.

And he ceased to mind acutely the slimy water, the flies and the ants, and developed a passion for shooting and trapping the snakes and the dingos. He discovered he was a natural good shot, and bagged a dingo the second week. The kangaroos and wallabies, especially the females with their baby bags and amazing leaps, began to fascinate him, as did the huge, ostrich-like emus and iguanas and carnies and other creatures, plentiful outside and in the paddock.

At the end of the second week a pack train, which continued on its way to a couple of locations farther on, brought him his next half-month's food supplies and firewood . . . and so it went for eight months, during which time Eliot had moments of feeling fairly sure he was meeting the test. He did not need the cushion of his family's wealth, nor the stimulus of being a Jew. Here, at eighteen, going on nineteen, he was a man on his own, doing a tough job satisfactorily, and getting paid for it. This realization made him rub his sun-bleached soft beard with mounting self-satisfaction and confidence. Now he could go anywhere, do almost anything.

In his second month on the job, Eliot commenced to kill from two to five dingos a week, thus boosting his wage to as high as six pounds.

VI

Occasionally, for days at a time, he worried intensely about his father. He could have written his mother, and probably received a reply in four or five months, but he did not write. One reason for this was that he did not know how long he might stay on the job; another, that he wanted utter isolation from his family, in order to test the mettle of his make-up over a period of time. He did not want his mother to send him another wad of money; it might tempt and weaken him. He was conscious of his weaknesses. Off and on he felt an overwhelming desire for a bed with clean sheets, a bath, a meal in a brilliantly lighted dining-room. There were sex tortures such as only solitude and loneliness can contrive in a youth.

At times he felt frightfully lonely. Also, at moments the place scared him. The yelps of the dingos at night sent shivers through him. His boyhood fear of death returned and held him in a cold sweat. A snake might wiggle itself to him while he slept. Or the horses and mules might break loose. One night a meteor hit a spot near No. 9, sending a terrific shudder through the entire plateau, and for weeks after Eliot wondered why it had not fallen on him. . . . But, as time went on, he had less and less trouble in subduing these fears and wild imaginings.

Physically he was thin, but hard. He could ride from eight to ten hours without feeling exhausted at the end. Once, for a whole week, while attending to his duties, he had recurrent and excruciating pains in his abdomen and he felt a big hard lump on the right side of his belly. He had no idea what this might be, so he pressed and massaged the spot. Then both the lump and the pain passed. Years later, in medical school, he realized that he had had an acute attack of appendicitis.

Now and then a local disease called the barku rot touched him. Due to the insufficient vitamin content of his diet, intense heat, and probably other causes, it manifested itself by nausea and vomiting, and in tiny cuts or scratches in his skin developing into large sorelike white wounds, which took weeks to heal. But Tim the Oxonian had told him about this, and Eliot was not worried. He studied the sick flesh, fascinated.

VII

At Harvard, and through most of his life prior to college, he had found it difficult to pick up a book, start reading it, and finish it. He had little use for magazines and newspapers. Now, by the faint light of a primitive lamp of his own invention, consisting of a piece of rag in a metal dish filled with mutton tallow, he read over and over again the scraps of paper in which his supplies had been wrapped. Then he began to ask the men of the pack train to bring him reading matter, and he perused anything and everything. He read every word, including advertisements, in the two- and three-year-old copies of *The Saturday Evening Post* and the London illustrated weeklies. Books were scarce in Innamincka, but, along with some pure trash, he got hold of a few by Kipling, which he liked for their vigor; and *The Jungle,* which he devoured with an interest verging on the personal, both resenting and approving it; and, strangely enough, a little volume entitled *The Discourses of Keidansky* by Bernard G. Richards, published in New York in 1903, after most of it had appeared in the form of articles in *The Boston Evening Transcript.*

Books and individual copies of books are apt to have strange careers. *The Discourses of Keidansky* sold three or four thousand copies in the years immediately following its publication, mostly in New York and Boston, then went out of print; and how or when a copy of it got to that remote sheep station in central Australia, hundreds of miles from a railway, and how it happened to be there and in fairly good condition more than ten years after its publication, will never be known. At any rate, it excited Eliot Steinberger, who read it several times with deepening interest.

It is a book about Jews, and particularly about Jews in the Russian- and Polish-Jewish section in Boston at the turn of the century. Keidansky is an immigrant intellectual and a curious duck living in that section, maintaining a precarious existence as a journalist. He is somewhat of a socialist and radical, but not really; a Zionist, but not really; and several other things, but none of them really. He is primarily a wit and eccentric (and there is room for argument if he is that), with opinions on nearly everything under the sun, but especially on the Jews, about whom he speaks from the inside. If he is nothing else, he is certainly a Jew.

Among the chapters, which are reports on Keidansky's views, are pieces with such titles as "Keidansky Decides to Leave the Social Problem Unsolved for the Present," and , "On Enjoying One's Own Writing." Although they were concerned mostly with poor Jews, workers and Ghetto-dwellers, they found a curiously keen echo in the millionaire packer's son, who rode the boundary at No. 9. However, the chapter on "What Constitutes the Jew?" in which Keidansky (or, rather, Bernard Richards) comes close to producing a classic, interested him most:

. . . And after we have read about him in the comic weeklies, have seen him delineated in popular works of fiction, caricatured in various publications, portrayed on the vaudeville stage, and have heard from the slum student of the Ghetto; after we have visited a few money lenders—on important business—and have listened to our minister talk patronizingly of him, telling pityingly of how he hath a great past and possessed more than a few commendable qualities, and of how he was, alas! doomed to damnation because he would not accept the religion that he hath given to the world; after we have bought clothing in one of his stores, taken a personal peep at the Ghetto, met a reformed rabbi, conversed with a distant descendant of his people, read the polite charges of his friend, the anti-Semite, and gone down and made beautiful speeches before him prior to the election; I say even after we have done these things, or some of these things have happened to us, we must still ask the question: What constitutes the Jew?

For, of a verity, he is so complex in his character, so heterogeneous in his general composition, so diverse in his activities, so many sided in his worldly and heavenly pursuits, so widely varying in his appearance, so wonderfully ubiquitous, and withal such a living contradiction, that even after we have made the above painful efforts to understand him, we are still at a loss to know—what we know about him.

He represents one of the ancient [groups of humanity] . . . and yet is as up to date as any; he reaches deepest into the past and looks furthest into the future; he is the narrowest conservative and most advanced radical; in religion he is the most dogmatic, sectarian, stationary, orthodox, and also the most liberal and universal reformer; he is a member of the feeblest and strongest people on earth; he has no land of his own and he owns many lands; his wealth is the talk and the envy of the world, and none is so poor as he; his riches have ever been magnified and exaggerated, his dire poverty overlooked. "As poor as a Jew" would be a truer simile than the one now in use. He is the infamous Shylock, the money-lender, yet he borrows as much and more money than he lends to others, only he pays his debts and so there is no talk about it; Christians and others who borrow from him go to court, denounce him, call him Shylock, and give him several pounds of "tongue," though he asks not for flesh, because it is not "kosher," and because whatever he is, he is never cruel. Come to think of it, what a fine thing the Shylock story has ever been for those who did not want to pay their debts!

He loans money to kings, and the kings oppress the Jews; he is the great concentrator of wealth, and he is the socialist and anarchist working ardently for the abolition of the private ownership of wealth; he is eminently practical, and he is ever among the world-forgetting dreamers, "the great host of impracticables;" he has no fine arts of his own, and he carries off the highest prizes for his glorious contribution to the arts of the nations. Now he is exclusively confined to his own Hebrew religious lore, believing that beyond it there are no heights to scale, no depths to fathom, and then he becomes a Georg Brandes, a great interpreter of the literatures of the world; his own literature is so Puritanical, so religious and chaste that there is hardly a single love song to be found therein, and then comes a Heinrich Heine. He is the slave of traditions and the first to break them; persecute him and he will die for the religion of his fathers; give him freedom and he will pity them for their crude conceptions and applaud Ingersoll; he is intensely religious and the rankest infidel; he condemns the theatre as being immoral, and he is the first to hail Ibsen and applaud him, even on the Yiddish· stage; there is no one so clannish and so cosmopolitan as he is . . . and these contrasts can be multiplied ·to the abuse of time and space.

If, then, he is everything and to be found anywhere, to be seen in all sorts of circumstances, in all walks of life and walking in so many diverse ways, making his way in such strongly contrasting conditions, how shall we know him? How shall we know what constitutes the Jew? He does not always abide in the Ghetto, and, things are coming to such a pass, that he rarely has the Ghetto appearance. I suppose that if our dear Mr. Zangwill had his own way he would fill the world with Ghettos. He could use them in his business. But perhaps the time is drawing nigh when we must have the books of Mr. Zangwill and other works of such excellence to preserve the most picturesque life of a unique people and save it from oblivion. . . .

Old-fashioned folk, like other things, go out of fashion. The old-style long garb, the "capota," will take itself away after the toga, and such is the awful power of civilization that even the time-honored skull-caps of the men and the wigs of the women are vanishing before it. Time, with its scythe, cuts down even the curling sidelocks and the long beards dear to tradition. Up-to-date fashion is a democratic tyrant, an expansionist invading and permeating all places and peoples. So we cannot count on these externals. Physiognomy is another thing by which to be misguided. Other outer details may help us as much as medicine can help the dead— or the living, for that matter. Then there are names. What's in a name? An opportunity for misunderstanding. One cannot even know himself by his name. All these artificial designations do not designate.

What, then, are the telling traits, the conspicuous characteristics by which the typical, representative Jew may be known? Now, I am blissfully ignorant of anthropology, and could not analyze scientifically, even at the risk of being destroyed critically. But through a certain accident—an accident of birth—I may be enabled to make a few suggestions, which I will offer with all due and undue apologies, of course.

First and foremost I should mention his wonderful versatility; he is the most versatile actor in this play called life. He has acquired this versatility throughout his wanderings, sufferings, trials and tribulations, and together with his prodigious adaptability, it constitutes the secret of his survival. Originally a being of the highest talent with the radiant glow of the Orient upon his brow, he had walked through the histories of many nations, and being persecuted by all peoples who recognized his talent, he received a most liberal education in the school of sorrow. Thus his abilities were cultivated and he learned to adapt himself easily to all circumstances and to create his own little world wherever he pitched his tent.

Mentally alert, keen of comprehension, quick to grasp any situation, almost too shrewd to be wise, practical to the detriment of his high ideals, calm, careful, cautious, calculating, hopeful in the face of despair, optimistic to a discouraging degree, often too regular and respectable to become great; intensely individualistic, proud of his past, anxious about the future, ever devoted to his cause, self-appreciatory, at times too sure of his capabilities, confident in the ultimate decency of things, deeply in love with life—are among the qualities that may be attributed to the Jew.

His isolated, peculiar and purely religious life, "the spiritual Palestine," which he has carried along with him in his wanderings through the darkness and cold of the Ghettos, has under all circumstances and in all the hazards preserved those fine domestic and social qualities for which he is noted. What can *now* be said about his domesticity, his love of home and care of his family; his sobriety, thrift, peacefulness and good deportment, the readiness with which he cares for his poor, his public spirit in the interests of his community—wherever that may be—his unequalled kindness . . . would be mere repetition; but these are nevertheless some of the undisputed qualities which constitute the Jew. Believing himself chosen of God, he has strong faith in the part he plays, the work he does, and the mission he is to perform with his being. And like others who have much faith in themselves, he has abundance of conceit. But let us not call it that. "Sublime egotism" sounds so much better, and besides, the line of demarcation between the two is so fine that it does not exist. The Jew is strongly individualistic in his social tendencies, and for that reason is often so progressive. He dares to deviate from the trodden path. He is not always in harmony with the rest of the community in which there is from time to time much discord—discord that sometimes amounts to war. Thus the persecution of the Jew often begins at home. His receptive mental attitude often brings him into the ranks of the most radical, despite his traditions, which would hold him back.

He has talent to waste, and much of it is really wasted because he lacks opportunity for cultivation and frequently has not the required concentration and application. Perhaps it is better so; for if all Jewish talent was brought out in the various forms of greatness, what would—what would the anti-Semites not say? They would say that the Jews have stolen their talents. For anti-Semitism is the cry of despair of defeated mediocrity, or it is the plaint of the blinded Christian maddened by jealousy because he has been beaten by the wandering Jew in his own game of trade, commerce, politics, or art. But the Jew is kind, his kindness is unsurpassed, and the Hebrew line in which his people are called "merciful sons of the merciful" is literally true. He pities the anti-Semite as he pities all who suffer and who are in want of the good things and the good qualities of life.

. . . This on the one hand and the strange world with its hard realities, with its stumbling-blocks and stunning blockheads, on the other, have created in the Jew a striking two-sidedness, a kind of duality and, if I may so call it, a sort of conciliation between the ideal and the real. This forms another trait by which you may tell him. Thus he is very practical, and still dreams, hopes for the restoration of Palestine, and loves his home and his country wherever he abides. He is an ardent Zionist and a good citizen at the same time.

. . . People must live, you know, and therefore they often live a living death. Not permitted to live rightly and happily, they still must live somehow. The instinct of self-preservation preserves much evil, but life is life. Those who have talent and are not permitted to use it for the good of all, use it for their own temporal good, regardless of the consequences. . . . They who walk in darkness find the ways that are dark. Over-praise is damning, and I want to be careful. The Jew has on the whole been far, far better than he has been permitted to be—and this, too, is one of the charges against him. He is a graduate of the school of sorrow *cum laude.* . . .

The Jew is a great possibility. Sensitive of and susceptible to all things, to the very color of the atmosphere around him, with a soul sharpened by sorrow and a mind of keenest understanding, he can become anything and everything, assimilate himself with any and all conditions, and illustrate life with a new meaning or adorn it with a worthy work. . . .

Along with the rest of *Keidansky* these words filled Eliot Steinberger, when he first read them, with a mingling of almost unbearable grief and profound peace.

One night Tim the Oxonian, who usually came in charge of the pack train that brought his semimonthly supplies, turned to Eliot in the lantern light under their mosquito net, and said, "You're a Jew, aren't you, Yank?"

Eliot answered in the affirmative.

"Your name suggests it." The Oxonian told him he was Irish. He had apparently never heard of the Steinbergers or the S. & S., and Eliot told him very little about himself. Tim was not really interested, or else thought he could imagine what had brought the young fellow to inland Australia. He seemed to believe that men were pretty much alike, whether of this or another nationality, Jews or Christians, "educated" or not. They were all engaged in "a blind struggle for something or other," no one could be sure what. He guessed it was to extricate themselves from their current environments and personal desires; but this struggle was stupidly conducted and tended only to complicate their situation. "I am now at the point in my personal philosophy," he said to Eliot, "where I believe the thing to do is to simplify oneself, reduce one's needs, demands, and cravings to the absolute minimum, and thereby make oneself fit to wage a quiet one-man war against the the world, which confuses and makes us into creatures we are not. . . . The life you and I lead here is perfect training for the struggle against the world's mad complexities."

Eliot agreed. Tim but articulated his own recent feelings and thoughts about life which he had been expressing differently, not quite so clearly and directly, in the verse he had been writing. He thought of making this idea his ideal. Then he re-read *Keidansky* once more, and it occurred to him he would have difficulty in realizing it—he might never be able to simplify himself. Jews were a complex people, closely tied to the world. Extreme. Many things at the same time. . . .

VIII

Every two months Eliot rode to Innamincka. The company required this, for the boundary riders had the tendency to go "off" on account of the loneliness, monotony and heat. At the outposts, as the paddocks were also called, they were forbidden to drink anything alcoholic, owing to the fact that drunkenness often resulted in getting "bushed" or lost, in being thrown off a horse and then "perishing" of thirst, mosquito, ant and snake bites, or sunstroke, or all of these; while at the sheep station they were allowed to get as drunk as they liked, enjoy a woman (a few aborigines—"black gins" or "lubras" they were called—were there for this purpose), and otherwise give vent to themselves for two or three days.

Each time he went "in," Eliot thought of sending a letter to his family, but always decided against it. Returning to No. 9, he brought his supplies for the next two weeks, including such reading matter as he had been able to pick up at the station.

He spent eight months as a boundary rider.

On his fourth trip to Innamincka, the Oxonian suggested he stay "in" for a while. Wild horses being herded in from the Bush had to be busted and trained into dependable boundary-riding mounts: would he try his hand with them? Eliot would; and he lived the next two months in the strange little community, breaking in the horses. This raised his pay, for he received his share of the £5 per horse broken in; and, more important, his self-confidence increased.

Then Eliot was assigned to a camel team in charge of an Afghan, whom everybody called Buffalo Bill. Thirty-odd camels carried the large bales of wool from the station and the shearing sheds on some of the outposts to the far-off railroad sidings. Till he learned it thoroughly, this new work was dangerous. The camels were very erratic as well as extremely enduring beasts; and the trips through the Bush, most of them requiring from two to three weeks, often strained his spirit and every fiber of his physical being. But he met the requirements of his job, and a little more. One day a twitch of an approving smile flashed across Buffalo Bill's dead-pan Oriental face; it filled Eliot with a light that glowed for days.

The European War had been on for two months when the news of it penetrated to the Bush and Eliot. Thereafter he got hints of events on the various fronts every two or three weeks. The wool business boomed . . . and Eliot, driving the camels, worried and wondered about his family. He was inclined to assume they had returned to America by then, but could not be sure. Was the Old Boy well again?

IX

Satisfied at last that he had passed the test, Eliot abruptly decided to quit his job. Without being in any great hurry about it, he thought he might return to the United States, and made his way to Melbourne with about fifty pounds to his name and the conviction that the thirteen months in the Bush had done him a universe of good. Now he might be able to live his life more or less on his "own terms as an individual and a free agent." What he meant by this phrase he scarcely knew, but it expressed—he was sure of that—a definite improvement in his character and morale.

However, he no sooner said this to himself than he let himself swing again to the other extreme of his station and atmosphere in life. In Melbourne he bought some fine clothes, put up at the best hotel and enjoyed to the limit its every convenience and luxury, at the same time wondering self-consciously how much all this had to do with his being a Jew, how much with the fact that he was born a rich man's son, and how much with the fact that he was just human. He met a troupe of American vaudevillians, caroused with them, and in a week was penniless again.

On the way to Melbourne he had half intended to cable his family to ask about the Old Boy and tell them he was all right; now once more decided against it. Nor was the lack of money for the cable the reason—he knew he could always go to the United States Consulate for aid. He dropped into the Depths again, sold his fine duds for one-fifth of what he had paid for them, went to Sydney, then starved for two weeks along the water front . . . till he was hired as a navvy, or laborer, on a railroad-building job between Dunedoo and Coonabaraban in New South Wales.

The hours on this job were as long as the wages were low, and the work was hard, mostly mucking and pushing a wheelbarrow full of gravel, but, after a few hefty meals in the labor camp, Eliot, now just twenty, managed to stick it out. The major part of his wages went to the camp boss for food and lodging; nonetheless, in three months he saved enough to return to Sydney and get passage on a San Francisco-bound freight ship.

What to Do
With Himself?

REACHING the Golden Gate, Eliot Steinberger was penniless again. He went to work on the docks and earned his trainfare to Chicago, where— dressed as a workingman, without necktie and socks—he all but fought his way through the cordon of bellhops in the ornate lobby of the Palmer House to the desk, and demanded he be announced at once to his half brother, Louis Steinberger, who chanced to be in his suite there.

Louis was popeyed with delight listening to his young half brother's account of himself since his disappearance. In turn, he gave Eliot the news about the family and the S. & S. Both were in a bad way. The Old Boy was not expected to live through the summer. He was still in Switzerland, as were his (Eliot's) mother and brothers and sister. "The old man believes you're still at Harvard," said Louis, "and I imagine your mother has worried a great deal about you, and has had a hard time keeping father from finding out that you disappeared." He mentioned some of the international and domestic difficulties in which the S. & S. was involved, said that personally he did not care very much what happened to the company, then talked excitedly about the potato masher he had just invented.

Eliot sent a long cable to his mother, who replied begging him to come to Europe at once if he wished to see his father, who was asking for him. Within a few days he was on the way over . . . but five days out he received a wireless: *Father died last night.*

The news plunged Eliot into a deep, self-condemnatory sadness, which kept him from taking any close notice of the year-old war. He was sorry for his mother, and glad to feel he served her as at least a slight solace in her grief. A few days after his arrival in Europe, he found himself with her and the Old Boy's body on a New York-bound ship. . . .

After the burial, Louis invited Eliot to come to Chicago to see whether he might not wish to become connected with the packing industry once more, "if only for the time being, in order to be doing something." Eliot went to Chicago, and Louis put him on a salary, but he could not develop any interest in the business. He knew he would never feel comfortable in it again, although now the other half brothers, who were officers in the company, no longer objected to him. They knew it had no future, and on one occasion, when he met with two of them, they joked about his being the "white hope" of the S. & S.

Eliot did not know what he could do with himself. Enroute from Sydney to San Francisco, his ship had stopped at a number of South Sea Islands, and for a while he had a notion to go back there with some of the money that would eventually come to him from the estate, but everybody discouraged him in this, especially his mother.

II

In 1916, a number of young fellows, sons of well-to-do families, who were friends of the Steinbergers, drew Eliot with them to Hollywood, which they thought had a great and exciting future. But Eliot was not interested in the movies—except in the lovely girls whom the industry attracted by the hundreds from all over the world. At various times during the ten months he spent in California he almost married. He had a wild time. But every once in a while he jerked himself up: was he slipping back into the pre-Harvard period? People introduced him as "the late Henry Steinberger's son" or as one "of the Steinberger packing family, you know." This annoyed him. Was his being a Steinberger to go on playing a central role in his life? The money coming to him from the office of the Steinberger estate: was it going to help him, or be a factor in his decline from the man he made of himself as a boundary rider, broncho-buster, and camel driver in Australia?

In January, 1917, Eliot quit Hollywood, partly in disgust with it and himself, partly in self-defense, lest the opportunities for wasting himself do their trick. He went East.

In the old Steinberger mansion in New York his mother was uncomfortable to the point of tears. The strain between her and the children of the second marriage continued. There were petty squabbles over the problems of the estate. Eliot did not care how the money was to be distributed, and the intra-family bickerings sickened him.

He was not yet twenty-two, and was about to receive fifty thousand dollars as part of his share of the estate. What would he do? He could not stand living in the mansion even to please his mother, and took rooms in a midtown hotel.

III

In February the United States severed its relations with Germany. To Eliot the European War had been at first a colossal stupidity; then, as he followed the events and caught glimpses of the ideas behind them, his sympathies had become strongly pro-Ally. That his father had been a native of Germany, and that its business rivals and the British Contraband Control had tried to brand the S. & S. as a "German company," had given him moments of uneasiness. Now he strongly approved of President Wilson's action. It stirred him.

A few days after, turning a corner on Fifth Avenue, Eliot ran into Phil Brooks, one of the "bums" he had known at Harvard five years before. Phil was excited, too. "We'll be in the war in no time at all, you'll see. We've got to think about it." He called a few more fellows; they had dinner and drinks in Eliot's rooms . . . and, one thing leading to another at a swift, typically American pace, early in March they and several more young men, who had been brought into the group, started to learn flying, so they would be ready for service when the United States Army or Navy was ready to take them in.

Eliot gave a large part of the money needed for the airplanes and hangars, the Long Island flying field, and the instructors' salaries.

When the United States declared war on the Central Powers in April, these young men were promptly accepted. Among the first fliers to go over, Phil Brooks and three others were killed in action early during America's participation in the war.

Recognized as a first-rate instructor, and against his repeated protests, Eliot was kept in the various air-training camps in the United States. Finally, he got over in the fall of 1918—too late to see combat action.

IV

Released from the service, now in his mid-twenties, Eliot asked the old question: what to do with himself? From the estate he continued to receive his share of the money which became available from time to time for distribution among the members of the family. What to do with it? Why should he be getting it? He hadn't earned it. . . .

Less than a year after the Armistice, his mother and sister and brothers decided to return to Switzerland to live. They urged him to come with them. He said he might follow them later.

He stayed in New York till 1922, blowing in much of his money ("to hell with it!"—one of his favorite expressions at the time). But what usually passed for "good time" gave him no real satisfaction. His life had no flow or rhythm. It jerked and squirted in all directions, and none.

In 1922, Eliot received a cable from his sister Ann: his brother Marshall had been killed in a fall from a horse. His mother was heartbroken, and Ann begged him to join them abroad at once. She hinted there were "other complications."

The family lived in an hotel outside Zurich. When Eliot arrived, his mother had partly recovered from the shock of her son's death. In the hotel, doing all he could to soothe her sorrow, was a middle-aged widower, Sam Berman, who had been her early-girlhood sweetheart in Norfolk. He wanted to marry her. This constituted the "other complications." A retired dry-goods merchant, Mr. Berman was well-off himself, and obviously his motive was not merely to marry a rich widow. The affair was close to pure romance. Eliot saw nothing against the man, and although the situation gave him a strange feeling, he thought remarriage might be the best thing for his mother.

For five years the devoted Sam followed her wherever she went, and finally, when in her early fifties, she consented to marry him. Now they live in their native Norfolk. To Eliot, who sees her and her husband about once a year, this is "rather wonderful and terribly funny. Also a little sad, in a way. Now and then it seems that all of us, my father, the years of her life with him and us, were just a kind of interlude, a passing incident. In Norfolk she took up again the friends of her girlhood and the whole thread of life as though it had never been broken. . . ."

V

Soon after Eliot got to Switzerland in 1922, his sister Ann, an exceptionally pretty and brilliant girl in love with a young Swiss who adored her, became afflicted with a serious case of acne, which in the next few years, in spite of all the efforts of medical science, ruined her lovely complexion and naturally affected her life drastically—a story all by itself, which I shall not even try to summarize here.

Her physician was Dr. Maxim Laubach of Zurich, a leading skin specialist with a volatile, hot passion for his profession. Eliot came to like him enormously. When he talked with him, or watched him treat Ann, or listened to him talk to her, he had a feeling he could define only as inspiration. The *Herr Doktor* was then already past middle age, a small man but tireless; a Jew with a bespectacled face, which flashed with quick, at once sad and humorous smiles, and seemed to accept the world in toto and with a fierce determination and a personal plan to help make it better.

In a few months Doctor Laubach and Eliot became deep friends.

Both because of Ann's tragic affliction and through her physician, Eliot became profoundly interested in medicine, and particularly in dermatology, as a science and practice. All at once he forgot himself. Without realizing it, he ceased asking what to do with himself. There were questions bigger than he and outside of him, inviting him to discover their answers. It was like no other challenge before. Listening to Doctor Laubach, he lost himself and found himself in the warmth of a great love, an enduring absorption. His being became a vessel to catch and hold what he heard. On the threshold of an endless quest, he experienced simultaneously breathless excitation and a deep quiet. He knew the quest would require infinite patience, reverence, almost; and he was impatient to acquire the technique and the habit of mind which would equip him for it. He plied Doctor Laubach with questions. He told him of barku rot, recalling how much the phenomenon had interested him at No. 9, and that he had wondered what the causes of the disease were. . . .

One day his new friend brought him a book containing the reprint of an address delivered by Sir Jonathan Hutchinson, the eminent English physician of the late nineteenth century, before the graduating class of a medical school. It included these words:

If I am not mistaken, the time is not distant when diseases of the skin, instead of being esteemed an unimportant, if not repulsive, specialty, will be regarded as affording almost unequalled opportunities for the study of morbid processes, and when they will take their proper place as introductory to the study of medicine; and before trying to understand diseases which are to a large extent concealed from observation, the student will attempt first to master those which are exposed to view. . . .

The scholastic record which had admitted Eliot to Harvard was not sufficient in the judgment of the renowned medical school in Zurich, whose requirements were extremely high. Besides, his Harvard record weighed heavily against his enrollment. But Doctor Laubach, a member of the faculty, helped him to enter in 1923 . . . whereupon he studied "like hell" through most of the ensuing five years, as he had studied in the "prep" school in Boston 'way back in 1911-12; only with a different motive and spirit—not to take the citadel of Harvard, which limited the number of Jews, but to be a doctor, a fellow and brother of men like Maxim Laubach. The third year he began to be considered the most brilliant student in the school.

This development resolved one of his main dilemmas.

But the rest of the inner drama of his quandary continued. Most of the time he lived in extremely modest student quarters in a poor section of Zurich and watched with deep interest the ways and problems of the people in the neighborhood, feeling himself part of it. Then, of a sudden, a powerful impulse would take him to St. Moritz, Monte Carlo, Nice or the Lido, where he took rooms in the most expensive hotels.

VI

In 1925, at St. Moritz, he met Peggy Bryce, a beautiful young divorcée of old-stock American ancestry, well-off, traveled, and constantly trailed by a squad of love-smitten males of various ages. At thirty-one Eliot was already bald (a family trait), but this did not diminish his attractiveness; and Peggy, bored by the attentions of the conventional playboys and would-be playboys who never pierced her intelligence, found him stimulating and agreeable company. He was moved to write poetry again and excel himself in love-making.

In the next few years, as a medical student, Eliot kept in touch with Peggy, who was increasingly fascinated by him. He sent her his poems. Every four or five months they met at St. Moritz or the Lido and had joyous times for a week or two at a spell. Then they quarreled and parted.

Eliot's quandary was one of the chief factors in these "fights" between them. After a few days in the lap of luxury, where Peggy felt completely at home, he began to get restless, then irritable, then (from her angle) somewhere between difficult and impossible; while to him she appeared "a spoiled brat." One of the two inevitably told the other to go to the devil. Whereupon Eliot would return to his room in Zurich and his studies, which he told himself were after all his real passion; and Peggy would go back to America or England, or on a trip to India, Japan or Greece.

A few months after each such incident, however, one of two things happened, or both. He cabled her the latest bubble of his love-churned poetic talent, or she communicated with him or suddenly appeared in Zurich. Once he had barely sent his cable when the postman brought him a letter from her: she was in London and coming to Switzerland in a fortnight. At another time a message that she was at a hotel in the city reached him as he sealed a letter to her and was writing her Florida address on the envelope.

They could not shake one another out of their respective make-ups, but his quandary, her high-strung temperament and the hangover of her first marriage, the fact that he was a Jew and she a Gentile, and diverse intangibles which stemmed from the other factors and intermingled, producing endless absurd but extremely real difficulties, kept them from marrying. Both their families objected to the affair: his, on the ground that she was a Gentile, a divorcée, a woman of the world; hers, that he was a Jew. This crossfire of objections caused nasty scenes on both sides, with unpleasant repercussions in the middle.

Eliot became once more aware that he was a Jew. From a secondhand bookshop in New York he procured another copy of *Keidansky*, then re-read again the chapter on "What Constitutes the Jew?" It once more simultaneously exalted and depressed him, and these complex "Jewish moods," as he subsequently recalled them, no doubt influenced his love affair.

With its sharp ups and downs, the affair went on through most of his Zurich student period, then continued in its seemingly uncertain way for seven years more: a decade, all told. Several times they decided to marry "next spring," "next month," "on next Tuesday" or "tomorrow"—then the explosion again, the intense and sudden difficulty, which neither could quite analyze and define.

On several occasions Peggy swore to herself and before friends and members of her family that "this time" she was really and finally done with him. Twice, to show how firmly she meant what she said, she came close to marrying another man. The second time she changed her mind only a few hours before the ceremony. "That lunatic," as she occasionally called Eliot, fascinated and absorbed her. Also, his manner and attitude challenged her feminine ego: she must "get" him. He was bald, but "wonderful;" she could scarcely say why. He made her angry, furious. There was a continual tension between them, simultaneously pleasant and unbearable. She wondered: was this part of "the Jew-Gentile business"? Was he so damnably interesting because he was a Jew? She did not know; she had had distant contacts with a few Jews who seemed rather dull; but she inclined to think that in Eliot his being Jewish had a great deal to do with his being interesting. One day in the seventh or eighth year of their tumultuous relationship he asked her to read his favorite chapter in *Keidansky*.

"Why," she exclaimed, "this is you all over!"

Now and then, talking with her across the dinner table in some *de luxe* hotel or café, he would casually refer to dock-walloping or living in the slums of London, to sheep-raising, dingo dogs, barku rot, Innamincka, camel-driving, puffaloons, kangaroos and emus, but modesty or some other inhibition kept him from tying up for her these bits of narrative into a coherent story. What he did tell her however, caused Peggy to wonder almost endlessly about him.

By-and-by, as they both grew older and started to realize how inevitable "this whole thing" was, the difficulties between them began to melt away. Their families gradually ceased to object. . . . And finally, in 1936, when he was already an established doctor in New York, they married, puzzled why they had not done so before; and their private life—full of stimulating tensions, most of them springing from his quandary and her high-strung temperament—has been very much of a mutual success.

Doctor Steinberger
—Continued

Eliot passed his "State exam" in 1930 and, toward the end of that year, opened his office in the Seventies off Park Avenue. By 1933 he was widely recognized as a "coming man" in the field. He had already published a number of papers in the United States, Germany, Switzerland and France, and was being asked to talk before medical societies. He became a lecturer in a medical school in New York City. He published his first book. He was obliged to move to a larger office.

I quote a few paragraphs from one of his earliest addresses which reveal his professional function and attitude, and suggest his thought processes in general:

It is an obvious fact that no organ of the body can have an independent life of its own. The more we learn, the more closely knit the interrelationship of organ to organ and of the part to the whole appears to be. . . . It is certain that the relationship of the skin to other organs is no exception to this rule. . . .

Many skin disorders seem at first glance and if regarded from the purely morphological and descriptive viewpoint, to be merely local changes in the outermost layers of the body's envelope. They seem superficial, both in actual depth of the pathological process and in fundamental significance. . . . The older dermatology was content to contemplate skin lesions in this manner. . . . [The] newer dermatology has learned to be aware of the deeper meaning of many seemingly only dermatologic manifestations.

. . . Dermatology has been benefited by the newer concept; so also has general medicine. The accessibility and visibility of the skin, the facility with which repeated histological and bacteriological examination may be made, have enriched our knowledge of many processes of general biological and pathological importance. Because the skin offers external, clearly apparent signs of the earliest beginnings of many diseases, it has been of incalculable aid in the study of the early and previously ignored stages of various general processes. For example, we owe almost our entire knowledge of the beginnings of cancer to investigations of the precanceroses of the skin.

Furthermore, skin diseases are frequently the earliest and most apparent danger signals of internal conditions. They are visible, often ugly and uncomfortable, as a rule disturbing, not to say terrifying to the patient. Many who will disregard a slight internal malaise or nondescript, vague general complaint will come to the doctor at the first appearance of a definite skin manifestation. I shall endeavor to show that the knowledge of the art of reading and interpreting these signs will often enable the physician to suspect underlying diseases of the utmost importance, and will sometimes lead to early diagnoses of otherwise unsuspected and often dangerous conditions. This will often permit the urgently required early therapy and may spare many a patient serious illness, long suffering; and may even save his life. . . .

This idea and attitude that Eliot Steinberger expressed (not originally) is now held by nearly all dermatologists. It drives the men who really belong in the field into intense explorations of the unknown. It urges on those who are just naturally alive—the slaves to, and would-be masters of, the wonder of life, its revelations and secrets, the reactions of its phases one to the other, the amazing chemistry of its processes.

II

One evening I dined with Eliot Steinberger when he was so full of a case with which he had lately dealt that he could not refrain from telling me about it.

"About a year ago," he began, "the people working in and patronizing a Bronx cleaning-and-pressing establishment, owned by a Mr. Ben Dunkel (to give him a name which is not his), began to be annoyed by an unpleasant smell which suggested something was mildewed in the place—like an old half-rotten, damp rag lying under the slop pail beneath the sink. The first measure was to throw away all the old pressing cloths and replace the pads in the pressing machines. But the smell persisted. Mr. Dunkel had the walls torn down, thinking there was something rotten or dead behind them. Nothing was found. . . . It was impossible to localize the stench. Now it was here, then there; now almost everywhere.

"The shop is a fairly large place, employing four full-time and three part-time pressers and a delivery boy. The workers began to quit on account of the smell, and Mr. Dunkel had trouble keeping the people he hired to replace the old employees, one or two of whom had been with him for years. The customers, too, complained of the smell; some who had long been patrons of the shop came back annoyed or irate, to tell Mr. Dunkel that they detected the strange smell in the clothes they had had pressed. . . . The poor fellow was getting frantic.

"Mr. Dunkel has a wife and several children. They were puzzled by the smell which was also present in the family apartment above the shop. It occurred and went. When at its worst, it sent all of them out of doors or to the movies.

"One of the boys in the family is going to Columbia and seems to have a scientific turn of mind. He determined that the smell appeared when his father was about. It was perceptible in the towels he used.

"Poor Mr. Dunkel bathed and bathed—to no avail. His morale was shattered, his business ruined, and he had to close the shop. He went from doctor to doctor. He entered a hospital and submitted to a series of thorough examinations. Everything about him that could conceivably be analyzed was analyzed. Everything was all right. His sweat was under strongest suspicion, but all analyses declared it normal. He appeared in perfect health.

"One of the doctors finally suggested he see me, and about three weeks ago

I read the history of the case which had been assembled for me. Naturally it interested me, and we had the man come in. My assistants put him through another complete examination, making all the analyses. No hint, no clue. But there was no doubt that the smell emanating from him was both peculiar and unpleasant.

"The problem fascinated me"—smiling—"so I laid my curious patient on the table and began to sniff him——"

Visualizing this, I roared.

Laughing, too, then smiling, Doctor Steinberger continued: "I was fairly sure that his body or his skin as a whole did not emanate the odor; so, assuming it had a localized source, I wanted, or I hoped, to determine that source. I started with his head, and learned the kind of hair tonic he used. Sniffing his chin and cheeks, I detected the last faint whiffs of his favorite after-shaving lotion; and so on. . . . Everything normal. . . . I had suspected his armpits, but his sweat was apparently normal there, too. . . .

"Then, focusing my olfactory powers on the right hand, calloused from handling the pressing iron—Eureka! I found the spot. It was beneath the gold wedding ring, which he had worn for twenty-two years. The stench there was very strong.

"How to explain it? Evidently an important change had quite suddenly occurred in his body. We cannot tell how or why. It cannot be detected by any of the analyses we now know how to make. But it subtly altered the composition of his sweat, which, when it came in close contact with gold, or with the particular alloy in the gold of which his ring is made, produced the odor! . . ."

We both laughed again. The case enthralled him. It was "amazing, wonderful." The chemical interaction of Mr. Dunkel's sweat with his gold ring was a part of the whole vast wonder of life, its nuisances and possibilities.

He concluded his tale: "I took off the ring and washed the finger; in a half-hour there was no trace of the smell. The man has not worn his ring since, and the odor is a thing of the past. . . . The surface or now-obvious phase of the case was very simple. The first requisite was tackling the problem directly, objectively. . . . Today I received a letter from Mr. Dunkel, thanking me: I saved his life, his family happiness, his business. . . . But, of course, I solved the problem only superficially. Assuming I am right that a change did occur in the composition of his sweat, the important question is: what caused the change? Then: will that change further affect him, in other ways, later on? And how? . . . And how many such mysterious changes are going on in all of us, altering our degree of resistance or susceptibility to serious diseases—to cancer, to tuberculosis, to mental depressions and manic states?"

III

Eliot Steinberger's mind throbs with queries apart from his work. Everything interests him. As one talks to him, he has a listening look about him, as though his ears were standing up. He is one of the best listeners I know—a rare quality in people who are also good talkers. His body is poised to catch every word and sound. Now and then his entire being seems concentrated in the pupils of his eyes. He listens with his head slightly tilted down, his eyes lifted wide, waiting, evoking and absorbing your words and meaning. And when he talks all of him appears to be thinking, speaking, responding. Yet his manner is not compulsive; it is inviting. While not egoless, the man is humble. He conveys to you his vitality, draws you to his quest. . . .

For years now he has been watching and studying events in America and Europe, probing into their underlying significance. Already in 1933, after a two-month tour of Europe, including Germany, he saw manifestations of a "disease" spreading through the Old World "and possibly the United States." He was unable to diagnose the disease but it was there and "most likely dangerous." Nobody of consequence was studying it and making moves to check it.

He spoke to me similarly early in 1938. In his capacity as an American citizen, one side of him held for some time, although more and more weakly, onto the traditional foreign policy of the United States of no foreign entanglements, while another side of him, with his dermatological objectivity, maintained "that the human world, very much like the human body, is all of one piece," and that America could not help being affected and involved or entangled.

In May, 1940, he could barely be restrained from offering his services as a flyer to the Allies. It was difficult for him to continue looking objectively at what he saw; it was hard for him to stand and do nothing. He responded as a Jew, a human being, an American who believed in Democracy, suffering "every blow and kick delivered by every Gestapo agent at every prisoner, Jew or Gentile, in every concentration camp." When he said this to me one day early in 1939 the curious expression on his face wontedly so finely balanced between amusement and near-despair abruptly turned all agony, and he "looked Jewish."

One of the most frequent subjects of discussions between him and me was the idea, on which we essentially agreed, that there really was no "Jewish problem" as something apart from the American and general human problem. He said that anti-Semitism was but a symptom of the disease he considered dangerous. Both of us held that "we would have to get together, somehow, soon," all of us who came or stemmed from the many lands of the Old World, who were Gentiles and Jews, white and black and yellow and red, Polish, Welsh, Irish, Slovenian Americans, etcetera, to acquire an insight into one another. But how to do that? So many elements of the American people set themselves apart. On an occasion a friend of mine who happened to be in the conversation addressed a remark to Eliot Steinberger that there was basis for the oft-heard statement that the Jews were clannish.

"I dislike to merely defend the Jews," he replied, ". . . but my impression, stating it as objectively as I can, is that their clannishness is, roughly, one-third a matter of their own impulse and making, a result of their desire to hang together communally and otherwise, and two-thirds imposed upon them by the attitudes toward them of the non-Jews. I married a Gentile, I mingle with Gentiles, and want to mingle with them much more and on a much more natural and agreeable basis than I do; but consider this: For years Peggy, a Gentile afflicted with the name of Steinberger, had difficulty in renting houses for our summer vacations. She was refused as a would-be tenant in Greenwich, Connecticut, on Cape Cod, and elsewhere; and finally we had trouble finding people willing to sell us a summer place which was not in a Jewish community. I resisted the pressure to drive me into Jewish clannishness at Harvard; I have been resisting it in New York and elsewhere in recent years—successfully, so far, perhaps only because I am more advantageously placed than are most Jews. Most of them cannot cope with it. They become clannish. . . . How long will I hold out? . . . I am supposed to be a fairly well-known doctor, but before I enter the home or hospital room of any of my influential or well-known or very wealthy Gentile patients I look at myself in a mirror if I have the chance, to make sure about my appearance. If there is no mirror, I examine myself as well as I can without it. I feel my necktie to make sure it is straight. All this because I am a Jew. I am conscious that I am on trial; not only I, myself, but Jews——"

IV

As I write these concluding paragraphs of his story (in July, 1940), Eliot Steinberger's quandary continues with fluctuating, confusing emphases on his various predicaments.

There is the personal predicament, which touches his profession. He and Peggy live in an eight-thousand-dollar-a-year apartment, which she furnished and decorated with superb taste, and they have a vacation home in the White Mountains. His large office includes a big staff and the latest equipment. He is continually training new doctors, whom he selects on the basis of their potentialities; some are Jews, others Gentiles, and more than a score of them are scattered all over the country working under his influence. He is suddenly an upperdog in his own right, ascending on his own power, and one side of him does not like any part of this success. He has, as I have said, a passion for his work, but the trappings, the hocus-pocus, the symbols, the rush of social life accompanying it annoy him. Also, something in him resents individual or personal success.

He does a great deal of free clinical work, but this does not settle his personal-professional quandary; rather it aggravates it. It carries with it an implication of charity, which he inclines to consider unsound.

Once he told me that but for Peggy, who appears perfectly at home in the atmosphere of success, he would "chuck up everything and get to fundamentals." He would go back, symbolically, to No. 9. There he had not been primarily a Jew, not a successful man; he had been accepted for what he was and what he did, he met his test as a man.

This was no pose, but the statement of an actual and frequent impulse; yet

he—the rich man's son, the Jew, the modern individual in an increasingly insecure world—also needs and enjoys, "in a way," the elevator of his success.

Actually, he does not want to go back to the experiences of his early youth.
No. 9, he knows, was not the answer to anything. It was a mere beginning; in
spite of the physical hazards, only a simple, direct test. Talking with me one
night, he recalled Tim the Oxonian's remark: "The life you and I lead here is
perfect training for the struggle against the world's mad complexities," and disagreed with it.

"The problem in the Bush," he said, "was the fight against the elements, in-
sects and snakes. All I had to do to survive was to use such wits and resources
of endurance as I had. In civilization, so called, the problem is that of one's
entanglement in the struggle of man against man, of one human organization
against another.

"In relation to this problem, the wish of most of us, perhaps most of the time,
is to withdraw. One has relatives, friends, wife, children; and the impulse is to
say: to the devil with everything else. One cannot succeed in this. One becomes
an ant running around on the upper link of the hobble chain. Below are the
links of one's other predicaments and weaknesses: clannishness, greed, sheep-
ishness, etcetera, all tied together by the instinct to live on, somehow, and
breed. . . . Perhaps one way to state the human problem is: how to stop the
vicious circling on the top link of the hobble chain and do away with the rest
of the chain—the prejudices, the impositions—that keep us from reaching our
goals? We are tangled up in one another's purposes, drives, compulsions and
lack of them. . . . How to be free and strong in a world of others who also
would be free and strong, but who, like oneself, are weak and pulling and
clawing at one another. In other words, how to end this pointless struggle? . . .

"It's easy to ask these questions and to criticize humanity. To do something
about it is another matter." He smiled, relaxing for a moment the intensity of
his dark eyes. "I can't be consistently objective myself. I get in my own way,
let others get in my way."

"How?" I asked.

"Well, in my work as a doctor for example, I am not doing ten per cent of
what I could do."

"Why? What do you mean—specifically?"

He shrugged and smiled again. "Well, let us say I am called into a consultation with Gentile doctors. What happens? Both they and I are aware of what I
am: a Jew. This mutual consciousness not only stands between us, but between
us and the case. Often, of course, I have nothing to contribute; sometimes I
have. Sometimes I am afraid if I offer something my Gentile colleagues do not
know there will be resentment against me as a Jew and against the Jews
generally. Of course I speak out anyhow. But, in nine cases out of ten, I am not
entirely free to give the best in me—everything I say is just a little distorted by
the fact that I am a Jew; not necessarily in content, but the way I say it. There
is nearly always this fear: if I am too right or too prophetic, it may create a

feeling not only against me but against Jews. If I am wrong, this will be remembered and magnified because I am a Jew. Occasionally I have, or think I have, clear evidence in the facial expression and manner of Gentile physicians that they fear that I, a Jew, may have some part of the answer they don't have; even though, as non-dermatologist, they could not be expected to have it. . . . By this I do not mean to criticize my Gentile colleagues any more than I mean to criticize myself. In fact, myself more than them; or, rather, neither. What I really want to say is that the consciousness of my being a Jew and therefore on trial more than the Gentiles and bearing additional responsibility both for myself and for all other Jews, is always with me to a greater or lesser degree and is often accentuated in certain circumstances such as a consultation with eminent and eminently non-Jewish fellow doctors. Then I (but usually no one else) become aware of certain strains and inhibitions which prevent me from being my natural self; I am conscious of being either too timid or too aggressive—in short, not myself. I don't know whether I am more or less efficient, better or worse, because of this feeling of discomfort and added responsibility. . . . This feeling is probably both beneficial and detrimental, sometimes acting as a spur or as stabilizer and sometimes acting as an impediment, according to the situation and/or the temperament of the individual.

"In 1931 I was in line for promotion to a leading position on a hospital staff; I was frankly told, 'We already have two Jewish chiefs of departments,' and they took on a Gentile because he was a Gentile. Two years later I became dissatisfied with my opportunities for the studying and teaching of dermatology; I thought of trying to get a teaching job in a small medical school which might lead to a four- or five-thousand-dollar-a-year professorship, and which might enable me to really delve into dermatology as a science in collaboration with specialists in other fields in medicine, and train young doctors. I discovered I did not have a chance. . . .

"But this may sound like bellyaching. Really, I am not talking only about myself, about Jews. We agree: there is no 'Jewish problem.' Anti-semitism is but one symptom. I know a brilliant Negro doctor in Harlem and another brilliant doctor who was born in Oregon of Japanese parents; their chances are slimmer than mine; they are not doing *two* percent of what they could do. . . .

"The waste of it! I think I probably feel," he smiled, "as my father felt back in the 1860's and '70's contemplating the waste in the butcher trade. Only the problem of the waste that bothers me is much more complex than was the one that drove him to rendering fat into tallow and oleomargarine. . . ."

v

Several sentences in his copy of *The Discourses of Keidansky*, which he let me read, are pencil-marked. There is a specially emphatic line under the words, *"The Jew is a great possibility."*

I asked him about it.

He smiled. "I don't mean that only the Jew is a great possibility. Man—humanity is a great possibility.

"The Jew is perhaps an intensification of humanity, of its inner contradictions, its powers and weaknesses. The Jew is extreme in many ways, 'a graduate of sorrow *cum laude*,' and as such somewhat of an over-clear mirror of the human breed as a whole. As I have said, he is on trial. So is the rest of humanity; only it does not know it as clearly as he knows it. Therein is the source of his great discomfort, also his advantage over the non-Jew. He exerts himself more; he must be good. . . . If only man generally realized fully he was on trial!

"In part because man generally does not realize this as fully as the Jew, the Jew is uncomfortable. At many points he, himself, is anti-Semitic. He does not like his 'clannishness.' He his discontent whether he is rich or poor; if rich, because others are poor; if poor, because he lacks even the illusion of security which wealth sometimes provides, and so he wants it and, in some cases, is apt to do almost anything to get it. In this his predicament and disposition are the same as the average Gentile's; only more so.

"While chasing around on the top link of the hobble chain, the Jew has glimmers of objectivity. He would like to stop the mad circling and make a beeline for his goal of creative function, but he doesn't—he can't . . .

"What are our prejudices, our contradictions and quandaries doing to us all? Why do we physicians labor and sacrifice our strength and our happiness and our lives to relieve suffering, and then see that others no different fundamentally from ourselves devote their minds and energies to the creation of suffering? Why are we, humanity in general, sick with hate, stalled, held back from creativity? What would be our possibilities—here in America, in the world—if we freed ourselves of them, all of us?" He spoke in an even, quiet tone, but his whole being was aflame with these questions. "What if we ceased to be primarily Jews or X-ians and become primarily men? What if we got off the hobble chain and became free agents, free to tackle the mysteries?" He smiled. "*That's* the great possibility that interests me."

FIGURES IN
THE AMERICAN MAZE

To the Editor of The Sun:—*Sir:* As a true American, descendant of the pioneers who turned this country from a wilderness into the greatest country the world has ever known, until recently, I say, why should we Americans have to support the horde of aliens who come here uninvited? One look around New York, and it is evident they are not Americans, nor even the kind of people one wishes to have known as Americans. Why should we, the people who really belong here, be asked to support these people? Let them stay in their own lands, or, if they feel they must leave, let them go to the many waste places in this world and do as my forefathers did. It means sacrifice, hard work and privation, and they have not enough of these qualities to do this. They want to come here and spoil the country we true Americans made, and politicians do all they can to bring these people here just to get their votes. They are selling the country for a mess of pottage.

It is the most disgraceful thing we American descendants of the original settlers have been obliged to witness. Let dependent aliens leave this country to us and our descendants. We are not responsible for them or their condition, and we did not ask them to come here. There would be no question of relief if we had not been too generous and allowed them to enter. It is time we asserted ourselves to protest vigorously against this foreign invasion. Americans they never can be.

Madison, N. J., April 6, 1940   A TRUE PATRIOT

If you allow yourself to judge the worth of a man by anything except his character, if you discriminate against him for any reason that is outside his own control, you are no true American.—EMMET FOX, in *The Historical Destiny of the United States*.

We have paid our price. We, and we alone, know what it cost to leave behind scenes and traditions and affections which clung close to the heart.—WILLIAM ALLAN NEILSON, immigrant from England, former president of Smith College.

Manda Evanich
from Croatia

THE village of Smisliak, in the township of Severin, was, in the early eighties, typical of many peasant communities in Croatia—then under Hungary, later a part of Yugoslavia. The land about the hamlet was not over-fertile; few families owned enough of it to live on its yield, and each autumn most of the menfolk left to seek earnings in Hungary, Austria, Germany and elsewhere in Europe. Some peddled notions and other petty merchandise. Some worked as laborers on highways and railroads, in quarries, forests, sawmills, and factories.

Most households in Smisliak were semiprimitive in setup and circumstances. They included from two to as many as five families, closely kin on their male sides, and were called *zadrugé*—family collectives. The food was cooked, usually by the oldest woman in the house, over an open fire on the kitchen's earthen floor; then served in the big-room from a huge common clay bowl placed in the center of the large table, around which all the members sat, armed with wooden spoons. Most of the clothing was home-spun of home-grown wool, flax and hemp, and sewed in the house. There were few petroleum lamps; evenings, pieces of kindling burned indoors, torchlike.

The Evanich family was one of the larger *zadrugé* in Smisliak. Old man Evanich and his five grown sons were illiterate; there was no school in the village. Four sons were married, living in the collective with their wives and children. Their dwelling was tight and their total income slim and uncertain; like Croatian folk generally, however, they possessed their share of the Balkan Slavs' "heart culture"—kindness, generosity, humor, fair play, a sense of personal and communal responsibility, and a matter-of-fact acceptance of one another's faults and virtues—and they got along. They owned a team of horses and, their work in the fields done, the old man and one of the sons hauled lumber between Severin and the city of Karlovac, while the other sons, who were all obliged to contribute some cash to the collective's treasury, went off, usually on foot, soon after the birds' flight south, to find work in distant lands to the north.

Mihailo, or Michael, was the third oldest of the Evanich sons; short, compact, powerful, in his late twenties, with a barrel-like chest, a large head on a low neck, thick arms and legs, and immense hands. In '78 he had wed the nineteen-year-old widow Manda Filipac, whose first husband, also a peasant, leaving her with a small child, Tomo, or Thomas, had died on a sudden the previous year in the Filipac *zadruga*, across the street.

A large, well-built, fabulously strong girl, Manda had first married at sixteen. She was an outstanding character in the village from the start. For one thing, she could read and write. Her father was a progressive, comparatively well-to-do peasant in the close-by town of Damalj, who had taught himself to read and sign his name. For another thing, even more impressive, Manda could best in a fight any man in the township. She did the work of any two. Logs in the woods she handled like fence posts; boulders like pebbles—such was the slightly extravagant legend about her among the village folk. Also, she was immensely religious, ascribing her strength to her health, which she considered a gift of God.

Manda was gifted, too, in the art of healing. Back in her native Damalj, her mother, who was part Slovenian, had taught her the mixing of concoctions of herbs, roots and berries which were effective with various common ills and diseases; and by the time she was twenty, using common sense and possessing infinite self-confidence, she became expert also at setting broken bones and treating open wounds. There was no doctor within a half day's walking of Severin, and in accidents and sickness people called Manda.

In 1880 she bore her first son by her second husband, naming him Stevo, or Stephen. A year later she had her third boy, Josip, or Joseph.

She was content, even happy, in the Evanich household; there was always plenty to do, and her mother-in-law and three sisters-in-law esteemed her, as did the entire village. She was an asset to the collective, to Smisliak as a community.

But times were hard. Drought. Poor crops. Little hauling of lumber. Men returned early in winter, lest they starve and freeze to death in the faraway countries; there was no work for them.

II

Amerika . . .

Suddenly, somehow, this name appeared in the village minds. Someone uttered it. *Amerika*. But it was still no more than a name. Croatians from and the vicinity of Dubronik or Ragusa, or Dalmatia, had been going to the United States long before this, as had Slovenians from Carniola, which was right across the river from the Severin territory, but, so far as known, no inland Croatian had gone over till then.

A Carniolan cattle trader passed through Smisliak, saying he knew a man in his village who had gone "across the big pond" to a place called Michigan, where he was doing so well working in copper mines that he allegedly ate meat and white bread daily and was able to send money home several times a year.

Feeling the pinch of hard times, the Evanich *zadruga* decided that one of their men should go to America for a few years and see what he could do. Manda's father, known to have some cash, was consulted, and he agreed to lend them the money for the passage if his son-in-law Mihailo went.

Mihailo was hesitant, for by then the village had also heard stories of shipwrecks and other accidents and situations in which hundreds of emigrants were said to have perished. At the end, however, when they learned that a couple of Slovenians from near the Croatian border were about to go too, Manda induced her husband to brave the journey to the New World.

The ocean trip took nearly a month, and in the fall of '82 Mihailo Evanich reached Houghton, Michigan; whereupon he worked awhile in the mines of a small copper company operated by the Ruppe family, Slovenian-immigrant merchants in Houghton County, who subsequently became very rich. The copper deposits of Upper Michigan, which presently turned out to be the richest in the world, were just being opened.

Mike, as he began to be called, was the first Croatian in Michigan, and one of the first inland Croatians in America. For a year he associated almost exclusively with Slovenians, whose language was similar to his Croatian tongue. He repaid his father-in-law for the passage and sent home some money besides.

His second job was with the Osceola Mining Company at Osceola, three miles from Calumet, the center of copper operations. There he found a number of young Slovenian-immigrant miners who, having no Slovenian boardinghouse in this camp, lived with Finnish, German and Irish families. On learning that Mike was married, and that his wife was a jewel as a housekeeper, they urged him to send her a *shifkarta*, or steamship ticket, and bring her over, promising they would become her boarders.

Although he had no intention of staying permanently in America, Mike considered this a good idea. At this time, too, he became afflicted with an eye disease which no doctor in Calumet or Houghton seemed able to diagnose and cure, and he was afraid of going blind. He believed Manda would know what to do about it. So he had one of the literate Slovenians write her to come right away, and to fetch the boys with her. Bringing over the children was also her prospective boarders' idea. They wanted her to stay in America awhile.

Motivated largely by her eagerness to cure her husband's eyes, Manda prepared to go at once. She saw no sense in taking the children along, for they would have been cared for in the Evanich *zadruga* till she and Mihailo returned home in a few years; but, in view of Mihailo's illness, there was no time to write to him and argue about this, and so the three little boys went with her.

Mike Evanich rented a dilapidated log cabin in a wood on the mine company's property. There were two rooms and a kitchen on the ground floor and a large bedroom upstairs. The cabin was almost unfit for habitation, but Mike and his Slovenian friends repaired it hurriedly, made bedsteads, tables, chairs, closets and shelves, and procured the necessary kitchenware and bedding.

III

When Manda got to Osceola with the children, late in the summer of '83, she found in her new home ten or a dozen men besides her husband. They taught her how to use the stove Mike had bought for her, for she had never seen one; as already mentioned, back in Smisliak food was cooked over an open fire on the floor.

She had brought with her a remedy for Mike's eyes, and they were well in two weeks.

It took Manda—now in her mid-twenties—a good while to become accustomed to this new life, which, in many ways, was cruder and harder than the life she had left behind in Croatia; and in later years she confided to her sons that during her first few months in America she had wept in secret every day. Huge black bears would appear from the dense virgin forest in back of the house. There were no neighbors.

The hard-working, hungry boarders, whose palate had been Americanized, demanded cakes, pies, cookies and other foods of which Manda had not heard in the old country. She had to learn to prepare them.

In winter the temperature often fell to twenty-five or thirty below zero, and snow piled up from eight to twelve feet high. She and the men frequently had to tunnel their way out of the house through the drifts. To make the boarders' beds upstairs, Manda was obliged to remove panfuls of snow from the covers. The well was some twenty feet from the house, and water had to be brought in, winter and summer. She had to be up at four to give the men breakfast and pack their dinner pails. Her usual workday was sixteen hours.

She found it strange to go to Mass in an Irish church.

In those mining communities, the custom was for the "boarding missus" to do all the cooking, baking, washing and ironing for the boarders. The washing included their heavy miners' work clothes and, once a week, their feet. For this she received three dollars monthly from each boarder. The grocery, meat and fuel bills were charged in equal proportions to the "boarding boss" and the boarders.

The weekly feet washing had originated in Upper Michigan some ten years before Manda's arrival. The story goes that there was a Finnish "boarding missus" who used to wash her husband's feet every evening as he came home tired from the mine; it refreshed him. Later, when some of her boarders threatened to move to another house, she offered, in addition to the usual services, to wash their feet, too, once a week. They stayed; men in other boardinghouses heard of this and, to keep them from moving, the missuses generally took to washing their boarders' feet. In a few years it became a tradition.

On top of all this, Manda was also the boarders' doctor. From the old country she had brought a bundle containing all sorts of roots and seeds, dried leaves, blossoms and mosses which, cooked in various combinations known to peasants in Croatia, were supposed to cure—and in many cases did cure—diverse afflictions. Men came to her with colds, earaches, stomach troubles, and rheumatic pains, or with crushed fingers and hands, broken arms, ribs and collarbones, dislocated shoulders or open wounds; or were brought to her from the mines with broken legs or hips, or caved-in torsos. Manda "fixed" them up.

In common with other copper-mine workers, Mike made $1.25 a day, and, with the income from the boarders, in two years he and Manda saved six hundred dollars. She began to see that America was a land of great opportunities and gradually ceased thinking of returning to the old country.

Near Osceola was a mining location called Raumbalton, where the subsequently famous Calumet-Hecla Company operated three mines. Wide-awake, shrewd Manda heard that the C-H was paying better wages than other companies and prevailed upon Mike to try to get work there.

The Cornish mine boss, on hiring him, inquired for his surname. Mike replied, "Evanich." The boss, who had to issue him a workbook, asked him to spell the name. Mike, who never had learned to write, couldn't. A Slovenian wrote it down in awkward hand; the boss misread it "Evans" and entered it thus in the workbook. Then and there, Mike ceased to be Evanich and became Michael, or Mike, Evans, was naturalized as such, and the whole family—now very large—has been Evans ever since.

Shortly after this the Evanses bought a house on the company property in Raumbalton for nine hundred dollars, and the boarders followed them there, all finding work in the C-H mines.

IV

Manda's departure for America had caused no end of talk in the Severin township back in Croatia, and by '85 a month seldom passed without one or more Croatians coming to Michigan. Among them were a couple of Mike's brothers and some of his and Manda's cousins—all eager to board with the Evanses, who built additions to their house.

Manda's workday increased to eighteen hours a day. There were no Slovenian or Croatian women or girls whom she could hire to help her, and she would not take on one of another nationality whom she would be unable to understand; so she did everything herself, up to the minute she gave birth to her first child in America—another boy. During her brief disability, Mike and the boarders attended to the household duties the best they knew how.

In those early years of hers in America, childbirth was Manda's only vacation. A new baby came on the average of every year and a half. All boys. Altogether she bore thirteen sons; and when her twelfth and thirteenth—twins—came in 1902, Theodore Roosevelt wrote her a congratulatory letter from the White House, which got into papers all over the country. One of the boys died in an accident in earliest infancy. Twelve grew to manhood. Eleven are still living. . . .

In the five years in Raumbalton, the Evanses saved twenty-five hundred dollars, and Manda—"always the brains, the moving spirit of the family," as one of her sons described her to me—realized it would be foolish for them to remain there. Every month hundreds of Slovenians and Croatian immigrants—generally called "Austrians"—were coming to Calumet, a few miles away. Copper was booming. Mike was reluctant to make a change, but, as usual, in time gave in to his wife's coaxing and they sold the Raumbalton cabin and bought a large house in Calumet. They tore out the walls on the ground floor, put in a twenty-five-foot bar and other fixtures, and—in 1891—went into the saloon business.

The Evans saloon, which they ran for more than twenty years, was essentially a Croatian and Slovenian immigrant worker's club. Working in the mine ten or twelve hours a day, he visited it once or twice a week, most often Saturday evenings, to down a few seidels of beer or a couple of bottles of wine in the company of his friends and fellow countrymen, look over the latest greenhorns, cash his pay check, get his mail, read his Croatian- or Slovenian-language newspaper, which came to him from New York, Pittsburgh or Chicago.

Cashing most of his countrymen's pay checks, the immigrant saloonkeeper not infrequently collected union and even church dues. As likely as not, he was the president or secretary-treasurer of some fraternal lodge which was the immigrants' social and insurance organization. The lodge meetings, like the rehearsals of singing clubs and numerous weddings, were held in the hall above the saloon. The saloonkeeper was usually a naturalized citizen and helped others with naturalization, instructing them so they could answer the examiner's or the judge's questions, and serving as their witness at the examination.

He was, in most cases, an ex-worker, either endowed with superior business qualities and economically ambitious or, like Mike Evans, married to an alert, dynamic woman. Often the patrons of his saloon trusted him more than they did the local banker—who was usually a native American—and asked him to keep their earnings in his safe. In many instances, too, he took subscriptions to foreign-language newspapers, had a steamship-ticket sub-agency, and sent money orders to the old country.

Sometimes he became a political strawboss, telling or advising the naturalized citizens among his co-nationals how to vote. When they got into trouble with the law he aided them in getting straight with the authorities. He knew some English and helped his people to understand America.

The Evans saloon was an immediate success, both as a business and a social institution. Manda saw to that. She worked harder than ever, attending to all important business matters, supervising a staff of girls—her and Mike's nieces, whom she had helped to bring over—while Mike—now in his late thirties and not overburdened with business acumen—worked behind the bar. Gambling was not allowed. Patrons who exceeded their drinking capacity were asked to leave, or were—sometimes by Manda personally—propelled out-of-doors.

Croatian women who came downtown to shop would park their small children in the Evans saloon.

The ill and injured continued to come to Mrs. Evans to be healed and mended. Her fame as a doctor spread even outside the Croatian and Slovenian groups to other nationalities. Occasionally she stayed up all night, brewing concoctions or applying compresses to ailing parts. She never lost a case, but sometimes—as when they brought to her a Croatian miner with both legs crushed—was unable to help and urged the sufferer to seek relief from a professional doctor or in a hospital.

She was active in church affairs, went to early Mass at least every other day, and became the leader in the movement to build a Croatian Catholic church in Calumet. She also organized the first Croatian women's fraternal lodge in America and served as its initial president.

By now, of course, Mrs. Evans understood a good deal of English and spoke some. Croatian greenhorns poured into the copper country and, needing jobs, begged her to help them with the Irish, Cornish and American bosses, some of whom were inclined to discriminate against the "Austrians" in taking on workers. She went to see the bosses, invited them to supper in back of the saloon, and the newcomers were given employment.

In the fall the Evanses made from three to four hundred gallons of wine and vast tubs of sauerkraut. They killed a dozen pigs and hung up the hams and the *kobase*, or sausages.

And there were the children, the locally renowned Evans boys, *Evansovi boysi,* who—healthy, normal lads—gave Mrs. Evans no end of work and worry. Back in the 90's and early 1900's, Calumet was a wild, all but lawless town; and to keep her sons under control she was obliged to be firm or even tough— "a regular Mussolini," as one of her adoring sons now puts it. To which she replies, "But I ask you: if I had let them do whatever they wished, where would I have been?" . . . She required them to return from school in a certain number of minutes, by the most direct route, then kept them busy helping behind the bar and in other departments of the Evans establishment.

She had them "organized like soldiers in an army." When they were in their teens, each day after school two of the youngsters were required to go to the mine shafts and pick up pieces of broken timber which were brought up and thrown on the dumps. This wood was taken home in a sled in winter, and in a wagon in summer, drawn by a team of big Newfoundland dogs. One of these dogs was in the family for twelve years, and Mrs. Evans often said that he hauled as much wood as her father's horses in the old country.

Occasionally, in sub-zero weather, one or more of the boys came home with a cold and high fever. Mrs. Evans made them undress, wrapped them in linen sheets soaked in water verging on ice, and, putting them to bed, covered the shivering bodies with a half dozen blankets. The next day the boys went to school again, perfectly well. Whooping cough she treated with onions cooked in liquid sugar.

v

The twelve sons, of course, constituted no petty economic problem. Mrs. Evans maintained a veritable "quartermaster department"—as the sons now call it—of which she was the chief purchaser and distributor. Twice a year she went to Chicago and bought at wholesale prices, as for a store, dozens of suits, overcoats, sweaters, shoes, stockings, underwear, and caps of various sizes.

The saloon, to be sure, yielded enough profit to cover these expenses, but what of the future? Some of the boys might want to go to college, others might need to be financed to enter business.

So Mrs. Evans studied the local copper-stock market, which commanded the attention of most of the rest of Calumet, including the majority of the workers. She talked with the men working in the different mines, who came to the saloon, and thus determined which stocks were wildcat and which sound; then began to play the market—at first with extreme caution, then more confidently.

By 1903 the Evanses were a well-to-do family. Whereupon Mrs. Evans decided that it might be best for them to get out of the saloon business. No matter how respectably conducted, it was not the soundest life imaginable. It came at least into indirect conflict with her religiousness. Also, she was forty-four and getting a little tired of working fourteen to sixteen hours a day. She had just had twins and wanted to devote more time to her sons. Mike was past fifty and very heavy. Off and on, he found it hard to breathe. Tending the bar, he had been obliged to drink more than he wanted or than was good for him; while for the boys, now ranging in ages between mid-twenties and a few months, Calumet was not the best place in the world, either. Her peasant background caused her to begin thinking of returning to the soil.

On the other side of Lake Superior the Canadian government announced its readiness to give away one hundred and sixty acres of good prairie land, in the province of Saskatchewan, to every male over sixteen years of age who would settle on it and begin to improve it. Manda and Mike Evans went to see this land, and returned enthusiastic. It was almost too good to be true, thought Mrs. Evans; just the place to raise a big family.

She had a colossal and lovely vision. Now they would take up nine hundred and sixty acres for Mike and five of the older boys, and later one hundred and sixty acres more for each boy as he became sixteen. Thus they would, eventually, acquire more than two thousand acres, possibly all in one piece, and they would live—all of them—the hard, free, clean, healthy life on that endless northern prairie. The section she had selected included a forest and a lake teeming with trout; there were prairie chickens, deer and rabbits galore, and grass grew up to one's waist.

Early in the fall of 1904 Mike and a few of the boys went to Canada, took up 960 acres, bought a team of horses and some farm equipment, and started to build a house and barn. Mike, however, had grown soft in the saloon business. Three months after taking up homesteading, with temperature at forty below, he caught a severe cold, which turned to pneumonia.

Though barely able to breathe, Mike decided to return to Calumet to have Manda "fix" him up. Dressing, he toppled over.

The boys brought their dead father back to Calumet for burial. Then they refused to return to Canada. Overcome with grief, Mrs. Evans was unable to argue with them, and the homestead idea was abandoned. It was the only thing she ever attempted that did not pan out.

They decided to keep the saloon, putting Tom, the oldest, in charge of the bar; and they retained it till Prohibition came, when Tom took to farming in Upper Michigan. Now in his sixties, he still farms there. The other eleven did not know that Tom was only their half brother till the youngest of them was past sixteen.

VI

I cannot tell here the full stories of the Evans boys—that would take a good-sized book by itself—but I want to give an outline of Steve's career, because, so far, it probably is the most interesting of the twelve and because I happen to know him best.

At seventeen, or along in the late 90's, Steve suggested to his parents that they set him up in the grocery business. They did, and he did well at it.

In 1900 Mike Evans had to go to court over a matter connected with the saloon which obliged him to engage a lawyer. This gave Mrs. Evans the idea of sending one of the boys to law school. Steve volunteered, took a three-year preparatory course at Valparaiso, Indiana, then entered the law school of the University of Michigan at Ann Arbor.

At home Steve had observed, with pain and a sense of outrage, the plight of injured workmen who came or were brought to his mother from the mines to have their bones set and wounds dressed. They received no compensation, even in case of total disability. The then-existing laws in Michigan, as in most other states, absolved the employers of all responsibility in such accidents, even if obviously due to a lack of precautionary measures and safety appliances. Now, as a law student, the young man made a special effort to familiarize himself with the laws and court decisions dealing with the employers' liability and related matters in other states and in foreign countries. During his final year in school he wrote an exhaustive treatise on the subject. He was admitted to the bar in 1906 and opened an office in Calumet.

His political-social-economic thinking was strongly influenced by the Republican leader in the neighboring state of Wisconsin, Robert M. La Follette.

In 1908 Stephen Evans ran on the Republican ticket for, and was elected to, the Michigan state legislature, which, under his purposeful leadership, then enacted laws requiring safety measures in the mines and industrial plants and defining the employers' responsibility to the workers who suffered accidents. Later, on the strength of his legislative record, Steve was elected prosecuting attorney of Houghton County, and in this capacity served the interests of the people with such loyalty and integrity that they reelected him twice.

At election time, Steve's chief campaign workers were his mother and brothers. During the day the boys pasted posters with his picture on fences, cliffs and telegraph poles all over the county. At night they folded campaign leaflets, stuffing them into envelopes for mailing, or distributed them from door to door.

Till the end of the First World War Steve's political future in Michigan looked extremely bright. He appeared almost bound to go to Congress, then likely to be elected governor of Michigan. After the war, however, the bottom dropped out of copper in Upper Michigan; the mines were exhausted, or so deep it no longer paid to bring up the ore; and by 1921—in less than two years— more than seventy-five per cent. of the people had moved out of the copper country. This made the place insecure as a steppingstone for anyone with polit- ical or business aspirations. So Steve joined the exodus and opened a law office in Chicago. Now, in his early sixties, he is one of the most highly regarded members of the bar in that city. But in Calumet and thereabouts people of all national strains still talk of him as a square shooter and the best prosecuting attorney they ever had.

After the death of their father and the abandonment of the homesteading idea, Mother Evans informed her sons that those of them who wanted to be- come educated would have a chance to go to college, while the others would be obliged to go to work and learn trades or find means to independence in one honest way or another.

In the ensuing ten years two boys besides Steve entered the legal profession. One of these, Frank, served a term in the Wisconsin legislature. Four became locomotive engineers. One is a salesman in a Detroit department store. One is in the purchasing department of the telephone company in Cleveland. One has a large garage and automobile and farm-equipment agency in a town in Western Pennsylvania. One is an official of the State of Michigan at Lansing. Six served in the World War; three were wounded in action.

VII

A good part of the Evans family moved to Detroit—"Deetaroit," Mrs. Evans pronounces it—even before the expiration of Steve's last term as prosecuting attorney. To the west of the city was a stretch of vacant country which looked good to the old lady. She bought a piece of it and built a house. It turned out a good investment. In the next fifteen years Detroit came to her. Mrs. Evans still has her home there, and four of her sons and their families live within walk- ing distance.

In 1919 one of the locomotive engineers, Andy, died in a boiler explosion while working for the Chicago, Toledo and Detroit Railroad Company. The company gave Mrs. Evans an honorary pass for life which is honored by all other railroads; and when her sons began to scatter over the middle states she started to make use of it. During the last two decades she has been spending about half of her time traveling and visiting her sons, daughters-in-law, grand- children and great-grandchildren who do not live in or near Detroit.

Mrs. Evans is eighty-one as I write, but in excellent health; not quite so strong, of course, as she was at twenty or thirty, but, if it is necessary, still able to lift and carry a hundred pounds or more, or to toss a burglar out of the house. She is a large woman, weighing more than two hundred pounds, and not fat. She moves with ease, does all her own housework, and entertains a good deal. She sees well without glasses. Her hair is just beginning to gray. She eats heartily and likes to take a drink in company. She stands out wherever she appears, and her sons and their wives and children generally recognize her as the head of the Evans clan. According to the latest statistics available, she has thirty-nine grandchildren and eight great-grandchildren.

Not a few of the younger Evans folk are alive partly because she saw them through their childhood illnesses. Even today she is constantly on call to the entire family. She has a bag packed all the time. If her son George telephones from Gary, Indiana, that the baby has a serious colic attack, she takes the first train down, brews a concoction of garlic, caraway seeds and olive oil over a low fire, and feeds it to the infant who recovers in two or three days.

When her sons—most of them now in middle age—overwork, they ask her to give them a massage. She is proud of the strength in her fingers, hands and arms, which is a prerequisite of a good masseuse. She is proud, too, that in important matters, including business affairs, her sons often seek her advice, even if they do not always heed it.

Now and then, of course, the world in which she moves is a little strange to her. She is all here, in America body and soul, seldom thinking of the old country, which she has not visited since coming over in 1883; and she is an American woman, a citizen of the United States, officially and actually. She is a fierce patriot. She has difficulty in being patient with people who want to change the American system of government and way of life. Every day she prays for the President, Congress and people of the United States, that they may have the wisdom and power to keep America America.

Yet, essentially, she is also still an immigrant woman from Croatia, old-fashioned in her ways and purposes and in her sense of values. Her English is still uncertain. All her sons talk fluent Croatian and, when alone with them, she speaks only her native language, and she calls them Tomo, Stevo, Juro, and so on, as they would be called in the old country. Most of her eleven daughters-in-law, however, and nearly all her grandchildren and great-grand-children know no Croatian, and their ways are not Croatian or immigrant, but something called "American," or "modern," or "streamlined," and to old Mother Evans, as she watches them, a bit bewildering.

She knows that they are all fond of her. A few are openly proud of her, others more or less secretly. A handful of them are a little uncomfortable when she comes to their homes, fearing some of their old-stock American friends may drop in and they will have to introduce to them their "foreign" gran'ma, whose English is broken and weighed down by a heavy accent, who once was a "boardinghouse missus" and ran a saloon, and whose name was not always Evans. Some of them are afraid their friends may find out it originally ended with -ich, and they begged me to disguise it. (Which I did. Their name now is not "Evans," but as "American"-sounding as that; and they came to it as I have told.)

Mrs. Evans knows all this and it would hurt her if she let it. But she knows the young people are facing serious problems, what with hard times and everything. She understands one of her grandsons who is moving into politics in his city and says it will be "just too bad" for him if his opponents learn he is "of foreign descent." But ——

Well, she makes no effort to think things out; she accepts them. Now and then a deep sigh escapes her.

She naturally derives immense satisfaction from the fact that all her *boysi* are self-supporting and a few of them well-off; that one of them drives a Packard; that she has enough money to live in comfort the rest of her life without becoming a burden to them; and that there is, apparently, no danger of any of her people ever going on government relief or needing charity. She is, in short, a fairly happy woman. But there are, as she calls them, two "tragedies" in her life.

One is that she never had a daughter. Her daughters-in-law are of several strains or backgrounds and of different religions. Tom married a Slovenian Catholic girl, Steve's first wife was of old New England Protestant stock, while his second wife is a Catholic woman of German parentage. Joe married a Protestant girl of German-French background. George, who is the first of the American-born Evans boys, married a Catholic Irishwoman. John's and Tony's wives are of German Lutheran descent. Luke's is an American-born Catholic girl of Slovenian origin. Phil and Ted married Croatian Catholic girls born in Calumet. Frank's wife is of English stock and Fred's is Welsh; both Protestant.

This is all right with Mrs. Evans, in a way. Such things are happening all over America—people of one nationality and religion mating with people of other strains and faiths. And it is not that all her sons' wives are not the best women in the world; she is most emphatic on this point. They seldom disagree with her on important matters. But, she says rather pensively, it would be nice to have a daughter with whom she could be deeply and consistently intimate.

The other "tragedy" is that none of the *boysi* became a priest. She sent three of them to seminaries, to see if they might not fit into religious life, but all three insisted priesthood was not for them. She still goes to Mass every day and is one of the pillars of the Croatian Catholic church in Detroit.

Unlike many old people and most old widows, Mrs. Evans is never lonely. There is always someone coming to her house. During her twenty-odd years in Calumet, she had brought over from Croatia something like eighty girls and young women, who then had worked in the Evans saloon till they married. Some were her or her husband's relatives. She is godmother to their American-born children, more than three hundred of them. Some of these, now between their twenties and forties, are scattered all over the United States, some functioning in prominent positions. The son of one of her sisters is a commander in the United States Navy. Others are air pilots, farmers, nurses, doctors, attorneys, government employees. One is an important permanent employee of the State of Michigan. One, a few years ago, was an all-American football star. One or two are in prison. The majority, however, are ordinary folk, many of whom have followed her, with their parents, to "Deetaroit," and still live there, or in Flint, Dearborn or Pontiac. Devoted to her, they often visit her to talk of the old days in the copper country and of the vicissitudes and mutations of their lives in contemporary America, in which she is endlessly interested.

From Bohemia:
Ma and Pa Karas

HELENA TOPINKA was born, in the late 1880's, in Kozlany, an average Bohemian town midway between Pilsen and Prague. Decades later it took on fame as the birthplace of Eduard Beneš, whom Helena then remembered as a pleasant-mannered boy two or three years her senior. His home was a few houses from hers.

During the nineties, when Helena Topinka was a child, her father was a well-to-do brewmaster who at various times leased and operated small breweries in different parts of Bohemia and Moravia. He was a proud Czech, a business man with rigid Central European middle-class standards and values: thorough, industrious, and honorable. He was deeply devoted to his large family, who moved with him from place to place under the impulse of his business.

Between Helena's tenth and twelfth years the Topinkas resided in Pomoklé, a town near Prague. Attending school there, she met her future husband, though at the time no one could have dreamed they would ever marry. His name was Frantisek Karas. A tall, husky peasant lad of Helena's age, he had a square, handsome Slavic face and a shy, agreeable way about him. His father owned a little house, two cows, a few acres of not the most fertile land in the near-by village of Buciny, and a trumpet which he played at local dances and weddings. This meant that young Frantisek was fathoms beneath Helena Topinka in social and economic standing, and their early acquaintance was mostly a matter of tentative grins and fugitive words.

Mama Topinka was a kind, patient woman whose main concern in life was her children, husband, and housework. She was raising her daughters, of whom Helena was the youngest, to become thrifty, efficient wives of middle-class, safe-and-sane Czech men like her husband and mothers of wholesome Czech children.

Till about 1900 everything was fine with the Topinkas. Then Papa Topinka experienced serious business reverses. Small breweries were being absorbed by large ones, and in 1903 the family found itself in critical circumstances.

Just then a female relative returned for a visit from Chicago, where she had lived for years and done well in marriage and business. She suggested that some of the Topinka youngsters come with her to the United States. She described America as a land not exactly inundated with milk and honey, as rumored by those of extravagant imagination or lazy disposition, but rich with opportunities for people not afraid of hard work, especially for industrious wide-awake young folk. She told of Bohemians in Chicago who occupied entire sections of the great and growing city: how they worked in numerous industries or engaged in businesses of all categories, and how the majority of the older families, as well as many recent immigrants, had advanced themselves from penniless greenhorns to owners of homes valued from a few to many thousands of dollars.

Helena and one of her younger brothers, Alois, decided to go to America. The Chicago relative offered to loan them passage money and, after some hesitation, the parents gave their approval. Their main misgiving was Helena's youth; what would she do in the strange, far-off country till some man worthy of her would want her for his wife? . . . When I asked her thirty-seven years later what had prompted her to make the decision, she said: "I was only a burden to my father; what could I have done at home? Wait for a man to turn up who might marry me without a dot? I figured I might do a little better in America than in Bohemia," which then was a subtly oppressed province of Austria. . . .

Helena Topinka was sixteen, growing into an attractive girl with a strong, full body. Her pretty red-cheeked round face was framed by a mass of brown hair. A faintly amused, discreetly quizzical look glowed in her hazel eyes. She had a simple, unassuming personality with a slow, kindly, yet direct manner.

In the old country Helena could not very well have become a servant girl, regardless of the urgency of her economic plight. It would have been a blow to her proud, class-conscious father and a subject for never-ending talk and eyebrow-lifting among all who knew the Topinka family. On arriving in Chicago, however, she discovered European class restrictions as to how one might earn a living did not count for much in America. Hundreds of Bohemian women in Chicago, now married, had on first coming over served for a few years as maids in old-stock American and German and Jewish American families. The Bohemian American Household Help Agency, whose office was in the heart of the Czech neighborhood, enjoyed a high reputation among Chicago's upper-middle-class housewives and had no trouble placing Bohemian girls as fast as they came over. It placed Helena Topinka in the home of Mr. and Mrs. Sam Levy as nurse to their three children.

In writing to her parents about this, she took care to explain and emphasize that this was all right in Chicago. America was "different." Although a servant, she was allowed, in fact expected, to wear a hat like a lady, instead of a kerchief, which was part of the uniform of European peasant and servant girls; and by-and-by Papa and Mama Topinka seemed to become reconciled to the idea. Helena and Alois sent them small sums of money and later helped to bring to the United States almost all of the other young Topinkas. Two of the boys died in France as American soldiers during the First World War. . . .

The Levys were also immigrants: Mr. Levy from Russian Poland, Mrs. Levy from Vienna. Their children were American-born. Mr. Levy ran a window-shade factory, and they owned a home in one of the better sections of the city where Jews were not excluded. Helen—as they called her—found them fine, openhearted people. They liked her very much too, while the children fell in love with her. Virtually a member of the family, Helena stayed with them for seven years, till all the youngsters had outgrown the need of a nurse . . . and she married.

II

Frantisek Karas' father had been a trumpeter in the Austrian Army, which had awakened in him a deep interest in music generally. Though he could not play it, he had a special fondness for the violin and wanted his oldest son, who evidently had a natural passion for it, to become a violinist. His wife sang Czech folk songs all day long, in the field, at her cooking, at the crib of her latest infant, wherever she was and whatever she was doing; and she also favored giving Frantisek a musical education. If they could only send him to Prague! But that was out of the question; they could barely keep the Emperor Franz Josef's tax collector from selling their little farm and two cows for taxes at auction.

Then, when the boy was twelve, the older Karas heard of a man in the adjacent town of Beroun who gave violin lessons. From his father he had inherited a small factory making files, shoemaker's rasps, and similar tools, but he was really a musician at heart. Peasant Karas took his son to see the man, who agreed to take him into his shop as an apprentice filemaker and give him three violin lessons weekly. The Karases considered this rare good luck, and father and son journeyed to Prague and bought a half-size violin for eight gulden, or about three dollars—all the money the family had at the time.

Young Frantisek stayed in Beroun for three and a half years, working in the shop and studying the violin. The two efforts were highly incongruous; often he could not get the sounds of one out of his ears while engaged in the other. Nonetheless, he became a fairly good filemaker and showed promise as a violinist.

Attaining his mid-teens, Frantisek realized he could not, in the long run, be both a filemaker and a musician. Also, there was no future to speak of in filemaking. No matter how expert he might become or how long he might work at it, he could not hope, anywhere in Austria, ever to make more than the equivalent of three dollars a week.

At this point, as in Helena Topinka's case, and almost at the same time, in 1903, a native of Buciny who had made what he considered a lot of money as a carpenter-contractor erecting houses for Czech immigrants in Chicago, returned home for a visit. He told the Karases of some American-born relatives of theirs in Chicago by the name of Kolar, one of whom had a harness shop while the other was a foreman in a factory turning out meat grinders, sausage machines, and other equipment for the stockyards. He met Frantisek, who by now was sixteen, a strong, attractive young man; and, returning to Chicago, told the Kolars about him.

The Kolars promptly wrote the Karases: would Frantisek like to come to America? If so, they would send the money for his passage. They implied that in Chicago the boy would have the opportunity to develop, according to his talents, either as a machine-shop worker or a musician.

With his parents' approval, Frantisek jumped at the chance, and he arrived in Chicago the same week as Helena Topinka—but the two remained unaware of each other's presence in the New World for several months. In fact, they had all but forgotten one another and their encounters during their school years in Pomoklé.

Frantisek Karas became Frank Karas.

His American-born cousin, Louis Kolar, the foreman in the meat-grinder factory, promptly found Frank a job in his department. The young greenhorn began at $10.25 a week and thought he would soon be a millionaire and organize an orchestra. Then a strike broke out in the machine industry of Chicago . . . and lasted eight months.

During most of the strike Frank Karas worked as pants-presser in a tailor shop at six dollars a week, which was a drop from the machine-shop wages, but still high pay to him. His employer was a Bohemian Jew, and nearly all the patrons were Czechs. Living and working in the neighborhood was almost like being back home in Bohemia.

The strike over, Frank returned to his former job at $10.25 a week, which in the course of the next two and a half years was gradually raised to $14.75.

Two days before he quit the pants-pressing job a young man who looked familiar to Frank Karas brought in a suit to be cleaned. He gave his name: Alois Topinka. They recognized one another, for Alois had also attended school in Pomoklé.

Alois told Frank that Helen was in America too. The following Sunday all three got together at a Bohemian affair . . . and thereafter Frank, now seventeen, had something to live for besides music.

He had started taking violin lessons the first week in Chicago. His teacher, with whom he studied for two years, was a Czech, Frank Kolbaba, who had a studio in the Bohemian section and later became professor of music at Washburn College in Topeka, Kansas. The lessons were seventy-five cents an hour. His second teacher, Horymir Chapek, also a Czech, who presently became a violinist of the Chicago Symphony Orchestra, charged a dollar and a half.

A good part of Frank's wages went for music lessons, for his fine full-size violin which he acquired on the installment plan, and for concert and opera tickets for Helen and himself. Often he rushed to his music lesson straight from the shop, which was even noisier than the little filemaking factory in Bohemia had been. The whir of the machines and the pounding of hammers lingered in his ears as he tried to play for Mr. Kolbaba or Mr. Chapek. His ambition to be a musician persisted. To produce music seemed to him more essential than to turn out sausage machines and meat hashers or even sausages and meat hash.

On the way to and from work he passed a United States Army recruiting office and one day noticed a special sign on the poster: "Wanted—Musicians for Army Bands." He talked to the recruiting sergeant, who turned out to be a German immigrant from Bavaria and assured Frank that if he enlisted he would have plenty of opportunity to study music. There were vacancies in the Second Field Artillery Band at Fort D. A. Russell, Wyoming, where, said the sergeant, the bandleader was a friend of his, Joseph Studený, a Bohemian born in Pilsen. The recruiter wound up his sales talk with the remark that the trouble with Army bands was they trained such excellent musicians that none re-enlisted. They all returned to civilian life and got jobs in orchestras and bands.

Frank Karas was nineteen; the enlistment was for three years. He had a talk with Helen. Would she wait for him?

He enlisted and was sent to the regiment in Wyoming, which soon after was ordered to the Philippines.

Frank was disappointed with the Army. It was all right as an army, but it had no real interest in music. The purpose of the band, even under a Bohemian bandleader as excellent as Joseph Studený, was mainly to emit rhythmic noises for marching and play "The Star-Spangled Banner" well enough to be recognized as the national anthem. Outside of an occasional officers' dance, there was no demand for string or orchestral music.

But Frank made the best of a poor deal. He took up the cornet and by the end of the enlistment, between kitchen police and fatigue duty, learned to play it well.

Helen and he exchanged weekly letters. On his release from the service and return to the States they were married in Chicago. Helen's father, who disapproved of the marriage on the ground that Frank Karas was nothing but a peasant's son with no clear future ahead of him, was gently reminded by her that this was America where one's background, whether peasant or aristocratic, was of slight moment.

III

Helen and Frank were twenty-two—and very much in love, citizens of the United States, with something like two thousand dollars to their name. They had saved this money serving Uncle Sam and the Sam Levys, respectively. They furnished a modest flat in the Bohemian section.

Chicago was full of excellent musicians, most of them Germans, Italians, Jews and Czechs, and Frank Karas soon realized he was not yet good enough either as a violinist or cornetist to find steady musical employment. As a violinist, he had, in fact, grown rusty in the Army. So he went back to the meathasher factory. He made fifteen a week and resumed lessons, now both in violin and cornet, with the best teachers in Chicago—Josef Karlovsky, Fred Weldon, and Noah Tarantino; and in 1911, partly with the aid of these instructors, began to get temporary jobs evenings with small orchestras playing in hotel restaurants, stock-company theaters and at special affairs. Sometimes he worked eighteen, twenty hours at a stretch. He took his tuxedo and razor to the machine shop, shaved and changed after work, and rushed to the Loop to play before dinner in some hotel lobby, then during the dinner hours in the restaurant, grabbing a bite between times. He joined the musicians' union.

In 1912 a machine clipped off a half-inch of Frank's thumb and he quit the factory for good. The accident only temporarily affected his ability to play and soon he found a permanent position as a cornetist of the orchestra in the famous Rector Café, where Irene and Vernon Castle, then on their first transcontinental tour, danced the Castle Walk on his first evening there. Frank received thirty-six dollars a week, and the future looked bright to him and Helen. Those competent of expressing such an opinion told him he was almost bound to get on the Chicago Symphony Orchestra; and he continued to take lessons.

The Karases' first-born, in 1911, was a boy, William; a year later came a girl, Elsie. Expecting to stay in Chicago for the rest of their lives, they bought a home. But a few months later—in 1913—hard times hit Chicago along with the rest of the country. For musicians the period was one of panic. Faced by a drop in business, cafés and hotels reduced or gave up their orchestras; while the motion pictures—which had, on the whole, not yet commenced to feature orchestra music—continued to take more and more business from stock and road companies, causing them to go out of existence and leaving their musicians jobless.

Except for brief engagements at long intervals, Frank Karas was out of employment the better part of a year. Determined to "make a go of it" as a musician, he tried to teach violin and cornet, and discovered he liked teaching. One of his first pupils was the daughter of Anton Cermak, one of the wealthiest Czech Americans in Chicago, who later became mayor and early in 1933 died of an assassin's bullet intended for President-elect Franklin D. Roosevelt.

But the few lessons Frank gave were not enough to meet the obligations on his new home and to support his family. In a moment of desperation, he entertained the idea of re-enlisting in the Army, but gave it up. He did not think Helen would like to live in Army posts and move wherever the regiment went; also, he could not forget the Army was not really interested in music.

Like all unemployed musicians, Frank Karas read the want-ads and notices in the monthly paper issued by the Chicago Federation of Musicians' union. Early in 1914 he came upon an item to the effect that the town band in Menominee, in northern Michigan, needed a cornet soloist. No salary went with the job, the band being an amateur outfit; but a good soloist would be guaranteed employment and a wage of fifteen a week in the local baby-carriage factory, whose general manager was interested in the band. Besides, he might pick up some extra money playing in the band when it was engaged professionally for occasional lodge affairs, weddings and picnics. Also, he might give lessons in cornet and other instruments, and thus add to his income.

Frank showed the notice to Helen. It looked good. Where was Menominee? They looked it up on the map: a small city on Lake Michigan's Green Bay. It would be nice to live in such a community. Of course that might mean he never would get on the Chicago Symphony Orchestra, but——

IV

In Menominee two more children were born to the Karases—another girl, Clara, and another boy, Frank.

The family liked northern Michigan very much—only the winters were severe, with snow piling up eight to twelve feet in November and lingering till April, and with temperature sub-zero for months . . . but in two or three years they became inured to it. Menominee was a pleasant, busy community with a population between ten and twelve thousand, including two thousand Bohemian immigrants and their American-born children. Many of these immigrants were old-time lumberjacks who, when the timber boom had petered out, stayed in northern Michigan to work at whatever was available.

Now in his late twenties, Frank Karas at once became a busy and popular citizen of Menominee. His cornet and occasional violin solos were a treat to the ears, and soon he had over a score of pupils. He was put in charge of the band and a string orchestra the boys organized. He worked in the baby-carriage factory only the first few years, and was treated with much deference, given a leave whenever his factory job threatened to interfere with his music. He made good money, and, having sold their place in Chicago, they bought a home in Menominee. The town was ideal for raising a family; everyone was friendly, and they felt much happier living in a small city than they had in Chicago.

Frank Karas took on more and more pupils, and he and his orchestra were out playing three or four nights a week, till early in the 1920's overwork brought him to the verge of a breakdown. It became imperative he give up for a time most of his activities, and several of them permanently. He tried vainly to do this. He had become so definitely a center of all musical life in Menominee and so intimately tied up with the cultural texture of the city that he could not, remaining there, gracefully extricate himself from it.

He suddenly decided—with the approval of the worried Mrs. Karas—to quit Menominee and accept the job of orchestra leader which had been repeatedly offered him by the largest movie theater in Escanaba, a city of sixteen thousand about seventy miles north of Menominee.

Escanaba was a town very much like Menominee: friendly, progressive, and American in the best contemporaneous sense that its population was a mingling of many strains, no one strain predominating.

The Karases sold the house in Menominee and bought one in Escanaba. Mr. Karas' new job took only a few hours in the evening, giving him a chance to rebuild his health. Then he began to take pupils once more—one or two a day, largely because he liked to teach. Lest he overwork again, Mrs. Karas kept him from taking on all who wanted lessons.

The four Karas children were growing into healthy, good-looking boys and girls, all going to school, and the family was one of the most content in Escanaba. Elsie and Clara were interested in music, studying with their father; Bill and Frank leaned more to mechanics and sports—to football and to boating and fishing on the lake, whose shore was but a few hundred yards from their home.

Thus till early in 1929, when the films—the talkies, with their "canned music"—plunged the musicians throughout the United States into another panic. Mr. Karas lost his job in the movie house, and the family's scheme of living was disrupted once more.

In the large cities this panic was fatal to the careers of tens of thousands of musicians; a few years later many had to go on relief and W.P.A. projects digging ditches and grading roads. To Mr. Karas in Escanaba, Michigan, the loss of his job was another piece of good luck, although it did not instantly appear so.

He promptly took on all the pupils who had been wanting to study violin and cornet with him, including a number of high-school youngsters. Presently his work with these boys and girls was noticed by the superintendent of schools and the high school principal in connection with the school band, and they suggested he qualify for an appointment as music teacher in the city school system by taking a State examination. He took the suggestion, got the appointment . . . and has been a school teacher ever since. He also became director of the Escanaba Municipal Band.

But before Mr. Karas was drawn into the school system, he and Mrs. Karas realized his income from violin and cornet lessons would not be enough to send the children to college. Bill and Elsie were finishing high school, while Clara and Frank would be ready for college in another four or five years. So Mrs. Karas decided to go into business.

v

They sold their home and bought a ramshackle little frame structure on a small lot near the Escanaba High School (a half-dozen blocks from the main business section) with the idea of turning it into a store which would cater to the approximately eight hundred students, most of whom passed the spot twice every school day, and some of whom, living in the remoter parts of the town, might get in the habit of buying part of their lunch there.

The Karases put up a tiny addition in front for the new store, made repairs on the old part, painted everything . . . and in the autumn of 1929 as school began Mrs. Karas opened for business. She carried "light groceries" for the chance neighborhood customers, but her chief trade was in pencils, notebooks, erasers, and other school supplies, soda pop, ice cream, milk, fruit, candy, cookies, pie, cakes, and sandwiches. The family moved into the repaired old part of the building, which included a fairly big kitchen with room enough for the dining table, a couple of small bedrooms and the bath upstairs, and the parlor on whose window Mr. Karas painted his name and "VIOLIN AND CORNET LESSONS." In back of the building was a yard with a few trees and space for a vegetable and flower patch.

The new store was an immediate hit with the high-school boys and girls. That first winter they named it "The Igloo," because their football team was called The Eskimos and because it was often approachable only through a tunnel cut into the deep, hard snow. It promptly became, and still is, an institution in Escanaba. The youngsters heard Mrs. Karas' children call her "Ma," and so in no time they all took to calling her Ma, too.

Now, in her mid-fifties, more than a decade after the inception of the Igloo, Ma Karas is a healthy, buxom, graying woman with spectacles and a mild, kind smile, which is an all but permanent feature of her smooth round face. She wears print dresses and New England aprons. Her movements are unhurried and unruffled even when The Igloo is jammed with youthful customers crying "Ma, give me a cone! Come on, Ma! . . . Ma, give me a piece of that pie; hurry up, will you, Ma! Do I gotta wait all day? . . . Here's the nickel I owe you, Ma, and don't say I never gave you nothin'! . . ."

The Igloo is open fourteen to sixteen hours a day, seven days a week, and the profit from it is meager—averaging eighteen dollars a week, which Ma does not need any longer, certainly not enough to work such long hours, for Pa Karas' earnings are sufficient to maintain them in comfort. But Ma goes on running the Igloo. She says she would feel lost if she gave it up. "I don't know how to play bridge. I'd wonder about the kids."

Ma knows most of the eight hundred high-school youngsters and an additional hundred or so of the younger children who live in the immediate vicinity of the Igloo. A good half she knows intimately; not by prying into the facts of their home life, but intuitively through her brief contacts with them as they come in from day to day for penny sticks of candy, milk shakes, pencils and erasers.

She likes the youngsters; but not in any sentimental way which may involve a semi-morbid "motherly" desire to fuss and fret over them, or imply they are young and therefore inferior and in need of her. There is nothing morbid or neurotic about Ma. Her mother instincts and needs have been, and are being, satisfied in her own family.

She does have a sense of responsibility toward her customers. And being a deeply disciplined and actively moral person, at the same time that she is natural, matter-of-fact and full of common sense, she has without any effort become an influence in their lives. They are open and responsive to her. They come to her with their difficulties and misunderstandings. Her manner encourages them to talk; she listens patiently to whatever they have to say. In turn, they listen to her and quote her to one another. They know she is more interested in them than in their pennies and nickels. She laughs with them; she can take a joke, but keeps an eye on possible mischief.

On the counter is a basket of eggs, and one of the favorite pastimes of the youthful Igloo clientele is to decorate them with faces, wisecracks, and dates. Ma tells them not to, but not very emphatically, and they slip on such legends as "Laid—1492," or "Ready to Hatch—Don't Buy Me." Another Igloo sport is to take an egg and play catch with it, tossing it from one to the other. By-and-by someone misses it, then comes Ma's inevitable exclamation: "What did I tell you!" They feel sheepish for a moment, gladly pay the three cents for the broken egg; someone gets the pail, brush and mop from the kitchen and cleans up the mess. Off and on Ma has to take the broom and literally sweep everyone out. Nobody minds; they all come back again.

Once in a while they make fun of her accent, which sometimes becomes quite heavy, or of her pronunciation of certain words. She takes this "kidding" good-naturedly and asks them to teach her, or how they think they would make out in the Czech language should they move to Bohemia.

Ma has no favorites. She gives no credit above a nickel, sells no cigarettes to youngsters of high-school age or under.

When the kids come to her for advice, she appeals to their intelligence. "Was that a smart thing to do?"—or, "What do you think you should do now?" She has a knack of simultaneously praising and scolding without raising her voice. One young man, now out of high school for several years, has been able to get an objective view of Ma's effect on him. "She used to make me feel at once proud that I was 'I,'" he told me, "and ashamed like the dickens that I wasn't better. I used to love to have her talk to me, even, if not especially, when she scolded me. . . ." The young people have no guards before her. They tell her everything; in many cases more than they tell their parents. She knows most of their boy-girl troubles and could be a source of endless gossip, but even her own family never learn what she hears in the Igloo.

Ma has no sympathy with classifying people, and especially youngsters, as "good" and "bad." To her notion, everybody is good for something; the question is, for what? Early in her career as the Igloo proprietress, she studied a boy who was labeled "bad" and she conducted a quiet campaign in his behalf for several years. At the same time she "worked" on him; nobody knows just how (she doesn't talk about it), but perhaps merely by showing an interest in him and asking him, "Was that a smart thing to do?" Mr. Edward Edick, the principal, is sure the boy straightened out during his last year in high school largely because of her. The young man has since entirely overcome the unfortunate circumstances of his family which were at the bottom of his early behavior. He moved to another town after finishing college, but he never visits Escanaba without calling on Ma; now and then he sends her a card, a wire and a gift on her birthday.

There are dozens of such and similar cases in Escanaba. They were told to me (not by Ma) in very general terms with the request that I do not mention them even that way; publicity might start pointless, if not harmful, talk in town.

Ma is interested in the kids' health and physiques. Those inclined to over-weight are discouraged from buying candy. Youngsters who come in for a piece of huckleberry pie at five-thirty in the evening are told it might spoil their appetites for supper.

Ma keeps track of the grades of scores of students. The backward ones she encourages to do better by promising them milk shakes or ice cream sundaes for marks indicating improvement. Sometimes she shames them into more effort—"if Johnny Smith gets A's, why can't you? He isn't any smarter than you, is he?"

Ma is interested in all school activities, but particularly in the football team, in part because both her sons have been on it. When the team plays a game, she promises the boys malted milks if they win. Sometimes they get the free drinks even after defeat, provided they tried hard enough to win. When play-ing out of town, the first thing the team captain does after the game is to wire Ma or call her long-distance.

Mr. Edick freely admits that but for Ma his job as principal of the high school might be a good deal harder than it is. A couple of years ago he asked her to come to a "pep" assembly. She thought he meant to have her sit in the audience. But Mr. Edick took her onto the platform and had her take the seat next to Mr. John Lemmer, the superintendent of schools. When the students saw her, they gave her the biggest hand anyone had ever received in that school. The ovation lasted several minutes. It embarrassed and surprised Ma. On Mr. Edick's insistence she has been attending occasional general assemblies and graduation exercises ever since.

The events in Ma's life, such as her occasional trips to Chicago, are reported in the high-school paper. Every now and then some student writes a poem en-titled "To Ma Karas." In the last eight years she has been honorary president of numerous student clubs. She is invited to class reunions. Three or four times a year various student groups give dinners for her, and Editor Bill Duchaine of the Escanaba *Press* sends a reporter and photographer to cover them.

During the Czech crisis in the fall of 1938, while Ma sat by the radio, tears running down her face as she listened to the reports of the drastic developments in Berlin, London, Paris and Munich, her young friends stood about her. "Don't cry, Ma!" ... "Don't worry, Ma; Czechoslovakia will be free again. ..."

VI

Bill Karas is twenty-nine, a modest-mannered young man, graduate of the Michigan College of Mining at Houghton, where he met a Scotch-Irish girl and later married her. He is the engineer in charge of the Delta County roads. He and his wife live next door to the Igloo, which is pleasant and handy all around. They have a baby; and when they want to go out, they take it over to Ma; while the daughter-in-law takes charge of the store when Mr. and Mrs. Karas take in a movie.

Elsie Karas is the teacher of singing in the public school system in Muskegon Heights, Michigan; early in 1940 she published her first song. Clara, who seems to be a copy of Ma in temperament, finished her college course at Marquette in 1939 and received a Michigan teaching appointment. Twenty and a six-footer, Frank is in the grip of an ambition to be a football coach.

All four of the Karas children are identified with Menominee and Escanaba, with Lake Michigan, the green woods, the deep snows, the cool summer winds. They speak of the complexity of circumstances which brought the Karas family to Upper Michigan with good-humored gratitude. They proudly "kid" Pa Karas, who, with but a few years of formal schooling back in Pomoklé, Bohemia, has become a school teacher in America; and their mother, who has become a local institution called Ma.

They are Americans. But they are conscious of their Bohemian background. They speak Czech. Their mother has told them scores of Bohemian folk tales. All four share keenly their parents' sorrow over the status of Bohemia since 1938.

Ma and Pa Karas are Americans, too; yet they are also Czechs and immigrants. On a wall in the little hallway between the kitchen and the parlor is the Czech national motto: "Truth Will Prevail." On festive occasions Mrs. Karas roasts a goose and serves it with Bohemian bread or potato dumplings and sauerkraut—a combination that tastes better than it may sound to non-Czechs.

Mr. Karas subscribes to *Svornost*, a Czech-language newspaper published and edited by my friend Vladimir Geringer in Chicago. On the Karases' bookshelves are several Czech books, including a biography of Dr. Eduard Beneš, which contains a number of pictures of the town of Kozlany, his and Helena Topinka's birthplace. Mrs. Karas likes to open the book and show these pictures.

When she shows them to some of her young friends in the Igloo, they remark that the houses in Kozlany are rather different from the houses in Escanaba. Ma agrees, but adds that in many ways Kozlany is in Bohemia what Escanaba is in Michigan or, for that matter, in America—an average town.

"Which house were you born in, Ma?"

She points to one of the largest dwellings, made of stone. Then the following exclamations and wisecracks are in order:

"Gee, whiz, Ma; do you mean to say you were born in this great big palace? . . . Let me touch the hem of your garment, Mrs. Karas . . . Now look where you live; right here in the Igloo. What a comedown, Ma! What a comedown! . . ."

They all laugh, including Ma. Whereupon Pa Karas, who is giving a music lesson in the parlor, raps on the wall, begging the racket cease.

The Finnish
Americans

JOHN STARKKU came to the United States in 1890 from a tiny village upon a narrow strip of land between two lakes in Finland, then a poor, little-known grandduchy of Czarist Russia. He was twenty-five, big and strong. His ambition was to get a homestead in the Hood River Valley in Oregon, because a man from his village had chanced to settle there a half-dozen years earlier and had since written home highly favorable reports of the place.

But it took John Starkku five years to reach Oregon. He stopped over in the copper country of northernmost Michigan, in Wisconsin, on the Iron Range of Minnesota, in the Dakotas, and in Montana and Idaho, working in mines, logging camps and sawmills, and on ore docks and railroad-construction jobs. He saved every cent he did not need to maintain his strength.

He arrived in the Hood River Valley in '95, settled in a log cabin he erected single-handed on a large homestead, married the daughter of one of the two Finns who had preceded him there, cleared the land little by little, and plowed and sowed. He dug a network of irrigation ditches and planted long rows of young fruit trees, till he had a great plantation. He worked hard and prospered, raising Oregon apples and prunes, cherries, pears, and several kinds of berries.

In five years his wife bore him three sons, who from the beginning showed signs of developing into husky boys and men; and, planning for their future and scheming how he might best invest what money he made, John Starkku bought more land as it became available for purchase adjacent to his homestead. By 1905 he owned eight hundred acres, all in one piece. The growing sons helped him gradually extend irrigation and plant more fruit trees.

Now all three sons are men in their forties and married, each father of a number of children, while the property, highly developed, has been divided into four ranches of nearly equal size, which are autonomous economic units within a kind of family co-operative, or federation, headed by the old man who at seventy-five is hale and sinewy, if considerably slower in his movements than he was once; still fit to work, when necessary, from ten to fourteen hours daily for weeks at a stretch. His own ranch is so situated that it borders on all three of his sons' properties. He planned things thus from the beginning. After his death (his wife passed away in 1937) it will be divided into three equal parts, which will be attached to the sons' farms. The original log cabin still stands: a crude, solid shelter, now used as a storeroom and tool shed.

Like the majority of the early Finnish immigrants, John Starkku was not an educated man when he came over, and was unable to analyze the forces that held Finland in a paralyzing vise and had sent him more than seven thousand miles away. He knew only this: there he had known mostly poverty and frustration, while, by comparison, here in Oregon he had, as he put it, everything: freedom to accomplish what he could.

With his wife, who had emigrated with her parents as a very young girl and knew next to nothing of her background in the Old World, he seldom and, as the years followed one another, more and more infrequently discussed the old country. He was a taciturn, inarticulate man, anyway. Soon, too busy to think of anything besides his ranch and family, he ceased to write to his relatives and lost all contact with Finland.

To his sons, when they were boys and very young men, John Starkku said little about his native land. And all through their youth they were not interested. They knew a little Finnish, having picked it up in their early boyhood when their father still spoke mostly his native tongue because his English was uncertain, but they did their best to be considered Americans and kept the scant knowledge they had of the language to themselves.

Their surname, with its double k, to say nothing of the u at the end, caused the youngsters some trouble in school and out of it, and occasionally people referred to them as "Finlanders." In 1917, to make sure he would not be regarded as "some kind of foreigner," one of the boys enlisted in the United States Army under the name of Stark. This seemed a good idea to the other two boys; after a while the whole family took on the new name, and in the ensuing decade they all felt more and more certain that the change had been a wise step. It had stopped all the questioning about their "nationality" and kidding about the monicker. It helped to make the three young men "full-fledged Americans." Two married old-stock American girls, the wife of the third one is half old-stock and half of Norwegian descent. There were a growing number of non-Finnish people in the Hood River Valley with whom they came in contact who did not know that they were "Finlanders." This, they thought, was all to the good.

Since about 1935, however, the Starks—the old man and his sons and the older grandchildren—have been having increasingly frequent moments of pride in the fact that they are of Finnish blood, and of regret—on the part of the old man and two of his sons, at least—that they had abbreviated, and thus Anglicized, their name. As an independent country since the First World War, Finland won the respect and admiration of the world, including and especially the United States, in the first fifteen years of its freedom; its achievements as a state and the accomplishments of its outstanding people were widely publicized, and the Starks have found it pleasant to bask in the reflected glory of "the old country."

In the autumn of 1939, traveling through Oregon, I met the family with the aid of a letter of introduction from a friend of theirs and mine who edits a Finnish-language paper in the Northwest and who had visited them the previous spring. We became rather friendly during the three days I spent on the four-in-one ranch, and I learned a good deal about Finland, for the Starks, including the non-Finnish daughters-in-law and perhaps a half-dozen of their children, now in their late teens, have been industriously delving into its story and culture during the last three years.

In 1936, his interest in things Finnish reawakened, the elder Mr. Stark subscribed to the newspaper edited by my friend; whereupon one of his sons started ordering books from a Finnish-American bookstore in Michigan. Then another of the sons got himself put on the mailing list of the Finnish Information Center in New York City, and in 1938 three members of the family took a trip to Finland, stayed a month, and returned enthusiastic.

On the parlor table in one of the four Stark houses I saw four books: the Bible, Emerson's Essays, the Finnish epic poem, *The Kalevala* (The Land of Heroes), in parallel Finnish and English versions, and *Hiawatha*, which Longfellow wrote under the influence of *The Kalevala*. I was shown a scrapbook of clippings about Finland, its problems and progress; about Sibelius, about Paavo Nurmi. I was asked to read a little syndicated piece Will Rogers had cabled from Finland one day in the mid-thirties, and which contained this sentence: "In Helsinki, capital of Finland, a traveler can leave his suitcase on the sidewalk in front of a hotel and come back hours later and find it there."

On a wall of the elder Mr. Stark's house was a map of Finland with a penciled mark on the narrow strip of land between two lakes whence he hails. He had little to say, but nodded once or twice while some of the others, including a grandson of his who is half of old Yankee stock, spoke of their "Finnish heritage"; and smiled when one of his daughters-in-law said that maybe some day they should "fix up" the old log cabin he had built forty-five years ago and turn it into "a kind of family clubroom or museum," into which they would put their "Finnish textiles, pictures, and books and make it look a little like a cabin home in Finland." The whole family referred to the sturdy, albeit now a bit lopsided, little building as *pirtti*—Finnish for log cabin. In the evening they played Sibelius on the gramophone.

When I was there in late October, the Starks were following closely the European developments which came in the wake of the Russo-German pact, and were worried and "getting warm under the collar," as one of them put it, over the Kremlin's pressure on the Helsinki government.

Two months following my visit to the Hood River Valley, when, to the intense and all but unanimous applause of the American people, the Finns gave battle to the Soviet forces with almost incredible bravery and resourcefulness, I received a Christmas card from the Starks. There were several signatures; one, in a heavy, awkward hand, was "John Starkku."

II

According to some of the more reliable estimates, the United States received since the middle of the nineteenth century about three hundred thousand immigrants of Finnish origin and nationality. No exact figures are available. In the immigration statistics most of the Finns were long regarded as Russians, while a considerable number of people who came from the eastern edges of Sweden and were officially listed as Swedes were actually Finns, or Swedish Finns.

Some of the above number, to be sure, returned to the old country, while others went to Canada, after living and working here for a few years; but the majority remained. Of the latter a third or more have died by now and the probability is that at present there are in the United States about 150,000 Finnish immigrants, whose American-born children, ranging in age from infancy to gray hairs, number perhaps two hundred thousand and there are perhaps another hundred thousand grandchildren, who are of Finnish descent through either one or both parents.

As it became rather generally known in connection with the Swedish-Finnish Delaware Tercentenary in 1938, the first Finns arrived in the New World a good two hundred years before the beginning of what is now called the New Immigration. The Swedish adventure, beginning in 1638, to start a colony on this continent included a major proportion of Finns, who were then under the rule of Sweden. With the Swedes, they settled over a region now included in Pennsylvania, New Jersey, Delaware and Maryland. One of the towns which they started, near the present city of Chester, Pennsylvania, was originally called Finland.

Among them were competent builders, woodworkers, agriculturists and men-of-all-work, and the rapidly growing number of Finnish Americans nowadays who, like the Starks of Oregon, are eagerly interested in the Finnish lore in the New World, maintain—to the occasional annoyance of Swedish Americans—that these early Finns introduced here the log cabin, which had been an institution in Finland for centuries and which subsequently played so important a role, both as a dwelling and as a symbol, in the life of the Colonies and the United States; and also rye, which had achieved a high point of cultivation and popularity in Finland long before that; and *sauna*, the steambath.

Like their Swedish contemporaries, these early Finns assimilated into the Anglo-Saxon, Dutch, and Pennsylvania German strains; but, according to the current Finnish American historians, a few of their descendants played important parts in the creation of the United States. John Morton, one of the signers of the Declaration of Independence, for instance, is said to have been of Finnish lineage, although the Swedish Americans also claim him, as they do Sarah Austin, a great-great-granddaughter of a man named Goram Kyn, or Keen. A member of the Swedish Lutheran Gloria Dei Church in Philadelphia, she made one of the earliest flags of the United States. It was presented to John Paul Jones, who hoisted it on his ship, the *Ranger*; and rendered historic because it was the flag that received the first salute given the Stars and Stripes in Europe. But the Finnish Americans say Sarah Austin's descent was Finnish, maintaining that her great-great-grandfather's name—later changed to Kyyn, Kyn and Keen—was originally Yrjänä Kyy, a Finnish name, if there ever was one. They further point out, with a good deal of supporting material, that many of the "Swedes" (their quotation marks) were really Finns in spite of their Swedish names.

All this is interesting chiefly as a manifestation of the newly awakened pride of the contemporary Finnish Americans in their history and heritage in the United States. To a great many it is all very important. It is the beginning of their background in America. The mouth of the Delaware is their Jamestown or Plymouth Rock, and in 1938 a number of them put up a hard and successful fight in Washington to have the part of the Finnish nationals in the New Sweden Colony officially recognized.

The new Finnish immigration may be said to have begun in 1850, when a couple of hundred adventurous Finns, making their living as fishermen and seamen along the coast of Norway and Sweden, heard of gold in California. There are now in and around San Francisco a number of families stemming from these men, who journeyed to the Pacific Coast around the Horn. The ninetieth anniversary of their arrival was celebrated at the San Francisco Fair in the summer of '39.

In the mid-fifties, during the Crimean War, about 150 Finnish sailors serving under the Russian flag left their ships in New Orleans, Philadelphia, New York, and Baltimore, because they saw no sense in risking capture by English vessels. Most of them had no difficulty getting onto American boats, and did so well that during the Civil War the Federal government drew about a hundred of them into its naval service. After the war many settled in the larger Atlantic port cities, especially in Boston, New York, and Philadelphia.

But what started the Finns America-ward in a big way was the shortage of labor in the newly opened copper country in the far reaches of Michigan's Upper Peninsula, which became acute about the middle of the Civil War. Several came over with the Norwegian contract laborers imported by the Quincy Mining Company of Hancock. They showed themselves to be exceedingly strong, hard-working people who took in their stride the sub-zero temperature that reigns over the Upper Peninsula for four months out of the year. So more were sent for, not only by Quincy but other companies.

Many of these Michigan-bound Finns, however, never got there, or it took them a long time to attain their initial destination. Stopped enroute by Americans anxious to hire them for military service in their stead, many allowed themselves to be hired. They fought and died in various battles. Some, too, went into Lincoln's army not as hired soldiers, but because they became partisan to the Union cause.

Most Finnish immigrants of that period, however, did wind up on the Upper Peninsula, and as a beginning the majority went into the mines. The towns of Hancock, Houghton, and Calumet drew them by the thousands, as did the iron camps in northern Michigan. And almost simultaneously they spread to Minnesota's Iron Range and other mining regions in the Northwest. Owing to their background as woodsmen in the old country, they were at their best erecting safety props in the pits, but excelled too as actual miners. Many found work in the new mills and smelters, on ore docks, or building railroad embankments through the virgin forests of Michigan, Wisconsin, and Minnesota with pick and shovel and wheelbarrow.

But, in spite of their competence in it, industrial work did not satisfy the Finns; or, rather, it dissatisfied them more than it did the Irish and Slavs, also numerous in the Michigan and Minnesota mines and smelters. Traditionally, the Finns are farmers, woodsmen, trappers and fishermen, with a passion for the open, silent places, and disposed to go into difficult enterprises without a boss over them; and so a large proportion of them got out of the mining and smelter towns and camps as soon as they saved enough to go on the land. Some did this by way of the woods, where they worked temporarily as timberworkers, or by acquiring, with a small down payment, a piece of land near the mines or smelter plants while still working in them.

Off and on, back in the eighties and nineties, a great elemental impulse seemed to seize entire groups or colonies of Finnish immigrants in places like Hancock or Calumet or Ishpeming, Michigan, or Ely or Hibbing or Eveleth, Minnesota, and they left the towns for the backwoods of those states to go into farming in cutover areas. The fact that some go-getting fellow countryman of theirs, who had blossomed out as this or that mining or railroad company's land agent, organized that impulse made it no less elemental. On a farm near Cloquet, Minnesota, I know a man, now very old, who once told me he had left the mines for farming in 1896 because underground he could not recite to himself as he worked a bit of *Kalevala* which he specially fancied:

> Then the aged Väinämöinen
> Spoke aloud his songs of magic,
> And a flower-crowned birch grew upward,
> Crowned with flowers, and leaves all golden,
> And its summit reached to heaven,
> To the very clouds uprising.
> Then he sang his songs of magic,
> And he sang a moon all shining,
> Sang the moon to shine forever
> In the pine-tree's emerald summit
> Sang the Great Bear in its branches.

The soil in northern Michigan and northeastern Minnesota is far from good, and fifty or sixty years ago, and more recently, it was worse, rocky and full of stumps. But the Finns were the folk to tackle it; much of it was rather better than what they had left in Finland. In the Great Lakes country one still hears it said that the language best understood by the stumps and boulders is Finnish. Starting literally thousands of farms of from forty to eighty acres, the Finns—along with some old-stock Americans, a sprinkling of Slovenians and Czechs, and a great many Swedes, Danes and Norwegians, most of whom came there initially as farming pioneers—did an epic job in clearing and improving the land and creating new communities and business centers in those remote parts of the country. And, unlike the Irish and Slavic immigrants who seemed to have been more industrial, the Finns stayed in those regions after the best times of the mining and timber industries had passed, and now form the backbone of their population. This is especially true of St. Louis County in Minnesota and large sections of Upper Michigan. The Finns stayed, in part, also because terrain and climate, the lakes, and the fir, spruce and birch woods in those regions are a great deal like Finland's. Summers are cool, winters are cold and dry. The extreme temperature from December to March is no serious matter to the Finns.

Here and there they improved the soil by burnbeating, a method which consists of burning the brush, the leaves and bark of felled trees, and the sod, while keeping the fire under control by beating out the flames with branches if they threaten to spread.

Beginning in the mid-seventies, some of the most resourceful and adventurous Finnish immigrants started, individually and in small groups, to make their way into the Far West and, discovering the vast, sparsely inhabited territories of Washington and Oregon, particularly the latter, wrote to relatives in Finland and in Michigan and Minnesota; whereupon others—like John Starkku—followed them. Still others went all the way west as workers on the new railroads. But many stopped enroute, almost anywhere, for no end of reasons, and started little colonies, usually as farmers, in the Dakotas, in Wyoming, Montana, and Idaho. They went through the typical American pioneer experience, living in sod houses, plowing with oxen, burning dung for fuel, fighting drought and grasshoppers.

At the same time considerable groups of them, coming over in a steady stream from the old country, paused in their journey in various sections of the Northeast, then decided to remain, with the result that there are Finnish settlements, both rural and within large urban centers, from Brooklyn to Detroit, in parts of New England, and in well-nigh every important lake and seaport.

The lumber industry drew waves of Finnish immigrants to Maine, where Yankee logging operators still speak of their physical endurance and sense of responsibility and timing which made them ideal for the hazardous work of lumberjacks. Others who had worked in stone quarries in Finland were attracted to New England by the granite industry. It seems, however, that the first Finns who got into quarry work in Massachusetts were inexperienced. During a depression about forty years ago, a group of young greenhorns starved while looking for work in and around Boston. Something impelled them to hike forty miles to Rockport, on the tip of Cape Ann, where a group of Yankee quarrymen noticed them digging beneath the seaweed for mussels and periwinkles, and eating them raw. The American workers fed the Finns and gave them jobs, whereupon the immigrants wrote home, bringing to Cape Ann more Finns, some of whom later moved to Fitchburg and Quincy, to the granite towns throughout the White Mountain region.

Still other Finnish immigrants whose search for work brought them to New England went into textile mills, chair factories, the machine industry. For a people who had had next to no mechanical experience in the old country they proved themselves, I am told by employers, extremely efficient in handling and making machinery. . . . The Finns seem to have done well in whatever field necessity and fate pushed them.

Finns, too, went into fishing on the Great Lakes. Seventy years ago the news of salmon fishing in the Columbia River began to excite a great many, who then made their way to Astoria, Oregon, and became pioneers in the salmon industry. In Oregon in the fall of '39, I spoke with men who recall the time when they used to cook fish for canning in huge crude cauldrons over open woodfires. Now several Finnish Americans are heads of large modern canning plants.

From Astoria, which is currently one-third Finnish American, the Finns spread into Oregon's hinterland and hewed their homes out of the big trees in the dense forests of the foothills of the Coast Range. Some of these cabins, made of trees from a foot and a half to two feet in diameter, still stand in the remote parts of the Clatsop County, of which Astoria is the county seat; and a few still are inhabited by descendants of the early immigrant settlers. There are numerous little towns, largely Finnish American, whose lives revolve around the general store, the post office, and the communal Finnish steambath.

Finns scattered thinly the country over, through a great variety of industries and pursuits. They are to be found in the Pennsylvania and West Virginia coal mines, in the rubber and glass plants and steel and tin-plate mills of Ohio, in the lumberyards of California. Great numbers of them work in automobile production in and around Detroit.

Once the government engaged a number of them to go to Alaska to teach the Eskimos reindeer breeding. During the First World War they were numerous in shipyards and munition factories, as well as in the United States Army and Navy. In the cities, especially in the East, thousands of Finnish girls and women became efficient household workers. A good many have gone into building trades, or have opened little retail businesses, especially in places where Finnish Americans are concentrated in large numbers. One of them worked out the plans for the beautification of the Detroit and Chicago water fronts.

But, as already suggested, these people's strongest inclination has been toward farming, toward small communities, toward the Northwest. Possibly half of the Finnish immigrants now live on the land and derive all or a substantial part of their sustenance from it, and perhaps one-fifth of all the Finnish Americans, immigrant and born in this country, are in the Northwestern states. Their number in the South is minimal.

Physically, many are large, blond, fair-skinned, and blue-eyed; but smallish and dark Finns are not rare.

III

The central motives of the Finnish immigration at its height were the same as those of the majority of immigrants from all other countries—self-improvement, liberty. Most of them were getting away from what appeared to them to be an existence devoid of worth-while future. The backwardness of the Russian Empire held Finland in a grip, the breaking of which few individuals could imagine within their lifetime, and hundreds of thousands of them decided the sensible thing to do was to escape from it. Many had no taste for serving in the Czar's army, and left their homeland before reaching the military age. Some were political "criminals" who escaped from Finland to keep the Czar's police from sending them to Siberia. And the great preponderance of those who came to America have never regretted their step, in spite of the fact that twenty years ago the historical process in Europe abruptly offered the 3,500,000 Finnish people who remained in the homeland a brief moment of opportunity to break the fetters of medievalism—a moment in which they achieved marvels with their little, none-too-rich country.

Most Finnish immigrants have markedly improved their lot in the United States, economically and otherwise, and their chief reactions to this country have been those of gratitude and loyalty. In 1898 an immigrant who settled in Minnesota wrote to his brother in Finland: "I have come to love this immense land, with its broad sky line, great lakes, limitless wilderness, and freedom."

But, of course, the history of the Finns in America is not all light, progress and triumph. In one particular, at least, the story of the Stark family in Oregon is not typical. The Starks have had comparatively smooth sailing; economically, their status is above the average Finnish American family.

In the last fifty years thousands of Finns, along with hundreds of thousands of other immigrants, have perished or been maimed in mine, quarry, and logging accidents. I am aware of numerous American Finnish families of four, five, or even six children that have been kept alive and raised by widows, almost incredibly resourceful and heroic immigrant women, now old, whose sons and daughters are scattered the country over. Many families have had drastic ups and downs even if the fathers lived, making bad starts, moving every few years, beginning over and over again.

And there were difficulties which more or less touched all of them whether they became well-off or not, because they were immigrants and Finns. Fifty, forty, thirty, or even twenty years ago, the average Finnish newcomer, male or female—like the average newcomer from any other non-English-speaking and socially and politically backward country—faced the very tough, if extremely vague, problem of adjustment of the stranger in a strange land. The difficulties involved in this cannot be readily understood by non-immigrants, or even by immigrants who came from England or Ireland, or from France or Germany.

He faced the problems of getting along with non-Finns, of "Americanization," of seeing his way through the jungle of forces generated by the Industrial Revolution and other dynamics of American life, of learning a language sharply unlike his mother tongue, of revising his character which had been created by conditions in the old country and was, to a greater or lesser extent, out of harmony with the atmosphere here.

For centuries Finland was the battleground between Russia and Sweden, and prior to the mid-1920's, when freedom finally gave the Finnish people a seeming chance to work out their own destiny, it was an ill-organized country. The struggle for existence against cold and famine and the effects of war was a grim business. Abrupt frosts destroyed grain and potato crops. I have met immigrants living here and there in the United States who recall bands of starving people in Finland traveling from village to village in search of food. Early in their careers here, these immigrants used to say to their American-born children, who were growing up under better conditions, "Don't laugh so much; soon you will be weeping." There was (still is) a superstitious feeling among the Finns that it was best not to be joyful and overhopeful, for some misfortune might come to spite them; and the majority had the outward appearance of stolidity and grimness, seriousness bordering on sullenness, lack of humor and spontaneous friendliness—characteristics which lent themselves to misunderstanding and unfavorable reactions on the part of the general run of old-stock Americans as well as people of the non-Finnish new-immigrant groups, including Swedes and Norwegians.

For decades the prejudice against the Finns was strong. They were called "Finlanders," and the word—like "Polacks" or "Litvaks"—carried a touch of derision. Their language (they belong to the Finno-Ugric linguistic group) had almost no relation to any other tongue heard in America. Many of their names were difficult: Hietakangas, Ruonovaara, Pyöriasaari, Syrjäniemi, Vitikko-huhta, Kalliokoski, Wuorijärvi, Parkkila, or Niskawaara, to list only a few which put great strain on non-Finnish tongues, and which made them seem more foreign or outlandish than were some of the other new people—the Danes, Norwegians, or Swedes, for instance, whose names were easily pro-nounceable.

Late in the nineteenth and early in the twentieth century, Finland was not known to the old-stock Americans or to the Irish, Cornish, and Slavic miners in Michigan and Minnesota, and there was a lot of confusion as to who the Finns were and whence they hailed. Many Finns did not like to talk about their old country and refused to, or could not, answer the hasty questions put to them by the momentarily and superficially interested—which made them all the more mysterious and misunderstood.

The Finns, too, are a proud, stubborn, obstinate people; which—a few decades ago—rubbed no few non-Finns the wrong way, including some employers or labor bosses, especially those who believed in driving workers, or yelling their orders at them. Finns resent attempts to drive them and are not inclined to tolerate being yelled at, but respond quickly to competent and responsible leadership.

I have mentioned the Finnish bathhouse—usually a log cabin, containing an oven made of boulders, which a woodfire of several hours brings to intense heat. Buckets of cold water are then splashed against the stones, filling the room with steam; and the idea is to stay in for an hour or longer, till one is practically cooked, meanwhile beating oneself briskly with birch or cedar twigs. The Finns take such a bath once a week, and call it soothing and invigorating. For climax they run out and dive into a cold stream or lake, or roll in the snow. To the discerning non-Finns this bathing is a mark, as well as an explanation, of their hardihood, good health and clear eyes; to most people in the old days, however, especially in the primitive mining towns and logging camps where bathing of any sort was somewhat of an idiosyncracy, it but underlined the notion that the Finns were a strange lot.

In the early days, too, before Finnish women began to come over in large numbers, men lived in camps and boardinghouses which, off and on, exploded with incomprehensible Finnish sounds and noises, for among themselves they expanded and gave fierce vent to the joys and pains in their innards. These outbursts occurred also in Finnish saloons, in which most of the drinking was of hard liquor and done in the thorough fashion that characterizes all Finnish endeavors, functions and pursuits. This was another thing that some blue-nose non-Finns had against them, neglecting to observe that the Finns also had a powerful so-called temperance movement, most of whose followers were— typically—not merely temperate but strict and passionate abstainers and teetotalers.

Coming from a country in which oppression and injustice prevailed, a good many Finns had, or developed here, leftward political tendencies; the ways of some American industrialists or their superintendents early in the century reminded them of Czarism back in Finland, and they became passionate believers in unions and went into the I.W.W. and Western Miners movements. They played important roles in the Northwestern mine strikes in the decade immediately preceding the First World War. As strikers they always stuck to the last. This caused certain mine operators and their spokesmen to brand the Finns in general as Reds, subversive, and what-not, although large numbers of them were in fact conservative, even ultra-conservative, eagerly involving themselves in all the anti-Red snares of private property, and warning their children that the wrath of God surely would descend upon them if they so much as set foot in the meeting halls of the "Socialists," who were immoral and Godless.

In Finland ninety per cent of Finns are said to be devout, churchgoing Evangelical Lutherans. The proportion of churchgoers among the Finnish Americans is considerably smaller, but they do have close to two hundred Lutheran churches in the United States, organized in a Synod, and a large school—Suomi (meaning Finland) College, in Hancock, Michigan—founded by the early immigrants to train pastors for their churches. With many Finns in America, as in Finland, Lutheranism is an intense faith, full of devotion and purpose, which has to do both with this world and the next. Lutheranism, in fact, explains much of the Finnish character. The Lutheran intensity hangs on in Finns who have drifted away from the church. They take it into unionism, atheism, stump-clearing, burnbeating—into whatever they do.

The basis of much of the early prejudice against the Finns was economic. Here and there in New England, for example, where they took over and made a fresh go of farms abandoned by Yankees as hopelessly unproductive, the resentment against them—as against the Poles—was strong and steady. In one Massachusetts community, the center of a region that includes many Finnish farmers, some of whom are also part-time or occasional quarry workers, the local newspaper has been "riding the Finns," as they put it, for decades; this in spite of the general admission that their coming has added to the town's economic energy. The Yankee editor-publisher simply "has it in for" them, even to this day, headlining every least impropriety, as he sees it, committed by a person of Finnish origin or descent. This is true, too, of an occasional Anglo-Saxon American editor in Michigan.

The Finnish immigrant's reaction to these unfavorable attitudes has usually been one of silent contempt. By and large, they did them no serious damage. In places they only made them a bit more clannish than they had been normally, and impelled them as individuals to proceed with even greater determination by their diverse routes toward self-improvement, usually by seeking for "the hardest job and the biggest pay," to quote Mr. J. H. Jasberg, of Hancock, himself a Finnish American, and one who is well-informed about his people; by going to night schools and libraries; by forming and joining cultural clubs and subscribing to newspapers and keeping up with events.

There is a steely, firmly positive streak in the Finnish strain; a quality for which the Finns themselves have a word, *sisu,* that has become well known in the United States since December 1, 1939, but is not adequately translatable into English. It is stick-to-it-iveness, and more. It is courage and endless resourcefulness. It is the ability to turn disadvantage to advantage, to do the impossible. It is almost a mystical attribute. One possesses *sisu* who, in the common American phrase, has "what it takes" to achieve things in the face of misunderstanding and disapproval, definite opposition or downright hostility.

I referred to the Finns' clannishness. Clannishness, as a rule, is not a specially desirable quality. There is a great deal of it in a number of the new-immigrant groups in the United States, as well as among the old-stock Americans. It usually is an ingrown, introvert, negative tendency, destructive of some of the best attributes of the groups and the individuals in them. It becomes a matter largely of neurotic intra-group bickerings and pettiness. And I do not mean to suggest that among Finns clannishness is free of these negative symptoms, but in their case the word is closer to being synonymous with co-operativeness than it is, so far as I can see, in any other new-immigrant group.

As sons and daughters of a country where the natural environment was extremely difficult, the Finns brought over a strong co-operative instinct. At first it expressed itself in mutual help. In the seventies and eighties, if a Finnish farmer in Michigan or Minnesota lost a cow or horse when he was trying to get a foothold on the land, his neighboring fellow countrymen made a collection and bought him another animal. The co-operative urge then caused the Finnish immigrants to form fraternal-insurance societies, which are found in nearly all other new-immigrant elements and whose purpose and basis was organized mutual self-protection in a strange country. It led them to join labor unions and start Finnish labor temples.

Very early in the current century, in spite of the Russian authorities' opposition to it, the so-called co-operative idea, which developed in England, took hold in Finland. Finnish immigration was then at its height, and the immigrants brought the idea over and began to organize co-operatives, through which they sold their products and bought what they needed at advantageous prices. Swedes and Norwegians, who in some ways resemble the Finns, became interested in the co-operative idea at about the same time; there is almost no doubt, however, that the Finns did more for it, or with it, in the United States than any other group. Among them it began to develop into a full-fledged movement already before the First World War.

Now the Finnish Americans have about seven hundred co-operative enterprises of various kinds all over the country—stores and supply houses, bakeries, hotels, restaurants and apartment and boardinghouses, feed mills, warehouses, garages, repair shops, gasoline stations, coalyards, sawmills, cheese factories, quarries, banks, farms, and so on. Their annual turnover runs into tens of millions of dollars. For some time now they have been drawing into them non-Finnish Americans, or have been urging and inspiring them to create co-operatives of their own. There is a saying that if two Finns are seen together they are either on the way to the *sauna* or to form a co-operative.

With Norwegians, Swedes, and, to some extent, the Danes, they have been the American pioneers in this economic movement, which, in large measure, is the explanation for the progress and internal peace and prosperity of Finland and the Scandinavian countries from about 1920 till the *blitzkrieg* days of 1940; and which, emphatically proclaim no few Finnish American addicts to the co-operative idea, is the one and only effective answer to the challenge of fascism and communism. Finns, as already said, do nothing halfway; and those who believe in co-operatives believe in them passionately and work energetically to spread them.

The clannishness of the Finns, that was enhanced in America by the prejudice against them, found a positive expression in co-operatives; and the co-operatives, in turn, explain much of the group's progress in this country. In central Massachusetts, for instance, the Finns have become successful strawberry growers on land that had been given up as unfit for agriculture not only by Yankee farmers but by the government, and this success is due mainly to their efficiently organized co-operative marketing. The same goes for the successful Finnish American poultry business in Connecticut and Rhode Island, where their co-operatives are well known. There are scores of such cases.

Lately I discussed the Finns with a Yankee who has kept an eye on them in New England for twenty years. Considerable prejudice against them, he said, was due to the fact that they seemed willing and eager to work harder than the Yankees, the Irish and the other elements; but much of it, too, was attributable to the Yankees' highly developed individualism and the keen opportunism of the Irish. For a long time the Yankees viewed the co-operatives as subversive, kin to socialism and communism. But of late much of this misunderstanding has evaporated. People of all backgrounds are beginning to see the Finnish Americans in their midst as an intensely and consistently constructive element, whose co-operative tendency in no way impinges on their individualism, their passion for personal freedom and self-sufficiency.

Up to a few years ago complaints were uttered that here and there the Finns were not "Americanizing" noticeably. They held overlong and too stubbornly onto their ways and customs, and many took their own good time in becoming citizens. Recently, however, people, including old-time New Englanders, have been saying that Finns may be in no greater need of Americanization than a lot of old-time Americans may be in need of Finnization.

IV

In 1923, Rev. John Wargelin, then president of Suomi College, wrote, in a little book, *The Americanization of Finns,* that a great number of the American-born sons and daughters of Finnish immigrants were ashamed of their parents. I have the same information from numerous other sources. This shame of parents was widespread as recently as fifteen years ago and was due, in part, to the already-mentioned prejudice against the Finns and the immigrants in general. But, in no slight measure, it must be ascribed, too, to certain ill-considered aspects of the "Americanization" movement, which was at its height about twenty years ago, when most of the immigrants' children were in their teens and early twenties; and which implicitly—and sometimes explicitly—scorned and fought everything that was not more or less Anglo-Saxon American. It stamped the immigrants from backward non-English-speaking countries as inferior in the eyes of their children, who were made fun of, or who experienced antagonism in various forms and in diverse connections, also on account of their difficult names, or because they lived in homes where certain "foreign" customs persisted. The youngsters blamed this antagonism on their parents, not on "Americanization." The result was conflict in the home. Boys and girls wanted to change their names, refused to learn Finnish, and did not want to know anything about Finland, even if some of the more articulate and better-educated parents were able to tell them about the old country.

Youngsters were uneasy and did their best that no non-Finn found out about their parents' old-country superstitions and so-called "charms"—such as the charm which consists of chanting the following verse in order to prevent one's fingers and hands from freezing in sub-zero weather:

> Cold, thou son of Wind,
> Do not freeze my finger nails,
> Do not freeze my hands.
> Freeze thou the water willows,
> Go chill the birch chunks.*

This shame and uneasiness produced in many young people feelings of inferiority about themselves for being Finnish. It prevented them from having, or developing, a sense of continuity, of worth-while background. It short-circuited their ambitions and talents. It kept them from developing self-confidence, from running for office, and assuming responsibility. They "Americanized" by shedding, so far as they could, everything that smacked of being Finnish, and by taking on only the superficial aspects of being American; and in point of character and personality many seemed to compare unfavorably with their parents, who were usually at a loss to know how to get along with their sons and daughters.

This sort of thing exists, or existed, to a greater or lesser extent in most new-immigrant groups.

In the Finnish group it is now almost entirely a matter of history. It slowly commenced to disappear about fifteen years ago, when, as already suggested, postwar Finland began to come into its own and receive so much favorable publicity in the United States that it caused prejudice to decline. It prompted many immigrants to talk to their children about things in the old country and about their early struggles in America. This inspired respect in the youngsters. It stimulated their further interest in Finland and particularly in the Finnish story in America. It gave them a sense of background or continuity. It led them to read *The Kalevala*, to delight in their parents' "charms" and folk songs, and to revive, as they did in several places in Minnesota and Michigan, the *Laskiainen* ("sliding downhill"), a Finnish winter festival, which includes skiing, sled- and snowshoe-sliding, bumpty-bumps, and sliding on spruce boughs and barrel staves; telling of legends, singing of snow songs, and eating of authentic old-country foods. It prompted them to participate in the old immigrants' "pioneer re-unions," whose purpose is to recall the early history of the settlements and commemorate the achievements of the trail blazers through the wilderness. It made them feel good as Americans who happened to be of Finnish descent. It helped them to become outstanding students in high schools and colleges, both academically and athletically, and generally to develop resourcefulness, give play to their talents, and move ahead in many departments of America's national life.

* For the translation of this verse I am indebted to Miss Marjorie Edgar of Marine on the St. Croix, Minn., who published an article, "Finnish Charms and Folk Songs in Minnesota," in the *Minnesota History Quarterly* for December, 1936.

Emil Hurja, the statistical wizard and one-time assistant to Jim Farley, is perhaps the best-known American of Finnish blood. He helped many of his strain to positions in numerous government offices in Washington, where, almost without exception, they are highly regarded for ability and character. Hundreds of others have advanced themselves in their localities as political and civic leaders, professional and business people. There are Finnish Americans in most Northwestern legislatures. Several are mayors of smaller cities. A few have been in Congress in recent years. Many teach in colleges and universities. A number of them are outstanding in architecture, engineering, mechanics. Some are officers in the Army and Navy. Others serve on merchant ships, especially on the Great Lakes. Many work as managers and clerks in co-operatives that were started by their immigrant parents. Few are in prisons.

The great preponderance of Americans of the Finnish strain now are quietly proud of their parents, of Finnish achievements in the Northwest and elsewhere on this continent, of "the old country," of their entire heritage which goes back to Finland and to "New Sweden" on the Delaware. This helps to make them into excellent individuals and citizens.

They belong to all political parties. Among them one finds an occasional ultra-reactionary or Babbitt or leftist crackpot in the least engaging sense of these terms, and there is a microscopic Stalinist element which even in 1939-40 sided with Earl Browder, the Kremlin, and "the Finnish People's government" at Terijoki; but the majority of Finnish Americans are progressive on gradualist, common-sense, middle-of-the-road lines leading toward general welfare in the United States.

Some are, or were, for the New Deal, or for certain phases of it; others oppose it, wholly or in part. A proportionately small number of them have been on jobless or AAA relief, while the great majority have been pulling through the bad years without help from the government. This is particularly true of the numerous groups among them who have farms near some industry in which they work off and on, and are completely dependent for their livelihood on neither one nor the other. A number of Finnish Americans personally known to me in various parts of the country have been against relief on the ground that it was given mostly as a premium on shiftlessness and incompetence. "Who got the most help from the government?"—to quote one man in Minnesota. "He whose farm was the most poorly managed and whose house and barn were unpainted, unrepaired, and dirty."

By and large, Finnish Americans are among the firmest believers in democracy, in government by law and tradition, rather than by men. They seem to be constitutionally incapable of hero worship and are critical of all public figures, especially of "great" and "successful" men.

Most Finnish Americans whom I know are amused by the fact that so much has been made of Finland's debt-paying habit. Their smiles and shrugs imply: Why shouldn't Finland pay her debt? Isn't that what every country ought to do, and every individual? It's the right, and also the wise, thing to do. Finland deserves no special credit for this. Besides, her debt is small and before the Russian invasion payments were no strain on her, and they were good publicity.

If at all possible, the Finn avoids getting into debt. If he can't help getting into it, paying it back becomes temporarily the central aim of his life. He is thrifty and has scant interest in keeping up with the Joneses. He buys on installment plan, but only if he is sure he can handle it. This, along with the co-operative spirit among these people, is the reason very few Finnish Americans lost their homes or farms when foreclosures were general back in 1932 and later.

The Finnish mind is realistic, balanced, practical, tough; this even when Finns engage in fanciful, romantic, quixotic, or idealistic doings. The idealists who go about the country organizing co-operatives, for instance, never go hungry, although they often work without pay. I know one of them who every once in a while takes a holiday from his co-operative evangelism and makes himself a few thousand dollars on some lumber deal, which then keeps him and his family going while he puts another co-operative on its feet. The political reformers of Finnish descent in the Northwest usually succeed in improving the local government because they know just how far to go. They do not wreck themselves. When a Finn takes a drastic step, he has usually organized his resources and made retreat possible. Twenty years ago a good many Finnish immigrants were pro-Bolshevik and some went to Russia, but in most cases left bank accounts in the United States so they could return in case the Revolution turned out to be a disappointment. The majority soon returned.

The Finnish Americans' reaction to the Soviet's attack upon Finland was inwardly intense and full of pain, but much calmer outwardly than has been the reaction of the majority of their non-Finnish fellow Americans. In Louisville, Kentucky, in December, 1939, an old-stock American woman burst into tears and became incoherent as she tried to express to me her sense of outrage over the event; while no Finnish American among the scores of those I met during that period was incapable of discussing it quietly, concisely, even objectively, without rhetoric about the glory that is Finland. Most of them listened to the raving comments of non-Finnish Americans about the reported Finnish performance against the Red Army, then pointed out that General Winter and Russian miscalculations probably had as much to do with it as Marshall Mannerheim or the bravery of the Finnish soldier, and said the coming spring would make things more difficult for Finland. All they were sure of was that the Finns would fight as long as they would have anything to fight with: "but, then, why shouldn't they? Isn't that the thing to do?" Their chief feeling was that the war was a tragedy.

The general American reaction to the Russo-Finnish conflict made the Finnish Americans into the favorite new-immigrant group in the United States. Everywhere non-Finnish Americans became interested in them. If jobs were to be had, they got them, more likely than not. People in New England, in the Northwest, and elsewhere went out of their way to point out the various virtues

The Thrill That Comes Once in a Lifetime   BY WEBSTER

From *The New York Herald Tribune* (March 6, 1940)
by special permission

of the Finnish strain and its contributions to the upbuilding of this country. But the deep realism and sense of balance which persisted in them impelled a good many Finnish Americans to remark as they listened to such enthusiastic talk that there were all kinds of Finns, including the kind that did not pay debts, or that was ruined by drink, or— They are a self-critical people.

I sent copies of a rough draft of this chapter to five Finnish Americans, three immigrants and two who were born in this country. One asked me to emphasize there was almost no crime among his people. One thought what I say "is all right." Three were afraid I was too favorable, and this not on the basis of modesty. "Why should we be singled out and given so much credit in developing the Northwest? Old-stock Americans and Swedes and Norwegians have really done more than we. Besides, why speak of 'contributions' when whatever we did was done really in the course of living our lives according to such lights as were ours?" . . . "I have no corrections to make, but couldn't you make it clear that our Finnish backgrounds or heritage probably is not superior to the backgrounds and heritages of other groups here? We may have a touch of this so-called *sisu*, but other peoples are not without it, either, and some of them have qualities which we Finns lack."

The Meleskis:
From Pomerania to Paradise

WHEN he decided to go to America, in 1907, Stefan Meleski was twenty-eight; son of a poor peasant in Hojnice, a village in Pomorze, or Pomerania, then held by Prussia. He was of medium height, thin, large-boned, with long arms and big hands capable of great strength and—despite the air of awkwardness enveloping his person—no slight agility and deftness. Mild, deep-sunken blue eyes lit up faintly his fair-skinned, sharp-featured Polish face. His bristly straw-colored hair was ever in revolt; giving him, when he was hatless, a touch of the comic.

He could not have been called good-looking, except, by the discerning, when his face suddenly—often, to all seeming, irrelevantly—broke into a grin which, as one got to know him, was a diagram of his character and soul. Slavs believe in the soul and refer to it more often than any other Occidental race. That smile revealed in Stefan qualities, or states of being, that one can suggest with such words and phrases as dignity, inner power, uncertainty, fatalism, peasant optimism, Slavic pessimism, a sense of tragedy; competence, longing to function and express himself through effort, and frustration. All these, and possibly others, were tangled in him, and were not unrelated to the unhappy situation of Poland as a whole, though Stefan himself was but remotely aware of it.

He had just served out a long term in the Prussian Army. Save for a few months at the start, he was not really a soldier, but a laborer who, because his hands craved that kind of work, developed into a carpenter and was then transferred to the quartermaster department, wherein he became the butt of numerous jokes and the object of occasional cruelty—although, of course, there were Prussians and other Germans with whom he came into contact, men and officers, who were as decent to him as any Pole could have been.

Stefan's personal problem—swinging mostly about his poverty and his love for Anna Przybylowicz—was typical of young Poles of his class and age at that time, when they were going to the United States by tens of thousands yearly.

He could expect no help from his father or elder brother, who was in line to become the owner of the debt-ridden Meleski homestead, with its tiny hut and few acres of clayey land. As a carpenter, Stefan could do only the rough work, which was so ill paid in Pomerania that he could not get married on what he might earn. So he wrote to his youngest brother Pawel, who, three years before, at eighteen, had emigrated to evade military service and was now a miner in Coalville, Pennsylvania. Would Pawel send him the ticket? Pawel sent it. Then Stefan and Anna had a long tender talk about their future.

Daughter of another poor peasant in Hojnice, Anna Przybylowicz was no beauty, without material assets or prospects, but a definite character, if there ever was one, with sound instincts, and capable of hard work, interminable loyalty and high courage. Her home stood by itself on the edge of a forest, outside the village proper. One wintry morning, when she was eighteen, on stepping out of the house she had found herself facing a hungry wolf, poised to leap upon her. Instead of flying into the house and bolting the door, she had seized the ax lying on the chopping block and swiftly, with amazing aim or luck and force, connected it with the beast's head, splitting it open. A few minutes later, Stefan, going on twenty-one and just summoned into the army, had come by on his way to work in the woods, and—to say no more of the wolf—had fallen in love with Anna then and there. He had been on the verge of doing this for some while before. On her part, she had liked his grin, and God knows what else; this sort of thing is as inexplicable in Pomerania as elsewhere. They had decided to marry "when we can." She had waited seven years, and the waiting had but emphasized the definiteness of her character, which, ruled by an unconscious woman purpose, was mostly unaffected by the Polish problem, peasant poverty, and other such vicissitudes of environment, history and circumstance that mold or tear apart more men than women.

Now, taking stock of their resources—no hard matter, for they consisted only of such things as youth and health—Stefan and Anna agreed that he would send for her as soon as he paid Pawel for his ticket and saved enough money to buy one for her. They did not know how long they might stay in America after she joined him. Possibly only till they had enough to be able to return to Pomerania and acquire four or five acres on a sunward slope.

II

From Ellis Island, Stefan went directly to Pittsburgh. There Pawel awaited him, then took him twenty miles to Coalville, where about eight hundred miners—mostly Poles, Slovaks, Croatians, Slovenians, Ukrainians—were getting up trainloads of coal for the steel mills in Pittsburgh, Canton and Youngstown.

The boardinghouse where Pawel lived was run by the wife of miner Julius Zwierzchowski. There were always between eighteen and twenty boarders, who slept in shifts on five iron double beds in two rooms. When the night shift finished breakfast, the woman set the supper table for the day shift.

Stefan's first name was promptly "Americanized" into Steve, as Pawel's had been into Paul. In fact, it was Paul who, all for "*amerykanizacja*," had enjoined the other boarders to call his brother "Steve" right off. They pronounced it "Steef." This change of his name was a trifle compared to other things he experienced on his arrival in Coalville.

He ate supper with the day shift. There were quantities of Polish cabbage soup, pork chops, potatoes, sauerkraut, white bread and butter, and beer, which the Zwierzchowski children fetched in buckets from the corner saloon. Compared to old-country fare, this spread amazed Steve, as did the fact that all the others at the table took it for granted.

Laughing at Steve's remark about this, Paul explained that, in relation to wages, good food was comparatively cheap in America, and that miners must eat well. Coal mining was harder than peasant toil in the old country, where, with the aid of endless fresh air, one could maintain one's strength with black bread, corn mush, cabbage, potatoes, sour milk, and an infrequent hunk of pork fat, hambone, or sausage. With a touch of amusement and the faintly superior air of a seasoned *Amerykaniec* toward a *grynol*, or greenhorn, Paul went on to say that most peasants came over with the idea of returning home when they saved some money, but the majority stayed, in big part because of the difference between food in American industrial towns and in European villages; while many who did go back presently returned to America, partly for the same reason.

Steve slept with Paul, who till then had shared a bed with another boarder. Lying in the dark that first night, listening to the eloquent snores of the weary men in the other beds, who fell asleep the instant they attained the horizontal position, Steve had a taut feeling in his chest. At the foot of the vast iron bedstead two brass knobs gleamed dimly.

Breakfast included baked ham, fried eggs, potatoes and onions, white bread and coffee. In his brand-new lunch pail, which Paul had bought him and Mrs. Zwierzchowski had packed, Steve found several *senwiczes*—sandwiches—made of white bread and meat.

He went to work in No. 2 Mine, where Paul and a few other Poles boarding with the Zwierzchowskis were employed. Paul was friendly with the Irish mine boss, Pat O'Keefe, who liked the "Polacks," as he called them, because they were strong, conscientious, hard-working men, and who attached the newcomer to his prop crew.

Steve then moved alone or with one or two other men through the corridors and caverns of the mine, putting up timbers, repairing the old props, laying new car tracks. The work was not strenuous, but very strange at first, for moments terrifying. But after a while Steve got used to being underground; only he had nightmares, in which rock and coal and earth came down on him in avalanches unevadable as the universe.

Now and then he put in a few days on the surface, erecting a shed or repairing something. Once, fixing the gate at the shaft mouth, enjoying the sun's light and warmth, Steve—the peasant in him—had this thought: Working underground was lunacy, not on the part of any one man, but on the part of all, of miners everywhere, and of the world that required coal and ore—a sort of collective madness. He remembered this thought for the rest of his life, because, as it occurred to him, he considered it clever and smiled to himself.

Steve's wages at the start were $2.08 for a ten-hour day, which in four months advanced to $2.76. They remained there for the rest of his time in Coalville. He could have become a miner and made as much as $3.62 a day, but he preferred to be a carpenter on the prop crew.

Depending on the fluctuation of grocery and meat prices, the boarders paid between $3.00 and $3.25 a week for food, bed and washing. Working as hard as any of the miners and far longer each day, Mrs. Zwierzchowski cleared nine or ten dollars a week, and thought she was doing well.

III

Steve paid his debt to Paul, then was in no rush to send for Anna. The men at the boardinghouse might joke about his eagerness to bring her over as they joked about another fellow, although this was not a serious consideration. Serious was his doubt whether he wanted to stay in Coalville and work in the mine for any length of time, or to stay in America for more than two or three years all together. Food was fine and the brass knobs on the bed continued to impress him, but—well, he didn't know what to think of America. Every few weeks he saw some Pole or Ukrainian or Slovak brought up with a broken limb, rib, collarbone, or cracked skull. This wiped the grin off his face for days. He noticed, too, that some miners drank heavily, and that the only well-to-do immigrants in town were the saloonkeepers and undertakers.

Men talked of quitting coal mining as soon as they saved enough to buy a farm either in America or the old country, but Steve saw that most of them would never realize their dream. It was hard to save money, and when you did accumulate some, you usually developed the ambition to possess more; when you got a little more, along came illness, or an accident, or a strike, or some glib-tongued swindler—usually a fellow immigrant—who wangled the hard-earned money out of you with promises of doubling it in six months; or you got caught in a complexity of other unforeseen circumstances, which appeared matter of course as they sneaked upon you—usually after you married.

As much as he loved Anna, with whom he exchanged semimonthly letters— which all began: "Over mountains and dales and over the endless ocean, I send you greetings, beloved"—Steve became afraid of marriage. He heaped wordless denunciation upon his soul; he was selfish, disloyal. Then, twisting the problem around, he argued with himself that Anna was better off in Hojnice, where things were green and air smelled of the soil. In Coalville, culm dumps and coal smoke dominated the scene. And the place was a trap. If she came, wouldn't they get caught here? Children. *Ach Boze!* Anna might want to start a boardinghouse and work eighteen hours a day, as Mrs. Zwierzchowski worked—and, in consequence, looked aged at thirty-one.

Steve mentioned these misgivings to Paul, who, though far from thoughtless and unobservant, was, at twenty-one, overfull of energy and youthful egoism. He liked mining, its risks and dangers. Most mine accidents, he said, were the men's fault; they were careless, dumb, awkward. Why hadn't he ever had an accident? Answer: He was careful and quick. When a lot of rock crashed down, he had got out of its way. He made sure the props were secure and the dust was watered down. Someday he would be a mine boss; Pat O'Keefe had as much as told him so. He was learning about mining and soon would be able to handle this confounded American language well enough to talk with the head boss. He had taken out his first citizenship paper. He would be the first Pole to become a mine foreman in Coalville, and make seven, eight dollars a day. "America she O.K." he told Steve. "Yoo vatch it my smoke!"

Steve's eyes and ears reveled in Paul. *Dobry chlopak*—a great youngster— good-looking, not a scarecrow like he, Steve; with a cool fire in his wide-apart blue eyes, a mane of tawny hair that curled and stayed combed, and wads of muscular flesh under the tight white skin of his straight, supple body. On Sundays he sported a blue serge suit, shoes that buttoned on the side, a derby or straw hat, a silk tie, a gold-plated horseshoe tie pin, and a silver watch chain with a boar's tusk for a fob. Never tired evenings, he usually dressed up after supper and went from one Polish saloon to the other—there were three—sometimes with Steve or some other fellow, sometimes alone. Once he confided to Steve that it was not so much his liking for beer as the pleasure he experienced pushing the swinging door and walking in, then up to the bar, and ordering. At the same time, Paul maintained a well-informed interest in the cause for a free Poland, was a member of the local lodge of the Zwiazek Narodowy Polski— Polish National Alliance—a fraternal organization formed by immigrants many years before to provide themselves with a sense of economic security in the New World; and read regularly *Zgoda*, the Z. N. P's weekly organ.

Paul urged Steve to bring over his Anna. They would make out somehow. He would board with them. One expression Paul used a great deal at this time was "Vat ta hell!" The utterance was accompanied by a jaunty cutting gesture.

When Steve had been in America six months, Paul fell in love on first sight with Ludmila Czernik, seventeen and pretty. Her father, Joe Czernik, also a peasant from Pomerania, had been in America for several years, a miner, living in the Zwierzchowski boardinghouse; Ludmila and her mother and two young brothers, Feliks and Jan, had just joined him in Coalville.

All the *swaszke*—matchmakers—approved, and Paul now insisted that Steve send for Anna. They would have a double wedding, one that Coalville would long remember. Then they would all live together—Ludmila and he, Steve and Anna, and the Czerniks and their two boys. Paul knew of a big house for rent; they might even have room for a few boarders.

Steve sent for Anna—and the double wedding lasted two days. A Pittsburgh newspaper carried a story about the uproarious, colorful affair, in which the entire Polish colony of Coalville participated, dancing polkas, mazurkas, *obereks* and *kujawiaks* to the music of an orchestra dominated by the concertina player, or "lemon squeezer." The paper printed photographs of both couples. Mentioned in the writeup was the fact, which the reporter had got from Paul, that Anna had singlehandedly slain a wolf at eighteen.

IV

Anna made a difference in Steve's outlook. His face now broke frequently into that grin of his, even as he worked underground. She did not mind the culm dumps or the coal fumes. Her imagination was livelier than his. The Statue of Liberty had brought tears to her eyes. The vastness of America, the possibilities of life here, impressed her. On a map of the United States in the Polish steamship-ticket agent's office in New York someone had pointed out Pittsburgh to her. It had seemed very near New York, within a stone's throw of the Atlantic Ocean she had just crossed; then she traveled all day on a train to get there! It was a sunny day in early spring, and the rolling land of Pennsylvania was turning green. Farmers were plowing for oats and corn; here and there, near lone white or gray farmhouses and cathedral-like red barns, were great fields of freshly turned soil. There was so much room in America; houses were kilometers apart. . . . And now, in Coalville, Anna talked of how Steve and she would go on the land, perhaps in a very few years. No, not return to Pomerania, to Prussian Poland, that beloved, miserable homeland of theirs; but on the land here— here in America. There was so much of everything; much of it not beyond the reach of ordinary folk like Steve and herself, provided they made some effort to get it.

Shabby and ugly outside, with cinders all about it, the dwelling that the three-in-one Czernik-Meleski family rented was adequate inside. The young couples each had a room; the Czerniks two. They shared the kitchen, with Mrs. Czernik in charge, and they ate together. There was also a little ground where they could raise vegetables.

The women immediately filled the extra space in the house with a half-dozen boarders. When more Polish immigrants kept coming to Coalville than the older boardinghouses could accommodate, they rented the house next door and took in thirty more. This expansion was chiefly Anna's idea, which sprang out of her ambition to make and save money quickly, so she and Steve could get on the land.

The two Czernik boys, Felix and Johnny, began to go to school in Coalville, and had difficulties at first because they knew no English. The Irish and Welsh kids jeered at them on the way to and from school, calling them "Polacks" and "Hunkies." But they quickly picked up the language and, as they took Uncle Paul's advice to swing at anybody who called them unpleasant-sounding names, their troubles decreased. Anna asked them to teach her the words and phrases they learned.

Anna got along agreeably with Ludmila and her mother. All three good, rapid workers, they respected one another. Now and then they paused in their washing and scrubbing, potato peeling and cooking, and exchanged looks at once happy and apprehensive—the latter especially after the first of their boarders had been brought home injured. Anna was not so afraid for Steve; Pat O'Keefe, who had come to their wedding, kept him more and more aboveground. Nor was she very worried about the cautious Mr. Czernik, who had never suffered a scratch in his five years as a miner. But, more than Ludmila, who was so blissfully in love she could not imagine that anything ill could ever happen to her young husband, Anna feared for the overconfident, boastful Paul.

One day late in spring, the two young women were gathering berries along the woods' edge beyond the railroad tracks, when Ludmila felt faint; whereupon Anna told her that she, too, was with child. Their babies, both boys, came in winter, ten days apart. Anna called hers Anthony, for her father in the old country; Ludmila's was named Joseph, for her father. They had a double christening in the just-completed Polish church of St. Stanislaw Kostka. Prior to that, the Poles had gone to the Irish church, where the parish priest had had a Polish assistant.

This was early in 1909. . . . "And for a year or so after this," Mrs. Anna Meleski told me thirty years later, "we were all content. Ludmila and I each had another child; girls, whom we named after ourselves, Annie and Ludmila. We had fun, kidding each other. . . . The children and boarders were lots of work, but we were all healthy and we were getting on. Steve and I had nearly five hundred dollars. We thought we needed two thousand before going on the soil. Good land in Western Pennsylvania or in Ohio was no longer cheap. . . . Steve took out his first citizenship paper soon after we were married. We learned a little English."

After becoming in-laws, Paul Meleski and Joe Czernik worked together in the mine. Paul called his father-in-law "partner" or "side-kick." One day a mass of rock crashed on them. It took a score of men, including Steve, hours to dig them out.

v

All three mines and both schools were closed, and Coalville followed to their graves "the best coupla Polacks that ever went down a mine shaft," as Pat O'Keefe, one of the pallbearers, finally characterized them.

From the Z. N. P., Ludmila and her mother received the sums for which their husbands had been insured, but a good part of that went to cover the funeral bills. Like most new-immigrant groups, the Poles believed—still believe—in elaborate, expensive burial customs.

Steve went about his work in a half trance. Pat O'Keefe had to yell at him, "Snap out of it, Steve!"

Anna sorrowed with the widows. She held them in her arms as they wept, took care of Ludmila's infants, and was tender with the two Czernik boys, now so pale and silent. The boarders helped her in the kitchen.

Steve could not meet her eyes. One day he suddenly said to her, "Annusia, I want to get out of here as soon as we can manage"; and she herself blazed up for a spell with a cold hate for Coalville and America.

Then, gradually, the routine of the household returned more or less to normal. Slavic fatalism ("*Co ma być to bedzie!* What is to be, will be!") helped the widows to accept their lot. The boarders began to talk at meals again, but occasionally, as one or the other tried to furnish the banter formerly supplied by the irrepressible Paul, they got unnaturally hilarious.

There were then in Coalville ten male Poles for every Polish girl or woman, and everybody knew that Ludmila, only nineteen and prettier than when Paul had wooed her, would not remain a widow long. Her two children would be no serious obstacle to her remarrying. Polish public opinion in Coalville also favored Mrs. Czernik's taking one of the older immigrants for her second husband.

And so it was. After the year's mourning required by their sense of what was proper and respectable, both daughter and mother wed again. Ludmila's new husband was Vincent Lesiak, an ex-miner who, being a bit more literate than the others, had opened a Polish insurance, real-estate, money-order, and steam-ship-ticket agency in Coalville; while her mother married Hieronim Mucha, a widower with a grown-up daughter, who ran a grocery store in town. Both Ludmila and her mother had turned down proposals from miners.

Meantime Steve and Anna had undergone a series of reverses. First Steve had pneumonia, which put him to bed for two months. When he got well, there was a three-week strike. Then Anna had to have her appendix removed, which cost a tidy sum. And finally, little Anthony had required the attention of an expensive Pittsburgh specialist to help him recover from an attack of scarlet fever.

Steve persisted in wanting to leave Coalville, where Paul's name was invisibly written on every piece of coal, every culm pile and every cinder path. But a farm now was out of the question. His peasant optimism, which used to buoy him a bit, now was suppressed under his other qualities—uncertainty, sadness, tendency to frustration. *Psiakrew!* He saw himself caught in Coalville, and developed a resigned attitude.

He loved Anna as much as ever, but could never tell her so again, even indirectly; he didn't know why. His little boy and girl he loved passionately, though no one could have proved this by his manner; but he wanted no more children. He looked twisted inside; his grinless face was almost ugly; his hair bristled wildly.

This made Anna uneasy. But two months after the appendectomy, which she called a vacation, she was younger-looking than she had been on her arrival in America, and her attitude toward her and Steve's problem was a positive one. They still had a chance in America.

Ludmila and Mrs. Czernik moved to their new homes, leaving the boarders to Anna. There were now forty of them. Anna hired two greenhorn girls and for more than a year worked frightfully hard. Off and on, her spirit and physical stamina came perilously close to caving in, but she kept them up, along with a cheerful front, with which she meant to shame Steve into a better attitude. Gradually she succeeded.

Toward the end of 1910, their savings amounted to seven hundred dollars.

One day Steve returned from work with a wide grin, looking handsomer than Anna had seen him look in two years. Pat O'Keefe, he said, was quitting his job to go as assistant superintendent of a mine in Galestown, West Virginia, not far from Pittsburgh, where the head superintendent was a friend of his; and O'Keefe wanted him, Steve, to come along and take a five-dollar-a-day job as a carpenter boss. The mine was new, opened a year before; the company was trying to make it "the safest coal mine in the world."

VI

Galestown was rather unlike Coalville. The population was largely white native American and Negro, with a good many Irish families and a mixture of Hungarians, Czechs, Slovaks, Slovenians. The Meleskis were the only Polish family there. Till two years before, it had been a sleepy little place, the center of an unprosperous mountain farm region; now people poured in. But to get a job a man had to come highly recommended for sobriety and cautiousness. Six mines were operating; the coal deposits were rich; the work, however, was dangerous because of the extremely gaseous condition in the mines, which had postponed the development and exploitation of the territory.

The Meleskis moved into a new three-room company house. On either side of them were a Slovenian and a Hungarian family, respectively, very nice people; but Steve and Anna decided to keep to themselves and save every cent possible. There was no chance of starting a boardinghouse; the company had a barracklike building with a cookhouse for the single men; and for a time Anna felt emptyhanded. She took to sewing and knitting. The children demanded more of her time. In 1912 she had another son, Stephen.

For three years Steve's work was largely aboveground, building breakers, trestles, tool sheds, blacksmith shops, garages, company houses. He was generally liked by the men under him, who were mostly immigrants. When he went underground, it was in a supervisory capacity. The safety work below was in charge of engineers, who called for Steve's gang when they got shorthanded.

It was steady work, and Steve was content.

Late in 1913, with the seven hundred dollars they had brought from Coalville, they were worth three thousand dollars—enough to go on the land. But where to buy their farm? They thought they would like to be near some Polish people and not too far from a town—Anthony was almost ready for school.

In Coalville both Steve and Anna had joined, and become insured with, the Z. N. P., and they received *Zgoda*, in which they read of occasional small groups of Polish immigrants who banded together for the purpose of going on the land. Most of these movements failed before they got started, for various reasons—insufficient funds, incompatibility, or some individual's dishonesty. A few, however, seemed to be successful; at least the people in them had escaped from the life in grimy industrial towns which had been against their peasant grain.

Early in 1914 Anna became interested in a Polish land-colonization scheme north of Tampa, in Florida. Twenty families had already signed up for it. A few had gone down to get the colony under way. Anna wrote for information and received a leaflet. The pictures of palms and Spanish moss, orchards and bungalows, were beautiful. The name of the prospective colony was Raj in Polish, or Paradise in English. The location was a lush bayou region of several thousand acres. The town of Parkersville, which had a school and a post office, was a few miles away. The sun shone three hundred and twenty days a year. It was warm in the summer but springlike all winter; ideal for families with small children. The land was cheap, but those joining in the enterprise should have, said the leader of the scheme, at least $2500 in cash.

Anna woke up nights, thinking of it. Paradise. Was it too good to be true? Something told her it might be all right. She and Steve discussed the proposition. All that sunshine *would* be good for the children. She was thirty; she hoped to have several more.

But the first four months of 1914 the work in the mines was especially heavy and urgent. Steve was putting in overtime, mostly underground in No's. 5 and 6, which were connected and occasionally referred to as the Twin Mines. Equipped with canary birds, miners were encountering alarming quantities of gas; engineers were anxiously extending the ventilators and sprinkling apparatus.

Toward the end of April, Steve and his gang were working in No. 6. Suddenly there was an explosion in No. 5, close by. Steve ordered his men to drop everything and get out. But it took several minutes before all were on the way. Meantime explosions in No. 5 and No. 6 followed in rapid succession.

Fire.

One explosion blew timbers through the No. 5 shaft mouth, scattering them over a radius of two hundred yards, wrecking a building. Men came out blazing, choking. Some of these died of burns soon after. The timbers inside the pits burned for days, and 181 miners were trapped and perished.

Steve lay in the overcrowded little hospital. The first week he was kept drugged. Then it seemed he had lost his mind. He raved, wept, gnashed his teeth. He cursed Pat O'Keefe, not knowing the man had died trying to get into No. 5 to help some of the men.

During those weeks, Anna's agony was almost greater than Steve's. Finally he was brought home. His body was wasted, but it was healing rapidly, leaving big scars.

His mind was fixed on returning to Pomerania. He told Anna to get the tickets. The doctor said the bandages would be off and he would be able to walk by mid-June; Steve wanted to sail immediately after.

Anna was partly sympathetic to Steve's idea. She had seen the carloads of coffins. The town was full of widows and fatherless children. Most of Anna, however, rebelled against returning to the old country. She felt that, in spite of everything they had experienced and seen, America, somehow, was all right; she and Steve and the children still had a chance.

But she could not fight Steve now. Feeling compelled to yield to him, she bought the tickets for a boat sailing on June twentieth, and as the date neared, she was more and more certain that the trip was a mistake.

On June tenth the last of Steve's bandages were off. He could walk.

Anna said, "Stefciu, let's think it over."

"No, no!" he yelled, a wild look in his eyes.

On the nineteenth they arrived in New York. Toward evening the agent took them, along with scores of other returning immigrants, to Hoboken, whence the ship was sailing at noon the next day; they were to be aboard by ten in the morning. From the ferryboat they saw the Statue of Liberty in the distance. Her light was on. Anna told Steve to look at the goddess, and he did, then scowled.

They spent the night in a cheap immigrant hotel. Anna did not sleep a wink.

In the morning she said very calmly, "*Sluchaj no!* Listen to me, Stefciu! You suffered so much, you are not yourself; you don't know what you are doing. You are desperate. Now I'll run this family for a while. Something tells me we will be sorry if we return to the old country. So we are not going. Our children were born here."

Steve stared at her, then yelled again. Remaining calm, Anna reminded him that she had the money and the tickets. The latter she would return to the office and cancel the passage. Steve yelled some more, then quieted down. He noticed that Anna looked a bit the way she had looked when she killed the wolf.

"But what are we going to do, Annuszka?" he asked helplessly.

"We are going to Florida—on the land—to Paradise."

VII

When the Meleskis reached Parkersville, Florida, the place sizzled in the hot sun. The children were uncomfortable, cross. On the train, Steve had swung between masculine resentment against his wife's dictation and his faith in her judgment; now, still weak, he slumped in a sweaty stupor.

Anna put up her family at the little hotel in town. Then she discovered that the Polish scheme for Paradise had exploded in a quarrel among the members of the group who had come down to get it under way, and the last of whom had left Florida, disappointed and disgusted, a month before. This was a blow.

"But here we were," she told me twenty-five years later, "and I had to do something."

She talked with Mr. Robinson, the local real-estate man who had dealt with the unfortunate Polish would-be settlers. He impressed Anna as a nice man, and said it was too bad the Poles could not get along and stick it out; here was an opportunity for some folk with a pioneering streak. No, he told Anna, it wasn't always so hot, and there was plenty of water the year round; these bayous were splendid. The ocean was six miles from the location.

Anna asked him to take her to the actual spot he was talking about, and Mr.

Robinson drove her, in a buggy, several miles outside the town. . . . Two and a half decades subsequently, when he was an old man, he told me that, although he had difficulty in understanding her broken English, his immediate impression of Anna Meleski was that "she had guts and meant business." . . . The trail ran through a jungly stretch of country with gray, sandy soil—in fact, it looked more like sand than soil. Yet things grew. It was a vast grove of low oak trees, beneath which spread a thicket of palmettos and other subtropical growth. Here and there were tufts of grass, and the ground was almost covered with acorns. There was an occasional pine tree.

They passed a roofless brick building; the walls were in semi-ruin. "An old sawmill," explained Mr. Robinson, "though God knows why they made it of brick. Before my time. There used to be lots of pine hereabouts."

He halted the buggy by the bayou to which they came—a cool, grassy clearing of several acres, a lovely spot. There were two shedlike buildings and a number of frames for tents in which the would-be settlers had lived and quarreled.

"The fight started," Mr. Robinson told Anna, "when one man, who apparently had the most money, wanted this entire clearing for himself. He gave up the idea, but then one thing led to another——"

Anna fell in love with the spot. Paradise indeed. But what could one do here in a practical way to make a living? Mr. Robinson said that, with all these acorns dropping throughout the year, the place was good for pigs. A man ten miles north of here, who had bought four hundred acres of land like this, now had hundreds of pigs, which gave him next to no work. He also had a few cattle, raised vegetables and chickens for his own use, and lately was beginning to clear a section for a citrus grove. Mr. Robinson said that she and her husband could have four hundred acres—a square piece of land with this clearing in its approximate center—for two thousand dollars cash.

They returned to town, got Steve, and drove back to Paradise. For the first time since the disaster, Steve's scarred face worked itself into a grin. They closed the deal the same day. Steve bought a horse and wagon. Next morning the Meleskis moved onto their land.

Under the challenge of this new situation, Steve's strength returned quickly. He and Anna worked harder, and longer hours, than ever before, but their toil carried with it more satisfaction than any previous effort of theirs. One shed left by the Polish group became their living quarters, another the kitchen, the third a chicken house. By mid-August they had their own vegetables. Steve bought some pigs and cattle and another horse; tools and farm implements. For a few of these he had to drive twenty-odd miles to Tarpon Springs, where a couple of thousand Greek immigrants were developing a thriving sponge industry, and where Steve learned that a world war had begun three weeks before because five weeks earlier somebody had pulled a trigger in Sarajevo. From the reports he read in the Tampa paper, he surmised that had they returned to the old country, he would surely be back in the Prussian Army, and that entire Pomerania was a scene of intensive military concentration.

Returning home that evening, Steve talked to himself in Polish, "How did she know something like this would happen in the old country? Or did she? She said something told her we ought not return. *Mój Boze!* Funny creatures, women! Now, what will happen over there? Germany . . . Russia . . . Poland—" He decided to get in touch with the Z. N. P. and resume getting the Polish paper.

When Steve got home and told Anna a war was on, she remarked, "*Widzisz!* You see! What did I tell you? . . . Mr. Robinson was here and said you can use the brick in that burned-down sawmill," which was not on their property. "He said he couldn't see who else might have any use for it. . . . What did you say? War all over Europe? *Mój Boze!*"

VIII

During the next two years Steve devoted two thirds of his time to getting the brick out of the sawmill ruin, carting it over to the clearing near the bayou, and building a large house—large because here was so much free brick and because Anna wanted a big home ("There is so much room in America") and, besides, she expected more children.

She had six more; nine all together. The first born in Florida was a boy; they named him Paul. Then came Frank, Michael, Mary, Felix and Josephine.

All through the war, Steve and Anna followed the events. A free Poland— Paderewski, Wilson, Pilsudski. They were glad when America got in.

When Anthony started to school that first fall, Steve got him a pony, which he rode daily to Parkersville and back. When Annie began school a year later, they put her on the pony in back of Anthony. Then, as the school-going part of the family increased, Steve built a cart for the pony which had room for five youngsters. In 1919 he bought a secondhand truck; two years later, his first car.

The pigs thrived on the acorns, and during the war Steve had no trouble selling them. He made money and, before the acquisition of the truck and car, needed very little of it. When the large brick house—which had some of the aspects of the better peasant dwellings in Pomerania—was completed in 1916, Steve had put into it only a couple of hundred dollars for cement and lime, what lumber he needed, doorknobs, hinges, windowpanes and roof tile. He had done the work himself; only Anna and little Anthony gave him an occasional hand.

The house finished, the work on the place was never very urgent or strenuous. Anna and the children could attend to it; and when, in the twenties, the Florida boom came along, Steve began to work as a carpenter in and around Tampa and Clearwater, making good money.

Four-fifths of the food they produced on the place. The property taxes were slight. Everybody was well; in their first ten years in Paradise the Meleskis turned over to Doc Ames in Parkersville $9.25. To attend her at childbirth,

Anna called a Negro midwife, who lived in a turpentine camp five miles away and who usually had her up and attending to her duties in three days.

When Anthony was fourteen, he branded "Raj—Paradise" on a piece of oak board and nailed the sign to a tree where the trail through the jungly wood turned toward the place. The sign is there to this day, the words on it dimly legible.

Anna loved the place more and more. Sometimes she did not get off it for an entire year. The few household necessities not obtainable on the farm Steve or the children bought in Parkersville. Every couple of years she made a trip to Tarpon Springs, every four or five to Tampa or St. Petersburg. From these trips she was always happy to return home.

But it was not till 1936 that she fully realized how fortunate she was. That year Ludmila Lesiak, with whom she had kept in touch, died in Coalville, and on a sudden impulse Anna went to Pennsylvania to place a bunch of flowers on the grave of her one-time sister-in-law, and see what had happened to people she had known. *Ach Boze!* What she saw simultaneously broke her heart and caused it to well with such gratitude for Paradise as she had not felt before. Over half of the town was on relief. She realized how tragically exceptional the Meleski family was.

By 1936 some of her and Steve's children were fairly on the way in life. In 1922, when Anthony had finished grade school, the Parkersville High School was built, and he attended it till 1926. Then, on the urging of a teacher, he went to the University in North Carolina. He graduated in 1931 and the next year got a position as a teacher of sociology in an Ohio college.

Annie went through high school, then to a nursing institute, and found a job in a Tampa hospital. She was a good-looking blond girl with a proud carriage. In 1933 she married a young doctor of long Southern ancestry.

Steve, Jr., liked the water and boats, and spent a lot of his time on the quay in Tarpon Springs. After he was twenty he occasionally hired out as deck hand on some Greek sponge-fishing boat. He was tall, strong, with a quiet manner and a grin like his father's. By the early thirties (as told in detail in the next chapter), sponge fishing was practically a monopoly of Greek immigrants who had begun to come over about a quarter of a century earlier, but young Steve was unable to see why an American of Polish extraction could not get into it in some capacity besides that of a deck hand. He talked things over with his brothers Paul and Frank, who had just finished high school, and with their father, who then built them a boat, and in 1935 the three boys became sponge fishermen. At first the Greeks looked at them with amusement; then with skepticism; by 1936 with respect.

IX

I happened to be in Tarpon Springs late in 1938, looking over the sponge industry, and met the Meleski brothers, who, fair, blue-eyed and blond, were rather conspicuous among the dark-haired, olive-complexioned Greeks. The crude boat which their father made for them, and from which they could only hook for sponges, had outlived its utility in 1937; now they owned a diving boat with a Diesel engine and the latest diving equipment. Now, too, there were four of them, for in 1938 brother Mike, next in age, had finished high school. They were a corporation, earning as much as ten thousand a year. All four struck me as keen, deeply agreeable young men. Talking with them, I became interested and asked them to take me to Paradise.

In the last twenty years, other pig farms have been started near the Meleski place. The animals are branded, and they feed on acorns freely over the entire area.

If one happened to stray by Paradise, one would not likely be impressed. One might look at the solid large brick house, because nearly all other farm dwellings in that part of Florida are wooden, small and rather ramshackle; then pass on. The grounds are somewhat untidy. There are dilapidated sheds, pieces of broken machinery, and rows of grapefruit, lemon and orange trees, which produce more than enough fruit for home consumption. Chickens, cats, dogs, goats and cattle wander about or lie in the shade of trees. The bayou is clear, cooling.

If one stops, however, and meets the Meleskis and takes a good look at the scene, the farm becomes an exciting place; the untidiness and haphazardness join house, bayou and surrounding jungle in producing beauty. Long, gray strands of Spanish moss festooning the boughs of the taller trees swing gently in sporadic breezes from the Gulf and help to give the atmosphere a unique charm, a lazy-active vividness.

I came on the Saturday after Christmas. I stayed all afternoon and evening, and returned the next day. They had no room to put me up, for all nine Meleski children were home for the holidays. The place grew on me as I learned the full story of the family.

In his early sixties Steve Meleski, Sr., is a hard, healthy, taciturn man. When asked how he likes America or Florida, he grins. The scars on his face are very prominent. His graying hair is wild as ever; he looks a bit comical. His English is halting, but he gets along with it when he must. With his wife and children he talks Polish almost exclusively. Is he an American or a Pole? Both; a man who came from Poland and became part of America. His neighbors, the nearest of whom is a quarter of a mile away, are all non-Poles, old-stock Americans, mostly from South Carolina and Georgia or native Floridans, white and black. He gets on with them. He was one of two farmers in that vicinity who considered the AAA *"cos zlego—something wrong"* and declined the government checks to decrease production of hogs. For years now Mr. Meleski has been driving the school bus between Paradise and Parkersville. When I was there on that first visit, he was in the midst of putting up a windmill-like contraption in back of the house, which was to produce electricity for home use. How many hogs had he? He grinned and shrugged his shoulders. "Too many; pork market down." But he wasn't worried. There were plenty of acorns for the pigs to feed on.

Mrs. Meleski is in her late fifties. She likes to talk. Her English is better than Steve's. The last twenty-five years, she says, have passed faster than had many a day in Coalville or Galestown while Steve worked underground. She is a deeply content woman. She can't explain what made her refuse to go to the old country in 1914. Otherwise her thoughts run swift and clear. People, she says, ought to live on the land; a majority of them anyhow. Living and working on the land makes folks sound. She is uncomfortably conscious that her family is superior in individual character and health to the average family in Coalville, whether Polish or of any other racial or national background.

She told me of her visit to Coalville—especially about the young people whom she remembered as children. The late Paul Meleski's first son, Joseph, had changed his name to Miller, practiced law in Pittsburgh, and was apparently ashamed of his Polish descent. His sister, Ludmila, was married to one of the sons of Mr. and Mrs. Zwierzchowski—both dead—who had been a miner, but was now on relief, suffering with miner's asthma. One of the Czernik boys, Felix, had died as an American soldier in France in 1918. His brother, John, married to a Slovak woman, was a miner who worked four or five days a month and thought it would be better to be on relief. And so on; every story was the same—sad, a little sordid. Few people in those small towns seemed to have very much to live for. Many American-born sons and daughters of immigrants "just chase around"—flivvers, movies, roadhouse dances, little else. Their parents used to believe in hard work; now there is no work for the young people.

Mrs. Meleski did not put it in these words, but she meant that to most young people in Coalville life was a chore rather than a challenge. A day was not a chance to do something, but a bit of time to kill. So many, she said, were satisfied to be helped by the government. They seemed "worn out, or something." This, she thought, was too bad. *Co zrobić?* What could be done for them? She used a Polish phrase, but spoke as an American concerned for America. What was it all leading to? Could the country afford to let character decline? . . .

Her first-born, Anthony Meleski, is thirty-three, now a full professor, author of two books, recently married to a girl from Texas who had been his student. He, too, is concerned for the future of the traditional America, with its spirit of individual and family independence and self-reliance. He is not dogmatic in his views, but feels that what his father and mother did probably is part of the answer to the question of what the American people ought to do. Get on the land—as many of them as possible—and become somewhere between twenty and eighty per cent independent of the immense whims of the industrial-economic system.

Annie and her doctor husband, with whom I also talked, had spent two months in Europe during the summer of 1938, most of the time in Poland. They had visited the village of Hojnice, and been deeply impressed by what they saw in the cities. Annie developed a strong interest in Polish literature and hoped her children, if she had any, would learn Polish and want to read Mickiewicz and Reymont in the original. In some connection, she said, "I am proud to be of the same people as Joseph Conrad and Madame Curie. . . ."

Mary, Felix and Josie are still in their teens, going to school. When he graduates, Felix will, in all probability, join Steve, Jr., Paul, Frank and Mike in sponge fishing.

Steve, Jr., is the captain of the boat and head of the corporation. Paul and Frank are divers; Mike tends to the diving equipment. Diving for sponges can be dangerous, resulting in bends, but the Meleski divers are careful and, so far, have been unaffected. Steve is in love with a Greek American girl born in Tarpon Springs.

When they go to sea for two or three weeks, Paul takes along a box of books, English and Polish. Annie, who until September, 1939, was on the mailing lists of Warsaw publishers, supplies him with the latter. He told me he had just finished *The Yearling*, the tale of a boyhood in the Florida Everglades. "The story of Jody," he said, "is a little like our own life was when we were kids."

x

I visited Paradise again early in March, 1940.

The new Poland had been conquered by Nazi Germany and Soviet Russia. I talked with Steve and Anna Meleski and two of their sponge-fishing sons. Their thoughts of Poland depressed them. Tears came into Mrs. Meleski's eyes as she tried to tell me how she felt about her old country. Then she said:

"I am more glad than I was ever before that we are here. God knows what is going to happen in Europe. *Moj Boze!* Maybe America is the hope of the world——"

Greeks Came
to Tarpon Springs

TARPON SPRINGS—twenty-seven miles above Tampa, in the sun-drenched bayou region surrounding the mouth of the Anclote River, whose banks are a lush subtropical jungle—is one of the early Florida towns. In the 1890's it had less than a thousand inhabitants, white and colored.

Most of the whites were Georgia "crackers," recent migrants to Florida, who, like the Negroes, led an uncertain, drab, casual existence. A few were Northern land speculators, mostly Philadelphians; and would-be fruit growers. Others were fishermen, farmers, trappers, and operators of turpentine stills, who rode in from the woods on Saturdays for a wild time. Dubious characters came and disappeared. Men carried guns, and Main Street had a frontier aspect—board sidewalks, saloons, hitching rails. One murder a year was the minimum.

A few wealthy Philadelphians, who dreamed of turning the town into a genteel resort, had winter homes a safe distance from its rough center.

In 1889 a tall, lean young Quaker, John K. Cheyney, came to Tarpon Springs from Philadelphia. Thirty-one, weary of the bank job on which he had spent a dozen sedentary years, and not sharing his father's interest in Florida land schemes, he lived much of his time in a boat cruising in the Gulf, occasionally going down as far as Key West. A pioneer by inclination, he wanted to get into "something new."

Below Ponce de Leon Bay and down by East Cape, young Cheyney ran into sponge fishermen. They "crawled" in crude small boats usually but a few miles from the coast, pulling sponges from the bottom of the sea with three-pronged steel hooks fastened to the end of poles twenty to forty feet long.

These sponge fishermen were "hookers." Their home port was Key West, the first and then still the only sponge center in the United States. Most of them were Cubans, Bahamans, mixed breeds—"Conchs," so named because they reputedly subsisted for the most part on conchs abounding in the Florida waters which they pulled up with the sponges. They were a clannish, sullen, suspicious lot. They put in at Key West to sell their sponges to packers and agents of Northern firms, then to blow their bankrolls and go out again for another load.

The sponge business as carried on by the Conchs caught John Cheyney's interest. What sponges really were—plant or animal—he did not know; they seemed to be both. When brought up they were slimy, smelly black balls of various sizes, very unlike the neat useful article one saw in store windows or bathrooms. But the business was obviously a man's game, and there was money in it. In a month or two the Conchs hooked a load in the most leisurely fashion and sold it for a couple of thousand dollars. Demand was greater than supply.

The young Philadelphian approached the Conchs with the tentative offer of a loan to expand the business and the suggestion to adopt Tarpon Springs as their port. Sponges, he told them, were doubtless to be had further north in the Gulf and Tarpon Springs was some three hundred miles nearer the Northern population centers which used most of the sponges. But, polite and quiet-mannered, he got nowhere with the gruff, contemptuous Conchs. Who was he, anyhow, to tell them where to hook sponges and which port to use? Hadn't they been operating from Key West since the fifties, and, before that, from Nassau?

In 1890 John Cheyney decided to try sponge fishing from Tarpon Springs on his own. When the strong winds ceased that autumn, he got himself a boat, hooks, organized a crew and went out. But the Gulf here was deeper than at Key West and it required longer poles and more effort to get up the sponges. Unfamiliar with the fine tricks of the trade, he hooked but few of them and made next to nothing on the venture. However, he could not rid himself of the idea that sponge fishing in Tarpon Springs had possibilities and continued to experiment on a small scale.

After a few years he decided to take a big chance. He went to Philadelphia, borrowed thirty thousand dollars and returning to Tarpon Springs bought and outfitted several boats. His crews consisted of men he picked up on Main Street and on the fishing wharf. None knew much more about hooking than he did; but, as luck would have it, be began to make a little money and his employees earned a good living.

He opened the first sponge-packing house in Tarpon Springs and took trips North to find a market for his goods and induce some of the buyers to come down once or twice a year. Whereupon the Conchs declared war on Cheyney. They burned his boats and thrashed his men. There were other difficulties— bad weather, the problem of keeping steady crews, the inability of the new men to find sponge beds quickly—and he lost everything.

Still the thing looked promising to John Cheyney. He charged his losses to experience, calmed his creditors and made a fresh beginning, learning as he went along. Thus till late in the nineties, when fear of the Spanish fleet during the Spanish-American War drove the Conchs to operate considerably north of the Keys and to use a cove near Tarpon Springs as their port.

In spite of his past encounters with them, the young Quaker welcomed the Conchs; they caused the Northern buyers and jobbers to come to Tarpon Springs. Some of the Key West packers moved up to do business, but Cheyney did not object to competition; he was that sort of man.

This went on for about a year—a period punctuated by bloody brawls between the Conchs and the other elements of the population. Tarpon Springs was a rougher town than ever.

The Spanish-American War over, John Cheyney tried to induce the Conchs to stay, but, tradition-bound and sullen as ever, they returned to Key West. He and some other American packers owning hooker boats at Tarpon Springs remained in the sponge business, and a few of the buyers continued to come down once or twice yearly, while others occasionally ordered by mail. But Cheyney was far from satisfied. The American crews were not nearly so good at hooking as the experienced Conchs, who could tell a sponge bed from the sheen on the water's surface or the smell of the air above it. It was only the man's strange attachment to the "game," as he called it, that kept Tarpon Springs now, at the turn of the century, from expiring as a sponge town.

In 1903 Cheyney went to New York to see his few customers, one of whom frankly told him that his packing was crude and suggested that if he meant to get anywhere in this business he would have to bleach his sponges as the Mediterranean packers bleached theirs; then he might find a ready market.

How did one bleach them? Where might he find a man who knew the process? The jobber told John Cheyney of a young Greek, John Cocoris, employed in a sponge warehouse on Canal Street. Cheyney looked him up. The ex-Philadelphia bank clerk and the Greek immigrant had a talk . . . and Tarpon Springs was off to a new start as a sponge center.

II

John Cocoris was a slight, unassuming young man of twenty-six. He had come to America in 1895 from the small seaport town of Leonidion on Peloponnesus —the great "Island of Pelops," south of the Isthmus of Corinth—where his people had engaged in the various phases of the sponge trade for centuries. The year before his meeting with John Cheyney he had gone for a visit to the old country and returned to New York with a bride. He had three young brothers in America—Gus, George, and Louis, all recently arrived greenhorns—who also were working for sponge concerns in New York, which were mostly in Greek, Jewish, German, Armenian and Syrian hands.

John Cocoris accepted John Cheyney's offer of a job to take charge of bleaching sponges, and he and his wife went to Tarpon Springs. Presently he sent for his brothers George and Gus.

The Corcoris boys told their new employer that hooking was not the best way to get sponges; back in the old country Greeks dived for them. A diver could go deeper than a hook, and the deeper he went the better sponges he brought up. Also, hooking was apt to tear them, while the diver usually got them up intact.

Now in his mid-forties, John Cheyney spent long hours with John Cocoris, whose English was uncertain, but who was full of the lore of the sponge. The young Greek told how the inhabitants of numerous islands in the Gulf of Aegina and along the southwestern coast of Asia Minor, as well as of some of the port towns on the mainland, had been diving naked for sponges from twenty to forty fathoms deep since before the time of Homer, who mentioned them in the Odyssey.

This "skin diving," said John Cocoris, was a dangerous way to make a living. Divers often came up minus an arm or a leg. Sharks. Off and on only the torso bobbed up. And almost worse than sharks was the terrific pressure of water upon the human organism at great depths. Some divers could hold their breath for as long as three and a half minutes, keeping their eyes wide open the while looking for sponges in the curious deep dimness, with a pressure of twenty or thirty pounds against their eyeballs.

The men dived with a large stone, which they held by the twine around it, and which pulled them to the sea's bottom with the speed of an arrow. They had the few minutes to pry the sponges loose; whereupon, releasing the stone, they came up with such force that they were sometimes flung five or six feet in the air. Bleeding from thousands of pores and from the nose and ears, the divers then plopped back into the sea, to be pulled, stunned or unconscious, into the boat and be relieved of the sponges clutched in their rigid, cramped hands. Skin divers aged early and usually suffered severe heart attacks before they were thirty.

Since about 1870, however, John Cocoris told John Cheyney, the more progressive Greek spongemen had taken to "scientific diving" in watertight rubber suits with steel-and-glass helmets and hose attached to air pumps worked by hand by men in the boat. This method was very successful. It enabled the diver to go much deeper than the skin diver and to stay down, not for a few minutes, but for three, four, five hours, depending on the depth. He could walk for miles on the bottom of the sea, gather the sponges as he found them, fill sack after sack, and send them up by a long, loose rope attached to him and the boat.

The Greek diving boats were specially made for this purpose. They included among their equipment glass-bottomed buckets, through which, when lowered beneath the surface movement of the sea, the divers were able to spot sponge beds far below.

As a boy John Cocoris had dived off the island of Hydra (an important place in the Grecian sponge industry) while working for his uncle, Panagos Vlahopulos, who owned five diving boats. So now—in 1904—he acquired an ordinary tarpon-fishing craft, named her "Elpis" (meaning "Hope"—the first Greek-owned boat in Tarpon Springs), rigged her up with secondhand diving equipment procured from the old country, and, taking the craft out, demonstrated to John Cheyney that diving was as sound an idea in the Gulf as in the Mediterranean.

"But I am no diver," John Cocoris told John Cheyney; "I haven't the heart for diving. Few men have it. And this boat is not the best possible trick for sponge diving. What we ought to do is bring over some real experienced Greek divers and some Greek diving boats."

Early in 1905, with a sum of Cheyney's money in his pocket, Cocoris went to New York to meet one Spiros Vouteris, a veteran sponge trader from the island of Aegina (another important Greek sponge center) who had just come

over on his annual business visit. He knew every man engaged in the trade
in the Gulf of Aegina and up and down the Aegean and western Mediterranean.
Cocoris commissioned Vouteris to send over a first-rate Greek sponge-fishing
outfit: boat, diving equipment, and a crew including two of the best divers he
knew.

The outfit reached Tarpon Springs early that summer. The divers were
Demosthenes Kavasilas and Stellios Bessis. Eleftherios Moutsatsas was their
life-line tender. The other two members of the crew were Pavlos Moutsatsas,
captain, and Milton Stathes, cook and deck hand. All came from the island of
Aegina.

In a few weeks they brought in six thousand dollars' worth of sponges.

The group interested in converting Tarpon Springs into a high-toned resort
rose in protest. They wanted no industry which would bring in a lot of "these
foreigners." But their protestations were in vain. John Cheyney and the other
Americans in the business, aided by John Cocoris, were determined to bring
in more Greeks and develop Tarpon Springs into a great sponge center.

It was not difficult to lure in more Greeks.

The crew of the first Greek diving boat wrote to everyone they knew back
on Aegina to come over posthaste—the bottom of these American waters was
thick with sponges and one did not have to dive half as deep for them as in the
Mediterranean. Within a month the news spread all over the Aegean and
reached the Greek islands off the southwestern coast of Asia Minor which were
then under Turkish rule.

Simultaneously, John Cocoris went to New York and talked with a number of
Greek leaders. The Greek-language newspaper *Thermopylae* printed a report
that the Gulf within a few score miles off middle Florida was a gold mine for
Greeks who knew something of sponge fishing. This was promptly copied by
other Greek papers in the United States and by the press in Greece—with the
result that all over America when Greek met Greek the talk was not, as
formerly, of opening a restaurant or flower shop where they happened to be,
but of going to Tarpon Springs.

III

By the end of 1905 over five hundred excited Hellenes had reached Tarpon
Springs. The ensuing year about a thousand more came. They were all single
or men whose wives stayed behind in the old country or wherever they had
lived theretofore in the United States. Mrs. John Cocoris was the only Greek
woman in town.

Greeks came from Boston, New York, Philadelphia, Chicago, Cleveland,
Atlanta. Some had been sponge fishermen in the old country; others were the
average run of Greek immigrants, bent on opening restaurants, coffee houses,
and grocery stores in the new Greek colony. There were too many of this
last category and after a while some returned whence they had come. At the
same time others continued to pour in. One Diamond Dick, a famous New

York Greek gambler of that day, came along with a few other such nonessential fellows usually found in any rush.

Among the newly arrived immigrants were many of the world's foremost spongemen. Some were the subjects of the King of Greece, others of the Sultan of Turkey, but all Greeks; some gnarled, squat, fleshy men edging toward middle age, with dark south-European visages, the sea graved deeply in their features; others almost excessively handsome youths, the proverbial Greek gods, with classic, olive-complexioned faces and strong, supple bodies. They were the divers and boatmen from the islands of Hydra, Halky, Aegina, Symi, Calymnos; bleachers, cutters, general sponge workers. And there came also cunning men whose background in the old country and in London and New York was the business end of the sponge industry, and who were bent on becoming brokers, packers, jobbers' agents, or—Ulysses-like—taking advantage of any other opportunity that might spring out of this dynamic situation.

Tarpon Springs was a changed town. Many of the new arrivals, unable to find quarters at first, slept outdoors. But they seemed to "belong" from the very beginning. Unconsciously, by virtue of their number and the suddenness of the influx, they all but took possession of the town. As though uncognizant of the older settlers, they gathered in groups on Main Street and along the fish quay, and talked loudly and excitedly in their rhythmic Greek. Most of them knew no English, except "Mister Cheyney," whom they credited with their good fortune of being in America. Evenings, the newly opened Greek coffee houses were geysers of incomprehensible noise. There were explosive shouts, which suggested that someone was about to commit mayhem. But this was just the Greeks' way of conversing, possibly only about the next day's weather.

At the outset of this abrupt development, not comprehending the tongue and gestures of the new arrivals, and feeling slightly out of place in their own town for the moment, the old residents were a little afraid of them, also a little awed by, and resentful of, their patent self-confidence and optimism. They did not know that Greeks facing the sea, or a task on the sea, always felt and acted this way. The Greece of Homer is far off, having scant bearing on modern Greece; yet there is a touch of it in the present-day Hellene. He is a remote inheritor of the cunning of Ulysses, the fearlessness of Achilles, and the inspiration and idealism of Plato, and in time of exaltation or crisis these qualities are likely to reveal themselves in him—though often very confusedly.

Two or three months following the first big spurt of the Greek influx the town commenced to turn into a busy, respectable, law-abiding workaday community. Everyone had a job, including the migrants from Georgia and the Carolinas, and the colored folk. The wild, rough element was somehow subdued by the presence and industry of the newcomers. The annual murders ceased.

The Greeks were all fanatically absorbed in boats, the sea, diving suits, air hose, air pumps, glass-bottomed buckets, sponges, the sponge market. This absorption had a well-nigh spiritual quality, a passion not solely material, something like the spirit of the American westward-going pioneers two or three decades before. It simultaneously vitalized, excited, and quieted all.

For forty years, in common with many other Florida communities, Tarpon Springs had been on the verge of something or other—an uneasy position to occupy for such a long time. Now the destiny of the place had been sealed and delivered. For the Greek divers were amazingly successful and most people connected with sponges were making money. Not a few Greeks had brought with them boats, diving equipment, and considerable sums of money, depositing five, ten thousand dollars in the little local bank (totaling perhaps $300,000); which had a general stimulating effect. The town began to take an almost single-minded interest in the new industry. By-and-by the general aspects of the place were affected. The wooden sidewalks on Main Street were removed, the thoroughfare was paved, and other improvements followed.

But now difficulties arose. Cheyney and the Greeks discovered that a Florida state law, which had been on the statute books for twenty years, forbade them to dive for sponges within ten miles of the coast of Florida. They learned the interesting history of this law. In the mid-eighties an English sponge house in London had organized an expedition of Greek divers to the waters along the coast of British Honduras to see if the sponge industry might not be developed in the Mexique Bay. Nothing came of this. However, a Syrian sponge trader named Arapian, a citizen of Florida and in close business relations with the Conchs, learned of the expedition and told them about it. The Conchs then engaged him as their lobbyist and in '87 he induced the legislature at Tallahassee to pass the law forbidding sponge fishing by diving within what they chose to define as the Florida state limit in the Gulf.

This law, which is still in effect although probably unconstitutional, caused no end of confusion and unpleasant incidents. Tarpon Springs boats were seized by sheriffs, crews were arrested and jailed. Tarpon Springs diving boats were surrounded by Key West hooker boats, splashed with gasoline, and set afire. For years a veritable war raged, with casualties on both sides. The Conchs removed buoys, causing Greek boats to go aground on sand bars or be wrecked on coral reefs. . . . Hostilities continue sporadically to this day. In 1935 a Greek diving boat with a full crew disappeared mysteriously, although the weather at the time was calm. Two years later a diver came upon its hull at the bottom of the sea. . . .

At the same time, in 1906 and '07, the government in Washington, stimulated by the Conchs' lobbyist Arapian, began to inquire whether the new Greek immigrants settling in Tarpon Springs were contract labor or not. John Cheyney, as the instigator of this migration, had to use all the influence he could summon to keep some of the best divers, boat captains, and life-line tenders from being deported to Greece, and himself from being fined and put in prison. Finally, an official opinion came through that the Greek spongemen were not contract labor as defined by the immigration law. They did not take away the employment of anyone who had been in America before them; and, in fact, did not earn their living in this country at all, but in the international waters of the Gulf.

Soon the sponge industry was raised from a gross of less than $100,000 to a million a year, most of which money stayed in Tarpon Springs.

IV

Late in 1906, Mrs. John Cocoris gave birth to a girl, Margaret—the first Greek American baby born in Tarpon Springs. The christening of this infant was the excuse for a communal celebration, a picnic, during which the old-stock Americans for the first time came in close social contact with Greeks, who were the hosts. Most of the Greeks as yet knew little or no English, but they invited everybody and nearly everybody came and had a good time.

There was dancing, singing. The food was prepared as in Greece. Wine, cheese and delicacies had been specially imported from the islands of Aegina, Halky and Symi. Nothing was too good for the occasion; money was no object. People who attended the feast, now middle aged or elderly, still like to talk about it.

The celebration marked the beginning of the second chapter of the Greek story in Tarpon Springs. During the next few years scores of men, deciding they were here to stay, sent for their wives, or returned briefly to their native islands to get brides.

Today Tarpon Springs has over one hundred Greek families. Most of them are large; for, as one of them put it to me, "Greeks are good producers." The majority of the children now are between their mid-teens and mid-twenties, some already married, in most cases to Greek Americans, and there is already the beginning of the third generation of Greeks. The total Hellenic population of Tarpon Springs is about twenty-five hundred, or well over half.

The Greeks belong to the Eastern Orthodox faith, and most of them—particularly those who go to sea—are deeply religious. Their old-country national background and their religion closely intertwine. In the early days a Greek priest would come from Savannah to christen the new boats, bury the dead, or officiate at important holiday services in a temporary church. He made a special trip to christen little Margaret Cocoris. In 1908, when it became clear that they, as a group, would make Tarpon Springs their permanent home, the Greeks built a church, dedicating it to St. Nicholas, the patron saint of ships and seamen.

When I was there late in '38, the priest was the Rev. Theophilos Karaphillis, a bearded, dignified man, father of a numerous family. He blesses each Greek sponge boat every time it leaves for the sea. For this he receives five dollars a boat. He and a lay teacher, Professor George Anastassiou, conduct the Greek School in the town's school building, teaching the Greek language and literature, the history of Greece, the dogma of the Greek Orthodox faith, and Greek dramatics and singing.

Every child born into a Greek home in Tarpon Springs, as he attains school age, is required to attend the Greek School in addition to the "American" or "English" public school. After the other children leave school at three in the afternoon, the boys and girls of Greek parentage are taught for two more hours daily by the Rev. Karaphillis and Professor Anastassiou.

Behind this are several factors and motives. One is the intense Greek national egoism. Another is that the Greek immigrants—like every other kind of immigrants—want their children to grow up into good adults. They, themselves, were brought up in a certain ethical-religious system in the old country; now in a new world, full of strange influences, they maintain their ethical-religious institutions to inculcate in the young what they consider the right or stabilizing values and standards. Another motive is the desire of the immigrant parents to hold onto their children who might break away from the home and the Greek community sooner if they knew no Greek and were unfamiliar with the history and language of Greece.

The intellectuals among the Greek Americans hold that Greek and American cultures are not incompatible. The American ideal, they say, is a human one, as is that of the Hellenic tradition. They trace elements of American idealism to ancient Greece. Now as Greek Americans or Greeks in America, they benefit from the actuality of American institutions; on the other hand, their Greek cultural background still contains elements which the American atmosphere cannot give their American-born children. So they also approve the tendency of well-to-do Greek American parents, in Tarpon Springs and elsewhere, to send their boys and girls to Athens for part of their formal education. . . .

Behind the Greek School in Tarpon Springs is the money and prestige of a local organization called the Greek Community, whose membership includes virtually the entire adult Greek population of Tarpon Springs.

The Greek Community of Tarpon Springs also has a powerful disciplinary function. It stands for the idea that one Greek's improper deed will reflect on all Greeks and, therefore, one should refrain from such behavior. As a result of this, the Hellenes of Tarpon Springs are partisan to law and order. It is a rare Greek who comes up in court there as the accused.

The members of the Community are assessed according to their income. The organization has a fund to help those in difficult straits. No Greek is a drag on the city of Tarpon Springs. Few are, or have been, on government relief; which is true of the people of Tarpon Springs generally, for the town rests upon a solid economic basis. The Depression affected the sponge industry very slightly. For nearly thirty years now it has been giving the little city an income of about three thousand dollars daily.

A local "gag" goes as follows: The spongers sponge on sponges, the rest of the town sponges on the spongers. The system is a success.

In the winter months, the sponge industry attracts a stream of sightseers and tourists who leave no little money in the overnumerous curio shops. Tens of thousands of people pour into the tiny city every January 6th, when the Greeks celebrate the Epiphany, one of the most ancient ceremonies. The early Egyptians, enacting it on the Nile, called it Blessing the Waters. Later, at Alexandria, it was observed in honor of the birth of Osiris. To the religious folk of modern Greece, it is the anniversary of the Baptism in the river Jordan. With the sea-faring Greek islanders it is a mingling of the Blessing of the Waters and the Baptism traditions. They brought it as such to America. Tarpon Springs immigrants were the first to start observing it regularly thirty-four years ago.

Gradually, as the city commenced to link it to sponge fishing, the Epiphany increased in local significance. The two Protestant ministers began to participate in it, and encouraged by the town as a whole, the Greek Community started to improve the details of the program. Now it is an elaborate ceremony compounded of religion, culture, patriotism, civic-mindedness, commercialism and showmanship. His Grace the Greek-Orthodox Archbishop of North America usually attends. Such ecclesiastic dignitaries as Archbishop Germanos of the Patriarchate of Antioch and Damaskinos of Corinth have come over to preside at the ceremonies.

By January 4th, all of the approximately one hundred and fifty sponge boats—many of them painted in the favorite colors of the owners' native islands —return home for the festivities and to be blessed by the Archbishop.

At dawn on the 6th, religious services begin in St. Nicholas'. The church is jammed inside, with thousands outside. The Liturgy, with its curious strong cadences, is chanted and sung. The Archbishop and priests are robed in colorful and elaborate vestments. At noon they move, followed by the populace (Greek and old-stock American) in procession, to the Bayou, a lakelike body of water with concrete walls and grandstands about it, suggesting a Greek outdoor theater.

The Archbishop reads the gospel story of the Baptism in Greek; one of the Protestant ministers reads it in English. A dove is released; whereupon the Archbishop tosses a gold cross into the water. The next moment scores of young men in bathing suits—in recent years most of them American-born sons of Greek immigrants—leap from the assembled sponge boats and swim swiftly to where the cross disappeared. There follows a tense minute while the youths churn the water, till one of them recovers the cross and, amid cheers, brings it to the Archbishop, who then blesses him and the sponge fleet and its crews.

This annual event, attended by increasing numbers of Florida's winter tourists, impresses even people who are not inclined to formal religion. The fact is that five hundred men who do the actual work of sponge fishing, who stay at sea three-fourths of the year, believe it is as necessary for them to come in for the Epiphany as for gasoline every two or three weeks. They believe that, should they miss the ceremony, something harmful or unpleasant will befall them.

V

The economic heart of Tarpon Springs is the Sponge Exchange—two quadrangles of low buildings connected by a passageway, each around a spacious courtyard. Very simple architecturally, the whole setup has a Mediterranean air. Here the sponges are stored by the boat crews and owners till they are ready to put them on the market, which is held every Tuesday and Friday in the courtyards.

Behind the 'change are the numerous packing houses, large wooden or brick sheds, interspersed with modest frame dwellings of the sponge-fishing folk.

Directly in front of the 'change is the quay, where the boats are moored and sponges unloaded. Boats come and go daily—with certain exceptions. None leave on Tuesdays, for Tuesday is an unlucky day; centuries ago the Turks defeated the Greeks on a Tuesday. And no boat leaves while a dead resident of Tarpon Springs remains unburied.

The spongemen have other superstitions. One is that certain persons harbor the Evil Spirit; and if such an individual appears at the quay when the boat is ready to sail, the departure is postponed. How they spot such a person, I could not learn. I was told it would be improper and futile to urge or order him or her (it usually is a woman) to go away. One cannot and should not meddle with the supernatural; the Evil One would return to the quay lurking in another individual.

Still another superstition takes this form: When there is a severe storm in the Gulf, the wives of the crew members on boats that are out go to church and sweep it, then throw the dust into the turbulent water. This is said to still the tempest.

For people from the island of Aegina March 23rd is a poor day on which to start out; nobody knows why. Others postpone all important work for the day if the first person they meet in the morning is a priest.

But all this, while deeply ingrained in them, especially in the older men, is also, paradoxically, little more than a superficial frill of their character as seamen and spongemen. Once they cast off from the wharf, they are realistic, efficient, matter-of-fact.

The key men in the actual business of sponge fishing, of course, are the divers. They are nearly all immigrant Greeks; the youngsters born in America eschew diving, which, while fairly remunerative, is dangerous work. Ninety per cent of soft-suit divers become afflicted, sooner or later, with the bends, a curious partial paralysis of the legs, for which there is as yet no real cure, although helium treatments have in some cases proved beneficial.

The number of divers on a boat is governed by the depth at which they work. Seldom going deeper than a hundred and twenty-five feet, deep-water men work alternately, remaining under water from twenty to seventy-five minutes at a spell. Those working at from fifty to seventy-five feet can stay down as long as six hours.

The diving equipment consists of two suits, two collars, and one helmet, the latter being interchangeable. The relieving diver is fully dressed, except for the helmet, which is removed from the upcoming man and immediately screwed on the collar of the one about to jump in. The length of the air hose and the life line are about two hundred feet. The air pump is operated by a rotary engine.

The rest of the crew consists of the captain, engineer, life-line tender (a most important man), cook and one or two deck men, according to the size of the boat. They work on a share basis.

On some of the boats cooks and deck hands are Negroes, several of whom speak fluent Greek in the dialects of the various Mediterranean islands.

Most boats stay out three weeks, then have to come in for refueling. The period while the boat is out is called a *gaza*, the root of the expression being the American word "gas."

The food aboard is simple, much the same as that of sponge fishermen in the Mediterranean: a cheese called *feta*, imported from Greece; salami, meat stews cooked ashore and preserved under a thick layer of lard, hardtack, coffee, and much sea food, which the deck hands catch or the divers bring up. Sea urchins are a favorite delicacy.

When the diver jumps overboard, he has (if he is sensible and careful) nothing in his stomach except possibly a half cup of black coffee and a few crumbs of hardtack. With the diving gear he weighs in the vicinity of four hundred pounds and can reach bottom as fast or as slowly as he likes, by pressing or not the air valve in the helmet with the side of his head. He is entirely encased, except his hands. Strapped to one hand is a short three-pronged sponge hook, to the other a sack made of fish-netting.

On a bright sunny day the ocean floor is indescribably beautiful—like a vast rock garden of softly blending colors. I went down but stayed very briefly. The beauty, the awful solitude, the huge fish about me, and the smaller fish nibbling at my naked hand were terrifying. On getting up again, I was glad to learn that everybody is scared the first time. It takes a year or so to begin to feel fairly at home below-water. . . .

As he walks about, the diver's movements are reported to the men in the boat by the bubbles created by the air he releases from his helmet. Other information he sends up by a code of signals to the life-line tender, who sits on the prow, holding the line, waiting for the messages from below. Two tugs mean that he wants an empty sack, which is then promptly tied to the line, which the diver, in turn, pulls down. The sack he has just filled comes up in reverse manner.

Three tugs signify "Danger!"—which usually consists of some mammoth fish that might swallow the diver in a single gulp, should he come in line with its mouth. In such a case, the diver squats or stands on the bottom of the sea, under the fish's belly. Some of these monsters are half a block long. One was cast ashore in 1937; a six-foot man measured only halfway up its thickness in the middle.

A single tug says "I'm coming up in a few minutes"—suggesting they get the next diver ready. He rises to the surface by simply keeping in all the air pumped into his suit.

As the bags are hauled up, the sponges are dumped on deck. The pulp or animal matter is squeezed out by treading on the ugly, stenchy balls with the feet. What is left is then strung on twine and hung between the masts in the sun and at night thrown overboard so the action of the water may complete the disintegration of the pulp. The next morning the batch is taken in again, the skin scraped off with a knife, and the sponges—which are the skeletons of the creatures—are once more hung up to dry. Finally they are thrown into a little hold, which, when full, contains from two to five thousand dollars' worth of sponges depending on their quality.

The divers get the largest share of the sale price. The good ones make about three thousand dollars a year. But none like the work, or at least think they don't. Many try to leave it; few succeed. They return and dive till the bends get them, or they suddenly drop of heart failure.

The pressure at a hundred feet depth is forty pounds per square inch. It presses the air that is pumped down to the diver into his blood. If the ascent is too swift, the release of pressure is too sudden; something happens with the air bubbles in certain veins in the brain, and the result may be paralysis or death.

I became acquainted with one of the divers on the boat on which I went out. A native of the island of Halky, he "Americanized" his name from Stathis Jounou to Steve John. He started diving in the Aegean Sea at fourteen; at forty-three he had been diving a total of seventeen years. Two years he spent—with about a hundred other Greek Immigrants of Tarpon Springs—in the United States Army during the First World War. He was wounded twice; once nine machine-gun bullets ripped into him, and he now has a silver plate in his hip. As a diver, he always comes up slowly and does not eat anything before going down or too soon after coming up, and has, so far, escaped the bends. But he has no feeling in the skin of his legs—a mild form of paralysis, which does not interfere with his walking.

He told me he made about four thousand a year, but was obliged to support two families—his own and his brother's. His brother had also been a diver. One day he came up too quickly; they took the diving suit off him; he felt dizzy and stumbled below to his bunk. When the deck hand called him for his turn to go down again, he was dead.

Steve John has tried twice to get out of diving. Once he got work in a Detroit auto plant. Unable to make enough money as an auto worker to support two families, he returned to Tarpon Springs.

When they get the bends, some divers return to Greece. Others remain in

Tarpon Springs. They walk about with curious staggering steps or sit on the benches in front of the bandstand. The majority have the look of punch-drunk prize fighters. Some have a little money; others live on allowances from the Greek Community. One or two receive direct relief. There are always several at the United States Coast Guard Hospital in Savannah, being treated with helium.

Eventually a shortage of divers is apt to produce a crisis in the sponge industry, unless there is a return to hooking. American-born boys do not go in for diving. The immigration quota from Greece is only three hundred and through that tiny loophole only one or two divers may slip in a year. Divers usually come in as visitors on six-month visas, which are often extended to a year; then they return to Greece.

The top men in the sponge industry are not yet seriously worried about this possible shortage of divers. American-like, they are not crossing bridges before they get to them. Some think that eventually non-Greek Americans, like the Meleskis, will go in for diving.

VI

Next to the divers, the business men of the industry interested me most. They are now all Greeks. There is not an old-stock American in sight anywhere in the game. John Cheyney turned a real-estate dealer soon after the First World War. He had seen the entire development with an objective eye. I asked him to state and explain the reason for the withdrawal or expulsion of the old-time Americans from the industry in favor of the Greeks.

"The reason is," he said, "the Greeks' unquestionable superior ability when it comes to sponges. Sponges are their work. They have been at it for two thousand years. We old-time Americans, as you call us, were novices. We had no business in it, not really, though some of us made money at it at first. Also, the Greeks were willing and able to work harder than some of us. So now the sponge business is theirs. Well and good. I am glad. They won it fairly, according to the rules of the business world. They belong in it, it belongs to them. . . . They are a great people, these Greeks. I am happy I had a hand in bringing them here. Fine citizens. . . . Johnny Cocoris comes to see me once in a while. . . ."

John Cheyney died in his eighties a few weeks after he talked to me. The Greek Community took a leading part in giving him a fitting send-off. Nearly everybody was at the funeral. Many of the Greeks wept at the grave. But for him most of them might not be in the United States. . . .

Twenty-five packers own the Sponge Exchange on a nonprofit basis. Twice weekly the sponges are dragged into the courtyards and offered for sale. The packers bid for the piles silently, by writing the amounts they want to pay on slips of paper bearing their names and hand them to the manager of the 'change. The highest bidder gets the sponges, provided the original owners are willing to sell them at that price. The procedure is eminently fair and aboveboard. One morning I witnessed about thirty thousand dollars' worth of sponges exchange hands. Everybody was satisfied.

The price of sponges is fairly steady from week to week. There is no surplus. A week or two after it reaches the quay, the sponge as likely as not is on its way to be sold to the person in whose possession it will end its career— perhaps to a house painter in Easton, Pennsylvania, or to a New York housewife for her bathroom, or to a British cavalryman in India for currying his horse. . . .

There are several outstanding men among the packers. One is George Immanuel, who came to Tarpon Springs as a youth with his father, who had been in the sponge trade in London. George worked for John Cheyney at first, then started out on his own. His home now is one of the most impressive in town. When I met him, his two children were in college. He is a Rotarian and a former councilman of Tarpon Springs.

Gus Cocoris, now in his fifties, is agent for a New York sponge house.

The 1938-39 president of the Sponge Exchange was N. G. ("Nick the Millionaire") Arfaras, head of the largest and most successful sponge-packing house in the world. In '39 he was also president of the Greek Community.

Nick Arfaras is a native of the island of Symi, which was under Turkey when he was born and now is under Italy, although preponderantly Greek. He came to America at the turn of the century when in his late twenties, and engaged in the sponge trade in New York. In 1905 he heard of Tarpon Springs and hurried down to see what the shouting was all about.

A powerful man, shrewd and intelligent, he thought, slept, almost ate, and lived sponges. He bought and handled only the best. In his plant from sixteen to eighteen hours a day, he personally cut or inspected every sponge he shipped. He began to set the standards of quality and established a system of classifying sponges which was accepted by the trade in America generally. By the middle 1920's he was "tops" in sponges. Today he handles over half of the Tarpon Springs product.

In his late sixties no one would take him to be past fifty. Still the most energetic and hardest working man in town, he is in his plant at five in the morning, three hours before any of his workers arrive, and leaves two or three hours after they go home in the evening. He cuts and trims tens of thousands of sponges with his own hands, and directs and oversees every detail in the handling of the hundreds of thousands of others. He walks about with a springy step in slippers, shirt sleeves, old trousers and suspenders.

Lesser packers envy and even hate him, but they know, too, that he gives the industry the stability it enjoys, and respect him for it. Believing the divers and the rest of the boat crews ought to have a fair income, he consistently bids high for sponge, which, because of the size of his business, he can well afford to do; and to get any sponges at all, the others must keep their bids near his. This is probably one of the chief reasons for the economic stability of Tarpon Springs as a whole. He seems not to care what anyone thinks of him.

After working sixteen hours in the plant, he often dresses up and dances most of the night, then is at work again at the usual time in the morning.

All the talk in his huge shop is Greek. His English is expressive enough, when he is required to speak it, but grammatically imperfect. I asked him how he accounted for the fact that all old-stock Americans had gone out of the business in favor of the Greeks. He shrugged his shoulders and smiled. After a while he said, "Americans like to sit in nice offices and give orders, then go play golf."

One day I walked with Arfaras along the quay. Nearly all the talk on the wharf, as in the near-by coffee houses, was Greek. Most of the boats moored at the dock had Greek names: *Aegli, Kalliopi, Evdokia, Kanaris, Socrates, Podromos,* and so on; but several, too, had American names: *Calvin Coolidge, George Washington, President Lincoln, Uncle Sam, Mayflower.* I had heard that he, Arfaras, had some business interests in Athens, and that his children had received part of their education in Greece. I asked him whether he considered himself a Greek or an American.

Smiling faintly, Nick Arfaras answered: "Well, I was born a Greek, now I am here in America. I am a United States citizen, of course. Nearly all of our immigrants in Tarpon Springs are naturalized. The Greek Community encourages them to take out their papers. America did great things for us. Here we are free to do things in a big way. Back in the old country life was held up. You couldn't move fast. Here there is freedom. Opportunity. Yes——"

He fell silent for a moment, pondering; then went on, "Let me tell you something. One night a few years ago I suddenly woke up. I ached with desire to be in Greece, to see my relatives and friends in my old country—see Greece—see Athens and go to my island of Symi. This ache to see my native country stayed with me for weeks. Finally, unable to get rid of it, I decided to go home. I used the word 'home' in my thoughts.

"I arrived in Athens. At first everything was fine. I met my relatives. Fine people. I went to Symi. I was glad to see everybody. They were nice to me. Beautiful scenery; everything fine for a while. . . . Then, I don't know just when, I began to feel different. Mind you, I love Greece with all my heart. Great country, great history; and I am loyal to the good things in my old country's tradition—I want to make that clear.

"But—I don't know what happened. When I left America I planned to stay in Greece—at 'home'—for three months and visit every part of the country. But I wasn't there three weeks before I wanted to go back to America. For no reason at all. At night I suddenly woke up in my hotel room in Athens, aching to be back *home* in Tarpon Springs.

"When I returned here, a month ahead of my plans, Tarpon Springs looked wonderful to me. Home. . . . So what am I?"

Nick Arfaras glanced at me, smiling.

The Tashjians:
A Family from Armenia

BORN in Caesaria, Turkey, in almost the exact middle of the nineteenth century, Hagop Aram Tashjian was the son of an Armenian engineer and builder, who was also a rock hewer and sculptor; Armenians are a versatile people.

To be an Armenian in Turkey at that time, and for decades after, was a crime sporadically punishable by death at the whim of almost any Turk; and at seventeen, to evade such a fate, Hagop betook himself to the wilds of the high mountain country in central Turkey, and hid there for months. Then he made his way by night to Marzovan, where he found refuge and the opportunity for education at Anatolia College, established some years earlier by Congregationalist missionaries from the United States.

Hagop developed into a tall, strong, dark-bearded young man and became a Protestant minister. In the mid-seventies he was made pastor of the little Congregationalist church in the walled-in city of Erzerum, the traditional capital and cultural center of ancient Armenia.

But by then Erzerum had scant connections with culture, Armenian or any other; its chief importance was as a Turkish military fortress, which the Sublime Porte used in its intricate, erratic game of power politics with Russia and Britain. This international game was closely linked to the violent domestic Turkish politics, in which the Christian Armenians, newly awakened to a national consciousness and desire for freedom, were—much like the Central-European Jews a half-century later—a kind of irrelevant but handy pawn, kick-about and scapegoat; a helpless object of the fanatic impulses of the dominant majority.

The youthful Rev. Tashjian quickly distinguished himself as a preacher and orator, and a year or two after coming to Erzerum he was invited to the Kurdish city of Bitlis, some days' ride away, to address the graduates of Mount Holyoke School, founded five years previously by the New England missionary sisters, the Misses Charlotte and Mary Ely, who were among the earliest graduates of Mount Holyoke College in Massachusetts. He was introduced to the eighteen-year-old Sophia Varjabedian, valedictorian of the graduating class and locally renowned for her beauty and fine character. They fell in love at first sight and were married at once. For their honeymoon they rode horseback from Bitlis to Erzerum, part of the way in sight of Mount Ararat, the great peak sacred in the Armenian tradition.

Sophia's father was a wealthy landowner outside Erzerum. He had sent her to the Ely sisters' school as much for safety as education. A few months after her graduation and marriage, during a flare-up in Russo-Turkish military activity, he was forced to provision the Sultan's army from his granaries; when they were exhausted, the Turks slew him.

Sophia was a girl of deep feelings and intense beliefs. These stemmed from her own rich and terrible Armenian background and from the rigid New England conscience and purposes of the Misses Ely. They enhanced her own Armenian passion for education and for self-improvement in this world as preparation for the next. As such she was an ideal mate for Hagop Tashjian, whose nature and character met hers at many points . . . and, in a sense, this story is a chronicle of a family's urge and search for education and self-development.

In the belfry of the little Congregationalist church in Erzerum hung an American bell. Near the edifice, in the center of a sizable compound, was the parsonage with a flower and vegetable garden and a two-room school, in which instruction was given in English and Turkish. In the seventies Armenian was periodically forbidden in Erzerum. Now and then, here and there in inland Turkey, tongues were yanked out of the heads of persons who had spoken the language.

As Armenians, the minister and his wife lived under all manner of restrictions. They could not leave the city without a special passport. He could not own or carry a gun, although any Moslem could attack him without fear of consequences. "Onward Christian Soldiers" he deemed a fine hymn, but was not allowed to have his congregation sing it; to Turks it sounded like incitement to uprising.

His and Sophia's little library was repeatedly scrutinized by all but illiterate military officers, to whom almost any word was apt to be a source of suspicion. "H_2O" in a chemistry book, for instance, once caused trouble because the investigator wondered why the initials of Sultan Hamid the Second were followed by a zero. Did that mean the ruler of the Ottoman Empire was of no account? Or about to be reduced to naught? Was there a plot? . . .

In narrow, immediate personal ways, however, the Tashjians were happy in Erzerum for a few years. The American missionaries, whose headquarters was across the way from the church, regarded them with growing esteem. All the woe that touched the young couple's life came from outside their sphere of activity, although, on the other hand, Rev. Tashjian developed tentative friendships with a few Turkish officials, who also regarded him highly.

The first Tashjian child—a boy, Haig—was born during the siege of Erzerum by the Russians, one of whose war aims (screening their passion for control of the Black Sea and the Dardanelles) was to free the Christian Armenians from Turkish oppression. Undecided about taking Bismarck's advice to Abdul Hamid to exterminate physically the nationalistic minorities within their Empire, the Turks were putting up a stiff resistance. There was starvation among the fifty thousand inhabitants, and all the cats and dogs were consumed.

Typhus killed thousands. But the little Tashjian family, somehow, survived. Though he had no formal medical training, Rev. Tashjian served as a doctor attached to the Turkish army through most of the siege.

II

Roaming through the city one day, when he was twelve years old, Haig—a slight, eager, wide-eyed lad—was attracted by the agitated voices in an open courtyard, where scores of Armenians had gathered to discuss a common problem. Along the walls stood a number of other boys about his age. They had also been drawn to the scene by curiosity and expectation of excitement. Suddenly a troop of Turkish soldiers appeared like a whirlwind of doom, and, amid wild blasts from bugles, with bayonets and sabers butchered nearly everybody there. Only a few escaped.

Haig was not touched. The soldiers did not seem to see him, perhaps because, for some reason, he did not get panicky and run. He happened to be near the exit, and slipped from the courtyard, then moved on to a less disturbed zone and finally came to where everything was quiet and all windows and doors were shut. He reached home and told his father.

Rev. Tashjian hastened his family, which now included three more children, to the missionaries' house. Over the entrance hung an American flag.

All that day mobs dashed through the city, breaking windows, crashing doors of Armenian dwellings and places of worship and business, looting and killing. But no harm befell the missionaries' home, nor any of its inhabitants or guests; and, with his child's logic, Haig concluded that the United States must be the safest place in the world. Hadn't its emblem protected them?

After this, the Tashjians' life in Erzerum was pierced with unending anxiety. The city was far in the interior; in the likely event of another massacre, it would be next to impossible to get to the coast and within sight of a ship which might offer them hope of escape.

All other Armenians in Erzerum were thinking the same thoughts. Their nation's ancient capital now was a trap. Singly, in twos and threes, people vanished. Taking months to make their way, in various disguises and by bribing Turkish officials, to Smyrna or Constantinople, they paid foreign ship captains to smuggle them to non-Turkish ports in the Mediterranean, whence some proceeded to England and the majority to America.

Educated by missionaries for lifelong work among his people in Asia Minor, Hagop Aram Tashjian, like his wife, felt duty-bound to remain, not to desert his fellow nationals in their plight. But a year after the Erzerum massacre he gratefully received a call to assume the pastorate of the Protestant church in Bardezag, a town of three thousand near Constantinople.

"Bardezag" means "little garden," and the place was not misnamed so far as young Haig was concerned. In later years he recalled it most vividly. The gentle, sunny slopes around it, with the extensive mulberry, fig, and olive groves and vineyards, touched the green surge of the Sea of Marmora. Nearly all the inhabitants were hard-working Armenians engaged in the traditional Armenian pursuits of silk culture, fruitgrowing, and rug weaving. Some were well-off, doing business with England and continental Europe. The few Turks in the community were friendly people, quietly going their own way. There were no soldiers; even the police and tax collectors were Armenians and one's neighbors.

But the most important part of Haig's new environment in Bardezag was the local American school. The headmaster was an old friend of the Tashjians, Dr. Robert Chambers, who had lived in Erzerum till two years prior to the massacre. The institution was a prep school for the subsequently famous Robert College, which—under the sponsorship of the American Board of Foreign Missions—was then beginning to have a profound effect on Asia Minor. Haig attended the school for four years, while the family were in Bardezag, along with his younger brother Armen, who—like the third boy, Edward, and the first girl, Armenouhie—was also born in Erzerum.

Another girl, Nouvart, and the fourth boy and last child, Souren, were born in Bardezag. There were six, all told.

In the mid-nineties the Rev. Tashjian was transferred to the Congregationalist church in Smyrna, "the window on Europe," and the family moved again.

In the interior of Turkey, Armenian massacres occurred off and on, sometimes as a matter of formal state policy, sometimes on the caprice of some bey or pasha, or as a spontaneous mob action, impelled by fanaticism or God alone knew what; and, a close and consistent observer of political and psychological trends, Hagop Tashjian realized the time was approaching when the life of no Armenian would be safe or worth living within the Ottoman realm. He and his wife meant to remain loyal to his calling and continue their work in Turkey (for Sophia Tashjian helped her husband in many of his religious and educational activities), but they felt it would be unfair to keep the children there.

They determined to give each of their sons and daughters as good an initial upbringing and schooling as possible, then send them out of Turkey, one by one, as rapidly as they could manage. They thought they had from ten to fifteen years, or till 1905 or '10, to carry out their plan, but possibly not that long. Sometimes at dusk when the piercing prayer cries began atop the minarets, the atmosphere became so tense one could not say when extreme terror might strike even the comparatively civilized coast cities.

The plan required what seemed to them great sums, and that worried the Tashjians. By the time they came to Smyrna there were eight in the family, and the pastor's salary was the equivalent of less than forty dollars a month (it never got beyond sixty). But they thought they would succeed—somehow.

III

Seeking to meet a foreign ship captain who would not demand the usual high price for helping an Armenian slip from under the Turkish rule, Rev. Tashjian spent some time along the Smyrna water front, where Sultan's soldiers were posted at intervals of fifty feet guarding against unauthorized arrival and departure of people. Armenians were not allowed to emigrate. The lucky ones among them escaped to other countries by various means and routes.

"Escaped" is the word. Armenians were a people in bondage to a numerically superior nation, whose purpose was to keep them in that status because they were resourceful, hard-working, and highly competent in a number of industries and pursuits which were a factor in Turkey's export trade and foreign exchange; also because they could be mulct through taxation, and because, as already suggested, they were a convenient scapegoat, on which the general run of Turks could practice their Moslem sense of superiority over the Christians and their talents for hate and carnage that were encouraged by some of the pashas and the Porte as a matter of internal policy.

As the oldest, Haig, going on seventeen, was first on the Tashjian escape list. He chose to go to the United States.

American ships entering Smyrna were few in those days, but early in 1897 Rev. Tashjian got into communication with the captain of a British freighter who was ready to help for a price within the family's means. The high-minded pastor, educated by righteously straightforward Puritan Americans, could not bring himself to engage in bribery personally, even to help his son; so a Turkish acquaintance of the family who made it a business to aid fleeing Armenians, took from him a sum of money and salved the palms of the port inspectors and guards. Then, one evening after dusk the signal came from the ship anchored in the bay; the bribed soldiers on the wharf looked at the crescent moon above the minarets; a rowboat with an English sailor at the oars gently touched the piling below, and Haig, carrying a small bundle, jumped in.

A half-hour later the boy was locked in a closet of the British captain's room, where he stayed till the ship was outside Turkish waters.

In England, Haig secured passage on a New York-bound boat for ten dollars. This low price was due to a rate war then being waged by American and European steamship companies competing for emigrant business; and, as it turned out, the accommodations, if they may be so called, were not worth more.

Having attended American schools in Turkey, Haig spoke fluent English, and when he reached the United States, he underwent none of the language difficulties which were common to hundreds of thousands of other immigrants pouring into the country at that time from more than a score of non-English-speaking lands. The inspectors on Ellis Island were, in fact, so impressed by the youthful newcomer's English replies to their Turkish and Armenian questions they passed him without asking if he had the twenty-five dollars required by law as a condition of entry. He would have been o.k.'d on this score, too; he had two dollars over the amount.

An interpreter on the island, himself an immigrant from Turkey, a Syrian, wrote down for Haig the directions to an Armenian café at Twenty-seventh

Street and Third Avenue. The corner was then, as it is today, the heart of the Armenian section of New York City.

The young man treated himself to his first good meal in weeks, consuming quantities of *midia dolma* (mussels in shells, stuffed with rice, ground onions, pine nuts, currants, and spices cooked in olive oil and served cold), *shish-kebab domatessli* (lumps of lamb and tomatoes grilled on skewers), and other Near Eastern foods. He rented a room upstairs, and for the next few months made the café his headquarters.

The United States was in a major economic depression. The café proprietors cautioned Haig; and, jobless, he lived on his twenty-seven dollars for almost two months. Rising at four every morning, he bought the New York *World* and studied the help-wanted ads, but everywhere he came, no matter how early, hundreds of men stood in line, seeking the job he had hoped to get.

By-and-by, no longer able to pay for his lodging, he asked the proprietors to let him sleep on the restaurant floor after the guests had gone. They agreed and in return he cleaned the place mornings before setting out on his daily job hunt. Due to insufficient food and endless walking in the streets, he lost much weight; his clothes and shoes were in tatters; he suffered pangs of homesickness; and, worst of all, doubts about America began to loom in his mind.

A greenhorn job seeker, he encountered some of the worst aspects of American life. In spite of the charity bread lines, he met up with actual starvation. One day a suicide from a third-storey window hit the pavement at his feet. Some of his experiences came close to being personal affronts. Back in Turkey he had been a member of the upper intellectual class of an underdog nation, son of educated parents, to whom no few people, even Turks, deferred; here he was just a plain underdog, rejected daily by people who were culturally inferior. Walking about or lying on the restaurant floor, he had spells of untellable loneliness.

At last, he got a temporary job polishing false teeth in a dingy East-Side dental office. Then, drifting as a rug peddler to New England where Armenians were settling in increasing numbers, he found brief employment in an Armenian rug-dealer's shop in New Haven. This was followed by months of extremely hard manual labor in a brick kiln near Springfield.

All this time, carrying within him the passion for education and advancement the elder Tashjians instilled in their children, Haig looked for a chance to continue his schooling. In Springfield he came upon the French-American College and enrolled. During the next four years, while attending college, he worked in succession as a porter in a barroom, a cuspidor polisher in a hotel, a flunkey in summer resorts, a rug mender and cleaner, and once more as a dental assistant.

People noticed him because he looked a bit "foreign," and, being intelligent and possessing an agreeable personality, he made friends among old-stock Americans who became interested in his future. In college and out of it, he now began to encounter America at its best: people who were drawn to strangers from the Old World because they were different and, being different, they might have something out of the ordinary to offer to them personally and to contribute to the evolving scheme of things in the New World.

At twenty-two, after a period of indecision during which he graduated from the college in Springfield, Haig decided to concentrate on dentistry. One of his new American friends, who was eager about his progress in the United States, had gone to a job at Ann Arbor, and Haig went there, too, and enrolled in the University of Michigan's medical school. He continued to support himself by working at odd jobs, which sometimes were too brief and overmeager for a sense of security, but he contrived to keep going. Members of the 1904 dental class recall Haig Tashjian as one of the better students, with a tendency to originality and experimentation.

For a couple of years he knocked about clinics and hospitals in Michigan, then opened an office in Kalamazoo.

At a dental meeting he met the late Dr. Charles H. Land, of Detroit, a pioneer in modern American dentistry (and also the maternal grandfather of Charles A. Lindbergh). The two became friends, and under the stimulus of occasional conversations with the older man, the young dentist engaged in original experiments and subsequently wrote a number of important papers for the dental journals.

Soon after opening his office in Kalamazoo the young man met at a picnic Miss Janette Reitler, who taught art in the local teachers' college and had brought with her a homemade date tart of amazing excellence. In no time Haig Tashjian discovered the young lady's other virtues and accomplishments. She was an old-line American, and was warned about marrying a foreign-born man, especially one stemming from so exotic a nation as the Armenians. She gave the warnings the consideration she thought they deserved; they married . . . and have had a good middle-class American life.

They own a spacious home, whose interior is embellished by several Armenian *objets d'art* and other symbols of the doctor's heritage. Around the house is a formal garden, locally esteemed a beauty spot, in which more than two hundred plants—some imported from the Near East, the Carpathians, the Alps, and the Arctic—take their turns to sport their varied blossoms from the earliest spring to late autumn.

Dr. and Mrs. Tashjian have a son, David, a graduate of the University of Michigan and the Massachusetts Institute of Technology, an engineer, married to a girl from Georgia.

Now in his early sixties, still practicing, Dr. Haig Tashjian is a thoughtful man, somewhat of a philosopher. In his introspective moods he likes to talk, with a mingling of amusement and sadness, about the complexity of his inner make-up, which includes all the glory and horrors of being an Armenian and the puritanical New England conscience that got into him, *via* his mother, from the Ely sisters. He keeps up with events in the Near East, and in many subtle and basic ways is still an Armenian, but in the uppermost layers of his mind he is nothing if not an American. He has been a citizen for nearly forty years, and is deeply concerned about many of our American problems. He gives much thought to the new-immigrant groups which now constitute more than one-third of the total population. "The stranger in the land," he says, "is still a question mark. The country used to say, 'What can we do to him or get out of him?' While the stranger often said, 'What can I get out of this country?' The question will have to become, 'What shall we do for each other, or, rather, together for America?'"

IV

At the turn of the century no great massacres of Armenians occurred and for a while the elder Tashjians were in no immediate haste to send the rest of their sons and daughters out of Turkey. Parent-like, they wanted to keep them under their wing as long as possible.

Their second son, Armen Haygooni, went to Anatolia College, Rev. Tashjian's alma mater in Marzovan. Mechanically inclined, resourceful and brilliant, at the age of twenty, after simply reading on the subject, he constructed the first wireless station in Turkey. He made all the parts himself, including the battery. Then, again after only studying the reports on how they were constructed, he built a complete x-ray machine.

All this came to the attention of the Turkish authorities, and the youth was investigated. His books and paraphernalia were confiscated; and it is anybody's guess what else might have happened to him were it not for the fact that he was a son of Hagop Tashjian, who was respected by important Turks, and that the Tashjians generally had the friendship of the American missionaries and educators in the Near East, whose utter sincerity, singleness of purpose, naïveté and flag awed the Turks in authority.

Lee deForest, the well-known New Haven electrical inventor and associate of Marconi, heard of Armen through one of his cousins who was a missionary in the Near East, and he expressed willingness to help the youth should he decide to come to the United States. But by then Armen was under constant surveillance, and "escape" seemed out of the question. After a concerted wire-pulling campaign on the part of his American friends and sponsors, however, he got a special passport and reached America in 1903.

But in the meantime deForest had lost a costly lawsuit against Marconi, and now was unable to give Armen any sort of material help. So, twenty-four at the time, the newcomer got a job teaching night school in Bridgeport. Then he entered the Massachusetts Institute of Technology, and during most of the next five years boarded with the Hartshorne family in Boston, who were actively interested in the critical situation of the Near Eastern minorities. What money he needed, he earned washing dishes in a Back Bay hotel from six to nine in the morning and from ten to twelve evenings.

Armen Tashjian was one of the outstanding students of his class, winning several prizes in mathematics. He had started out to be an engineer, later changed to architecture, and finally got his M.S. degrees in both engineering and architecture. He wrote a thesis on reinforced concrete, then a new idea. He lectured on it and took out a patent on his device called the "Rivet-Grip Steel."

In 1912 he became a member of Walker & Weeks, a firm of architects and builders of Cleveland, which soon after was renamed Walker, Weeks & Tashjian. Since then he has taken out numerous other concrete and steel construction patents, and has developed into one of the most successful architectural engineers in the United States. In the last two decades his "Rivet-Grip Steel" has been important in many large concrete construction jobs the country over. It was used in the building of every Federal Reserve Bank in the country except one and it is popular in vault construction in America, England and elsewhere. Armen Tashjian has a factory in Cleveland called the Rivet-Grip Steel Company.

His other important inventions are a floor-molding called "Conduo-Base" and a prefabricated insulating panel or slab, the "Armenite," both extensively used in modern building.

During 1917-18 he was often called on by the United States government for advice and special services in steel-testing and other technical matters. He designed a concrete ship and offered it to the government, which considered it; however, the war ended before a decision could be made.

Some of the buildings and bridges he has worked on are the Federal Reserve Bank in Cleveland, the Cleveland Public Library, the Delaware Bridge, the Indianapolis War Memorial, the Memorial Bridge at Bruges, in Belgium, and numerous post offices erected since 1920 all over the United States. He is a former president of the Ohio Institute of Architects. In 1938 he gave up his Walker & Weeks partnership, and is now, in addition to his other functions and interests, consulting engineer for the Union Metal Manufacturing Company of Canton, Ohio, specializing in steel and concrete foundations.

His wife is the former Flora Beardslee of Cleveland. They have three children: Betty, a 1940 Smith College graduate; Peggy, a graduate of Laurel School in Cleveland, who has been studying ballet and has danced at benefit affairs since her early teens; and Armen, Jr., who is not yet ten.

Armen, Sr., is now in his late fifties. His home on Fairmont Boulevard is one of Cleveland's show places. The most important room in it is his laboratory, wherein most of his inventions took shape. He still spends several hours there daily.

v

In the mid-nineties more than four hundred thousand Armenians were massacred in the interior of Turkey, and in the ensuing years Rev. Tashjian and his wife, working from Smyrna, played a heavy role in taking care of Armenian orphan refugees. They evolved the foster parents' plan, since used by other nations afflicted by wars and other orphan-producing misfortunes. This work impressed all foreigners in Turkey, but particularly a group of Germans conducting a large orphanage in Smyrna. Later these Germans, working through their Embassy in Constantinople, inveigled the Turkish foreign office to give the Tashjians' eldest daughter, Armenouhie, a passport to go to Germany, where she attended a fashionable girls' boarding school in Duesseldorf on the Rhine.

Armenouhie was strikingly beautiful, socially graceful, at once dynamic and tactful, and unusually talented in several directions, but especially in the arts and languages. Her fellow students vied with each other to be her hosts during vacation time. From the private school she went to the teachers' college at Kaiserwerth, also on the Rhine. On her graduation, she was offered teaching positions in Germany, but, since Turkey again appeared tranquil, her parents asked her to return home to Smyrna for a while.

One day a cloudburst drove Armenouhie to seek shelter under the eaves of a house, where a number of drenched Americans were huddled against the wall. Among them were Mr. and Mrs. W. H. Hartshorne, of Boston, mentioned awhile ago in connection with Armen. Mr. Hartshorne was president of the International Sunday School Association, leading a group of more than a hundred delegates to Jerusalem on a chartered steamer. After the downpour subsided Armenouhie invited the shivering Americans to her parents' house near by. They enjoyed the sincerity and simplicity of the Tashjians' hospitality, and invited Armenouhie to visit them in New England and see if she would not care to live in America.

She arrived in the United States soon after Armen and spent the summer on the Hartshorne estate at Marblehead. She sent a statement of her qualifications to several schools and received seven offers of teaching positions and, putting them all in a hat, drew one that took her to Cleveland as head of the German department of a private girls' school. She was barely twenty at the time.

In her third year in Cleveland, she had her tonsils removed. It was Valentine time, and noticing that the girls in school were sending amusing or silly pictures to one another, Armenouhie made a humorous pen-and-ink drawing of a surgeon performing a tonsillectomy and sent it to Dr. John Ingersoll, who had operated on her.

The doctor asked her if she would like to do some work for him: he needed to have some medical pictures drawn. Armenouhie had no experience in this field, but she was observant and the drawings she turned out under her new friend's direction were not bad. Whereupon, impressing on her that good medical artists were extremely scarce and in great demand (there were only two in the United States at the time, both immigrants from Germany), Doctor Ingersoll suggested she let him teach her further. She began to attend his operations and sketch the diseased parts and what he did to them. The pictures then appeared with his articles in medical journals and caused several doctors to inquire about the artist.

Among these was Dr. George Crile, the famous Cleveland surgeon, lecturer, teacher, and author who was in need of a medical artist. Armenouhie was at this time considering going to Vassar or back to Germany, where positions had again been offered her. But Dr. Crile urged her to enter Johns Hopkins for a year as a special student in anatomy. There were then no courses in medical art anywhere in the country, but Dr. Crile thought that, being quick and intelligent she would "pick up enough anatomy" in a year to perfect her technique as a medical artist. Since then Johns Hopkins and other American medical schools have instituted special courses in the subject.

Within a year Armenouhie Tashjian made herself into a useful member of Dr. Crile's staff. She attended his operations, which doctors from all over the world came to watch. Her ability, beauty, and charm were noticed by many of them. The Mayo brothers wanted her to come to Rochester.

Armenouhie was with Dr. Crile for three years. During this time she developed the process of making almost microscopic drawings on film which were then projected on the screen by lantern at lectures. She accompanied her employer to medical meetings and conventions.

In 1913 Dr. Crile sent Armenouhie to Alaska to do a few pictures of the brain cells of salmon, which he needed for his new book *Brain Cells and Surgery*. In Seattle, waiting for her boat and being entertained by some medical friends of Dr. Crile, she met young Dr. Otis Floyd Lamson, formerly of the Mayo Clinic, now practicing in Seattle; son of a wealthy Western family, tall and blond, a one-time All-American football player from the University of Pennsylvania, and the only bachelor at the party. Armenouhie and he were paired. . . .

The wedding was to be in Trinity Cathedral in Cleveland, where Armenouhie used to sing in the choir. But just as the groom was to leave for Cleveland, a prominent official of Northern Pacific Railway went down with a ruptured appendix and insisted that Dr. Lamson and no one else operate on him; whereupon, since the operation had barely saved his life, the patient and his family further insisted the young doctor stay close by till all danger passed . . . and the railroad magnate ordered his private train sent to Cleveland for the bride-to-be.

They were married in Seattle in 1914.

During her first pregnancy, Mrs. Lamson wrote a "diary" of the unborn child, ending with birth. She illustrated it, Macmillan Company published it under the title of *My Birth*, and it began to be used as a textbook in biology classes in several medical colleges and many nursing schools. Ten years later, on the request of Cornell Medical School, it was revised and reprinted under the title of *How I Came to Be*.

The first-born was named Robert after Dr. Robert Chambers, erstwhile of Erzerum and Bardezag. Robert's middle name is Bardezag. A graduate of the University of Washington, he is now in his mid-twenties and engrossed in aeronautics. A few years ago he won second place in a nationwide essay contest in aeronautical sciences and received two years' intensive training at Boeing School for Aeronautics at Alameda, California. In March, 1940, he was commissioned in the United States Army Air Corps.

The Lamsons have two other children—Otis, twenty-two, a student at the University of Washington, who is interested in mechanical engineering and worked in the General Motors plant in Flint last summer; and Armene, nineteen and beautiful, attending Scripps College in California. The boys are blond; their sister is dark. Both Bob and Otis, Jr., are passionate sportsmen, sailing on Puget Sound, and skiing on Mount Rainier.

For two decades now Mrs. Lamson has been one of the most active people in Seattle, engaging in philanthropy and civic and cultural affairs. Her most important function is, perhaps, as director of the Free Parental Clinic she founded. In this capacity she once saved a twelve-year-old boy from spending his life as a criminal in the State penitentiary and simultaneously secured for delinquent minors in the State of Washington the right to be tried only in juvenile courts regardless of the seriousness of their offense.

She is also the founder and honorary president of the Seattle branch of National League of American Pen Women, founder and president of the Women's Auxiliary of the American Medical Association in her state, president of the Seattle Civic Opera Association, a director of the Seattle Symphony Orchestra, a member of the Committee for the National Foundation for Infantile Paralysis, a director of the King County Chapter of the American Red Cross, and vice president of the Women's University Club. She is active, too, in the Lighthouse for the Blind and the local Music and Art Foundation. In connection with the latter organization, she inaugurated sixteen years ago the annual Children's Christmas Festival in Seattle, which in 1939 was attended by six thousand children.

She is also one of the founders of the Town Meeting, a lecture forum in Seattle. She lectures occasionally and writes frequent articles for local publication and for English-language papers issued by Armenian groups in the East. Currently most of her time and energy go to the foster parents' plan in Seattle to help the Chinese children orphaned by the Japanese invasion—the plan whose technique was evolved, as already mentioned, by her father and mother in Turkey forty-odd years ago.

VI

Nouvart and Edward Tashjian came over next, close together, a few years before the First World War. Their brothers and sister who had preceded them to America helped them financially, while their passports to leave Turkey were procured with the aid of American educators and other influential foreigners in Turkey.

Nouvart was the first woman graduate of International College in Smyrna, which ordinarily accepted only men. Like most of her brothers and sisters, she knew a half-dozen languages and was not an entire stranger to about as many others.

She joined Armenouhie in Cleveland, enrolled in the librarian's course at Western Reserve University the first week there, and two weeks later won the highest mark in the examination for librarian. From the Library School she went into the cataloging department of the Library of Congress in Washington, where her natural orderliness and methodical and systematic tendencies came to good use. In 1915 the St. Paul Public Library became under her charge the first public library to institute the Library of Congress classification system.

Two years later, when the United States had been in the war for six months, the War Department in Washington made a frantic call for a person with a genius for system to take charge of the Army Ordnance Department's Record Division, which was in a chaotic state due to oversudden expansion; and, on the suggestion of some people in the Library of Congress, Nouvart Tashjian was sent for and put in charge of a vast continually expanding office, beginning with over one hundred civilian employees and soldiers.

While in St. Paul, she had been interesting herself, in her spare time, in the local Y.W.C.A.'s handicraft courses and for a while had conducted the handicraft page of a Midwestern farmer women's magazine. After the war there was a desperate need for teachers of occupational therapy and Nouvart taught handicraft for a short time to disabled ex-service men in Saint Elizabeth's Hospital in Washington.

During the next five years she edited the Arts and Crafts department of the *Modern Priscilla* magazine and wrote a book on Armenian needlepoint lace. Then she returned to library work, taking charge of the catalog division of the Public Library in Kansas City and teaching a course in cataloging. Now for several years she has been head of the cataloging department in the New York University Library on Washington Square.

Also a graduate of the International College, Edward was not yet twenty when he came to the United States. At first he worked in factories and as a lumberjack in Maine and harvest hand in Manitoba. Then, earning his living with odd jobs he took a four-year engineering course at Wisconsin, after which he enlisted in the Twenty-third United States Engineers and went to France.

Following the war, Armen took Edward into Walker, Weeks & Tashjian, and some years later the Ohio Battle Monuments Commission made him its representative abroad during the building of the great concrete American Memorial Bridge spanning the Scheldt River in Belgium and commemorating the achievements of Ohio's Thirty-seventh Division. Essentially as much an artist as an engineer, he was partly responsible for the interesting aesthetic aspects of the bridge, which have received favorable comment in both art and engineering journals.

Since 1933 Edward Tashjian has been a government engineer, working on many new concrete-and-metal post offices, which he designed, and on other public works projects in various parts of the country.

VII

The baby of the family, Souren Barkev, was born on the day when the muezzins from the top of minarets throughout the country called the faithful Moslems to hear the Sultan's *ferman* or decree, which began, "The government has decided to exterminate the Armenians." His parents named him Souren Barkev, meaning "saved from the sword."

The imperial decree was not carried out literally, and the boy went through all the schooling available in Smyrna, including the International College. He was scheduled to come to America early in 1914. His ambition was to study medicine. Passport difficulties delayed him; then the war broke out, making it virtually impossible for any of the Sultan's subjects of military age to leave Turkey. He was pulled into army service but, with a number of other young Armenians, his fellow students in the American college, vowed never to fight against the Allies.

Late in 1914 began the Golgotha period of the Armenian agony. There were almost daily massacres, punctuated by mass deportations of men, women and children into deserts, where they were left to die. There was the forty-day incident on Musa Dagh described by Franz Werfel in his famous novel.

Souren witnessed massacres and, even as a Turkish soldier, barely escaped death from Turkish swords a number of times. Finally, on the Dardanelles front, he deserted and, after a series of adventures in a two-oar skiff among the islands in the Aegean Sea, was pulled aboard a French man-of-war, which took him to Italy, where he was interned as a Turkish subject till after the war.

In 1920, Souren arrived in the United States. His brothers and sisters came to his aid; they had developed a chain system of helping one another. He went through medical school at the University of Virginia and did postgraduate work at the University of Pennsylvania and in London. On the completion of his studies he received a master's degree in proctology, in which he now specializes in Seattle. At Virginia he was one of the outstanding and most popular students, and was elected secretary of his class for life.

His wife is the former Miss Margaret Cahalan of Yakima, Washington. He is a Kiwanian and a perennially enthusiastic American, active in Seattle affairs.

VIII

Rev. Hagop Aram Tashjian died during the war. For an Armenian in Turkey at that time his death was amazing—in bed, of illness due to overwork.

After the war, the children tried for three years to get their widowed mother out of Smyrna, which meantime had come under Greece. It was a time of deep, dark confusion in which the fate of an elderly Armenian woman was of no importance. Also, Sophia Tashjian herself, while eager as all life to see her sons and daughters who were doing so well in America, was in no haste to leave Smyrna. The city swarmed with Armenian refugees needing her help.

In 1920, the Greco-Turkish War burst out, and two years later Smyrna was burned.

One night, after a week of sheer horror, Sophia Tashjian, a woman past sixty, was driven with thousands of others onto a strip of sand wedged between the flaming city and the sea. Hundreds died from the intense heat of the conflagration and the lack of drinking water. Mrs. Tashjian was caught in that trap for five days. She had no food, nor a drop of anything to drink. Thirst swelled her tongue to three times its normal size. People went insane. She lived and retained her balance of mind and sufficient energy to stumble into the launch from a French ship that had steamed into the bay.

She was taken to Athens, and her experiences were reported in the American press along with the fact that she was the mother of five American citizens and one immigrant, Souren, who still had three more years to wait for naturalization. The United States was then adjusting its immigration laws, and some doubt appeared whether she could enter the country. Was she a Greek or Turkish subject?

Finally, President Harding—the man of poor judgment in many matters but of good heart and decent impulses in purely human situations—cut the red tape, ordering Sophia Tashjian admitted into the country as his "personal guest." She arrived in 1923. Later her immigrant status was established under the law.

Mrs. Tashjian went to Seattle and alternated living in the homes of her daughter Armenouhie and her son Souren. She told how just before the burning of Smyrna, she had barely missed dying in two massacres in which hundreds met horrible deaths. In one, Tefik Bey, a Moslemized Jew who was a high Turkish official and had known her husband, ordered the soldiers to release her. In the other, a Turkish soldier yelled to his comrade who was about to split her head with his sword, "Let her go! What is the use of killing an old woman like that?"

Two years after coming to America Mrs. Tashjian suffered a stroke. But she lived for eight more years. Before she died in 1933, at seventy-one, she liked to sit by a window in her son Souren's house from which the snow-capped Mount Rainier was visible on clear days. She said this American mountain reminded her of Mount Ararat . . . of her honeymoon trip on horseback from Bitlis to Erzerum.

The Old Alien
by the Kitchen Window

TO HIS multitudinous family, relatives and friends, Anton Kmet is Oché Toné—*oché* meaning "father" or "old man" in his native Slovenian tongue, while Toné is the familiar abbreviation of his first name. He is an old man, no doubt about that.

His shrinking frame hunched over, his nape pushing down between his protruding, age-sharpened shoulder blades, and his legs crossed limply, Oché Toné sits all day long upon a hard, squeaky old chair by a small window in the kitchen on the ground floor of his house at 6208 Schade Avenue, in Cleveland, Ohio. He sits from ten to fourteen hours daily, and looks into the yard, in which there is nothing much to see; and, looking, he pulls at his corncob pipe and puffs with a slow, determined rhythm; and, sitting and looking at nothing much at all, and smoking, he thinks his thoughts.

Now and then he grunts or chuckles to himself as if to punctuate the things going through his head, or he lifts the large, tremulous paw that rests on his thigh in a faint, vague gesture in the general direction of the cosmos, or he makes a remark to his wife or anyone who happens to come within the range of his voice, which is rather limited. Except for this and for the sucking and puffing at his pipe, he is perfectly still, often for hours at a spell. Sometimes he does not even smoke, but only sits and thinks, and frequently, no doubt, he just sits. He is in good health; only he is very old.

Within a period of three weeks during the late winter and early spring of 1940, sitting by the little four-pane window, Oché Toné celebrated six anniversaries—the eightieth of his birth in the village of Ajdovec, near the town of Zuzemberk, in Lower Carniola, then a province of Austria; the fiftieth of his arrival as an immigrant in the United States; the fiftieth, too, of his beginning to work for, and getting on the pay roll of, the American Steel and Wire Company on Fortieth Street in Cleveland; the forty-eighth of his marriage to Karolina Novinec, who had come to America a year and a half after him from the village of Veliki Lipovec, also in Lower Carniola; the forty-seventh of the birth of the first of his eleven children, a son; and the twenty-fifth of his retirement on a monthly pension from his job, when he had decided that he had done his bit in the world and sat down in that chair (then new and free of squeaks) by the kitchen window, to gaze out and smoke and think from daybreak until nightfall every day of the week, week after week, month upon month, year in and year out; and to wait for his pension check, which the postman brings him once a month without fail.

As Oché Toné sees his life, now that it is tightly wrapped in old age, these anniversaries cover or suggest its high spots. Among them roam all his thoughts and talk. There is only one other important fact in his career, as he sees it: he is not a citizen of the United States, because he did not want to become one—a fact closely linked, however, to his notion that he is *neké vrsté Amerikanec vsé eno*, a kind of American, anyhow.

He understands some English but does not speak it. His medium of expression is a Slovenian peasant dialect, but he uses many American-English words twisted into Slovenian forms to fit his tongue. In his speech, for instance, a "house" is a *gauz*, "shoes" are *shukhi*, "street" is *shtrit*, and "beer" is *pir*.

He likes to tell "facts" about himself, which he has told so many times now that to him they are more true than truth itself; he has a surprisingly good memory, and each time he retells some of these "facts" he is more impressed by them than he was at the time of their occurrence. He is not hard to listen to, although, in common with most old people, he repeats himself a great deal. Off and on, when he catches himself repeating a bit of his life story in too close succession, he says something to this effect, "Eh, why not! I am like an old horse tethered to a pin in the ground, making the same steps all the time. At this stage of the game you don't go leaping into new adventures, so the old ones have to do."

His story, however, is not without significance, if that is the right word to attach to anything pertaining to an old man who has never been anything but a laborer. Perhaps I should say that parts of his story are typical of many aged immigrants who have been in America a long time without becoming citizens, and who are now dying at an increasing rate—albeit Oché Toné is apt to live to be a hundred. He wants to.

II

At thirty, on landing at Castle Garden in New York Harbor, Toné Kmet was what Slovenians call a *korenjak*, one who might be described as a "giant," or one constructed on a heroic scale. He was six foot three and all bone, blood, muscle and hide; strong and straight as a pillar holding up the ceiling in a church, and not hard to look at otherwise. He had a shock of dark-brown hair, an aquiline nose, an impressive mustache, and a bold, challenging look in his hazel eyes.

Kmet means "peasant" in Slovenian, and he was a peasant. He had no schooling but knew how to read a bit and to sign his name in an emergency. He had decided to come to the United States because he was his father's second son, and as such, along with all his younger brothers, obliged to leave the village and find a place and function for himself somewhere else. In the village of Ajdovec, a half-century ago, and before and since, things were tight and set economically, and only the oldest son was encouraged to remain at home. Fifty years ago, America was still a fairly new, though intensely interesting, idea in Carniola; but when Toné emigrated a score or more of Ajdovchani were already scattered through the various coal and steel and iron towns in the United States.

Toné Kmet had served for a number of years in the Emperor Franz Josef's army, and was none the worse for that experience. As a soldier, in fact, he had picked up a little German, which was useful to him in Cleveland, where a good many factory bosses were German immigrants from Austria and Germany.

From New York, Toné traveled in an immigrant train. At the depot in Cleveland, most of his fellow passengers were met by relatives or friends, but no one came for him. Not that he expected anyone. He had a slip of paper bearing the address of a number of the boys from the village of Ajdovec who had preceded him over; so he was not worried. But he was a bit bewildered by all the hubbub. His bundle over his shoulder, he stood outside the depot, watching the people jam themselves into the horse-drawn streetcars, and wondering which way to turn. Then a great dray loaded high with beer kegs drew up in front of him and the driver leaned downward from his lofty perch and yelled at him, "*Ti s' pa Kranjc, al' nis'*? You're a Carniolan, aren't you?" (Carniolan is usually synonymous with Slovenian.)

"*S'm*," answered Toné. "I am."

Showing a broad grin, the driver invited him to hop on; he would take him wherever he was going. He also was a Slovenian immigrant, three years in America, and said he could always tell a *rojak* or fellow countryman on sight. "There's something about us!" He delivered beer to saloons in the Slovenian neighborhood and often picked up newcomers when he happened to pass by the depot.

He dropped Toné at Feliks Novinec's boardinghouse, where most of the other Ajdovchani lived. Feliks was the brother of Karolina, whom Toné married two years later, soon after she came over.

Two of the Ajdovchani at the house were employed in the American Steel and Wire Company's mill on Fortieth Street, and the morning after he arrived they took Toné Kmet along and told him to join the job-seeking crowd in the yard. Taller by a head than almost anyone else on the scene, he was among the first hired that morning, and assigned to a German straw boss, who put him to work with two other laborers. The job consisted of putting great bundles and coils of wire from a platform into freight cars.

Mochan kot hrast—strong as an oak, Toné Kmet tossed the coils and bundles as though they were trifles. The straw boss noticed this immediately and called the boss, who called the assistant plant superintendent, who called the chief superintendent, who decided that with Toné around the other two workers had nothing to do, and, indeed, were in his way; so he ordered them taken off the job and left Toné alone to do the work of three men. This, Toné continued to do with the greatest of ease; in fact, he thought the job was somewhat of a sinecure, and soon he received a higher wage—twelve cents an hour, while the other laborers were paid only ten.

He worked from ten to twelve hours daily, but not infrequently overtime stretched his workday to sixteen and occasionally even to eighteen hours. Some-times his muscles creaked with fatigue when he took himself home, and he felt a little groggy, but thought he was doing all right, and America looked good to him.

III

Strong and good-looking, several years younger than he, Karolina Novinec caught Toné's eye, as she did the eyes of the other single boarders, immediately after she arrived from *stara kontra*, the old country. By-and-by, after he had made his intentions clear to her, she decided to marry him because he looked "steady."

Now, nearly half a century later, when he gets someone to listen to him, Oché Toné likes to tell of those days:

"To get married and start a home was no great stunt then. Sometimes I got only fifteen dollars on payday, which came every two weeks, but that wasn't bad. You managed on seven or eight dollars a week. If there was a lot of *obertaim*"—overtime—"and I brought home eighteen or twenty dollars, that was something to let the neighbors know about in some roundabout way so they could not accuse you of bragging, and they said, 'You're making good money, Toné; you and yours won't starve.'

"Living was cheap then. Naturally, when we got married, we had to furnish the flat. *Zlomka,* believe it or not, for thirty-five dollars we got everything we needed. Nowadays a young couple have to have four or five hundred dollars to set themselves up. Of course, our tastes then were not so high; we were satisfied with less than people are now: which may be good or bad, I don't know. But things really were cheaper then, in relation to wages. For three cents you got a quart of milk or a pound of meat. . . . Cleveland wasn't nearly as big a town then as it is now. Houses were thick only to about Fiftieth Street; there were a lot of farms within walking distance of where most of the Slovenians lived, and you could get a four-hundred-pound hog for four dollars; then there was enough meat and lard to last the winter and well into spring, if you did not have too large a family or too many boarders. If you went into a butcher shop and bought a few pounds of pork or beef, you got free of charge all the tripe and lungs you wanted to take along; the butcher was glad to get rid of such stuff. . . . And any time of day you could step into a saloon, buy a glass of beer for a nickel, and eat your fill off the free-lunch counter. *Ya-ya,* this was a wonderful *kontra* then . . .

"My wife and I rented a flat with two extra rooms; we put beds in them and took boarders, young fellows who were coming over from *stara kontra*: which helped. We were all content."

This last is one of his favorite sentences, with which he concludes most of his narrations about the old days. "We were all content." He rolls it off his lips with all the finality of a priest's "Amen."

IV

For ten years Toné Kmet tossed the great bundles and coils of wire from the platform into the cars. Then he was promoted to a "better" job in the cooling department, where wire was treated in chemicals. The work here was much less strenuous and by now this, too, was all right with Toné Kmet. He had got to be forty and the heavy work on the platform had taken something out of him. Also, since the new job involved some responsibility, the pay was higher, "which didn't get me mad, either."

One day the chemists and several of the bosses were experimenting with a dangerous new chemical. They warned the men to be careful, and Toné heard and understood them all right. In a moment of bravado, however, meaning to impress the bosses, lest they should have forgotten that he was still a *korenjak* and that this work of handling these wire coils and bundles continued to be pretty much of a snap to him, he pushed a big bundle into the trough with his foot, as though he were kicking a lump of earth into a furrow. The iron platform on which he stood was wet; he slipped and, trying to regain his balance, lurched with one foot into the strong acid solution.

He was pulled out and his leg was quickly immersed in a vat containing another solution, supposed to counteract the first; but even so the leg was affected. A doctor treated him immediately, and he was taken home in an ambulance (a horse-drawn one, of course, for this occurred in 1901). He was laid up for several months. The doctor came to see him at first every two days, then once a week . . . "and I got my wages just as if I were working."

As already reported, when he was a young man, Toné's eyes held a bold, challenging look. They did later on, too. But that look was directed personally only at individuals who might want a fight or seek to vie with him, and to situations such as a great pile of wire bundles on the platform that had to be heaved into the cars by quitting time. By and large, it had no reference to institutions, such as governments or industrial mills or companies. Way down deep in him, peasant-like, Toné was a humble fellow in most respects; in fact, rather frightened, obedient, and "grateful"—grateful for the least demonstration of decency or generosity toward him. Or, at least, that was one fairly definite streak in his character (there were others). So, since his pay was nearly always a trifle higher than the other laborers', gratitude was always part of his feeling toward the American Steel and Wire; and now, with all the good treatment he received following the accident, which he realized was entirely his own fault, he became clearly a "loyal employee," a "company man."

During the late 1900's and the early 1910's, there were a couple of strikes in the mill, but he never joined them. He felt miserable about this, especially since he knew he was called a scab, but he could not bring himself to go out. Eventually, too, his nonstriking became, to no small extent, a matter of policy between him and the company, for in 1910 the American Steel and Wire entered into a pension plan under which the workers retired on partial pay after twenty-

five years of continuous employment; and going on strike was interpreted by
the company as an interruption of that continuity.

What helped to alleviate Toné Kmet's unhappiness during these strikes was
that a good many of the men in the mill felt and acted as he did; and the
strike leaders, as a rule, did not really expect or count on those who were
working toward a pension to go out.

v

Like most peasant immigrants, in whom the property instinct was strong, Toné
and Karolina Kmet aspired from the start to live in a dwelling of their own.
To realize this on his laborer's wages was no easy matter, especially since a
child was born to them on the average of every two years. But in 1907 they
bought their first home, a small, cramped one-family house. Toné then acquired
a couple of lots, mostly because everybody else he knew was plunging into real
estate; and with Cleveland expanding at a great rate, he sold them in 1911 for
three times the price he had paid for them. The following year he disposed of
his house, or rather the corner on which it stood, for the building itself was
worthless, and bought the substantial residence on Schade Avenue in which he
now lives.

Karolina bore the eleven children, three boys and eight girls, during the first
twenty years of their marriage. To say nothing of keeping up the payments on
the house and lots, it was a problem to feed and clothe so large a family, for
the cost of living, of course, did not stay at the 1893 level, when they married; yet all eleven children achieved adulthood and ten are still living and,
in their various ways, doing as well as most Americans of the lower-middle or
working class.

The oldest son, Anthony, Junior, commonly also known as Toné, started to
work and contribute to the family income when he was but twelve. He served
in the First World War, then trained himself to become a coremaker, and got
a job with the United States Aluminum Company. He worked there till 1939,
when in consequence of his war experience he suddenly died. He left a widow,
who is a Slovenian immigrant, and two daughters and a son who are still in
school.

The oldest daughter, Lina, was the first to marry. Her husband, Frank
Turk, is a Slovenian born in Germany, where his parents had gone as emigrant
laborers shortly before he was born. He was also trained to be a coremaker
and works at that trade to this day. He and Lina, in their mid-forties, have
eleven children, the youngest of whom is a few years old. Three of their daughters are married, and employed in the Richman Brothers' clothing factory, which
is renowned for its satisfactory working conditions.

The second daughter, Mary, wed a grocer on St. Clair Avenue, which is the
lifestream of the Slovenian section in Cleveland. The Depression hit him hard;
when he was forced to sell either his home or his store, he sold the latter. Now

he is a night watchman, while Mary cleans offices downtown. They have a boy and two girls, all grown up, two of them working.

Frances, the third daughter, was only sixteen when she married John Svete, a young fellow fresh from the old country. Also a coremaker, he too works for the United States Aluminum; and Frances has been with the General Electric now for fifteen years. They live in a house of their own and have three daughters, one of whom is married.

The fourth of the Kmet girls, Rose, married in 1935. Her husband, Janko Rogelj, an immigrant from Slovenia, is in the general-insurance business and is an official of the South Slavonic Catholic Fraternal Union, secretary of the Slovenian gymnastic "Sokol" society, president of the Slovenian National Home on St. Clair Avenue, which is the center of the neighborhood's social and cultural life, and a writer of short stories and articles for the Slovenian-language publications in the United States. The Rogeljs rent the upstairs part of the old folks' house, and have one child.

The fifth daughter, Tonca, or Antoinette, married in 1930. She has a boy and a girl. Her husband, John Bukovnik, is an immigrant who came over young and served as an aerial photographer in the First World War. Now he is a successful commercial photographer.

Vidé and Joe, the two boys born after Tonca, are single men, now in their late twenties, both coremakers with the United States Aluminum, turning out airplane parts. They live with the old folks, as does their youngest sister, Gertrude, who, also unmarried, works at General Electric.

The other two daughters married American-born boys of Slovenian parentage. Mila works at Richman Brothers, while her husband is boss in a small factory. Bertha's man is an employee of the New York Central Railroad. Mila has no children. Bertha has a daughter.

Taking after the old man (for his wife is medium-sized), all the children are large people, as are almost all of the grown-up grandchildren, whose total now is twenty-four. And they are a handsome lot, both individually and together. Most of them resemble one another.

On Sundays and holidays the ground-floor apartment in the house on Schade Avenue, especially the kitchen, is full of the Kmet family, children and grandchildren. But they almost never come all at the same time. There is scarcely room for them.

American-born, all ten of the Kmet sons and daughters are, of course, American citizens; and having attended Cleveland's public schools, they speak fluent American English as it is usually spoken on their social level. But they know also their parents' Americanized peasant-Slovenian dialect, in which they occasionally kid and josh them for not being citizens.

VI

Why Toné and Karolina Kmet did not become naturalized is a little story by itself.

During the 1890's and the 1900's, and in fact all the way up to the outbreak of the First World War, Cleveland—most of the Slavic newcomers pronounced it "Kleh-veh-lahnd"—was the destination of so vast a stream of Slovenian immigrants that it eventually became, and is to this day, "the second largest Slovenian city in the world," the first being Ljubljana, the capital of Carniola, which at that time, say, forty years ago, had a population of thirty-odd thousand. And it was natural enough that in this new element men appeared who made themselves its leaders.

While most of these leaders were not wholly devoid of motives and intelligence which could stand the test of time, the characteristics which received the strongest and freest function in the exercise of their leadership were aggressiveness, business acumen, blatancy, general cunning, selfishness, and readiness to play the game with their environment, which was never of the best, never overcharged with those motives and intelligence which could stand the test of time, either. They made themselves the local political "bosses" of their people, both of the Republican and Democratic parties, and played second fiddles to the big "American" politicos, some of whom were old-stock Americans, while others had Irish and German backgrounds. The leaders of the Slovenian immigrants in Cleveland, as in other cities where they congregated, were no better and no worse than the leaders of other new-immigrant groups or, for that matter, than American political life as a whole.

They were the men who were first to become "Americanized"—Americanized, that is, in point of picking up the English language and in terms of the current surface values, rather than in reference to any basic motives or propulsions of the Republic. They were naturalized, of course; and, under the urging of their old-stock and German- and Irish-American superiors in their respective political parties, they became a force in the naturalization of their people; for their effectiveness as political strawbosses depended on how many of their fellow countrymen were citizens and eligible to vote.

In the early nineties, when Toné Kmet had been in Cleveland about three years, there rose to such a position of leadership in the Slovenian neighborhood along St. Clair Avenue a man whose name in the old country had been Jurij Bostijancich, but who "Americanized" it to George Boston. A big, rotund but not obese man, with a large, florid, and jovial face and small, close-set eyes, which squinted full of mysterious, would-be humorous meaning, he was a typical-looking ward heeler. This even in the matter of such details as the plug hat he wore low on his forehead or over to one side, and the cigar in the corner of his mouth. As an industrial worker, years before, he had suffered an accident, and now had a wooden leg, which did not detract from his picturesque jauntiness.

Possessing considerable talent for imitation, Mister Boston, as he liked to be called, was out to do in America as Americans did. A citizen of several years' standing, he spoke English; not the best, perhaps, but good enough for his purposes. Except in the matter of pronunciation, it was not much worse than the English of some of his superiors in the party machine.

Typically, too, Mister Boston ran a large poolroom, which was the favorite rendezvous of those Slovenian immigrants who "spoke English" and were "Americans" and "sports." The boss encouraged, almost required them, to speak English and become citizens. Noncitizens were all but barred from the poolroom, unless they came to ask how they might become naturalized.

Mrs. Boston was an immigrant woman, but also an *"Amerikanka,"* as some of the less "Americanized" of her fellow countrymen referred to her. She served as an interpreter in courts and generally as her husband's political lieutenant.

Mister Boston and most of his close side-kicks during those early days in Cleveland's Slovenia are dead now, but no few people along St. Clair Avenue still recall him; and their accounts of him are varied and contradictory, though all are in favor that the six feet of American earth should be light upon his immigrant remains. There is no doubt that, with his knowledge of English and his contacts with the more or less influential people downtown, he helped many of his fellow immigrants out of jams in which otherwise they would have been helpless or at a great disadvantage. Nor that in rendering aid he sometimes helped himself in tangible and immediate ways, although, when he died during the 1930's, he left nothing of any consequence in the way of property. Nor is there any doubt that, to keep his contacts and perpetuate his ability to help his people, he had to "deliver" on election days; and that, to "deliver," he worked hard at inducing the foreign-born to become naturalized, for getting noncitizens to vote or citizens to vote more than once was a difficult and risky business. Nor can it be denied that, in this latter effort, he did no little good, causing people to learn English and come a trifle closer to the American process, even if it was in a way one cannot fully approve. He made people go to night school and, in the course of twenty-five years or so, was directly responsible for the naturalization of thousands.

The worst that can be said about Boston is that his motives were mixed and his methods a bit crude.

Toné Kmet had been five years in this country when Boston—who was still referred to as Bostijancich by most of the Slovenian immigrants, and who continued to speak Slovenian when among those of them who did not understand English—came to see him on a Sunday afternoon and said, abruptly, "Look here, Toné, you take a day off tomorrow and come downtown with me."

Surprised, both by the visit and these instructions, Toné asked what he would do downtown.

"I want to see you get your citizenship paper," said Boston.

"What kind of citizenship paper?"

"American citizenship paper, of course. Don't worry about anything," Boston hurried on. "I'll pay your carfare downtown and back, and I'll also buy you a couple of beers and a couple of stogie cigars."

"But I can't speak English," said Toné, "and I don't know anything, I am just a peasant, a laborer tossing coils of wire; how can I get a citizenship paper?"

"Don't make yourself any dumber than you are, Toné," smiled Boston, squinting at him meaningfully, "and don't worry about anything. I'll fix everything. You'll get your paper rightaway, and in the fall, when election day comes around, you'll be able to vote like a real American; see? You come down to my poolroom at nine o'clock; there'll be a bunch of other fellows who are going downtown with me."

The suggestion—which was practically an order, for Boston believed that was the way a political boss should talk, especially to greenhorns—bewildered Toné. He could not believe citizenship papers could be obtained *kar takolé*—so easily. In the old country it took ten years for a county to recognize a man from another county and extend to him the *domovinska pravica*, the "right of belonging." He was sure Bostijancich was somehow in error, or that he, a politician, had something up his sleeve; and so he did not go to the poolroom that Monday morning.

Besides, a thought shaped something like this started to bump around in Toné's cranium: He was a foreigner here; what did he know about American affairs? He was uneducated and had the notion that many things were far beyond his powers of comprehension. Except for the words and phrases pertaining to his work in the wire mill, he knew no English, and he had no intention of learning the language at his age, for it seemed extremely difficult, and as a laborer he got along well enough without it; and he felt a laborer was all he wanted to, or could, be. Despite all the boldness in his eyes, Toné was a humble soul, a little man, a former peasant, now a manual worker: why should he presume to want to have a hand in the important decisions of this great country, which, according to rumors, stretched from ocean to ocean? Boston had said he could vote in the fall if he got his paper now; but vote for or against whom or what? In the mill, the bosses talked as though the Republican party was better for the country than the Democratic party. They said there was always more work when the Republicans were in power than when the Democrats were in; and if this was true in the matter of work, he inclined to think they were right in preferring the Republicans, who, like the Democrats, were a sort of abstraction in Toné's mind. He was dimly conscious of the great complexity of American matters; and who was he to figure these things out so as to be able to vote on them? . . . But this was not only humility; it was also a kind of peasant shrewdness or sense of realism, which led him to accept naturally his limitations. "You can't expect a frog to fly like a swallow. You can't cut an oak beam out of a white pine. . . ."

The ensuing Sunday, Mister Boston dropped in again and, clearly annoyed, demanded to know why Toné hadn't showed up.

Toné decided he did not like the man's manner; besides, he had learned that the politician had Anglicized his name and his reaction to that was: why should a Slovenian, any Slovenian, fake it and pretend to be "English"? Also, he had heard that this so-called Boston, who was really Bostijancich, was a Democrat, and on this score Toné was inclined to respect the mill bosses' opinion: they certainly ought to know whether there was more work during a Republican or Democratic regime: and what counted with Toné was work and more work—*obertaim*.

But Toné Kmet controlled himself and did his best to be polite to Boston, who was a guest in his home, though he hadn't invited him. He said he did not aspire to citizenship because he feared when it came to voting he would not know how to vote.

"You don't have to know how," retorted Boston.

"I don't understand," said Toné, although he was beginning to understand so well that he was getting hot under the collar.

With a quick ingratiating smile, Boston said, "All you'll have to do will be to vote as I tell you; *vish*—see?"

Toné "saw." He shook his head sharply; then his lips slowly clipped off these thought-measured words: "If that's how it is, I don't intend ever to become a citizen. I don't want anything forced on me, least of all citizenship. You keep your paper. All I want is to be left alone and have a chance to work. If I work as good as I can and try to behave as a man should, I am as good as any citizen of any country; *vish*?"

Boston left and did not bother him again.

A simple, honest *dolenjska dusha* (Lower Carniolan soul), Anton Kmet stewed over this incident for years, and he worked up within himself a definite idea, a sort of complex, against applying for citizenship, which he could not overcome even when he began to suspect his attitude was a bit foolish and he probably should become a citizen despite the Mister Bostons. There was in this also an element of typical Slovenian peasant stubbornness and contrariness. . . . And since Toné did not take out his papers, Karolina did not, either.

VII

Toné Kmet was always careful in the matter of his health. Even as a young man he ate and drank moderately and never ate anything warmed over. He avoided drafts. In 1910, at fifty, after a long cold which had "got into his bones" and forced him to go to bed for a couple of weeks, he became a bit of a hypochondriac. With no slight uneasiness, he had been noticing that many people in America died in their forties and fifties, whereas in the old country men and women had the tendency to live to be eighty and ninety. And Toné Kmet had an idea that he wished to live a long time even—and, in a way, especially—in America; he liked the place more and more. He had half a notion then to quit working. In fact, he sent word to that effect to the mill. The bosses, who had known him for two decades, came to see him and told him not to be a fool. What was the big idea, anyhow? He had twenty years of service to his credit; in five more years he would be entitled to a pension. They raised his wage from fifty to sixty cents an hour, and he went back to work for another half-decade—chiefly because, on careful thought, he realized if he quit now the family might have the devil of a time making ends meet; the house was not quite paid for and the two children who had begun to work were not yet earning very much.

At fifty-five, however, or early in 1915, Anton Kmet came home from work one day and said to his Karolina that he was *zmatran*, tired, tuckered out. No, he was not ill, so far as he could tell; but his legs, somehow, felt heavy and awkward. He would stay home the next day, or maybe the rest of the week. Maybe even longer. Maybe——

He sat down on that chair by the four-pane window in the kitchen, then got to thinking all over again about living and working and dying. Why should he work any more? He had done enough, hadn't he? Wasn't the wire he had handled stretched all over America, holding things in place, keeping cattle in their proper pastures? He still owed a number of payments on the house, but now there would be no difficulty in meeting them: four of the children were working and contributing toward the family expenses. What was the sense of his going on lifting and tossing those bundles and coils of wire which seemed increasingly heavy? In a way, he was tired of that, bored with it. And he was just generally tired. *Zmatran.* Funny, how weary his legs felt. He was fifty-five, an age not to be taken lightly in America. Even in the old country it was the beginning of a sort of twilight in one's life. Here, in this land of rush and strain, twilight was apt suddenly to snap and become night, with no evening. This was how Toné Kmet figured. Why couldn't he just sit on this chair by the window in the kitchen, and take things easy, think a bit, look back a bit upon his life, talk with Karolina when something occurred to him, and watch the children grow and develop? Why not? There was no reason at all.

And the idea of the pension check fascinated him. At moments in the past he had not quite believed he would ever get it. In the old country only government employees received pensions; people who were educated and seemed to amount to something, while he, Toné Kmet, here in America, was only a laborer. Back in Carniola (then still in Austria), only the government or the Emperor Franz Josef paid pensions; here some of the companies seemed to pay them, too. Of course that was America for you: a great, fantastic place. Who could understand it, or why things happened the way they did? That *he*, once upon a time of Ajdovec, near Zuzemberk, should get a pension, was a trifle odd, to say the least. In the past, he had at once believed and disbelieved he would receive it; now, sitting in the chair in the kitchen at fifty-five, he decided to retire in part also to test this pension plan. He would see whether or not this outfit called the United States Steel and Carnegie Pension Fund, of which the American Steel and Wire Company was a member, was a fiction or the real thing.

The mill bosses came, three or four of them, and joked with him again about being a quitter, and at his age, too—why he was just a chicken, a mere youngster! But Toné Kmet did not care what they said. He was through working in the mill; and repeating several times his request that they would please see about his pension, he smiled to himself when they laughed at him . . . and sat, smoking, with his legs crossed . . . and looked out of the window into the little yard, where there was little to see, for the time of the year was late February, and the trees were naked; there was nothing on the clothesline, and the snow that had drifted against the fence several weeks before was grimy with soot from the chimneys. . . .

One morning about a month after this, the postman brought a long, narrow envelope, and Anton Kmet opened it. There was a check. He looked at it a long time, studying it, feeling the crisp paper. There was the name of the United States Steel and Carnegie Pension Fund in heavy print; there was his name, ANTON KMET, typewritten in capital letters, all correct; there were a couple of signatures at the bottom; and there was the amount in figures and words: twenty-one dollars and forty cents. It looked all right. Carniolan skepticism, however, is a formidable thing, and Anton Kmet did not even yet quite believe the check was genuine. Maybe the mill bosses were playing him a trick. They were great jokers.

He sat by the window, and, keeping the check for several days, he looked at it every once in a while. Finally he called for pen and ink, as had been his wont on paydays, endorsed it, and sent his son Toné to cash it at the corner grocery store.

Young Toné returned with the cash, which the old man counted and pocketed. Then, still not entirely sure the check would not bounce back, he waited a week, whereupon he counted the money again . . . twenty-one dollars and forty cents, which was something . . . enough for all his needs from month to month.

And the check has been coming ever since; for twenty-five years, now. Oché Toné looks for it every first of the month, or on the second if the first happens to be a Sunday or holiday; yet, in a way, it freshly surprises him every time he pulls it out of the envelope. He studies it on each occasion. There is the name of the Fund; there is his name, always spelled correctly; and there is the amount, always the same. He notes the occasional change in the signatures at the bottom, and wonders—half seriously, half humorously—what has happened to the man who signed it before, whether he has died or quit or been discharged, for Oché Toné imagines that people even in such high and extraordinary places as the United States Steel and Carnegie Pension Fund have their troubles.

Then he puts the check on the table, which is within reach of his chair, and leaves it there till evening, glancing at it every once in a while between pulls at his pipe, and chuckling and grunting to himself. In the evening, one of the children—Vidé, or Joe, or Gertrude; or Rose or her husband Janko who often come down from their apartment—usually asks, "Oché, do you want me to get the check cashed for you?"—whereupon he grunts in the affirmative, and ink and pen are brought to him, and he takes several minutes to adjust his spectacles and scratch his John Hancock, and says, *"Tu jé papir, tu!"* which might be translated "This is a piece of paper that counts for something!"

This is the regular ritual. For twenty-five years, this has been the rhythm of his life, rising to the monthly climax of the check, which continues to give him immense satisfaction. *"U stari kontri so samu drzhavni uradniki dobivali penzijé,"* he says. "In the old country only state officials get pensions."

VIII

More than nine-tenths of the daytime in the last quarter of a century he has spent in that chair by the kitchen window. He never gets tired sitting there. He has been out of the house on the average of less than once a year. On an occasion, years ago, he rode in an automobile, but did not like it and never got into another car. He is full of eccentricities of that kind, of "funny things and ideas," as his family describe them; but thinks he is entitled to them. One of his principles is: let everybody live his own way.

He is also full of "jokes," which amuse him more than anyone else. Twenty years ago he announced that his calluses had moved from his hands *nekam drugam*, somewhere else, and has been repeating that remark, with much merriment, ever since. The day I visited him he wore a pair of pants he has had since 1921, and he gave me a full history of the garment, including the number of times Karolina had patched up the seat. The sweater he had on was ten years old.

Karolina cuts his hair, which is gray and inclined to stick out a bit wildly in several directions. He shaves himself a couple of times a week. He used to have a straight razor; recently, however, since his hands have begun to shake, his sons Vidé and Joe bought him an electric shaver, which he considers a wonderful trick—*"kaj sé budu l'djé vse domislil'*—what will they think of next!"

Since his retirement, Oché Toné has not moved a finger to do anything apart from attending to some of his personal needs: which is also typical of him. He worked hard and well during his active period, doing two or three men's work; now his aim is to make a good job of idleness.

He has made it a good job from the start. To sit down was his peasant idea of taking a rest, of idling. Of late years he sits for another reason: he must unless he decides to lie down, for his legs have become difficult to negotiate. He can still use them, but not much. They are old and tired. He needs a cane, which, when not in use, hangs over the back of his chair. Not that this disability bothers him. In fact, it is a source of amusement to him; he hasn't got much use for his legs, and will have less and less, anyhow. They are still good enough to get him from the bedroom to the kitchen and back, and to the bathroom: which is practically the entire range of his movements. All he wants to do is sit.

When I last saw him, in June, 1940, he had not been out of the house for two years and had no immediate plans to go out. The house was newly painted the previous summer, but Oché Toné does not yet know what color, except by report. It does not really interest him. One of the "funny things" about him is that he is not interested in anything outside and not in very much inside the house. He has not been upstairs for twenty-two years.

He is a curious sort of football fan. Early each fall, the radio is put on the table before him and he listens to all the games he can. He does not know the game; what thrills him is the excitement in the voices of the sports reporters. When the voice comes fast and loud, he clutches the table's edge, saying, "*Zdaj jih pa dajejo!* Now they are giving it to them!" He never knows, or cares, who is playing whom, or who is being beaten.

He is interested in his vast family, but largely in the purely human everyday phases of their lives; not so much in how much they have or earn as in the fact that they have and earn something, and in what sort of persons and workers they are. Every few days he spends an hour or two enumerating his children and grandchildren by name and in order of seniority. If he catches himself making a mistake, he stops and starts all over again. This gives him a deep intimate joy, and serves as a checkup on his memory, as well as an exercise for it.

One of his favorite grandchildren is the Rogeljs' little girl who spends much of her time downstairs and likes to crawl over him, pat his straggly hair, trying to put it in place, and examine his ears, see if his neck is clean or if he needs a shave. She, too, gets a thrill out of his electric shaver. They have grand times together; and their laughter, as his son-in-law Janko Rogelj describes it, is *kot bi imela oba medena usta*—as if they both had mouths of honey.

The old man's diet is simplicity itself. He always has on hand a supply of prunes and of *kranjské klobasé*, Carniolan pork sausages, which a number of butchers in Cleveland's Slovenian section make the way they have been made for several centuries in the old country. These sausages and prunes are the mainstay of his diet. In the morning, after transferring himself from the bed in the room adjoining the kitchen to the chair by the window, he usually takes a cup of coffee and a piece of bread, which he dunks; and an hour or two later, a dish of prunes and a glass of milk; then a cut of sausage, which he chews with his few remaining teeth, or another dish of prunes, or another glass of milk, whenever he feels hungry, which is every four hours. He has no regular meals.

Until a few years ago he used to drink moderately. In the fall he would buy a couple of barrels of wine, which would be put into the cellar for him and then be brought up by the gallonful twice a week. The gallon would stand by the right hind leg of his chair, and whenever he wanted a drink he would reach down and pour himself a glass. A few years ago, however, he began to feel vaguely unwell and called a doctor, who suggested it might be advisable to give up his wine and drink, instead, a couple of quarts of milk a day. This was a blow, for Oché Toné was born *pod trto*—literally "under the vine," as Lower Carniola is a wine-growing country; but, out to live as long as possible, he did as the doctor advised him.

Oché Toné is not a very religious man, at least not formally so, although forty-odd years ago, as a young man, he took a big hand in building the first

Slovenian Catholic church in Cleveland. He has not been to church in a long time. . . . In 1936, when his daughter Rose and her husband Janko were about to make a trip to Carniola, Karolina suggested to him that he give them five or ten dollars for the priest in Ajdovec or Zuzemberk who would say a few Masses for those of his relatives who had died in the old country since his departure for America, and he said he would give the matter consideration. He pondered for several days, then announced he had decided against paying for Masses for them. "If they are in Heaven," he said, "they are all right; if in Hell, a Mass or two won't help them; and if in Purgatory, let them wait a while—that's what Purgatory is for." He is not stingy, but does not believe in throwing money away.

IX

The spring of 1939 was a hard period for Oché Toné. First, as already mentioned, his son Toné died. Then his Karolina, in her early seventies, went down with gallstones and had to undergo an operation, which put a pall on his lightheartedness for a while. In her absence he lost his appetite for *klobasé* and prunes and milk, but regained it with her return from the hospital. In a few months, she was her hardy old self again, taking charge of the Kmet household.

Oché Toné continues to take good care of himself, and barring accidents or serious illness, is apt to live for a long time yet. He is old, and looks it, but the core of his life is vital and healthy. His will to live is strong, but not intense; not such that its intensity might devour him. Life to him, when all is said and done, is a rather pleasant joke, and he sees himself deeply involved in it.

So he chuckles a great deal, and many of his remarks are touched with a dry, tongue-in-cheek humor. Some of his seemingly childish or naïve notions, attitudes and actions, including much of the ritual with the pension check, are really sly, indirect commentaries on his own amusing and essentially satisfactory existence; commentaries by which he is himself convinced. There is in him a bit of the artist, which is to be found in most Slovenian peasants. His sitting by the window is an act; he is an actor in a role he himself has created, and he goes on writing his own lines. He has the artist's eye for effect.

Now and then he requests his son-in-law upstairs to come down; he wants to ask or tell him something. His questions are roundabout, not neatly phrased, wandering in all directions, but seldom unclear or pointless after one gets on to the habit of his mind. They are hardly questions at all, but ramblings of an old mind with a streak of humor.

"Sit down, Janko," he said one day in connection with his several anniversaries early in 1940, "pull over a chair, come close here, so I don't have to talk so loud. . . . I've been thinking, Janko, about this office where my check comes from, this United States Steel and Carnegie Pension Fund. What is it? What kind of a place is it? . . . Well," answering his own question, as is his wont, "I imagine it's an office in some great building, high up near the clouds, with desk and writing machines and water coolers, like the office of the American Steel and Wire mill, which I saw a few times. And there they sit, whoever they are; they sit by their desks and writing machines, and make out checks and sign them, and then they send them out—like gods in heaven. And what I want to know, Janko, is this: what am I to them? Am I just a name, someone on their list of names? For twenty-five years nobody has come to see me. No questions are asked. They must be *vsevedni*"—omniscient—"or how do they know I am still around? They must be gods; no?"

He chuckled.

"Besides, where do they get the money to send me? Do they ever say to themselves: when is that old buzzard on Schade Avenue in Cleveland going to die, so we can stop sending him money? Here I am. For twenty-five years they've been sending me $21.40 a month. That's a lot of coin. Where do they get it? They must be gods, *vsemogochni*"—omnipotent. "Their checks are good. There hasn't been a bad one yet. . . . Of course, Janko, another explanation may be that they are just Americans. Smart people, these *Amerikanci*"—chuckling again.

"But jesting aside, Janko," he went on, "wouldn't you think that they would get tired paying me all this money, with me sitting here, not doing anything, getting calluses in the wrong place, just sitting; or that they would run out of money, even if they are Americans? Not that I worry about them. It's their business. I did my bit. . . .

"And you know what, Janko: something else has occurred to me. Maybe those strikers were right. Maybe the American Steel and Wire didn't pay us enough for our work, not even me, although my wage was always a little higher than the others'. Maybe I did work too hard, crowded my years together too fast with *obertaim* and doing two or three men's work, and it may be that now I'm getting only what was my due all along because I worked in that mill for twenty-five years. Of course, it may be that they did not figure I would live so long and get the best of them in the deal. Maybe I'm getting more than my due. If so, the joke is on them; eh, Janko? The whole thing is funny, if you come to think of it. Me getting a pension! It's a joke; but maybe only to me. So I want to live a long time yet. I enjoy it so. What are jokes for but to be enjoyed; and if I die, who would enjoy this one?"

x

On one of my visits I mentioned to Oché Toné that there were people in the United States, including members of Congress in Washington, who were disturbed about the aliens and noncitizens, and that some wanted to deport all the foreign-born who did not have their naturalization papers, while others wished to pass laws requiring all noncitizens to register and be fingerprinted.

"*Taku?*—So?" said the old alien by the kitchen window. He was silent for a few minutes, smoking, looking out of the window. Then he chuckled and said, "Papers, papers! God gave the fish freedom in the sea and lakes and rivers, and birds all over the earth, but from a man somebody always wants some kind of paper." He smiled, shaking his head. "But, *nu,* maybe I was wrong in not taking out the citizenship papers; mind you, I don't say I was; I just say maybe I was. Let me tell you, though, what you do: you bring those people here on the first of the month, any month, whoever they are; you bring them and I'll show them my American paper, which says that I worked all right and did what was expected of me. I didn't ask for this paper. I didn't pay for it; Bostijancich, or Boston, didn't have to use his pull to get it for me. I worked until I did enough for one man's lifetime, and America has been giving me this paper once a month now for twenty-five years. . . . You tell those people, whoever they are, to come to my house and I'll show them. . . . But, of course, if they want me to get registered and—what do you call it?—fingerprinted, if that will make them feel better, I'll be glad to oblige, even if I have to go out of the house to do it. . . ."

He fell silent again, sitting and pulling on his pipe, and looking out into the yard, where a sparrow sat on a limb of a tree close to the window. Then Oché Toné chuckled again, "Look at him! They call him an American sparrow; what makes him American? Has he got his papers? Is he registered? Listen: back in Ajdovec, in lower Carniola, I saw sparrows which were no different." The chuckle broke forth again with real gaiety. Then: "A sparrow is a sparrow, a man is a man, *al' né*—isn't that so?"

The Hollanders:
They Made Their Pella

TWO Chicago salesmen were driving over the undulating prairie of southeastern Iowa. It was mid-May in 1939. The man not driving dozed off after they passed through Oskaloosa and slept for sixteen miles, till an abrupt halt of the car yanked him into wakefulness. "My God," he exclaimed, his eyes popping at the scene before him, "what's happened—*where* are we?"

They were in the center of a town. About them was a gay milling crowd of people, young and old, male and female, clad in the costumes of Holland, wooden shoes and all. The driver had been obliged to stop the car because scores of these costumed folk, with water pails, brooms and long-handled brushes, were busily (and hilariously) scrubbing the pavement of the square, though it apparently did not need it. And the place, wherever one looked, blazed with tulips of many colors. They grew in vivid profusion in the park, along the sidewalks, on lawns in front of and about the homes.

"It's a town called Pella," the driver informed his startled companion. "According to an item I read in the Davenport paper last night, they are having their annual Tulip Festival. The street-scrubbing is part of the program. It's a Dutch town. . . ."

The population of Pella is thirty-three hundred, about ninety per cent of Hollander origin or descent. The community, fairly well known within a radius of a hundred miles or so, is usually described as Dutch or Hollander, but it is also a very American place. Its story begins in The Netherlands during the reign of William I, about a hundred years ago, and revolves around the life of a man named Hendrik Peter Scholte (pronounced *Skolté*).

II

Scholte was born in 1806 in Amsterdam of a Dutch mother and a German father, a successful manufacturer and trader, who died in the boy's mid-teens. Young Hendrik was reared in an atmosphere of wealth and culture. Art, books, and intellectual discussion (most of it religious in quality or direction) were prominent in the Scholte home. The lad's tutors were the best available in Europe. He was tall and thin, earnest and quick of mind. His early ambition was to be a painter, and he entered the Academy of Arts in Amsterdam.

The family plan was that his brother should step into their late father's business shoes, but then he died too, and the mother's death followed within a month, leaving Hendrik the sole possessor of a great fortune. The conduct of the factory and the trade office was in the hands of managers whom the

elder Scholte had trained for their positions, but their ways and policies disturbed the young man who was independent of mind and temperament. The
conditions of labor under them he considered appalling. Workers received
scarcely enough to hold body and soul together. Living in hovels, they were
dying of the "white plague," or tuberculosis. Young Scholte tried to humanize
his concern, but came upon seemingly insurmountable obstacles. The managers
opposed him as a visionary. They pointed out, all too convincingly, that the conditions he disliked were organic with the whole situation in Holland and in
Europe at the time and that no one man (certainly no mere boy) should aim
to, or could, alter them.

Bewildered, vaguely miserable, he sold the firm, intending to restrict himself
to art. He was then one of the wealthiest young men in The Netherlands. Presently he married and proceeded to beget a family—three daughters. By his mid-
twenties he was a recognized artist. A number of medals were bestowed on him,
a few of his pictures hung on important walls in Amsterdam.

The serious quality of young Scholte's mind and feelings deepened. He began
to think art would not continue to satisfy him. The world, including Holland,
was an interlacement of urgent problems—economic, social, political, religious,
spiritual—which amounted to an all-around crisis and, to his mind, a solution
could not be evolved by painters or through art.

Free to follow any course, Hendrik Scholte abandoned art and entered the
University of Leyden, then a center of intellectual ferment. He joined a discussion group, which met twice weekly at an inn near the university and was
disposed to inquire into any and all questions. The ideas and instincts of most
of these young men were a mingling of conservatism and radicalism. Scholte
told what he knew of the conditions of labor in industry. Another was familiar
with the effect on the well-to-do of the high-taxation policy by which the King
was endeavoring to liquidate the large national debt contracted during the wars
of the preceding decades. Erstwhile wealthy homeowners starved to keep their
properties from being sold for taxes. Middle-class families were being driven
into the working class, then were unable to find employment. Only the very
rich, like Scholte himself, were able to withstand this economic assault; but even
they were becoming uncertain as to their future. What to do about it all? The
King was said to be cognizant of what was happening, yet persisted in his
policy.

Several of the young men, including Scholte, planned to become ministers of
the Gospel, believing they could best serve humanity and Holland as religious
leaders. They were Dutch Reformed, but deeply disquieted by the developments
within the Church, which was part of the State. In the eyes of these young
men of Leyden, to whom the Bible was the sole authority, the ministers—
acting as officials of the government, which paid them, rather than as men of
God—were straying in unscriptural directions, verging on skepticism, hetero-
doxy and blasphemy, thus throwing the people into spiritual-intellectual con-

fusion, rendering them incompetent to think clearly on social, economic and political conditions.

The young students sitting around the great oaken table in the inn groped for ways and means to check this. Scholte's feelings were especially strong. Ministers ought to be God's agents and leaders of the people, not mere lackeys of the House of Orange.

Accordingly, when he had been ordained and given a pastorate at the age of thirty, Scholte developed into one of the foremost protagonists of the cause to separate the Church from the State, to keep religion in Holland strictly scriptural, and to lead the people out of their economic and social chaos. As he saw it, religion and economics were related; meager compensation, brutal labor conditions, extreme poverty, and illness destroyed the moral character, and therefore were anti-God. In spite of his wealth and culture he rapidly emerged as a man of the people. Endowed with all but inexhaustible energy, a resonant voice and wit, he preached three or four hours at a time; and, eager for a clarification of their and Holland's problems, men and women of all classes came from near and far to hear him.

The young Dominie was also a man of action. When the dike broke, he rushed to the scene and worked side by side with his people. When someone's holdings were about to be put on the block by the King's tax collector, he took charge of the case and prevented dispossession. If there was no other way, he paid the taxes himself. He moved about the country like something elemental and preached wherever he found a crowd to listen to him, often in the street or in the fields.

And so it went for twelve years. The Separatist movement, which was at once religious and political, assumed considerable proportions. Although during the previous two centuries Holland had been an asylum for religious dissenters from England, France, and Central Europe, its government now instituted a relentless persecution of the new sect. Pastors were removed from their posts. Scholte and other leaders of the new faith were fined, imprisoned. But their congregations increased.

Finally, in 1839, the King reluctantly issued a decree recognizing them. Whereupon the persecution took other, more subtle, forms. The Separatists were ostracized socially, boycotted and plotted against economically. By the mid-forties, seeing that the State was determined to ruin them individually and thus destroy their movement, many, including Scholte, commenced to think of emigrating.

III

With this in view, Scholte formed in 1846 an organization called, simply, the Association. It included about one hundred and sixty families, or approximately eight hundred persons of all ages. Half of them were rich and desperate to save their wealth and the right to their personal religious inclinations. Close to a hundred single adults were servants of the well-to-do in the group. The moneyless were assured financial aid for the voyage and settlement, wherever they might go. Most of them were, or had at one time been, farmers or artisans. Some thought the Association should emigrate to "that jewel in Holland's Crown," Java, but the Dutch government did not want them there.

The previous year another group of Separatists, similarly motivated, had gone to America under the leadership of Dominie Albertus Van Raalte, a man of Scholte's cut, who had founded a Dutch colony in southwestern Michigan. Scholte corresponded with him and with others elsewhere in the United States. He read books about America and grew ever more enthusiastic about leading the group to the New World. He consulted with the American minister in Amsterdam, who urged him to go to Iowa, "a great, rich level territory" about to be admitted to statehood.

Meantime, changes occurred in Scholte's private life. His wife had died, leaving him with the three growing girls. One of his most devoted followers was an elderly rich woman, the mother of a beautiful daughter, Mareah, aged twenty. The young lady was a product of a Parisian finishing school, an accomplished musician, somewhat of a painter and Bohemian, and interested in the new movement chiefly because her mother was. Just forty, the Dominie fell madly in love and married her.

Mareah admired his character, his power and fire as a preacher and leader. She became a tender foster mother and made the Dominie happy in his home life. Though she severed all active contact with Bohemia, to her husband she was an echo of his own artistic youth. He called her *Kind* (child) and granted her every wish.

The first year of her marriage Mareah led a dream life as the mistress of her husband's spacious home. Everything she wore came from Paris, specially made for her. She ordered Parisian garments for her foster daughters. She played the piano, painted, looked exquisite, and was charming. She knew several languages, including English, and read widely. The works of Dickens, which were coming out in installments, fascinated and amused her. She believed his characters of the London slums could not possibly exist, nor the slums themselves, and considered the author a great and perverse inventive genius.

In his sermons, the Dominie spoke of a small Christian sect which fled Jerusalem in A.D. 66, when the city was besieged by the Romans to quell the revolt of the Jews, and found refuge in Pella, a little town east of the Jordan within the kingdom of Agrippa, where the group then led a peaceful life, worshiping according to their preference. Mareah's insight into Separatism and its problems was meager, and although the Dominie seemed to be saying something to the effect that they, too, were going to Pella—to a new Pella in the New World—she thought it all a story, an allegory, an expression of his cleverness.

But one day he suddenly informed her that "at last everything is settled and ready." In common with the others in the Association, he was selling all he possessed except some of the articles they might wish to take along. They were going to America.

Mareah swooned.

When she revived, the Dominie was bending over her, calling her *Kind*, and begging her to be brave. There was nothing to fear. America was a great, free country where they would be welcomed. The New World was full of Pellas; and should they not find one to their full liking, they would make one. America had room for thousands of new cities and towns. Mareah wondered if America, a new country, might not be "rough and wild." In Paris she had heard rumors to that effect. Was there music, art, refinement where he meant to look for their Pella? He answered Providence was with them. He was but an executive of the Will of Heaven, which had a special interest in the enterprise of the Association. There was nothing to worry about. Should their Pella lack in music, art, and the refinements of life, they would supply them.

Her fears relieved, Mareah started to take a hand in preparations for the departure. Going about the house with her husband's clerks who were cataloging the thousands of articles to be turned into Dutch guilders for use in America, she came upon many things with which she could not part and ordered the servants to pack them. One large chest was filled with old silverware; a barrel with Delft china, another with sentiment-weighted whatnots. Her maid Dirke she ordered to pack her wardrobe trunks, and sent an urgent order to Paris for more dresses for herself and her foster daughters.

The Dominie, too, found it heart-wrenching to part with all manner of belongings: books, pictures, pipes, snuffboxes, documents . . . and it required a stout dray to take the Scholtes' baggage to the pier in Amsterdam, to be put on a Boston-bound ship. The heaviest piece was a strongbox brimful of gold; it took four men to carry it.

IV

Dominie Scholte and his wife and daughters and their servants crossed the Atlantic on a "fast" ship to get things under way in America for the Colony, as the Association was now renamed; he was empowered to use his own judgment about everything pertaining to colonization. The voyage required nearly a month. They reached Boston early in May, 1847, and went to Albany, where they were well received—first by people of Dutch background with whom Scholte had corresponded, then by the community through its newspapers, churches, and leading citizens.

Mareah was impressed.

For days everyone discussed the fairly accurate and highly sympathetic newspaper stories of the Separatist movement in The Netherlands and the report that Dominie Scholte's followers were enroute to Baltimore in four chartered vessels—the *Nagasaki*, the *Maasstroom*, the *Catharina Jackson*, and the *Pieter Floris*. The voyage was compared to that of the Pilgrims' *Mayflower*. Everyone was interested, kind, eager with advice and offers of help. The Dominie was invited to preach in a leading church in town, and, in spite of the fact that English rolled awkwardly off his Dutch tongue, his sermons made a strong impression. So, too, did his wife's beauty. Mareah observed that here was form, elegance, breeding; why, the place had almost as much character as The Netherlands. If only this were their Pella——

Newspapers the country over picked up the story of the new Dutch immigrants, who were said to be mostly well-to-do farmers and craftsmen, and the Scholtes received invitations from many places. Before they left Albany, the Dominie was officially greeted by the legislature, and writing of this later to friends in his homeland, he exclaimed, "How different from Holland! In the land of our birth branded and treated as a despised congregation, misunderstood by everyone, shoved aside, trampled upon and bruised; in the land of strangers and, above all, in its respectable part honored and treated as a gift of God to improve their country!"

In New York City and its environs the Dominie was able to accept but a few of the invitations extended to him to preach before Dutch Reformed congregations, whose sympathies were with the Separatists rather than with the official church in The Netherlands. It was clear that he could easily get a permanent pulpit in the civilized East, where Mareah would be happy.

But the man was essentially a pioneer, conscious of his duty to the Colony, which, he felt, might scatter into directionless ways without his continued leadership. Newspapers had emphasized that these immigrants had gold, and Scholte was deluged with offers of free land accompanied by all manner of transparent schemes. "Sharks" approached him, some of Hollander origin or descent. He knew that individually many in the Colony would be ready prey for them.

But where to take the group? The Hollanders who had gone to Michigan urged him to join them, but Scholte decided against that. The part of Michigan where Dominie Van Raalte had taken his people was said to be thickly wooded and cold in winter. Scholte wanted a level, unwooded country, like Holland, with a moderate climate.

He went to Washington and, calling at the Land Office, "I found the higher Government officials," as he wrote subsequently, "so ready and willing to help me in every way that I could hardly trust my own experience, and I was involuntarily driven to compare them with the officials in Holland—a comparison which did not redound to the credit of the latter country. Not only did I not encounter any gruffness, not only was no greedy hand extended, but I found the greatest modesty and willingness in answering my questions . . . Printed documents were given me free, while a few days later a set of maps of the various States indicating the unsold Government lands was sent to me at New York, also without cost."

Scholte decided to take his people west. What little he knew of Iowa appealed to him.

Finally the four ships arrived in Baltimore: the first late in May, the last early in June. The crossing had taken between six and seven weeks, and the ships had gone through storms and dead calms. Each had a leader, trained by Scholte, who was in charge of maintaining order and discipline as well as education and religious life aboard. Education included the history, customs, and government of the United States. The number of passengers on each vessel was about two hundred. Two adults and eight children died during the voyage, most of them from injuries suffered during a storm; a half-dozen babies were born. When the vessels were put into the customary two-week quarantine, the English captain of one of them said, laughing, to the health officers, "You might as well let these people right in. There can be no disease among them. All the way over they prayed and scrubbed. My ship's never been so clean since she was new."

More publicity followed, stressing again the chests of gold, and more "sharks" came swarming about the Colony. But none of the immigrants were rooked. They did nothing without consulting Scholte or one of the subleaders.

Now arose the problem of transporting the Colony. The distances in America were enormous. There was a railroad from Baltimore over the Cumberlands to the Pennsylvania Canal, so Scholte got his multitude into several trains; then onto canal boats so squalid that even these Dutch immigrants could not make them clean, partly because they were "packed like herrings"; then onto the Ohio River steamboats, only slightly better in cleanliness and accommodations . . . and on up the Mississippi to St. Louis. The distance by these inland waterways was a thousand miles. The trip took nearly a month. Several more people died and a few more children were born—the first American citizens in the group.

Mareah was ill most of the way. She kept asking, "Where is Pella, Dominie?"

"Be patient, *Kind*; have faith."

St. Louis was a booming frontier town of thirty thousand. A few of the local Dutch Americans banded themselves into a reception committee and hastily put up barracks for the travelers. The Colony planned to stay there for at least two months, till Dominie Scholte found their Pella or the site for it in Iowa, or God knew where, and a way of getting them to it. The transportation facilities westward from St. Louis were even worse than from Baltimore to St. Louis.

Scholte left Mareah and the girls with the Colony in St. Louis, where the young woman suffered agonies at the endless signs of crudeness and lack of formal culture and elegance. Then he and four of his closest collaborators in the adventure rode horseback for a full month over the prairie, following buffalo tracks and Indian trails . . . till they finally found the location that appealed to them.

It was between the Des Moines and the Skunk rivers, a stretch of largely virgin earth, where the grass grew above a man's waist and only a few trees stood here and there. In places the rich black topsoil was two feet deep. As a start, Scholte purchased eighteen thousand acres at the government price of $1.25 an acre. To acquire so much land all in one piece, it was necessary to buy scores of claims of American settlers who had preceded him there.

The tract was to be divided among the colonists. Near the middle of it, on a slight rise of ground, stood a cabin inhabited by a settler, whose title was bought.

Close by were Indian dwellings. Scholte picked this as the center of the site of the new town. He printed the word PELLA on a board, and fastened it to a tree trunk near the hut. Then he engaged a number of American settlers who claimed to be competent rough carpenters to procure lumber and erect temporary houses and barracks . . . and he and his four companions started back for St. Louis.

v

"Have you found Pella, Dominie?"

"Yes, *Kind,* I found Pella," he replied, his heart sinking at the thought of her reaction to the extreme primitiveness of her new home. He did not expect the buildings he had ordered put up to be anything better than sheds. But he did not tell her this. The cultured European in him sympathized with her; the pioneer in him, however, relished the thought of taking the Colony to the spot he had selected, and building a town. He dried Mareah's tears and bade her again to have faith and be brave.

From St. Louis the Colony went by steamboat up the Mississippi to Keokuk, "The Gate City of Iowa." The journey took two days.

In Keokuk they were surrounded by crowds of curious and well-meaning folk and more "sharks" interested in the gold in those black iron chests with the heavy locks over which a score of husky Hollanders stood constant guard. A downpour of several days depressed the immigrants, but Scholte and his lieutenants went about purchasing wagons, horses, oxen, food, tools, and other supplies.

The Colony then plunged into the roadless prairie, which but ten years earlier was almost the exclusive domain of Indians and the buffalo. The oldest white settlers, nearly all old-stock Americans from New Jersey, had been there only six years, and settlements, whose primitive appearance brought fresh tears to Mareah's eyes, were small, few and far between.

Iowa had just become a State.

For one hundred and twenty miles the soft, yielding earth muffled the rumble of the Hollanders' wagons and their horses' hoofbeats. The axles and sideboards squeaked under the weight of chests, barrels, bundles and strongboxes on top of which perched children and women. Some of the men rode horseback beside the wagons, others walked. The tall grass swished about them.

To the Americans along the way, the caravan was a strange sight, a subject for talk years afterwards. The immigrants still wore their Hollander costumes, including wooden shoes; and all were incredibly neat and clean. The men doffed their caps in greeting; the women, with their pert white Dutch caps, nodded and smiled, and the children shrieked with excitement or wailed in discomfort.

The time was late in August, 1847, and the sun pressed down with its great purpose; only an occasional breeze stirred the grass, causing the prairie to leap into life with a vivid beauty that lifted even Mareah's low spirit.

On the fifth day Scholte said to Mareah, "Tomorrow we will be in Pella, *Kind*."

Next morning, before the caravan continued, Mareah had Dirke open the wardrobe trunks, and she and her foster daughters donned the finest Parisian garments and bonnets they owned, all of silk and lace, with flowing ribbons. Later in the day, as the Colony neared its destination, the onlookers by the way gasped at the loveliness and elegance atop the chests of one of the leading wagons. Approaching the location late in the afternoon, the Colony began to sing psalms—the only songs recognized by the Scholte branch of the Separatist movement.

Then, suddenly, as they saw the Dominie's crude sign, their spirits wilted. On the high ground, which was to be the center of the new town, still stood only the lone pioneer hut, with the few Indian tepees a stone's throw away. There were no new shelters the Dominie had hired the American settlers to build for his people.

So *this* was their Pella! A number of women sobbed; Mareah, in her Parisian finery, among them.

The American settlers, whose claims the Dominie had bought, appeared, explaining they had not expected the Colony so soon; they had been busy getting in some of the crops and preparing to clear out, and they were plumb sorry they hadn't put up the shelters. They helped the weary Hollanders to unload. . . . Then it was night.

Deferring to Scholte as their leader, the Colony gave his family the little pioneer cabin. As Mareah entered it, she was still sobbing, ashamed of herself for it, but unable to bring her grief under control. As a defiance to this primitiveness that had engulfed her, she ordered the servants to open the silverware chest and the barrel containing her china. The food they had was scant and crude, but she meant to have the first meal in this horizonless wilderness on Delft plates! And now fell the hardest blow: every piece but six plates of the exquisite set was broken!

Mareah stopped sobbing. She ordered the pieces put back into the barrel, to be saved. She took hold of herself . . . and kept hold of herself the rest of her life in America, until her death fifty years later. She never became a pioneer woman, never reconciled herself to her fate, but she put up with it, always maintaining a dignity toward it and everything and everyone in her new environment. A lady——

VI

The Dominie did not learn about the china till the next day. He was now in his element as a pioneer and leader, in the full grip of his *belief*. There was work to do. The old settlers had hogs, cattle, chickens, potatoes, grain and winter hay for sale, and with other men he spent most of that first night and next day buying supplies.

Then it was Sunday and, conducting an outdoor service, he preached a long, impassioned sermon, the substance of which was: In God is our hope and refuge. Here we will make our Pella. . . . The first sentence had been adopted in Holland as the motto of the Colony; it now became the motto of the new community.

On a sheet of paper Scholte drew a plan for the town, naming the streets Independence, Liberty, Peace, Inquiry, Perseverance, Reformation, Gratitude, Experience, Patience, Confidence, Expectation, Accomplishment—virtues which the Christian, the Separatist, the Hollander, the future American in him deemed important. Without much squabbling, the land was divided. By general consent Scholte took one of the best tracts, on the north side of the future square.

Thus Pella got underway.

It was too late to plant anything that year. Most of the energy that first fall and winter went into erecting temporary shelters and into hog raising. Some of the families, especially the less well-to-do, made dugouts or sod houses, then common among the American settlers in southern Iowa and in adjacent Nebraska.

The Dominie put up a church, which was to be unaffiliated with any organized church or sect as long as it stood. And he built a large house on the square, a half stone's-throw from the original settler's hut. When it was finished, Mareah asked him to pave the path from the hut to the new dwelling with the broken pieces of the Delft china! . . .

The Hollanders' first winter in Iowa was unusually mild, and by the spring of 1848 Pella began to look something more tangible than an idea. Scholte started a bank and brokerage, a newspaper called *The Gazette* ("Independent in Everything"), a lime and brick kiln, a sawmill. He became the local land agent and the notary. He was the town's leading citizen from its inception to his death, twenty-five years later; a man of God and a man of property fused into a personality with a touch of greatness.

To help the town achieve a self-continuing civil government in accordance with the American democratic setup, and so they might be able to vote in local elections before becoming full-fledged citizens under the naturalization laws, Scholte secured permission from the government to have the male adults, about two hundred of them, publicly declare void their allegiance to the King of The Netherlands and swear their loyalty to the United States. The ceremony was conducted in the language of Holland. Most of the men, as they assembled in the square, still wore their Dutch caps, velvet jackets, and wooden shoes. One American eyewitness of this proceeding reported in the Burlington (Iowa) *Hawk-Eye*: ". . . All appeared to feel the weight of responsibility they were about to assume. No tribute could be more beautiful or complimentary to our institutions than to behold the men of Pella coming up in their strength, on the Prairies of America, and there . . . with brawny arms upraised to heaven . . . eschewing forever all allegiance to the tyranny of king-craft."

That first winter the Pella farmers produced beyond their needs and sold twenty-five thousand pounds of ham and bacon and five thousand pounds of lard. They began to make a sausage common in Holland, which soon became known in the Middle West as the Pella Bologna.

In '48 Iowa soil was deeply responsive to the Hollanders' toil, the crops were good, the animals fat and sleek. The ensuing winter, however, was extremely severe, with the temperature ten below for nearly a month, and the people of Pella, having assumed the previous year that Iowa winters were regularly mild, were unprepared for it. Several children and a few adults died, along with scores of cattle and horses which had been inadequately sheltered.

Spring brought heavy floods, but the '49 crop was abundant; and just as the Hollanders were worrying how they might get their surplus products to Keokuk and St. Louis, along came the California Gold Rush. Groups of men rushed right through Pella, eager to pay any price for food supplies to last them through the wilderness ahead. Only a few Pella-ites joined the rush.

The next few years brought other ups and downs, including an unaccountable outbreak of cholera and a locust invasion. By the mid-fifties, however, Pella was upon a firm economic basis. Old-stock American pioneers began to settle in and near Pella, while every year a few hundred new immigrants from Holland, who had heard of the good fortune of Dominie Scholte's original colonists, came over. And with the laying of roads, which were soon followed by railways, Pella became the center of a large and prosperous farming region.

As the immigrants started taking out their citizenship papers, Scholte developed into a man of consequence in Iowa politics. In 1860 he went to the Republican National Convention and took a hand in nominating Lincoln, with whom he later became personal friends, visiting him frequently in Washington. During the Civil War many Hollanders from Iowa served in the Union Army, and when word reached Pella that Lincoln had been assassinated, Scholte, then in his early sixties, suffered a heart attack . . . and was never again entirely well.

He died a few years later.

Shortly before his end, he received a letter from King William II of Holland, apologizing in effect for the attitude of his predecessor, William I, toward him and his people, and explicitly inviting him and them to return to The Netherlands, where they would be guaranteed liberty. Hendrik Peter Scholte replied he was sorry, but obliged to inform His Majesty that their return to Holland was out of the question. By now most of the emigrants were full citizens of Iowa and the United States, enjoying various degrees of prosperity, but in every case the degree was higher than they had known in their native land. Former maids and manservants and poverty-ridden day laborers owned thriving farms with buildings worth thousands of dollars. They would regard with amusement any suggestion that they voluntarily give up what they had created and acquired.

VII

Mareah Scholte bore eight children. Only two attained adulthood. The early deaths of the others were chapter endings in the story of the first twenty-odd years of her life in the United States.

Pioneer America went deeply against her grain. She liked the large house the Dominie had built for her, but, all the occasional appearances to the contrary notwithstanding, she was never really at home in it. She loved nature and frequently wandered over the prairie, picking wildflowers, often running like a girl with her foster daughters. The flower she loved best was sweet mignonette because it smelled "like home in Holland." Its delicate scent made her weep, and she used it—secretly—to induce the flow of tears that relaxed her nervous system pent up by homesickness.

She loved to finger the bric-a-brac she had brought from Holland that had not broken, and often caressed the remaining Delft plates. She painted, but with little sense of release or fulfillment. Perhaps the deepest source of self-control during those early years, even more than her sense of pride and devotion to the Dominie, was her growing passion for music. She had always been an absorbed, knowing listener and a sensitive interpreter. A few years after they came to Pella the Dominie ordered the best piano procurable. It thrilled him, when he was not too occupied with his affairs, to watch her fingers on the keyboard and listen to her playing. Alone and lonely (which was most of the time), she practiced for hours. Liszt was her favorite composer. . . . But something was amiss; she could not say what. Iowa was not Holland or France, although of course there were moments, hours, entire days in her home life which were joyous, marked by laughter, form, and good conversation.

Consistent to the last, she continued to pattern most of her clothes on Paris styles. To the distress of some of the members of her husband's congregation, she cultivated her loveliness and was always the flawlessly charming lady. One day the rather straight-laced, puritanical deacons of the church called on the Dominie to complain against her in vague, awkward phrases. Finally they averred that she was too beautiful to be a preacher's wife.

The Dominie listened with a serious mien. Then he said, "I agree with you, Brethren, she *is* too beautiful to be my, or any preacher's wife. But I have her, she is my wife, alas!—what do you advise me to do with her? Shall I poison her—and if so, what sort of poison shall I use? Or would you recommend I take her down to the Skunk River and, like a good Christian, push her in?"

The deacons departed in haste.

Mareah found it amusing for the rest of her life to recall this incident.

Hendrik Peter Scholte's death plunged her into intense grief. Then came a feeling of disconnection with something terribly vital and real, which was followed by a sense of release, that led her into a state of confusion and disorientation. She was in her early forties, still beautiful, and rich. What to do with herself now? The thought of returning to Holland or to her "dear Paris" occurred to her, but she did not consider it long. Way down in her somewhere, despite all the disappointments, she had become strangely attached to America. Here was Pella; she had seen it begin and grow; she was part of it, it was part of her. Here all her children were born and most of them were buried. Here her three foster daughters, whom she loved, were happily married, raising their families. . . . Just now, however, she had to get away from Pella for a while, if only for a year or two; the old women's gossip as to what she might do annoyed her.

She went to Detroit, where a friend, a former Pella girl who was part of the city's musical world, had been urging her to come for a visit. The immediate purpose of the trip was to find a good music school for Dora, her exceptionally talented ten-year-old daughter, in whom she saw an extension of herself.

In Detroit—a small city in the seventies, but very much larger than Pella— Mareah Scholte found a school for Dora, associated with the local musicians, began to play the piano in a small orchestra organized by her friend's husband, and generally lived an interesting, satisfying year.

She was obliged to decline several proposals of marriage.

In school little Dora made a special friend of one of her teachers, Robert Beard, a young man in his twenties, who had given up business and professional baseball to become a musician. He was always attentive to both the little girl and her beautiful mother, whose passion for music matched his own.

Suddenly, Dora took ill. Recovering slightly, she wanted to "get well in my own room back home in Pella" and insisted that Bob Beard come with them. Almost immediately on reaching Pella the girl died, and her death threw Mareah into despondency. Everyone tried vainly to console her. Finally Bob and music succeeded. He stayed on in Pella, then begged her to marry him. . . . After some hesitation, she did; whereupon the old women's tongues of Pella wagged, but not forever. The town commenced to respect her individuality if not to understand her.

Sometime after her marriage to Bob Beard, her first-born, Henry Peter, married an old-stock American girl, Leonora Keables, and they took half of the Scholte House, as it had begun to be called, while the Beards took the other half, which then resounded with music from morning to night.

Mareah and Bob Beard were a happy couple for over twenty years. Except for a few die-hards, the town accepted them. Bob got along excellently with Mareah's foster daughters, their husbands and children. He became close friends with his foster son, Henry, who was older than he, and with Leonora. He and Mareah traveled considerably, attending concerts in Chicago, Philadelphia, New York and Boston.

But a good part of every year was spent in Pella. Mareah planned to go to Europe someday, but, growing old, she felt more and more that Iowa was where she belonged. "Why," she would say, "I knew this place when it was just prairie!"

She reminisced about her life in Holland after marrying Scholte, their voyage to America; their visits to Albany, New York City, Baltimore and Washington; the journey to St. Louis; the trek into Iowa. She made fun of herself; she had been a "softie," "a little goose." She spoke admiringly of pioneers who had done the hard, dirty work, and hoped that someday a book would be written about Pella. The artist in her saw the place as a dramatic story.

During the last ten years of her life Mareah became profoundly interested in the life of the town: in newlyweds, in new houses and newborn babies. She liked to talk to the latest immigrants from Holland, to help them. She was particularly tender to the young women who seemed homesick for Holland. She took a hand in civic matters and was liberal with her money. Her one-time maid Dirke had married a man who now owned a farm several miles outside Pella, and Mareah often drove out to see her and take her things. Returning from her New York and Chicago trips, she would bring gifts for dozens of people, and sometime half sigh, half exclaim that it was good to be back home among her own. The children of her son Henry were a particular source of joy to her. . . .

Then one day in 1892, returning from a walk, during which she had looked very young and spry in her silk dress, she collapsed. Just before the end her mind reverted to her unhappy earlier years in Iowa, and her last words, spoken to her friend and daughter-in-law Leonora, were, "I am dying a stranger in a strange land."

VIII

Pella now is a quiet prosperous community, the economic and religious-cultural center of a Hollander-inhabited farming area twenty-odd miles around it. The descendants of the Scholte group are third- and fourth-generation Americans, but—in common with the immigrants, who came here in the last fifty years, and the second generation—most of them still refer to themselves as Hollanders, distinguishing themselves from the "Americans," and speak Dutch in addition to English.

But there can be no question as to their loyalty to the United States. Hundreds of them, immigrants and American-born, were United States soldiers in the First World War. They are a bit clannish, however, and many who live on the farms drive to Pella for their supplies even if Oskaloosa or Des Moines are nearer. In the Pella stores they can get things which are "Hollander": sausages, smoked beef, rusks, Sint Nicolaas cookies, cheeses (imported and domestic), and wooden shoes. Except for festive occasions, when they don Dutch costumes, all wear "American" clothes, but some still like wooden shoes for work in the garden and fields.

The original Scholte church is gone; so is Separatism. The separation of state and church and religious liberty being actualities in the United States, that cause waned even in the Dominie's lifetime. Now most of the Hollanders are back in the Reformed Dutch Church, which owns the local Central College, a liberal-arts institution.

Religion is taken seriously in and around Pella. Sundays everything is closed but one drugstore (they take turns staying open), and two or three gasoline stations. There are no Sunday movies; in fact, the one movie theater barely exists. A good many people spend the better part of their Sundays in Pella's numerous churches, praying, listening to sermons, and singing psalms. There are evening services on weekdays. Religion is the center of the culture of the town and region. In many families the Bible is read through aloud every year. Reformation still hangs heavy over the psychological make-up of the people.

The Pella-ites are a very definite people. "Americans" of the old-stock Anglo-Saxon, German, Czech, and mixed strains occasionally get annoyed with their overfirm conservatism which reveals itself in their politics as well as in their reluctance to adopt modern farm and housekeeping methods. Perhaps they are a bit phlegmatic. But there is a great stability in their lives, in Pella as a community, which some of the non-Hollanders in town find pleasant, reassuring. Vernon Bobbitt, one of the old-stock American teachers at Central College, told me he would rather live in Pella than anywhere else. Life there has "a quiet, slow rhythm, a definite charm."

The great majority of Hollanders in and about Pella are solid people, hard-working, independent, self-reliant, constructive, proud. The Depression, of course, hit Pella, but there was no urgent relief problem. In town nearly every family lives in a home of its own with a flower and vegetable garden about it; outside the town the Hollander farms compare favorably with those of the non-Hollanders. In fact, like the Poles and the Finns of New England, the Hollanders of Iowa are making a success of farms once given up by old-stock American pioneers as failures. They, including the womenfolk, are willing to work harder.

Dutch cleanliness is no mere phrase in Pella.

The town has a "dank-hole," which is supposed to be the jail, but it is used almost exclusively as a hostel for itinerant hoboes. Most townspeople when parking their cars in the square do not bother to take out their ignition keys. A Hollander's word is his bond. The Des Moines department stores require no references from Pella folk who want to charge their purchases. In Pella itself much of the business is done on credit. Every quarter they ask one another, "How much do I owe you? How much do you owe me?"—then they subtract and one of them pays the other the difference. The Pella Dutch Americans are not great go-getters; money, to them, is not the most valuable thing in the world.

IX

The Pella Historical Society is promoting the movement to help keep the young generation of the town and its vicinity spiritually linked to the tradition and morality of their parents, grandparents and great-grandparents who came from Holland. The Society maintains a museum and sponsors the annual three-day Tulip Festival in mid-May, which had startled the suddenly awakened salesman. Improving annually as a show, the festival is attracting more and more people from increasingly distant sections of the country.

Next to the churches, the Scholte House is the most prominent place in town. There the eighty-one-year-old Mrs. Leonora Scholte sits in a chair in the middle of the old parlor, a cane by her side, and receives and talks to all who come, inviting them to go into the Dominie's room or to any other room they wish and see what is there to see, then come back and ask her questions. She is one of the old-stock Anglo-Saxon Americans who have become "Hollandized." When she says "we," she means "we Hollanders in Pella." She is identified with the group. She loves to tell the tales that make up the history of Pella. The house is a veritable museum of things associated with the beginnings of the community, and Mrs. Scholte knows the history and significance of each object. Two of the six Delft plates that did not break are still there, and the Dominie's books, pipes, snuffboxes, inkwells, quills, notebooks and boxes of documents, awaiting a biographer.

Every forenoon at ten Mrs. Scholte serves coffee to whoever drops in; this is a Hollander custom. Sundays she serves supper to all comers; there usually is a crowd. There was when I was there in the summer of 1939.

"Mother," as she calls the late Mareah, is the favorite subject of the present mistress of the Scholte House. But others in town still talk about her, too; perhaps because she was so untypical of the group. She is brought into nearly all accounts of "the old days." Because she was different and apart, her life—almost more than the Dominie's—lights up the story of Pella in the consciousness of the community.

X

Mrs. Leonora Scholte invited me to come to the 1940 Tulip Festival. Unfortunately, I could not go. Instead, I wrote my friend Vernon Bobbitt to send me a report of the event. He replied:

"On Friday, May the tenth, about nine thousand people crowded Pella. The Des Moines paper that morning carried headlines about Germany's invasion of Holland. No one quite believed the news. No one realized the importance of it. It was like a faint rumble of something far-off. All of us Pella-ites were busy in the streets and around the houses, doing our bits in the *Tulpen Feest* program.

"In the afternoon some of the people became very much upset, especially those who have relatives in Holland. Some cried. Many could not sing the gay, jolly songs they had rehearsed for weeks.

"At three o'clock the residents and visitors gathered before the *Tulp Toren* [Tulip Tower] in the town square and bowed their heads while the organ played *Wien Neerlandsbloed*, the Dutch anthem. I glanced up and saw tears running down many faces. A deep seriousness held the crowd as one of the local ministers read the cablegram which had just been sent to Queen Wilhelmina: 'Tulip Time festivities of people of Pella commemorating their Holland ancestry profoundly saddened by crisis in our mother country. You have our deepest sympathy and our prayers for Divine guidance in this trial.' The scene was poignant.

"At the evening program two hundred citizens in Dutch costume enacted the scene of the original immigrants renouncing their allegiance to Holland and swearing their loyalty to the United States ninety-three years ago. As they went on their knees at the base of the *Tulp Toren*, a large American flag was unfurled to superimpose the flag of Holland . . . At the close of the ceremony we all sang 'America.'

"For a few days after the Festival there was not much talk about the war, although it was rapidly becoming the major concern of everyone. Many now feel that Wilhelmina did right in relinquishing her power to save bloodshed and property; that Holland wasn't strong enough to withstand the power of Nazi Germany, and that it would have been folly to try to resist. The Hollanders are not a demonstrative people, so it is hard sometimes to tell what they are thinking, but I believe down in their hearts they hold a hatred for what Nazism represents. There are a few, however, who have tried to rationalize and say, 'What will be will be.' These are being severely criticized in the community.

"Last winter we in Pella prided ourselves on the fact that the war had not become an issue in the conversation of the people. We were neutral. The war was none of our business. That is gone now.

"Yesterday I asked a laborer here, who has sisters and brothers in Holland, if he thought the United States should try to rescue the fallen countries in Europe. He said no; he had come to America to get away from war and had no desire to go back. Another man dislikes the British 'economic dictatorship over the Continent and the colonial world' so much that he is disposed to try German domination for a while, although he has no love for the Nazis and their methods. He is rather confused; but England generally has few friends in Pella . . . Any number of young men, however, say they would volunteer to help the cause of democracy if that could be done. They, too, are confused. But there is no one in town who is not for preserving and continuing the American way of life, and most of them know what they mean by that phrase even if they have difficulty in expressing themselves. How could they help knowing? After all, the American way permeates the history and life of Pella. . . ."

A YOUNG AMERICAN
WITH A JAPANESE FACE

They lurk upon thy shores, California!
They watch behind thy doors, California!
They're a hundred thousand strong,
And they won't be hiding long;
There's nothing that the dastards would not dare!
They are soldiers to a man, with schemes of Old Japan.
Look out, California! Beware!

Chorus in *Anti-Japanese Hymn of Hate*, popularized by certain California and Eastern newspapers in 1916 and thereabouts.

Without hesitation we join the ranks of those who argue that the Japanese can be assimilated, and the more thoroughly we study the situation, the more powerful is the conviction that the debate about the Japanese would cease to be a debate at all if only all who argue against them could come into personal contact with the second generation of young men and women.

—PAUL B. WATERHOUSE, *Can the Japanese Be Assimilated?* (1924)

He Begins
His Story

I AM an American whose story in this country begins on Angel Island, here in the Bay of San Francisco. Before that, of course, my background is Oriental: Japanese. My parents arrived in the United States during the period of the great Oriental influx between 1890 and 1924.

[*He was twenty-three, five feet five, compactly built, and neatly, inexpensively dressed. His full round face was Japanese, but more expressive than are generally the faces of Japanese born and raised in Japan. . . . He had written me some months before I visited San Francisco: he wanted to tell me what it meant to be an American with a Japanese face. Now, late in April, 1940, he sat in my hotel room.*]

In 1923 earthquake and fire destroyed an ancient temple near Tokio, and with it the complete genealogical record of my maternal ancestors for the last eight hundred years. I have no feeling of loss there . . . yet lately this long ancestry does hold an interest for me.

During these eight centuries my mother's family lived in and around Tokio. They were, and still are, of the higher and wealthier middle class. There were generals, an admiral or two, ministers in the government, ambassadors, an artist, a writer of verse, and, I do not doubt, knaves of all species.

My maternal grandmother, now past her middle nineties, was nine when Commodore Perry "opened the doors of Japan"; my mother was her youngest child. I have an uncle who owns a bus line running out of Tokio; an aunt with a coffee plantation in Java; several other aunts and uncles about whom I have no definite information; and dozens of cousins, the older of whom are attending universities and academies, or are fighting in the China "incident."

To me, they are so many characters in a misty, faraway fairy tale, and I have no feeling for any of them, except for a cousin, a boy two or three years my junior, whom I dislike . . . although, on second thought, "dislike" is not really the word. Not long ago he wrote to us from his naval training station and said he was getting ready for the day when the mighty Navy of Nippon would repulse the attack of the American Navy. He wrote in English (as practice, I suppose, for as a future officer he is required to study the language), and my first reaction on reading the letter was that the punk had a hell of a nerve making a crack like that. I had a good mind to write him the United States Navy had no intention of attacking Japan; and, furthermore, if it ever came to any kind of a showdown between the two navies I had not the least doubt of its outcome. Then I decided it would be silly to write to him; he was a victim of the dogmatic nationalistic "education," the poison that was being pumped into him, and had no chance of knowing differently. I guess I pity more than dislike him. He sent a snapshot of himself—a good-looking boy, and I imagine he is not a bad fellow generally. Perhaps all he wants is the chance to live and do and be something—like most of us.

II

My father's line winds among the islands off South Japan. His people were mostly of the merchant class, and as such despised before the beginning of modernization in the 1860's. For that reason they probably did not think so much of themselves, but I imagine a record of his ancestry exists—or existed —somewhere, too.

He ran away from home at thirteen, and went to sea as a cabin boy. Later he became the ship's cook, and, it appears, a good one. His independence and wanderlust were infringements on the family tradition, and resulted in his father's disowning him. After nine years of sailing to various ports of the world he reached California. This was in 1900; he was twenty-two. He quit the sea, and started on a short career as a transient agricultural laborer, working in fruits, nuts, and vegetables up and down the State.

In 1904 he struck up a friendship with another Japanese immigrant, the black sheep of a Tokio family . . . and the two of them joined the United States Navy. They were not American citizens, although Japanese could yet, though not easily, be naturalized at that time; the Navy was still accepting recruits who were aliens, including a small quota of Orientals.

My father knew very little English, but soon after joining the Navy became chief cook on the gunboat *Bennington*, which blew up in San Diego Harbor in 1905. Sixty-five men and officers were killed. My father saved several men and came out of the disaster a sort of hero. One of the rescued was a high-ranking officer. He praised my father and promised him a citation, but died of burns before anything was done about it. Some of the other men were cited for bravery, but my father's act—due, perhaps, to an oversight or some confusion—never was officially recognized. This made him angry at the Navy. He was transferred to another ship, on which they also made him a cook— I think in the officers' galley; but when his hitch was up, he did not re-enlist.

My father had another claim to fame during his naval service. Owing to his Judo training before he came to America, he was for a time a wrestling champion; whether of the fleet or only of his ship, I am not sure.

Out of the Navy, my father worked for a few years as a fisherman, farm laborer, section hand, and lumber-mill worker. Finally he took a course in a tonsorial college in San Francisco, then proceeded to establish himself as a barber with a shop of his own in one of the communities across the bay.

He chose this particular town because no other Japanese lived there then (he had difficulty in getting along with most of his co-nationals) and, also, because a naval station and naval anchorages were close by. He figured that as an ex-Navy man with a reputation as a wrestler and hero he could get the sailors to patronize his shop. He opened it in a little two-room lean-to building near the Navy landing. At the station he had friends who helped him distribute his business cards and advertising leaflets.

His Japanese friend from Tokio had re-enlisted and, serving on a ship based in San Francisco Bay, also aided him in getting patrons. He showed him a picture of his sister, and told him about her. They engaged a go-between in Tokio to arrange matters . . . and in 1913, after he had made a start as a barber, my father returned to Japan to marry.

My mother did not see him, nor even a picture of him, till the day of the wedding; in fact, did not know she was to be married until a week before. She was twenty-one, and a sort of reservist or supernumerary lady-in-waiting to the Empress Dowager. This is a nominal honor for the daughters of the "better" families; she never saw the old Empress.

Although they were married in Japan, my mother entered the United States as a picture bride. This was either the only or the easiest way for her to get in. They remarried in San Francisco, whence he took her across the bay to his barbershop. He had furnished the other room, in back of the shop, as their living quarters, while the tiny back porch was boarded up and converted into a kitchen.

My mother and her parents were under the impression that my father was a rich business man in California. It was a shock to her to discover that he was only a barber—a low trade; in Japan, I believe, only women are barbers. But she had no way of backing out without upsetting her family in Tokio. Besides, her brother, the American gob, talked to her to the effect that her husband was a man with no inconsiderable future before him: was not his shop full of sailors all the time? He argued that America was not Japan; here a barber was as good as a banker. So my mother resigned herself to the situation.

In 1915 the first baby came: a girl. The eighth and last child arrived in 1932. I was number two, the first son, born in 1917.

III

During and right after the First World War, our family was well-off. The naval station teemed with sailors, and in 1919 or '20 my father was worth something like fifteen or twenty thousand dollars. Also, we had acquired ownership of the little building where we lived and my father had his shop. As Oriental aliens, our parents could not own property in California; so, with the aid of a Japanese lawyer in San Francisco, the deed was made out in the name of my oldest sister.

My father always used to drink and gamble a bit; now, suddenly, a year or so after the war, something hit him and he commenced to devote himself wholeheartedly to liquor, cards and dice, to the frequent exclusion of almost everything else, and to the general embarrassment and agony of his family. There were great blackjack and crap games on paydays at the station and along the water front in town, and a few times my father won considerable sums. Then he felt the compulsion to celebrate, and his shop was closed for days at a stretch.

To the Japanese intemperance is no vice. The trouble is that they are poor drinkers (such, at least, has been my observation), and my father was no exception. In back of his mind, I suspect, was the idea that drinking with the sailors of the United States Navy made him an American, which he could not become officially under the 1906 discriminatory provision of the naturalization law barring Orientals from citizenship. He was a curious mixture of pro-American, anti-Japanese and pro-Japanese sentiments and attitudes; a mixture which changed with the winds and the years. At this time, immediately after the war, he was very pro-American and, by virtue of his association with the bluejackets, if nothing else, considered himself superior to other Japanese in the United States.

The money he had accumulated barbering and gambling during and right after the war soon went. But he continued to drink heavily till about five years ago, when advanced age, spurred on by a serious operation, caused him abruptly to reform. He is now in his sixties, and a teetotaler.

When our family was in comfortable economic circumstances, between my third and sixth years, we used to eat mostly Japanese foods, which, since they were nearly all imported, cost more—contrary to popular belief—than even the best American foods. These delicacies were ordered in quantities from a Japanese importer in Oakland. Perhaps the only cheap item in the diet was rice, grown in California. In those days, too, my father drank *sake*, smuggled off Japanese ships entering the bay, which was also expensive. (Personally, I don't see how anyone can drink the stuff; it tastes like ether.)

Then, with the money gone, we settled down to the living standards of other immigrant families around us, Italians and Portuguese, Filipinos and Mexicans; although I believe we always lived a little better than did the majority of Mexicans, with their eternal chile, tortillas, and beans. As we grew poorer, we ate mostly American foods, with increasingly fewer Japanese items. We children gave up chopsticks; our parents continued to use them, even when eating macaroni, hamburgers, or oatmeal.

The room in back of the shop was big enough for my father and mother, but as the children began to arrive the situation became serious. Extra beds had to be installed . . . and now there are three beds in the combined living-room, dining-room, and bedroom. When the population reached peak, nine persons slept in that one room.

Saturday nights pots of water were heated on the little kitchen stove. The big round wooden tubs were brought in from the back yard and filled with steaming water. Father was first to undress and get in. He soaped and scrubbed himself for fifteen minutes or more. Then my oldest sister went in with him, and he soaped and scrubbed her; and so on down the line till all of us had bathed. We rinsed ourselves in the other tub and on our final emergence looked like boiled lobsters. Mother was last; she took her bath alone after we were all in bed.

Since the Japanese have no "funny" sex ideas, all of us undressed and bathed and moved naked about the room in full view of one another. My parents, however, are more "Americanized" now; they let the younger children who are still at home take their baths in privacy, behind a curtain which Mother rigs up for the purpose. . . . Now only six people, my parents and four younger children, inhabit the tiny place; the four oldest of us are away from home. . . .

As for clothing, we all wore Western clothes. The only Japanese articles were the house slippers. None of us has any Japanese costumes, except Mother —her wedding dress, a lovely, if a little faded, kimono decorated with Japanese designs or symbols. My father had a Japanese wedding costume, too, but he threw it into the sea on the trip from Japan, just before reaching San Francisco. He kept the wedding photograph, however, and it hangs on a wall in the room.

There are no other pictures in our home, no Japanese prints or mottoes, and definitely no picture of the Emperor or of the sacred, snow-capped Fujiyama. In his shop, on the shelf above the stack of towels, behind the gas water heater, my father has a little statue of Buddha.

Father
and Son

IN MY early boyhood, when my father had a little too much to drink but not enough for stupor or sleep to overcome him, he often turned mean and sometimes violent. My mother was a type of Japanese beauty, and he was extremely jealous of her. Sometimes he would get it into his head that she must not go out of the house alone, even for a walk around the block or to the store. As a gob, sowing his wild oats in Manila, Honolulu, Panama City and Barbary Coast, he acquired the theory that all white women were bad; now he was determined that his wife must not come in contact with any of them or any of his sailor friends. His jealousy carried him so far that he resented the children getting more attention from her than he did. Even though the marriage had been arranged, he did love her—in a fashion.

No doubt it bothered him, too, that my mother was of a higher social class than he, and that he had deceived her parents as to his standing in America. To keep her, he probably felt he must terrorize her; and to do that, he had to drink.

On her side, living in a strange land, in a town with no other Japanese, my mother did the best she could, mostly by obeying him. She is a tiny person, weighing less than a hundred pounds, but there is something in her one could call strength, discipline, Oriental fatalism, womanly endurance. I don't know what it is; perhaps a mingling of all these qualities.

But to be fair to my father, he also had his nice moods and attitudes, and was capable of great tenderness toward my mother.

II

Up to 1924, when I became seven, I was just one of several children in the house; outside our home, I was just another "foreign" child, an offspring of "that Jap barber." When I began to go to the American public school, I knew almost no English.

The second or third day in my educational career, the teacher came home with me and tried to discuss my language problem with my mother, who could not understand what she wanted. My mother called my father, who was working on a customer in the shop. When he came in, the teacher was seated in a chair, her eyes surveying with anything but approval the tight, crowded scene about her, while my mother and I stood apprehensively near her. The teacher tried to explain to my father what had brought her to the house, but he, too, had difficulty in understanding her. Finally he nodded a few times and bowed Japanese-like, and she left.

For some reason, this incident caught my father in a tender spot and touched off in him something that made things hard for me thereafter.

My oldest sister, also, had known no English when she started school the year before, but had, somehow, gotten by. She was a self-effacing little girl, and I suppose the teachers did not notice her until after she had picked up a bit of English. So now, finishing with his customer, the old man poured himself a tall drink of bootleg and, after a long silence during which he kept looking at me, demanded to know why the school woman had not come with my sister but had had to bring me home. Of what worth was I, anyhow?

My mother coming to my defense only made matters worse. I was no good, he declared, because she sheltered and pampered me; and, mocking her upper-class status in Japan, he wondered what one could expect from her kind, anyhow. He drank some more, and tried to talk English, then continued in Japanese, for, as he explained, we were too dumb to understand him in English, which he implied was a superior language. He raved about how humiliating the incident was. That an American teacher should come to his house to complain about the stupidity of his son—and his first son, at that! How would he ever live this down! . . . Another swig from the gallon. . . . Then, flying into high rage, he kicked me across the floor between the beds.

I mentioned that my father was a conglomerate of conflicting attitudes toward America and Japan. Sober, or when but slightly ossified, he had mo-ments—brief, it is true, and infrequent, but still noticeable—when he spoke derisively of Japan, the Japanese, and their customs and traditions, and worked himself into a nihilistic mood in which he wavered uncertainly, but very vocally and emphatically, between two worlds, Asia and America. One day years later, when he was in this frame of mind, my second-oldest sister over-heard him burst out contemptuously, "Japs, goddamn' Japs!—Japs, goddamn' Japs!—" repeating these words over and over, in English. . . .

Now, however, as I whimpered picking myself up after he had kicked me, his rage turned into sadistic passion, and he seized me. I was a disgrace to the race of Nippon! I was not his son, but only my mother's; and she was of the good-for-nothing upper classes. I was unfit to be his heir. He was a hero, he was; hadn't he saved ever so many Americans in the *Bennington* disaster? His Japanese blood had made him courageous. I had no manly Japanese virtue of any sort! In an attempt to remedy this lack, he hung me by the feet to the two-by-six rafters that cut the ceiling of the room in half, and whipped me with an old razor strop. I hung there, head down, for five or ten minutes; it seemed ages. My mother could do nothing. Huddling in a corner with the other children, she probably prayed to her ancestors.

This turned out to be the inception of my service as the object of my father's suddenly awakened sadism, which I imagine was mixed up, somehow, with his being a Japanese, an Oriental immigrant in America who was confused and ill at ease here; a victim of his own inadequacies, of his social inferiority in reference to his wife, of his jealousy and other undefined passions, of the looks of his face. I dimly recall that one day sometime before the beginning of this unhappy period I caught him posed before the mirror in his shop, pulling at the skin around his eyes this way and that, as if trying to straighten them, experimenting how he might look as a Caucasian. It may be, too, that the furious anti-Japan propaganda then at its height in this country, and especially the cartoons showing the Japanese as monsters and ogres, had something to do with it all. Years later I heard that some of the gobs at the naval station, who did not like him, gabbed irresponsibly, mostly in a "kidding" way, that he was a spy. This must have played havoc with him, and mixed him up—his loyalties, instincts and attitudes—to the point of occasional near-insanity. . . . At any rate, as he would drink oftener and more heavily, he would pinch my forearms with a pair of rusty old pliers to determine if I could take it without whimpering. I lacked the necessary Japanese fortitude; and the louder I yelled, the harder he squeezed.

One day, unable to endure this any longer, my mother ran away with us children; there were four of us then, all still rather young. The poor woman had, somehow, gotten hold of a little money, and we went to Japanese Town in San Francisco. She was going to get a divorce. But even before she called on the Japanese lawyer whose advertisement she had seen in a Japanese-language paper, the fear of upsetting her kin in Japan with such an action got the best of her. After she saw him, the lawyer communicated with my father, who came to San Francisco. Sober, contrite, he begged his wife for another chance, which she granted him at once, and we all returned home.

He promised not to beat and torture me any more, but was unable to straighten out his feelings about me. In fact, his resentment of me mounted. Now he blamed me for his wife's attempt to divorce him. He never mistreated any of the other children. How to explain this? Probably it had some connection with my being his oldest son. Perhaps some atavism or tradition made him secretly expect great things from me, and those expectations were shattered by the teacher's bringing me home; which, in conjunction with other things in him, caused him to go berserk so far as I was concerned.

III

My uncle stayed in the Navy till he retired in 1924, when he went to live in Japan on his pension . . . which, incidentally, he still receives. It is considered a large sum by Japanese standards. Now a man past sixty, he is living in style and comfort in a suburb of Tokio. . . .

Before he returned to Japan, however, he came to visit us and my mother told him about the difficulty between my father and me; and, wifeless and childless, he asked the old man to give me to him in adoption. He said he would take me to Japan, give me his name and a home, and see that I was educated. I would be his son and heir. At first this idea appealed to my father.

He agreed to commit me to his brother-in-law. Good riddance. Then he changed his mind. He never explained his decision, but I suppose he did not want me to have any advantages over the other children.

So I missed being a Japanese by a hairbreadth!

But this incident suggested to my father another idea, which soon became an obsession: he would get rid of me in some other way without affording me any advantage.

With my mother's consent, I was put into what appeared to be an orphanage. I do not recall much about the place; I was just seven, and the episode connected with it is wrapped in a sort of cloud. There was a building all by itself in the country. We youngsters worked in the fields in the daytime and slept in the yard under the stars, waking up mornings under blankets heavy with dew. But not long after I got there one of the children died in the solitary-confinement room of what appeared to be mistreatment and lack of food and water. The county officers came, arrested the people in charge of the "home," which was really a scheme to exploit us kids; and we were sent wherever we had come from.

This did not alter my father's determination to get rid of me. I had been at home a few weeks, making myself as inconspicuous as possible, when he returned drunk from a speakeasy one afternoon and instructed my mother to make me presentable as quickly as she could. In a little while, he said, an American, whom he had just met again after many years, was coming to look me over with the view to adoption. This man had served with my father in the Navy, and was one of the sailors my father had saved in the *Bennington* disaster; subsequently he had put in several enlistments in the Army, mostly in the Philippines, where he had lately received his retirement and adopted a Filipino boy, of whom he was exceedingly fond, and for whom he now sought a playmate.

My prospective father was a genial and expansive man. He was also drunk. Boisterously he exclaimed I was just the pal for his little Filipino lad. He would adopt me, a son of the man who had saved his life; we would all go to court tomorrow and make it official. I would have his name; he would be my father. He gave me a silver dollar and sent my father out for more liquor.

The stuff my father brought back laid out both of them by nightfall. When the American woke up the next morning in the same bed with my father, he had a violent headache. Getting up, he emitted a terrific groan, and my oldest sister, who knew English, understood him to say that he thought he had been poisoned. He left the house before my father awakened, not to be heard of since.

When my father came to, he raged again over this new and unmistakable demonstration of my worthlessness and undesirability, but did not touch me.

Finally my mother decided that for my own protection I must be sent away once more. She communicated with the lawyer in San Francisco whom she had seen about the divorce, and asked him to find a good place for me . . .

and on a lovely California spring day in 1925, as I was going on eight, I found myself in a red touring car and on the way somewhere.

It was my first automobile ride, and I would have enjoyed it were it not for my inability to keep tears out of my eyes. I sat alone in the back seat with no idea where I was going, and terribly lonely. The driver, whom the lawyer had hired for the trip, had nothing to say to me.

After a three-hour ride, the car turned off the highway, then passed between two rows of tall eucalypti. My mother had said I was going to a beautiful place, and I knew this was it.

The automobile halted within a few yards of a great crowd of children, most of them wearing the institutional gray-blue uniform. It was the time of the day, near sundown, when the entire two hundred were lining up outside to go into the mess hall. At the sight of me, one of the boys let out a yell, calling attention to me; everybody looked, fell silent, and stared.

Many had never seen an Oriental face, or at least not one belonging to a person as young and small as I. Their stares, which were like one concentrated glare from four hundred eyes, paralyzed me with embarrassment. I could not move. One of the adults, who emerged from this sea of eyes, kept inviting me to come out of the car; then, as I did not move, lifted me out.

I lived at this institution for the next nine years.

IV

The place was for youngsters from broken homes and poor families, delinquents, stepchildren, orphans, illegitimates, and the like. For a while my mother sent, through the lawyer, small amounts of money for my keep; the rest I earned working. She never wrote to me, because when I entered the "Home," as we usually called it, I did not know how to read Japanese (I only spoke it, in a fashion) and she knew no English.

In all the nine years, I was the only child of Japanese parentage in the institution. There were several Negroes, a couple of Indians, an Egyptian, numerous Mexicans, and many orphans with nothing known about their origin, while the rest were mostly native sons and daughters of California with New England, Midwestern and various European and Near Eastern backgrounds. The superintendent called the Home a "league of nations" . . . and after that first myriad-eyed once-over (which was perfectly natural, of course) I had no serious difficulty there owing to my Japanese origin. I was completely accepted, and my long close association with these youngsters may be the main reason for my own freedom from racial and cultural prejudice.

There was a seven-hundred acre ranch about the Home, with grazing cattle, orchards, vast vegetable fields, and eucalyptus, pepper-tree and scrub-oak groves. We were in a little valley, with broad slopes all about us. Behind the large stucco-administration-and-school building were rows of wooden cottages for the children, teachers, and other employees. Over to one side were the various shops, the laundry, the power plant; a quarter of a mile away, the large cow barn, the garage and field-implement shed, and the chicken coops.

In a few days, I felt as though I had been there a long time, and began to take part in the activities of the community, which, in spite of the certain obvious and serious but unavoidable limitations of such a place, was humanly agreeable. The people in charge were sensible on the whole. They maintained discipline, but there was never any hint of cruelty or browbeating. We were considered people. The food was plain but ample. And, all in all, my boyhood there was not bad. Each of us had to work at something but we were never required to work harder or longer than the strength of our years allowed.

Of course, the place could not give that unquestioning love which children need, and in my case it could not overcome the salient fact, which overhung my thoughts and feelings like a vague threat, that I was an orphan although my parents were alive.

There were all kinds of youngsters, including a good number who were tough or "bad"; and, coming in contact with all of them, I learned—among other things—to fight for my rights as an individual. I had a good many battles, but very few on account of being a "Jap." In nine years, I was called this name not more than a dozen times, usually in extreme anger or exasperation, when my antagonist, if I may use that word, had exhausted all his other resources in trying to get at me. I was, as I say, generally accepted; for, regardless of origins, youngsters are naturally democratic when not trained or influenced by their elders to be otherwise. When I was challenged on some point or issue, all I had to do was to prove myself, my ability and worth. The thing to do was stand up and face the situation; whereupon I was all the more "O.K."

The beauty of this institution—and, in my gratitude, I can pay it no higher compliment—was that the superintendent and most of his staff made no concerted effort to turn us into angels or goody-goodies. Within certain necessary limits, those of us who were tough or "bad" were at least tentatively free to retain and practice those qualities. There was no spying or snitching, or nearly none. There was no consistent active opposition to our fighting things out "behind the butts" with our fists. We had our gangs or cliques . . . and after my thirteenth year, or thereabouts, when I had learned English so I used it as well as any of the other boys, and I had grown a bit and developed my body, I became one of the leaders.

I was hard but small and my reach was short, and I lost fights because the other fellow had longer arms, or was bigger or stronger or a more experienced boxer; but that was not important in our little world. What mattered was that I did not run away from scraps, and that, thanks to my reading vast quantities of adventure magazines, I was full of ideas for "adventures," including doings which were tacitly forbidden by the regulations. The fact that I was never caught doing anything I should not have done (which was true also of most of the others of my gang) gave me enormous prestige among the fellows;

which, in turn, was of incalculable value to me as a growing boy with my unsatisfying past.

Of course we practiced deception and tricks of all kinds to be able to "adventure" over the countryside at night while we were supposed to be asleep in our bunks; but this, I am sure, had no permanent bad effect upon me— although one or two of my boyhood friends who engaged in these doings with me are now in San Quentin. This may be the fault of their environment before they came to the institution, or to heredity; I don't know.

There were rules in the place which seemed silly to me then, and still do; such as the rule against whistling and ballplaying on Sunday. I believe the superintendent himself did not like them. They were a concession to the religious supervisor, a bitter, frustrated person, of whom he was afraid (my only serious complaint against him). I disliked this supervisor from the beginning and finally became openly antagonistic to him when he tried, fortunately in vain, to start a spy system. One day he called me a heathen and a "Jap," which, I suppose, put the finishing touch on my conditioning against organized religion. I have not entered a church of any kind since leaving the institution.

But to continue the list of its good points: sports were generally encouraged, and, off and on, we held various county championships. One boy who played on our ball team and was a minor hero in the place is a major-league rookie this year. Some of the youngsters were trained in raising beef cattle, and they won prizes at both county and State fairs. And our band was considered the best within a radius of seventy miles.

The elementary education was given us on the premises, and two of the five teachers were good. One was very patient with me at first when I still had to learn English, and continued to be helpful and stimulating right along. Those who wished to go on with their education were enrolled in the high school of the near-by town, a community of about ten thousand, and were taken there and brought back daily by bus.

I was quick in my studies, and by 1930 I completed all the schooling the institution had to offer me.

v

One day the Japanese lawyer in San Francisco who had arranged for my coming to the institution visited me unexpectedly. As soon as he appeared a rumor flew among the boys that he was my father—my "Jap father," one of them put it.

The superintendent called me to his office, then left me alone with the man, whom I dimly recalled seeing before when my mother applied for divorce. He began to talk to me in Japanese . . . and now I made a strange discovery. I did not understand a word he was saying! Learning English, I had forgotten my original language, or else something had happened in me which amounted to that. Perhaps something had pushed what knowledge I had had of Japanese out of me. . . . At any rate, as the lawyer spoke in my mother tongue, there was just a faint and distant rumble of meaning in me.

I told my visitor that I did not understand him: would he please speak English? For a while, ignoring my request, he persisted in talking Japanese, and I gathered from his manner that he did not believe me. Then, annoyed, he did start to speak in English. Was I ashamed of being Japanese? I said no, I was not; and what business of his was it anyhow? (I was just coming into my "tough" period. I had but recently established myself as the leader of my first gang.) I was terribly uncomfortable.

He ignored my remark and, gazing at me, expressed his sadness over my shame at being Japanese. I got angry at this and pointed out that if it came down to brass tacks I was not really Japanese at all; I was an American—and what did he think of that? I began to hate his dead-pan Japanese face.

Speaking English with an accent so strong I barely understood him, the lawyer tried to lecture me. I urged him to "can that stuff" and demanded to know what had brought him to look me up in the first place.

He gave me his card, explaining he was an emissary from my mother. I began to feel queer all over. The lawyer asked me: would I care to return home? I was numb, and made no reply.

The past few years, particularly since my eleventh year, I had done very little thinking about home. I had been getting more and more adept in ignoring my history. I was busy studying, working in the fields, playing ball, puffing into a saxophone in the band, reading adventure stories, and scheming activities for my gang. Besides, as I have suggested, there was an active undeliberate effort in me to forget things. The cloud of my past drenched me with a miserable feeling only when someone like the religious supervisor called me a "Jap."

The lawyer repeated the question: did I wish to go home?—adding it was part of my mother's message to me. The rest of the message, he continued, was to this effect: that my father still drank, but less and less as the years advanced on him, and had thoroughly reformed in other respects. He was good and gentle to my mother and to my brothers and sisters, and was sincerely sorry for all the abuse and injustice he had inflicted upon me. But my mother, the lawyer went on, did not insist on my coming home, nor did my father. If I liked it at this institution, and I wished to go on with my education, I was free to stay and do so. My parents asked me to make my own decision. Again: did I wish to return? He paused for my reply.

I heard myself yell out, "No!"

The lawyer talked some more. I repeated my answer, even louder. He asked what reason for this decision he should convey to my family. I did not reply. Not that I did not care. I was on the verge of tears, but I could not permit myself to cry in front of this man with the expressionless face; so I was tough and contrary.

Should he say that I wanted to complete my education here? I nodded and left him. That night I woke up with my face wet. I had been crying in my sleep.

VI

Soon I was back to normal, and I enrolled in high school.

The school had about a thousand students, a little less than half of whom came by buses from the ranches and small hamlets located within fifteen miles of the town. There were a few Chinese American youngsters, and a Hindu or two, but I was the only Japanese American. I mixed fairly easily, although I inclined to be a little shy at the start. The reason for this was not so much racial as that a faint stigma attached to pupils who came from the institution.

By-and-by I regained confidence and became a very active part of the student body. I was on the basketball, tumbling, and swimming teams. My scholastic record was good. I never considered myself anything but an American— except now and then, I must say, when a wave of confusion swept over me, and I did not know what to think or feel about anything. This happened sometimes at night; or in the shower room after a workout in the gym, when my Japanese body was conspicuous among the white bodies; or when some white girl, adolescent and self-conscious, suddenly moved away from me as though something had bit her.

But this confusion bothered me less and less. In my last year at high school I had friends in town who invited me to their homes. Our relations were entirely natural. I was elected to offices in the Honor Club, the Athletic Club, and the Senior Class.

When I started going to high school, I ceased wearing the institutional uniform and had to buy my own clothes. I was also obliged to earn my own keep. Hard times had hit my family, and my mother could no longer scrape together the little sums she had been sending through the lawyer the first few years. I worked on the institution's farm and picked fruit in summer on near-by ranches. But my total earnings amounted to only about two hundred dollars a year, which was just slightly more than enough to cover my obligations. It left me only about fifteen cents a week for spending money—much less than my friends in town had at their disposal. So I could not keep pace with them and join in all their doings. This bothered me throughout my high-school years.

In 1934 I was graduated among the first four in scholarship. I was not yet eighteen.

I had a talk with the superintendent of the institution. He was very considerate, and suggested I stay there until I decided what I wanted to do next. I owed the place about fifty dollars for board and lodging; so for a while I picked fruit in the valley, then worked as a stonemason's helper in town for a few months.

I wanted to go to college; in fact, my ambition to continue my education was very intense; but how would I finance myself? Should I work at anything available for a couple of years, and save every cent possible, till I had, say, eight hundred or a thousand dollars, and then enroll? Or should I take the bull by the horns and try to work my way through college right off?

I decided to do the latter . . . and early in 1935 I came to San Francisco. I was healthy and full of self-confidence. But I no sooner got to the big town than I encountered difficulties with which I did not know how to deal.

VII

I needed a haircut, and went to a barbershop. The barber glowered at me. What did I want? I told him. "Nothin' doin'; get out!" In the town I had come from I never had a hint of anything like this, so I asked for an explanation. He sneered and said, "We don't cut any Jap's hair here, see? This is an American establishment!" I said I was not a "Jap," but an American. He said, "Aw, go tell it to the marines!" I said I was born in this country, right here in California, and that made me an American. "To me it don't!" he shot back. For a moment I saw red, and I wanted terribly to sail into him. That would have been the thing to do at the Home; here, something told me, it was not.

I walked out, hurt and bewildered. Goddamnit, I *was* an American, *not* a "Jap"! . . .

Then I discovered that the signs "Rooms to Let" were not addressed to me. The landlady of the fifth house where I applied for lodging took me in. She was an Armenian woman who spoke very little English.

I had arrived in San Francisco with twenty dollars. For two weeks I walked about twelve hours every day. No job——

Off and on, I found a curious comfort in the thought (accurate enough) that I failed to get employment not merely because I had a Japanese face but also because of the countrywide Depression and the recent general strike and other capital-labor troubles which kept industry and business in San Francisco in a state of jitters. I felt a wavering, indirect gratitude to Harry Bridges, whom the newspapers and the big employers blamed loudly for the situation.

Of course I could not live on this consolation, even if I gave up the idea of entering college at once. I had to begin to earn something. I tried to get ordinary labor. . . . *"Nothin' doin'!"* . . . One labor boss informed me casually, "I wouldn't have anything for you even if you was an American."

Walking about, I came upon the rather shabby, rundown district which is Japanese Town in San Francisco. There were Japanese signs over all the stores. I could not read them. Most of the people in the streets were Japanese. They spoke Japanese. Arches, with lights on them, were rigged up over the streets as I supposed they were in the cities in Japan. . . . I felt a stranger, a foreigner.

I entered a barbershop. The barbers were women, and after I got into the chair I was sorry I had gone in. The woman talked to me in Japanese;

she knew no English. I indicated with pantomime that I wanted my hair cut only in back and around the sides. She nodded, then talked to her fellow barber, no doubt about me: how strange it was that I did not understand Japanese. I tried not to listen; did not like the sound of the language—but I could not help hearing them, and there was the rumble of meaning in my head, similar to that I had experienced when the lawyer visited me at the institution; only it was even more remote. Touching a residue of understanding in me, their words made me miserable. And the barber's touch on my neck, as she put the towel about me, sent shivers all through me.

I had felt intensely strong and compact when I arrived in San Francisco; now, in this chair, having my hair cut, I felt as though I were cracking up, falling to pieces, turning soft and weepy. That my father was a barber suddenly loomed up as a tremendous fact. Should I go home? Of course this question had occurred to me before since my arrival in San Francisco, but not as sharply as now. . . . Should I ever go home again? I did not know.

VIII

Almost desperate, I wrote to the superintendent of the institution I had just left: could he help me? He had told me to let him know how I was getting along. He happened to be coming to San Francisco that week, and when I saw him I told him I was willing to try anything. Through some connection, he got in touch with a Japanese organization conducting a school for Japanese boys, which needed a sports counselor and coach, and—to my immediate and intense discomfort—I got the job. Since the superintendent had gone to so much trouble to find it for me, I could not refuse to take it.

There were over a hundred boys in the school, and the first time I saw them they all looked alike. I really could not tell them apart! And the names were beyond my grasp. . . . Suffice it to say that I did not make good. I knew my sports, but my lack of knowledge of the Japanese language was a serious matter, from the viewpoint of the school's director and his assistants, all natives of Japan. On my part, I considered the whole staff cheap, smug, and ill-mannered; they acted as though they had done me a favor in taking me on. The food in the place was awful: rice for lunch, rice for dinner, and rice crispies for breakfast. I saw so much rice in four weeks I did not touch it again for years. And I did not like it at all that many of the kids, although born here, knew next to no English.

But the crisis occurred when I was ordered to kowtow to my superiors every time they and I came within a certain distance of one another. I told them to take a running jump into the bay, and quit. How was I to know that in the better Japanese circles custom and good manners require a bow when greeting one's elders? But had I known it, I would not have bowed anyhow. I was an American; what did I care about Japanese customs? I still don't bow. It is either a handshake with a "hi-ya" or nothing! . . .

So I was where I had been on my coming to San Francisco, except that now

I had thirty-odd dollars, my month's salary, in my pocket. That would be enough, I thought, for five weeks or so, and in that time I was sure to find something. . . . But it was tough. Nothing; nothing.

IX

I got frightfully lonely—"scared" is the word. One day I found myself on a ferryboat going across the bay. Not having seen my home for nearly ten years, I had only a vague idea of its location. But I found it. It looked poor, small and shabby.

Through the shop window I saw my father sitting idle in his barber's chair. I did not really recognize him; I just assumed it was he. He looked very old. As I learned later, he had come out of hospital but a few days previously. In the window was the same sign "Closed for Business" we used to put out years before when he was too drunk to work.

I walked around the block. Should I go in? Would the old man recognize me?

I decided to enter by the back way.

My mother recognized me at once, with a little gasp. She was very still a few seconds, looking at me. Then she closed her eyes and smiled as though she had been expecting me. Three months before, through the lawyer, she had received a notice from the institution that I had left for San Francisco.

My mother had aged, too. She was so thin, so little. She came scarcely up to my chin. I could not understand what she was saying in Japanese and she knew no English.

There were several youngsters in the room, my brother and sisters. At first I barely saw them. They all stared at me, and whispered excitedly.

My father shuffled into the backroom from the shop. He said something in Japanese, perhaps inquiring what was going on, who I was, and what I wanted. He did not recognize me, partly because his eyes did not immediately become adjusted to the darkness of the room. I saw him clearly. He wore Japanese slippers over bare feet. He was only a shadow of the figure he had been ten years before. He was much smaller than I. Like a gnome.

When informed who I was, he folded his arms and his head dropped on his sunken chest, and he began to talk in a jumble of Japanese and English. I gathered that he thought I hated him. Finally he sat on the edge of one of the three beds that crowded the room, and, clutching a brass knob, asked me to forgive him for his mistreatment of me. He said "the booze . . . the booze . . . the booze" (repeating the words) had made him vicious and brutal. But that was all over now, he said; he had ceased drinking.

I felt dreadful over this, but managed to pat him on the shoulder and take his hand, which was weak and small and cold. Then he folded up on the bed and cried. After a while he picked himself up and shuffled back into his shop, perhaps to have words with the little Buddha on the shelf behind the water heater.

My mother was so still; she just looked at me. I think she was pleased by my physical appearance. During the first half-hour or so we did not speak for minutes at a stretch, and the fact that we could not understand one another was not the only reason. Even the children became quiet. Every once in a while my mother's hand went out from her, as if involuntarily or reflexly, to touch me. It felt strange to be so near to her, and I could hardly look at her. An intangible sort of loveliness hung about, or shone through, her little person. I have since noticed it in other middle-aged and aging Japanese women. Their lives as immigrant women and mothers of American-born children have not been easy. . . .

My mother tried desperately to make me feel welcome. She was distressed over my inability to understand her. She put food before me, but it had no reference to anything I had ever tasted: or was this only my imagination? Every swallow nearly gagged me.

I began to notice my brothers and sisters whose eyes continued to be fixed on me. Every move I made caused a stir among them. By-and-by I counted them. Four; all born after I had left home. One was only three, a tiny fellow sitting in the middle of one of the huge beds. They made me uneasy. . . . The younger children still affect me that way a little. They do not yet recognize me as one of the family. Talking to me, they still say with emphasis "*my* mother" and "*my* father," as though implying they are not also my mother and father. In turn, I do the same, not only when I am with them, but otherwise. . . .

On that first visit the other three members of the family were not home. My oldest sister, I was told, was a servant in San Francisco. I could not understand where the second oldest sister was. And the brother who came after me was out delivering papers.

The two senior children in the house acted as interpreters between my mother and me. She said she hoped my feelings about my father really were not bitter any longer. I found it difficult to say anything, but said they were not: I bore him no grudge.

She asked me to come home to live with them; they would make room for me. This caused a flutter among the interpreters. One whispered to another, in English, "Where will he sleep?" I declined the invitation. I said I would crowd them too much. But my real reason was that I did not belong.

I stayed only about an hour. I said I had to get back to San Francisco, to see someone about a job. I promised to come again soon.

When I found myself in my room in San Francisco, I had no idea how I had got there.

A Job
and College

THAT winter—1934-35—can't be laughed off easily. *"Nothin' doin'!* . . . *Don't hire Japs!* . . . *Sorry, we don't take on any Japanese!* . . . *I couldn't use you if you was a white man!* . . ." My feet still hurt when I think of all the walking I did up and down the hills of San Francisco. I was really frightened. Didn't I belong here at all? But, damnit, I *was* an American! If not, *what* was I? I was no "Jap"! This *was* my country. I *did* belong! . . . Then there were times when my brain and feelings went numb. Occasionally a flash would come through the numbness: I've got to fight this thing out! But I could not shake off the dead mood. The only thing that shook it off for me was a visit to my home, although I did not begin to call it that again for some time.

During that period I went home about every ten days. There I *had* to liven up and assume a front. My parents' looks, pathetic beyond words, needled me into an intense awareness.

I met my oldest sister. She had been ten when I left; now she was twenty. She worked as housekeeper in a millionaire spinster's home near the Presidio, making thirty a month, which helped to keep the family in food. She was also paying my father's doctor and hospital bills. . . . Such was her role in the family; it still is. Since she was the oldest, the heaviest burden fell on her. She was the "little mother" to the four youngest children. It was she who taught them English before they started going to school, then helped to make things easier for them all along the way. Totally unselfish, she always places the needs of the family before her own. I suppose a person who has played that kind of a part in life is inclined to put himself in a suffering-martyr light, and this sister does that once in a while. I feel for her. She is good-looking, but there is a weight on her spirit. She has artistic talents, but probably will never allow herself a chance to develop them. Once she went to an art school for a while, evenings; then gave it up because she could not afford the fees. She still works for the same millionaire woman, making forty a month now, and continues to give more than half of it to Mother. . . .

Remembering me as a little boy (and, I suppose, also because she is the sort of person she is), she was the only one of my brothers and sisters who indicated at once she was glad to see me and accepted me without reservations. I was unaccustomed to personal affection, and this made me miserable in a strange way, but I also liked it. She was frank and direct with me. Instinctively, she got wind of my economic crisis, which I tried to hide before the family, and asked me had I tried to get a job in some home. No; what kind of a job? As a houseboy or valet, a servant: and she said this very matter-of-factly. She added that lots of Japanese young men became house-boys and valets. Some people called them schoolboys, even in cases where they did not go to school, and even when they were men in their thirties and forties. They received anywhere from thirty to fifty a month. She told me what they did for those wages: cleaned house, pressed clothes, served meals, sometimes cooked, ran errands, and so on.

I had difficulty in controlling the resentment her suggestion kicked up in me, but replied—fairly quietly, I think—that I did not care to become a domestic. I wanted to be an employee in some office, shop, store, factory, restaurant or business house. My sister laughed and said: what difference did it make whether I was called an employee or a servant? I told her she did not understand how a man looked at that sort of thing.

In her way, my oldest sister was very good to me. When I ran out of funds and she began to see my reason for not wanting to live at home, she asked her mistress for an advance and gave me a little money. I saw it made her feel wonderful, but it was humiliating for me to accept her help.

I fought against her idea . . . but, to shorten a long tale, one day I regis-tered at a Japanese household employment agency. Then I was sent to place after place, perhaps a dozen in all, till I was finally taken by a couple who lived in a lovely apartment in a building high on the side of a hill, with a superb view of the bay—although, in a way, I took them as much as they took me. I could have been hired at several of the previous places to which I had been sent, but was not because I did not like the people on first im-pression, and deliberately behaved improperly during the interviews.

I did not like the job, but stayed on for two reasons. *One:* I realized this was in all probability the only position available to me in San Francisco which would enable me to go to college. *Two:* my employers tried from the start to be considerate of my peculiarities, as they must have seemed to them.

The boss, as I called him, was a successful business man in a field the Depression did not affect seriously. He had a keen instinct about people, which led him to suspect right off that I hated being in a servile position. He discussed me with his wife; then they both spoke to me, to the general effect that when they got to know me better I was to consider myself a mem-ber of their household.

To say that I was difficult is putting it mildly, and I still marvel at their patience with me. Now and then, during my first two years with them, they would put me in place, which pushed me to the brink of quitting; but they also made frequent concessions. For example, the previous houseboy had worn a white coat when serving them. I rebelled against this so much they let me have my way, except when they had special guests.

Although I knew I could not possibly expect anything more, I resented the tentativeness with which they took me—"when we know you better, you may consider yourself a member of our household." I was on probation. Hell with 'em! I decided to develop a tactic toward them. I would get from them as many concessions as possible and do my work so they could find no fault. I would be aloof; answer their questions, as far as possible, yes or no.

I started in college in the fall of 1935. By then my attitude toward my job was formed—a sort of to-hell-with-it philosophy, which I maintained for the next two years. I told myself the job was a means to an end, and in a way it was a cinch. The cook was an elderly Finnish woman, who had been there for years; she seldom had anything to say outside the line of her work. I saw that she took me impersonally (I was the houseboy, that was all), and I returned the compliment (she was the cook, and that was all). My work consisted mostly of cleaning, waiting on table, and odds and ends; four or five hours a day all told, except on the cook's day off, when I prepared simple meals according to her instruction. For this I received thirty a month; later, thirty-five, which was ample to see me through.

II

When I entered college, I had no definite plan. I was too young and green to try to blueprint my future; also too self-conscious and lacerated by my job-seeking adventures and resentful of my process of adjustment as a houseboy.

I did not quite admit this to myself, but somewhere in me I knew that the world in which I was living was a mess so far as I was concerned, but no more so than I was a mess within myself. Very early in my sociology class I came upon the phrase "marginal man," which described me fully. I was neither here nor there; an orphan who was not an orphan, a "Jap" who was not a "Jap," an American who was not really an American. When this occurred to me, I told myself it was funny and laughed, but it also cut into me.

I did not know whether I liked the college or not. What I noticed, I think, first of all were the "Japanese" and "Chinese" students (I thought of them in quotes) studying in their special corners at their special tables in the library. When I came on the "marginal man" phrase, I labeled them with it, then amused myself tossing them about in my mind, complicatedly, as "Japs" and "Chinks" who were not "Japs" and "Chinks" although some thought they were, as Americans who were not really Americans, and as orphans in relation both to America and Japan or China who did not know they were orphans.

Finally I said to myself, "To hell with 'em!" A couple of the "Japanese" students tried to approach me, but my manner kept them off. For a while, when I passed their table in the library, some would move as though to make room for me, seeming to take it for granted I belonged among them; but, avoiding their eyes, I would pretend not to see them, walk past, and pick a chair in some corner or against some wall, without a table. There I would feel uncomfortable, without letting myself figure out why. Sometimes it was a half-hour before I could concentrate.

By-and-by I decided I did not like the college any better than I liked my job, but I could not apply quite the same philosophy and policy toward it that I had toward the job. It touched and stirred all sorts of areas in me. Several of the subjects I took interested me. I could not help noticing the students, both individually and as a body; but, afraid they would learn I was a houseboy, I would not risk approaching, or being myself with, them. So I lived in a shell, in a state of hidden and futile rebellion against everything, and studied hard. I kept even the professors at arm's length, although one or two of them seemed disposed to talk to me.

I had a small but quiet and comfortable room in my employers' apartment, and usually read till one or two in the morning, sleeping four or five hours a night (I had to be up at the ring of the alarm clock at six to attend to my duties as a houseboy). I got excellent grades. By-and-by, however, that ceased to give me any real satisfaction. I never told anyone my grades, lest I be called a bookworm. I was full of ridiculous fears and notions like that, but outwardly, I think, I looked always poised and cool.

The first two years everybody on the campus left me alone. Now and then in my room I brooded over the thought that the students—the white students —were purposely steering wide of me, glad I made no effort to get in with them.

Only once in a while, riding in cable cars to and from school, getting a beautiful view of the city and the bay I felt momentarily relieved, detached—really quiet and at ease.

But there were other things—vague, elusive, ill-defined—which were part of my inner confusion. After taking the houseboy job, my home across the bay at once drew and repelled me. Its drawing power, I suppose, was the fact that, while I was there, it gave me a sense of being wanted. And it drove me away from it by the threat of uneasiness and pain it caused me every time I visited it. I saw there other aspects of the same thing that was troubling and confusing me. That overcrowded room in back of the barbershop was a cultural battleground, and the battle—Asia *versus* America—was a sordid business, which, I thought then, could resolve itself into nothing worthwhile.

Once, early in 1936, I witnessed what seemed to me a petty but nasty spat between my father and my oldest brother, who was seventeen then. My father thought he had caught my brother making a grimace in the direction of the little statue of Buddha in the barbershop. The old man fumed with indignation while the boy denied he had had Buddha in mind when and if the grimace had come to his face. As the old man apparently paid no attention to his denial, my brother finally blurted, in English: what did he care about his silly old Buddha anyhow! Which produced a new explosion. My brother walked out of the house, and anger all but consumed my father;

one or two of the younger children snickered at the whole incident; and my mother held her face in her hands in a gesture of helplessness.

Scenes like this—what could they lead to? They bewildered me, and made me sorry for my mother and the kids, especially for her. I could still communicate with her only through the translators. Once I asked her why she did not quit pretending to her family in Japan that we were rich, and sending them gifts which they did not need and she could not afford to buy. She said that what I suggested was impossible. Everybody in Japan had the idea that nearly everybody in America was successful and rich; she did not want her relatives to think or suspect we were failures.

I was sorry, too, for the old man, although, every now and then, when he happened to come near me, I went all taut as though with fear of him—an echo of his treatment of me in my early boyhood. . . .

So during my first two years in college I went home infrequently. But sometimes I sent Mother five or six dollars, and occasionally a gift for her or my brothers and sisters. Now and then I sent the old man a carton of cigarettes. My oldest sister in San Francisco, whom I characterized as a "slavey" in my mind, I saw as seldom as possible.

This went on for two years. Then things began to happen.

III

The second or third week of my junior year, a fellow whom I had seen around the previous two years and who was a newly elected student officer stopped me on the campus and swung his hand over my shoulder with a great show of belligerency, then laughed—rather foolishly I thought at the moment.

I was a very superior and well-contained person, and he seemed to me mildly idiotic as he stood there before me; but, instead of continuing on my way, I deigned to ask him, "What's the idea?"

He was a head taller than I, and, looking down at me and grinning, he said he had tried to knock the chip off my shoulder. I knew what he meant instantly, but, feeling of a sudden simultaneously foolish and miserable, asked him anyhow.

"The chip," he roared. "The goddamn' thing's big as a log! A bunch of us have been noticing it the last two years, and personally I don't know how you stand it. . . . What I'm drivin' at is that I think you're a dope."

I said, "Is that so?"—or, rather, "Zatso?" as I used to say it in the orphanage.

"Yeah, zatso!" said he. "I wanna talk to you." And he launched into me, the while I looked at the green grass at my feet. What kinda goddamn' lug was I, anyhow! Was I a student in this college or wasn't I? Why wasn't I myself? Why in hell didn't I do somethin'—join clubs, play intramural sports, go to games, take an active hand in the student-body affairs? . . . "Come on, what do you say?" He stuck out his paw.

I could not help taking his hand, and suddenly all my resentment went; I felt incredibly alive.

IV

That evening, as I served dinner, my boss asked me what I was grinning about. Had somebody died and left me a million yen? (His occasional "kidding" of this sort always had a Japanese touch like that.) I had not realized I was grinning, and his question embarrassed me a little. His wife then guessed maybe I was in love. "Bring 'er around," said he, "and let's see what she's like." They "kidded" me so much I was annoyed, at the same time that I was pleased.

This broke the thin ice between my employers and me which my "policy" toward the job had created, although for several months before this we had been getting along all right. I had obtained all the concessions from them I could possibly expect, and had decided to become reasonable. I was free to arrange my time in accordance with my changing class schedule. I could take anything I wished at any time from the refrigerator. And so on. I had practically the run of the place, and I really liked my bosses, especially him.

The only thing that had been more or less a pain in the neck was that my Japanese face had the tendency to stimulate my employers, particularly him when he and I were alone in the apartment, to ask me questions about "your (that is, my) people." Now and then, in fact, this had disturbed me acutely, and not only because I could not answer them merely with yes or no. In my customary aloof manner, I had tried to suggest to my boss that the Japanese immigrants in America and the Japanese Americans were not particularly "my people"; but, somehow, although he was very bright and quick, he had not caught on. He did not quite believe that I knew no Japanese.

Now, although I still did not like the subject, I found myself making attempts to reply to his questions. Little discussions and arguments resulted. He was as ill-informed as I, but one thing led to another, and by Christmas that year—'37—his questions and our conversations about the Japanese stirred my own thoughts in that direction. At first I felt queer about this. Then I said to myself: after all, my background *was* Japanese! Why pretend it wasn't? Why try to evade it and go around waiting for and dodging blows, feeling guilty as though I had a secret shame and sorrow; insisting I was an American, which of course I was anyhow, but by this insistence denying to others and myself that I was also of Japanese parentage—a pretty obvious fact? For the first time I saw myself. The only reason I felt ashamed (and I realized I had felt so), and therefore afraid and resentful, was that I had been trying to conceal what I could not conceal, and should have accepted as being as natural and perfectly O.K. as the fact that I was an American. The student officer was right: the idea was to be what I was—myself.

Before I knew it I found myself deeply interested in the Japanese Americans, and in the whole mess in which they found themselves, both in reference to America and Japan. At the library and in second-hand bookstores, I found such books as *The Japanese Problem in the United States* by a man named H. A. Mills, published in 1915, and *The Japanese in America* by Charles Lanman, which had come out in the 1870's. As I now realize, some of this stuff was pretty lame as writing or history or sociology, but it fascinated me. It broke down more barriers in me, made me begin to see I was not alone and peculiarly apart, nor were the other Japanese Americans. It gave me moments of awareness of our common need in this country to understand one another. . . . Late in 1937 I came on a new book just out, *Americans in Process: A Study of Our Citizens of Oriental Ancestry,* by Professor William Carlson Smith, of Linfield College; which, although rather academic, excited me very much. I began to read on Japan, its history and culture, and decided to major in Oriental history. I suppose part of this decision was also practical; I had half an idea I might teach this subject some day.

So by 1938 I became more or less qualified to talk to my boss. Previously I had believed I did not care what he thought on the subject. Now, as he put it, I began to change his slant on matters Japanese and Japanese American. He would exclaim, "You don't say!" or "Well, I didn't realize that!" He told me he had always had the idea that the "Japanese" (by which he also meant the Japanese Americans; I could not break him of this) were "mostly good only for domestic work," and that they never could be assimilated. Now he read with interest *Americans in Process,* which I brought him.

This began to affect our personal relationship. When his wife was out, he made me set a place for myself at the table with him; then, if we got into a hot discussion and it also happened to be the cook's day out, he would help me clear the table and dry the dishes in the kitchen as I washed them. Eventually I used to go to shows and night-spots with him. He was a regular guy; only now and then, when we were alone, he turned suddenly self-conscious and terminated our discussion with some unnecessarily abrupt order —which amused and irritated me.

As we talked, and he read the books I brought him, he soon reached the point where he started to re-educate his friends. I came to know some of them very well: important business and professional people in the Bay District. He had a lodge on the Russian River, where he threw big stag parties in the summer, during which he worked up stimulating discussions and arguments about Japan and the Japanese, using me as a foil and the authority on the subject.

The boss' wife did not know he had taken me in on so intimate a basis till the fall of '38, just before I began my senior year. Then she acted for a while as though she believed it was all a mistake on his part. But she was what he called a good sport, and decided to put up with his friendship with me.

Her father had been an Army officer, and she had inherited many of his biased viewpoints. This was especially true when it came to the subject of the potential danger of a Japanese attack on the Pacific Coast, which, of course, affected (if not created) her ideas about the Japanese element in the United States. I persuaded her husband to subscribe to *Time, Harpers,* the *Living Age* and *Asia,* and we noticed that she brought into her statements points from articles on the Orient in these magazines. Of course she continued to be anti-Japanese in many ways, but not much more so than were her husband and I.

For Christmas they always gave me a gift; and, in turn, I got them something of modest value like a book or a poinsettia. In 1938, I gave him a Japanese painting (the kind that is on silk and rolls up) and her a few Japanese dwarf plants. This gift stimulated her interest in Japanese floral arrangement to the extent that she took a course in it. Then she acquired and studied illustrated books on Japanese gardens and made several special trips to the Japanese Gardens in Golden Gate Park; while all winter and spring, coming to the conclusion that the Japanese militarists were one thing and Japanese culture another, she read books dealing with Japanese art, religions, and ways of life—Lafcadio Hearn's things, *Story of Genji*, Arthur Morrison's *Painters of Japan*, the Binyon-Sexton *Japanese Color Prints*, Brinkley's *Japan, Its History, Arts and Literature*, the Waley volume of *Nō Plays, The Daughter of the Samurai, Bushido, The Soul of Japan.* —She bought scores of books and started a shelf for them.

After a while it got so that she—having, of course, more time to read than I had—became the expert on Japan and started to instruct me on my background! One day I overheard her say to her husband that a new world had been opened for her. . . . When I graduated last year, and left their employ, they gave me a new convertible coupé for a graduation gift, and I suspect it was originally her idea

v

Simultaneously my attitude to my family underwent a change.

In the autumn of '37, after that talking-to on the campus, I suddenly saw my mother and father and brothers and sisters not so much as a family involved in a sordid and difficult situation as a group of interesting individuals.

I have mentioned my oldest sister, the "slavey." She appeared to me in new colors. She could be gay and good company.

My brother born immediately after me and I had a little trouble getting next to each other. He had been six when I left, and of course he remembered me, but only as a seven-year-old boy who had always been in trouble with the old man. Now, however, the distance between us gradually shrank and we became friends on a tentative basis; and after a while the tentativeness began to go, too. If it has not yet completely disappeared, it is probably less his fault than mine.

After I was sent away, he was obliged to assume responsibilities usually devolving upon the oldest son. He began to sell papers before he was eleven, and brought his money home. He ran errands and, speaking better English than any of the other children, was generally the family's ambassador to America.

He finished high school the year after I came home, and was near the top in the list of graduates. With no work to be had, he clashed awhile with the old man, who did not understand the economic situation and was constantly throwing it up to him that he was not earning anything. Then he left home and roamed about the Bay District, till he got a job as a salesman in a Japanese art-goods store in San Francisco. He was paid forty-five a month for a ten-hour day and seven-day week, and sent five dollars home. Six months later, the boss, a native of Japan, discharged him on hearing that he had contributed money to the Chinese cause at the outbreak of the war in 1937.

After that my brother became a transient fruit picker, working with the "Okies" and "Arkies" and with Mexicans and Filipinos and Hindus all the way from Santa Clara Valley down to El Centro. He was unable to find another job after the fruit season, and joined the CCC for six months. Most of his pay was sent home, but Mother saved it for him; then he entered a college in Southern California. This was in 1938. His CCC savings, of course, are gone by now, and he is working his way through school. I am sure he will make it; he is very ambitious. His current part-time job is in a vegetable market in the town where his college is located.

He is active in student affairs. He mingles with students of other backgrounds (old-stock American, Jewish, Armenian, Italian, Mexican, and Slavic). The whole complexity of the second-generation problems, which are his own, interests him. He attends conferences on the subject. He gropes for answers and always wants to do something about things that catch his attention. In common, it seems, with most young Japanese Americans, he has a sense of humor. One of his ambitions is to travel all over the world someday, especially in the Orient, "to see what makes the damned thing weak in so many places," as he puts it.

He seems a natural-born leader and politician. He plans to run for membership on the executive committee of the student body. The opposition has been trying to brand him a Communist, but he maintains that his platform of equal representation for all racial and religious groups is good Americanism. At the same time, he is proud of his Japanese cultural background. He speaks fluent Japanese. When he was in the CCC, he had to "sock" a couple of fellows in order to get their respect; after that he got along fine. A year ago he had the tendency to go overboard in his contempt for whites. He has largely outgrown it, although his current ambition to get on the student executive committee is not unrelated to it. We had an argument about it, but he was—emotionally—unable to see my point that, since they were all Americans, it was not really important who was or wasn't on the committee so far as races and religions were concerned, and that all his excitement about this was defense mechanism. . . . He has a very likable personality, a self-confident attitude and a dynamic push behind an independent, individualistic manner.

The second sister, the fourth child, graduated from high school at the head of her class and is a life member of the California Scholastic Federation. She is perhaps the best adjusted of us all, and seems never to have any conflicts. A possible explanation of this is that she has always been my father's favorite. Shrewd and cute, she got her own way even to the extent of leaving home at the age of seventeen to attend a business school in San Francisco. But in the end she did not go into office work; no non-Japanese firm would employ her, and she did not care to work in a Japanese office, if for no other reason than that Japanese lawyers and business men tend to pay their employees very little. So now she, too, is a housekeeper in a wealthy home here in the city, and also helps with the family finances, though not so much as my oldest sister.

She does not greatly mind being a servant. I suspect this is because she is very good-looking and popular, and free to marry any time she says yes. She is generally liberal, high-spirited and positive in her ideas and responses, and engages in arguments and discussions with other second-generation Americans of Oriental parentage as to what they could or ought to do about their problems.

The other four of my brothers and sisters (two of each) are still in school. The oldest of these, a girl, will be graduated from high school next June [1940], but I do not know her plans for her future if she has any. Last summer during vacation, she worked in a Chinese chop-suey place in Oakland (my father, who is very pro-Japanese now, was told it was an American restaurant). In school, nearly all her friends are Chinese American girls and boys; but my father is ignorant of this, as he is of the fact that my youngest brother's closest pal is a Chinese American lad. Awhile ago, this boy's mother tried to break up their friendship, but did not succeed. . . . (On the whole, the Asiatic war plays a less serious role in the life of the Orientals in the small towns than it does in San Francisco, where there are more of them and they are better organized. And I suppose the older Orientals who were not born in the United States cannot be blamed for reacting strongly to the issues seven thousand miles away. They are closer to Asia in spirit and culture than to America, which bars them from citizenship. It is different with us, the second generation; even if our problems of adjustment, of finding jobs, and of getting along with other elements in our population are tough, we are closer to the Occidental ideas and ways than to any other kind. And we are citizens.) . . .

Before, I had been reluctant to get close to my older sisters and brother, as well as to the rest of the family, because I did not (at the same time that I did!) want to know what had been going on during the nine and a half years of my absence. Now I quickly got the whole picture from my oldest sister, who also helped me to recall the details of the situations at home prior to my departure. We speculated on what had been the matter with the old man. I learned that, with me out of the way, he had improved vastly in the ensuing couple of years. He continued to drink, as I say, till shortly before I returned, but became generally more benevolent and after a while even remorseful over the way he had treated me. But even so life was difficult. Having established a reputation for drunkenness, my father had fewer and fewer customers, and there was little or no money. The Depression made matters serious.

On top of that, as the children grew up and went to school, came what I have called the cultural conflict. Despite his growing benevolence, the old man wanted—and still persists in wanting—to be the traditional pater familias, the big I-am; while the children, developing considerable independence and individualism naturally proceeded to reduce him to a futile would-be tyrant. As they became American, he became more and more Japanese and conservative. This development reached a climax with the China war; and the struggle to which I became a witness increasingly shows him the loser. His erratic ideas are a bit hard on my sisters who are still at home. Every now and then he becomes very dogmatic on the subject of their going out with young men. This leads to frictions, which tend more and more to end in laughter behind his back. To reduce these occasions to a minimum both in number and intensity, the children deceive him right and left. When he succeeds in thwarting their inclinations and purposes, they have ways of getting even with him.

One of my sisters, about sixteen, has the job of listening to the news over the radio every night and reporting in translation the progress of the Chinese-Japanese War to my father, who now knows less English than he did, say, fifteen years ago. If my sister is angry about not having had her way that day, she tells him that the Japanese have just lost a big battle. If she feels kindly disposed toward him, she tells him the Japanese have scored a victory in the north and another in the south, or that Chiang Kai-shek is down with the grippe. A Japanese division is usually annihilated on nights she is not allowed to go out of the house.

My mother has been a silent, helpless bystander in the struggle, with her sympathy largely on the children's side. Several years ago she realized they were becoming something called "American," and adapted herself as well as she could. In doing this, she had to rip up the rigid Japanese family pattern that had been woven into her mental and emotional processes. Now she generally respects her sons' and daughters' American urges, purposes, and inclinations. She even aids them in their tricks on the old man.

Our parents are Buddhists. Most of the children, however, attend Protestant churches. My oldest sister leans toward Christian Science. A few years ago religion was a source of much trouble in the family. Now, however, our parents are resigned to our deviations. My father insists only that the children respect the little statue behind the water heater. They generally ignore it.

Gradually, late in '37 and in '38, I began to perceive this cultural situation

as less serious and sordid than it had seemed earlier. In spite of and because of
it, the family had a certain unity and character. Now I see this quite clearly.
There are bickerings, deceptions, outbursts of indignation, and a lack of respect
for the old fellow. But there is also morale of a sort in the family. There are
standards of behavior which cannot be called low. The youngsters still at home
help one another get out of jams. They all love Mother, although in many vital
respects she is a stranger to them. They are Americans; but the idea is not to
hurt the old Asiatic couple if it is avoidable.

During my last two years in college I moved toward the pleasant realization
that, when all is said and done, we were more or less all right; at least as good
as could be expected. Our future was not rosy, but neither was it hopeless.

I said this to myself instinctively, emotionally, although I really had very
little basis for this optimism in myself as a member of the family. I do not,
even yet, quite belong. It is difficult to make my brothers and sisters understand
that my slight aloofness, which I cannot get rid of, and of which they mildly
and occasionally complain to one another, is not because I am ashamed of
them, but because my somewhat drastic boyhood left an inhibition toward full
participation in the family life. I expect this will pass in time, or my kin will
gradually get to understand me better. I get on well with them as it is.

VI

Meantime, too, during 1937-39, a great deal happened to me at college. I continued to receive good grades, and got in close contact with two of the professors. I began to make friends among the students, and joined in their bull
sessions. At the beginning of my senior year I was elected president of the
International Club. My class made me chairman of the Valedictorian Committee for Graduation. And, most important, through my new contacts I became interested in the second generation in a more definite way.

I mentioned the "Chinese" and "Japanese" tables in the library, and other
signs of the tendency to segregate. Negroes also had a corner in the library.
And there was a Jewish clique, and one of Armenians. For two years I had
tried to tell myself that I did not give a hang about this. Now, beginning in
'38, it commenced to irritate me, especially the Oriental part of it—especially
when I chanced to hear at various times Japanese and Chinese Americans
complaining that it was not much use to try to mingle because the whites put
on an aloof and superior attitude toward any attempt of that sort; and after a
while I began to believe the second-generation Oriental was at fault in this.
Many stuck in their shells, as I had stuck in mine before the aggressive white
student officer had tackled me. I realized that to establish contact or friendship with Oriental Americans, the non-Oriental students had to take the
initiative, and I asked myself: why should they? With so many interesting
people in the world, why should the Caucasian Americans put themselves to
the trouble of trying to penetrate the individual shells of the "Japanese" and
"Chinese" students, and to break up their campus cliques?

My new friends and acquaintances included boys and girls of every variety, but most of them were white.

One day a member of the "Japanese" clique stopped me and delivered himself of the information that I was not regarded well by his group because I did not go around with them but did mingle with the others. This struck me as funny, and I laughed. The fellow demanded an explanation. I asked him if my having a Japanese face obligated me to associate only or mostly with people who were similarly blessed or afflicted. No-o-o-o, he said, uneasily . . . whereupon it developed from his further remarks to me that his group objected most particularly to my going around with the "Chinese" students.

I corrected him: the students to whom he referred were not Chinese, but Americans like myself, except that their faces possessed characteristics commonly described as Chinese; and went on to elucidate that I associated with them because I found them interesting and otherwise agreeable, which was the reason, too, for my association with the Jewish, Italian, Armenian, Yugoslav, old-stock, Greek, and other kinds of white Americans, as well as the Negro with whom I occasionally talked. But, said my inquisitor, the "Chinese" all hated Japan and the Japanese. I felt obliged to correct him again: they all hated not Japan and not all the Japanese, but only or chiefly the imperialists and militarists of Japan who had invaded China. I added I had no objection to that particular emotion on their part, it was a general American sentiment; and, being just then in a very precise frame of mind, I asked him again not to refer to Chinese Americans merely as "Chinese."

Looking back now, I know that I must have sounded very objectionable, even smug and fatuous in a way, and do not wonder that for a time after this I was in deeper disfavor with the "Japanese" clique than before. I was declared a smart aleck, a wise guy, a hairsplitter—not unjust titles, for the new development in my life caused me, somehow, for a while to be severe with these people. I was getting the notion that, in connection with my employers and my new associations in college, I had hit upon a suggestion for the solution of the Oriental Americans' problem; and was on the way of developing a high opinion of myself. To try to excuse or extenuate this might only make it worse.

One of my friends was a charming young lady of Chinese grandparentage (her father and mother are natives of San Francisco, as she is herself). She interested me for a number of reasons, not the least of which was her loveliness. She was passionately attached to the Chinese cause against the Japanese invasion, which was all right with me as far as that went. . . .

Things grew really interesting between us when I raised the question whether she was Chinese or American. There was no doubt that, although third-generation American-born, she was inwardly identified with China, which she had never seen, more than with the United States, where she lived; while I, who was only second-generation, had no feeling of affinity or identification with Japan, at least not as a state (despite my growing interest in Japanese history and culture). She admitted—in fact, insisted—that she was Chinese (what else could she be? hadn't I ever taken a look at her face?), and then she added that she guessed she was also American "in a way . . . but not really an American, because Americans don't let us Chinese, or you Japanese, be Americans, real Americans, even when we are born here . . . because this is a white country and they don't let us get into things; and do things—" I am quoting her verbatim, if only in part; and when she explained herself thus, her face, which usually was alive and something to write home about, went wan and sad and frightened, reflecting her inner confusion.

On my part, I could not bring myself to tell her that I was a houseboy; the feeling of inferiority pertaining to my job stayed with me to the last. I talked to her abstractly or academically on what I thought could be done to improve one's relations with the non-Oriental Americans, many of whom, I said, were ready to receive us on terms of equality after we proved ourselves. I went on that because of the very tangible and obvious physical differences the situation was difficult for all concerned; more so for us, to be sure, but not easy for the non-Orientals; and I said that the problem was to find a technique of meeting and mingling, or getting together and working on, and with, one another. But, womanlike, the young lady dismissed my ideas as those of a dreamer and idealist; I did not know what I was talking about. The things her parents had had to go through because they were Chinese! She would not tell me what those things were. Instead, she quoted the ancient Kipling gag about the West and East and the fate of the twain never to meet.

Once I asked her for a date; she said I would have to wait until after Generalissimo Chiang Kai-shek had driven the Japanese out of China. Why? Because her mother would disown her if she learned she went out with a Japanese. . . .

VII

I spent my Easter vacation in 1938 trying to write an essay on the Oriental Americans. I held that the first thing for us to do was to realize that our situation, while difficult, was perfectly natural; in fact, inevitable. I saw it this way: we are of the most recent immigration, and so still in the acute stage of adjustment to the country, as the country is, in turn, in that stage in relation to us. We have our problem, to be sure; but what can we expect? We *are* marginal people, but more important than that fact is the need for us to see that we are that naturally. To cease being marginal, we must proceed from this realization, the only point from which we can proceed. We must look both within and outside ourselves, especially for the good and weak things within us. We must start working against our disadvantages—which, to repeat, are perfectly normal: but their being normal does not mean we need to put up with them. In America it means the exact opposite. It means we must try to overcome them. If we but try, we will do something. We must prove ourselves. All the people, groups and individuals, who came here had to prove themselves. We must stand up and face the situation, and not withdraw from it and lie down, or sneak around it with various dodges. . . .

But I did not finish the essay. I felt sure I had a piece of an idea which probably was not all askew; it was a little too much for me, though. Trying to write it, however, I came to a personal realization—that, in spite of my face, I was not so much a "Japanese" or Japanese American as a fellow who had spent nine years in an orphanage although I was not really an orphan, and that I had come to these conclusions, which I was trying to put in black-on-white, because of that. I had been obliged to stand up in the orphanage, face the situations and problems as they developed, and fight things out within myself and with the others, who were always ready to meet me halfway—even if only to fight. After the fight, whether I won or not, they accepted me as one of them.

The purpose of the International Club, of which I was president at this time, was to bring together students of various backgrounds and discover subjects of mutual interest. It was started a few years earlier on the suggestion of one of the professors. But it was misnamed. It was not "international" at all, but intra-America. Most of the members were average young people found out here on the Coast: a few Chinese, several Jews, a Filipino, a couple of Negroes, and the rest just plain Americans, old-stock and mixtures of all kinds of strains. For a while I was the only Japanese American in the group. We did not care what anyone's political beliefs were as long as he respected the other fellow's. We had a few crackpots who preached extreme ideas and methods in the name of progress, but nobody did anything about it. They were heard.

One day another "Japanese" student joined the club. He was older than I, and had just transferred from the University of California. He had been active in the "Japanese" circle there; now he suggested that I help him organize a Japanese Students' Club on our campus. He pointed out that all colleges and high schools in the State with any number of "Japanese" enrolled had a club for them as a group. I asked him what the purpose of this club would be, and he replied, a bit impatiently, that it would "foster better relations between the Japanese and American students." I reminded him that, whether they realized it or not, the "Japanese," as he called them, were Americans too; and refused to co-operate with him. In fact, I said if he went ahead with his idea I would actively oppose him.

My reasons were that it would be harmful for all the "Japanese" in the school to get into one club. It would not "foster" anything but segregation. I told the would-be organizer that the thing to do for the *nisei*, or the second-generation "Japanese," who were not Japanese but Americans, was to spread out and join other campus clubs as individuals. For instance, they could come into the International Club. In this way they would meet more of the non-"Japanese" students on closer terms and get acquainted with them, and the other way about.

He said I did not know what I was talking about. At the U. of C. the

"Japanese" students were "up against it"; they were discriminated against to the extent of not being able to find living quarters in Berkeley. Why, even one of the professors who was a "Japanese" could not rent a place in which to live!

I said that might be so across the bay; in this college most of the non-Oriental students were unprejudiced on the whole, and many were more than willing to associate with us: and I *did* know, from intimate personal experience, what I was talking about. Anyway, the Japanese Students' Club was not organized.

At the same time, I knew that the International Club, as it was, was a woefully inadequate organization. At our gatherings and meetings, we touched only on the externals of the things which I recognized as constituting a problem. To deal with the externals, that is, to read papers on the contributions of the Yugoslavs and Italians to the fishing and fruit-growing industries of California, etcetera, was the tradition of the Club. How to break this tradition so we would get *inside* the problem? As president, I felt it was up to me to do something: but I did not know how. Also, I was afraid. Being ashamed of my houseboy status was part of the inside of this thing. Could I let it become public? No; I was still extremely touchy on the point. My difficulties with the charming "Chinese" girl were part of the problem. Could they be discussed? Hardly. . . .

VIII

In the last half of my senior year, I felt impelled to explore the *inside* of the "Japanese" situation in San Francisco. I sought the company of the members of the "Japanese" clique in college, most of whom turned out to be all right, and who in turn, appeared to discover that I was not as bad, not quite as "stuck up," as they had thought; and through them, as well as by other means, I got into the Japanese and the Japanese American circles off the campus, where I caught at least glimpses of the inside picture. I went about Japanese Town, where it was a handicap not to know the language; but the residue of understanding in me was more and more responsive, and off and on I suddenly knew what some sound or word or utterance meant. This gave me a curious, lingering thrill.

Nearly everybody whom I contacted wished to know why I did not speak, or at least understand, Japanese. The usual explanation I made was that my father and mother were also American-born, and we had spoken only English at home when I was a boy. I was urged to learn it. The *issei*, the Japan-born Japanese, lectured to me: "After all, you are Japanese; you must know the tongue of your people, or you will be a foreigner among them"—which is exactly what I felt I was when among the natives of Japan, many of whom spoke no English, and even when among some of the *nisei* who, by virtue of their upbringing and despite their American birth, were closer to Japanese than American ways and customs. It was only my face that admitted me in their midst.

My replies to their urgings that I study Japanese were mostly to the effect that I was in the United States and intended to stay; what good would it do me to spend years learning a difficult language destined to be used here less and less? I was told I was wrong. Japanese would be essential to me not only socially but practically, for I would never be able to break into the economic field dominated by the whites. I was destined to be able to make a living only if I clung to the Japanese element, of which I came; and to work in the office or the plant of a Japanese firm I would have to know the language.

I caused much amusement and became the target of no little criticism because I did not know how to use chopsticks. In explanation, I repeated the fiction that my parents were American-born, and we had used spoons and forks when I was a child.

Learning that I went to college, many Japan-born persons warned me about the difficulties ahead. Some frankly disapproved of college education in this country for the nisei. It was bad; it took the young people just that much more time to meet reality, to recover from the four years' sojourn in the Ivory Tower, and to find themselves. Many nisei college boys and girls, I was told, became disillusioned with the "Japanese" group's present status in this country, which they could not possibly hope to improve in their lifetime, and so they became futile and objectionable, unfit even to be houseboys or kitchen-maids.

I said I was unable to see how any group with the educational attainment of the second-generation "Japanese" could permanently be kept down. I held that if a person became outstanding in any line, he would be accepted in this country when the need for his talents and skill arose; and that the thing for the American sons and daughters of Japanese parents to do was to aim toward competence and excellence. I was informed I did not know what I was talking about.

I browsed about in the Japanese art-goods stores in Chinatown, and got acquainted with numerous nisei college graduates, including a Ph.D., who worked as salesmen in these establishments, and are popularly known among the second generation as the Grant Avenue Slaves, because they work ten to twelve hours daily seven days a week, selling cheap art pieces to tourists, who stroll through the "picturesque Chinatown" at night. For this they get from forty-five to sixty-five a month. The employer can always get a fresh supply of job-eager A.B.'s, and so has few labor complaints. Another reason for the low wages in these stores in recent years is that Japan's invasion of China has not been well received by the American public, and there is now in effect a partial boycott on Japanese stores.

The conditions I have described as existing in my own family I found rather general in Japanese American homes. There were cultural conflicts in varying degrees of bitterness between the issei and the nisei, the latter rebelling against the old-fashioned autocratic family control, the former trying desperately to hold onto their offspring about to be snatched from them by the little-understood forces that were America. Nearly all the young people called themselves "Japanese" and most of them spoke the language; but in many ways, both definite and elusive, they were Americans of a kind, products of the democratic atmosphere of the public schools and city streets. Almost without exception, girls resented the male-domination idea, and in many cases were not backward in showing that resentment. Just as sharp was the girls' opposition to the old-country tradition of the mother-in-law's control over their married life. They wanted to live by themselves as any American couple would, but few—only the more economically independent—were able to do this.

One evening I sat with a fellow in a sukayaki restaurant, when an elderly Japanese came over and asked my companion, whom he knew slightly, if he was still unmarried. He was; so the man proceeded to cross-examine him about his past and current circumstances, then said he knew of a very fine girl whose parents were well-off and seeking a husband for her. She was American-born, but had lived in Japan for many years and was "in every way as good as a Japan-born female." He was a go-between, perhaps a little desperate to make a bit of money. My companion told him if there was no objection he would look for his own wife, thank you.

I heard of a case where Japanese parents induced or forced their nineteen-year-old American-born daughter to marry a forty-five-year-old Japanese-born man. Out of family loyalty she endured him for a month, then left him with his old-fashioned ideas. In another case, reported in the San Francisco News, a young girl committed suicide rather than be forced to marry a man she did not want. Such instances occur every now and then, but less and less often. Attempts on the part of parents to force or arrange marriages for their children are becoming rarer. The nisei have put up a terrific struggle against them.

Many second-generation girls, especially the good-lookers, are independent—my second sister, of whom I have told you, for one. They set high standards for their future husbands. If such are not immediately at hand when they become of age, they postpone marriage.

The male Japanese Americans' ideas about women are not different from those of the young male population of the United States as a whole. Their criteria of feminine pulchritude are Western, and their eyes are peeled for pretty girls of medium height, with straight and not pug noses, straight legs and slim ankles, well-developed bosoms (which many Japanese girls, unfortunately, lack), and a pleasing personality. They may talk loudly of blondes; but that is simply an American custom. They are ready to settle for a brunette, even if she is not Hedy Lamarr—especially if she possesses some of the previously enumerated attributes; and many nisei girls qualify.

My family is probably average also in point of economics, morale, and group solidarity. Daughters work as maids in "American" households and bring "American" family ideas and household methods into their own homes. The girls are in great demand for domestic work, because they are able and clean, and because when they dress in Japanese costumes in the evening to serve dinner, they add to the color of the occasion.

Where there is a Japanese business worth taking over, there is usually a Japanese American son ready to take it over. He speaks both English and Japanese; he must, for the business often depends solely or largely on Japanese customers. With so many second-generation youths out of work it would seem that these nisei boys who step into their fathers' business boots are the best off economically.

In other departments of life, the tendency of the great majority of the young Japanese Americans is toward Western or American practices, forms, patterns, and ideals which they pick up from their environment, mostly in school, but also from books, newspapers, radio, and the movies. They are partial to American music, dances and sports. A glance at the English sections of the Japanese-language papers reveals this.

Many Japanese Americans change their first names in an effort to become "Americanized." In my family this is true of all eight of us. Takeshi becomes Thomas or Tom; Jiro, John; Mariko, Mary; Haruko, Alice; while almost any Japanese name starting with "F" is made into Frank. The long first names are also shortened (sometimes by the "American" children in school) into such nicknames as Mas, Shig, Yosh, Tosh, Tots, Min, Aki——

Because of the boys' Western criteria in the matter of feminine beauty, and the girls' response to the charms of Spencer Tracy and Clark Gable, there is naturally some interest in intermarriage. Mixed marriages occur (the couples must go outside California for the ceremony), and I have come upon a number of them. They have all the appearances of being successful, but perhaps the husbands and wives involved in these unions with which I am familiar are rather above-the-average in intelligence, character, and economic standing. The children are good-looking and they do not appear to have any serious personality complexes. But nearly all Japan-born Japanese seem to oppose intermarriage, as do most of the second generation, the latter chiefly on the grounds that it causes great social difficulties, which it is hard to overcome unless the couple have a lot of money. (There is no problem, it seems, money cannot solve!) . . .

On one extreme, a large number of the nisei are, or try to be, intensely "American." They have adopted American conventions with a vengeance, but this does not solve their problem. Off and on, under certain circumstances, some are ashamed of their parents' culture, and sometimes even of them as persons. The majority in this group, as in my family, have given up their elders' Buddhism and Shintoism, and become Christians of various denominations, but mostly in the conventional, occasional-churchgoing fashion, although some have also embraced Christ in a fierce personal way, and turned strict puritans and rigid moralists in the Western sense. Many in this category seem perfectly adjusted young men and women. This is especially true of the small minority who have attained the middle-class economic status. But their faces remain Japanese; and I have been told that some in this "Americanized" element suffer occasionally before the mirrors in the privacy of their rooms, for their standards of facial and bodily characteristics also are "American" or Caucasian. . . . Here I touch on matters that call for several Dostoevskis. . . .

On the other extreme, in much smaller numbers than in the first, are second-generation people who tend or pretend to accept their parents' old-country traditions. Many do not differ noticeably from their fathers and mothers; in fact, some strike one as almost more "Japanesey" than their elders. They accept the practice of arranged marriages and other customs of Japan. They are Orientals religiously. Some are unhappy, but remain submissive.

Although technically of the second generation, most of this group are not really nisei, but so-called *kibei*—American-born sons and daughters of Japanese immigrants who were taken or sent to Japan at an early age for their education. At present there are thousands of these boys and girls in Japan. When they come very young, they get along, and are accepted by the people of Japan. The older ones, however, are suspected of American democratic diseases, and are watched.

Many kibei return to the United States. They cannot find other employment, so they take refuge in the domestic- and personal-service field. A few are well-educated and have obtained positions with the larger Japanese firms through the home offices in Japan, or with Japanese consulates and the Japanese Embassy in Washington.

One kibei I met interested me particularly. Externally he was "Americanized." He wore Western clothes even in his home. He spoke good English. He liked to eat T-bone steaks and strawberry shortcake, and had a passion for his new Buick. When I first talked with him, however, all his ideas were in terms of Japan first, last, and always. He hated the whites, British and Americans, and believed in the "destiny of Japan"—a phrase he loved to utter. Once, to see what he would do or say, I made a remark about the Japanese soldiers: that they must be damn' fools to fight in China for fifteen cents a day, barely enough to buy a package of cigarettes in this country. He took this as a personal insult and for two months did not talk to me. . . . Then, when I chanced to meet him one day, he stopped and addressed me. To make sure he was not confusing me with someone else, I referred to our last conversation. He looked embarrassed, and apologized for his attitude at the time; since then he had modified his views to quite an extent. He had gone so far as to entertain some doubts about the invincibility of the Japanese Army, and to conclude that the China war was a blunder.

I learned the reason for this change. His father wanted him to return to Japan and enter the Army. At this point he balked. He said to me, "I believe in family control, and many Japanese customs and ideas are good, but there are two things about the Japanese system in which I definitely do not believe. First, I am going to pick my own wife. Second, I'll be damned if I'll fight in

China for fifteen cents a day! I am an American citizen by birth, and they can't make me join even if I go back to Japan to live." Thus, when it came to practical matters that touched his personal life, he agreed—by implication, at least—that the American way was superior.

The majority of the nisei belong to neither of these extremes, but move, confused, between them; marginal people, neither here nor there, torn between two cultures, finding no function or satisfaction in either. They break away from parental control, but—well, they run into endless rows of *buts*, both in themselves and in their environment. In most cases they are unable to adjust themselves fully to the Occidental group. Their economic predicament is serious. Some become bitter: what's the use! A few cease to care, or so they say. They develop an exaggerated sense of humor, and laugh at their situation and at the squirming of their fellow nisei.

But many in this group, also, turn back partly to the Oriental background and start to study its better points. A considerable number, too, rebel and organize to demand their rights. My brother, whom I mentioned, is an example of this group. They find partial expression in such organizations as the Japanese American Citizens League or in various local political and college clubs. Owing chiefly to these organizations many are beginning to vote.

Most Japanese Americans, of course, are more or less content with their looks, but, as I have suggested, the exterior aspects of the Japanese face and physique are a rather general and serious psychological matter—much in the way the black skin and the crinkly hair are to the Negroes.

The people of the Japanese race, of course, do not all look alike. There are wide variations among them just as there are among any large group. On the average, however, the Japanese are considerably shorter and generally lighter in weight than the whites. The average male, I think, is about five feet two, while the female is an inch or so shorter. In general, the trunk of the Japanese body is well proportioned, but its relative disproportion to the limbs is marked. The legs are short and squat, probably due to the fact that their posture for sitting has been a kneeling or squatting position in Japan. The length of the head in ratio to the trunk is also a little longer than is the case with most Europeans. The eye sockets are small and shallow, and the eyes appear oblique because of the higher level of the outer corner, and the overlap of the upper lid on the lower.

The hair, as a rule, is black and straight. The hands are small, but their fingers are long and delicate. The shape of nose differs widely. The flat nose is not as general as commonly believed. The skin is usually light-brown with a tinge of yellow, but there is great variety also in color.

All this applies mostly to the foreign-born. But, from my observation, as well as on the basis of some existing tentative scientific data, I do not doubt that the variations are even greater in the American generation. First of all, the latter seem to differ considerably from the parents. According to tests which have been made, the American Japanese are taller and heavier than the Japan-born Japanese. This is attributed to environment. Maybe the food in this country is the chief cause for the greater height and weight. It is very rare to find an American-born boy or girl who, on reaching adulthood, is shorter than his or her father or mother. I am not tall, but taller than my father; two of my brothers are taller than I am.

Among the nisei the color of hair is tending to be brownish, while their skin is lighter in general. But the chief difference between the foreign-born parents and their American-born children is in facial expression. The older people have "Japanesey" dead-pans, whereas many of the American generation can display a great variety of emotions facially. The young people doubtless have a better sense of humor. The Japan-born folk have other "Japanese" characteristics. They are stolid, and rarely "let their hair down in public." The nisei are capable of no little spontaneity.

After mingling with the Japanese and the Japanese Americans for a couple of months, I had no trouble spotting one from the other on sight. Among the nisei there are also differences due to climate. The San Francisco fog, for instance, seems to be giving Japanese Americans a lighter skin pigmentation than that of the Japanese American in Los Angeles. Those who grew up in Hawaii are still darker than the Angelenos of Japanese descent.

It was this sort of information that I felt the International Club should examine and discuss. I knew the Negro and Chinese Americans had similar problems, as, I suspected, did (in milder forms), the Jewish and Armenian and Italian and Greek and Yugoslav and Portuguese Americans; problems which were important because they touched vitally their personalities, abilities, and functions; and I thought that they were, or should be, the concern of everybody, for they were subtly affecting the whole country through the second generation. But how to bring them out, even before the tiny college club of which I was president? I tried to talk about it with two professors (philosophy and sociology) who were interested in the club, but I got nowhere. The thing still scared me. It was too close to my own predicament. I was personally no better than the club; in fact, I was a personification of its weaknesses.

At the time, however, I could not admit this to myself. I rationalized it: I was graduating shortly and there was no time to do anything.

IX

In May I graduated, and I cannot summon sufficient modesty to refrain from adding "with the highest honors in my class."

Partly to provide further documentation for my idea that the non-Oriental Americans, or at least some (the best) of them, were ready to meet and mingle with us Oriental Americans, I got together a party of Japanese American fellows and girls, including my two oldest sisters, and took them to the large downtown hotel where the Graduation Ball was held. The girls of our group made a hit. While wearing regular evening gowns, they had accented their Oriental looks for the occasion, and all my non-Oriental friends were asking for introductions so they could dance with them. The dean of the college said it was the first time any "Japanese" had come to one of the big dances of the college, and he was pleasantly surprised.

What I am saying, I realize, may be little more than surface assurance, whistling in the dark. The mere fact that I mention these things reveals my uneasiness over the situation in which we find ourselves. The fact, however, is that throughout the dance we all had a very good time, and I see no reason why other Japanese Americans cannot do what we did. Our participation in the affair suggests a method of progress. Usually, when nisei go to school dances, they stick together and dance mostly with one another. Of course, everywhere things will not work out as well as they did with us in San Francisco, where Orientals and Oriental Americans are allowed to enter and dine and dance in nearly all the better hotels, restaurants and night clubs; it is mostly the lower-type places that have discriminatory rules against them. Elsewhere, you might be barred; but there is nothing like trying. If you don't try, you are licked right there; licked so bad you don't even know you are licked.

"What a Country!
What a Country!"

AFTER graduation, my employers asked me what I planned to do. I said I did not know, and that was the truth. Along with the developments on my job, and with the slant I had got on my family, the last two years in college had been marvelous; now, suddenly disconnected from the place, I was scared—although that may not be the exact word. I was uncertain and worried. I knew my college was not the world, and felt that the ideas concerning Oriental Americans I had developed there might not work out at all in San Francisco or in California in general. I had a notion that what I wanted to do right off was to get out of San Francisco, away from everyone I knew. I wanted to think and get a perspective on things. My bosses thought that was all right and, besides the new car, they gave me five crisp, brand-new twenty-dollar bills "for gas" . . . and I was off.

I drove about for a month, seeing California from one end to the other, and exclaiming to myself: "What a country! What a country!" I visited the institution where I had been an "orphan" and had a chat with the superintendent, who put me up for a few days in the guest cottage.

I went south, and spent a week with my brother. We had long discussions about the second generation. We got closer to each other than ever before; I liked him. A few times I called for him in the vegetable market where he worked, and was impressed by the attractive pictures into which he and his boss' son, also a nisei, had arranged the carrots, squashes, scallions and cauliflower on the stands. The arrangements were downright beautiful. Art. It occurred to me that this might be the Japanese in them, the tendency to fashion the simple everyday things into patterns of beauty. Later I noticed this aesthetic expressiveness in the vegetable and fruit markets run by Japanese immigrants and their children all over Los Angeles. I thought: why shouldn't the instinct for form in these people . . . in *my* people . . . be directed into other channels? Surely there wasn't any too much of it in America. . . .

My brother and I spent several days roaming about in the Japanese Section in Los Angeles, which is much larger than the one in San Francisco. I had a feeling the inner story here was the same as in San Francisco.

I met some of my brother's non-"Japanese" friends. There was an Armenian American boy who grew up in a house near William Saroyan's home in Fresno, where Armenians, it seems, are discriminated against even more than the Japanese in San Francisco or Los Angeles. The story behind this prejudice is long and sordid, a study in communal psychosis, all tangled up in the eco-

nomic factors of Fresno and its vicinity and the fruit-growing industry. . . .
There was a young man from San Pedro whose father and uncles were immigrant fishermen from Dalmatia, and who had endless trouble because his
name was Dragulovich. . . . There was a Negro boy——

II

What a country! . . . I went to work picking fruit and nuts . . . and at the
end of August I was back in San Francisco with more than a hundred dollars
and a car which, without a scratch after four thousand miles, suddenly became
an economic burden in the big city, for it had to be put in a garage. But I
loved it, both for itself, for the way it ran, and because it was a gift from my
ex-bosses; and I wanted to keep it.

The past three months I had given my future much thought, but was still
undecided as to what I wished to become or do with myself in the long run.
Once, as I suggested, I entertained the idea I might teach Oriental history
and culture; teaching continued to appeal to me, but I had—at least tentatively
—given up Oriental history and culture as my subject. In my senior year,
philosophy had begun to attract me, and eventually, I thought, I might want to
teach philosophy with a focus on America and the problems of democracy. I
might want to write in that field. But to do that, to become a philosopher
(as to become an Orientalist), I would need to study further, perhaps at the
U. of C. or Stanford or one of the Eastern universities: which would require
many years and a good deal of money.

I had decided I was in no hurry to make a choice. I was only twenty-two.
What I wanted immediately was a job of some sort for a year or so. I wanted a
full taste of the normal, everyday, year-to-year American world: in business or
industry. (This is how I talked to myself.) I knew it was going to be tough to
get such a job, for it was not likely San Francisco had changed much in the
past four and a half years in reference to the Japanese Americans, but I meant
to tackle the situation that had licked me before and turned me into a houseboy.
I felt strong and ready for anything. I was older and better educated, and I
assumed the odds against me were not as heavy as they had been in 1934.

The first week I made some preliminary inquiries. I went around to nearly
all my friends, including three of my former professors, and asked if they
knew of any place where I might try for a job. One after another they said
they were unable to give me any leads. I did not go to my ex-employers
because I felt they had already helped me enough. At least that was the conscious reason; under it was a fear which subsequently turned out to be justified.

I took the San Francisco business directory; I had a portable typewriter; I
bought a ream of paper, then wrote twenty-five letters of application a day the
first two days of the week and spent the next three days visiting the firms
to which I had written. (Saturdays and Sundays I went home or spent with my
sisters or friends in San Francisco.) I received not even one reply. In the past
eight months, or since early in September, 1939, I have sent out over a thousand

letters and have seen almost as many heads of firms or their employment managers. . . . I am still at it, though less energetically than I was at the start.

Most of the personnel managers and employers proper receive me politely enough, but they explain that, hell! business is "all shot" due to the war in the Orient, or to the one in Europe, or to Roosevelt, or to "this alien bastard Harry Bridges," and for that reason they are taking on no new employees or workers. On top of this, I am told, my difficulty is that I lack previous experience or specific training along some vocational line. A frown usually appears on their faces when I say I can learn in a short time (as I certainly can) any work not too technical or complicated. A few frankly tell me that it is the policy of the firm not to hire Japanese because it might disturb the harmony among the rest of the employees. "But I am not a Japanese; I am an American." When I say this, they smile helplessly and repeat they are sorry, they have nothing against me personally but they haven't anything for me.

Back in September some of my Japanese American friends warned me there was little hope of getting into an "American" firm with my limited equipment. They knew only of a few exceptionally competent and well-trained Japanese American engineers and technicians who had such jobs. I was not convinced as to my own slim chances, and determined at least to try. I know of Japanese American youths who believed on mere hearsay that they had no opportunity of landing anything, and did not even bother to apply. I at least have the satisfaction of trying!

One day I met one of my college friends, who mentioned that he had heard the Stock Exchange was hiring a number of inexperienced "boys" for runners. I hurried down to the personnel office. The woman at the window asked me what I wanted. I said I wished to see the placement manager. She gave me a long look, then said, "Janitors and building helpers apply on the first floor." I explained I was looking for a commercial or office position. A sympathetic glow lit up her face, and she said it would not be much use for me to apply; the chances of a Japanese getting an office job there were extremely slim. I made my routine correction that I was an American, not a Japanese, which confused her and the sympathetic light fled from her face. A week later I met the same friend, who told me that So-and-so and So-and-so, two of our schoolmates (non-Orientals, of course), had been given jobs there the time I had tried to apply.

I have had dozens of similar experiences, and they fill me with mixed feelings of anger, of uncertainty, and—when I drop all my defenses—of deep and general bewilderment. I forget the ideas I had built up the last year in college, and ask myself: what *is* this? Is the problem racial or economic, or both? If both, which is stronger?

Now and then I feel that my trouble is not mostly racial, for I have tried to get employment in numerous Japanese export-import businesses, with the same result. I was told they could not use me because I did not speak and write Japanese. I have learned, too, that Japanese Americans had no future

in Japanese firms in this country. The policy is to import the employees
needed for higher positions from the main offices in Japan. Another factor
in this part of the melancholy picture is that I was never really disappointed
or crestfallen when I failed to get a job with a Japanese firm. I wanted to work
as an American in an American business or industry.

Then I say to myself that the difficulty is, or appears to be, almost wholly
racial. But the next moment I catch myself and wonder. I know that nearly
all unemployed Japanese Americans tend to rationalize their predicaments
on this basis, then stew in the thin, sour juices of their frustration; but this
gives me no satisfaction. I tell myself over and over again that this is a
complicated difficulty, which stacks up something like this:

San Francisco has a long tradition of anti-Orientalism which still lingers
on among the unthinking and uneducated groups, and even among the
educated. It was in this city that a furious agitation went on against the
Japanese from 1900 to 1924. At one time (in 1907, I think) an attempt was
made to segregate the children of Japanese immigrants in one school, but
national public opinion was against such an undemocratic practice, and the
City Fathers were forced to withdraw this plan. Acts of violence also occurred during this period (principally over property), and some newspapers,
notably Hearst's, were loud in denouncing "the Japanese threat" in California.
Politically, such organizations as the California Joint Immigration Committee
led by V. S. McClatchey, pushed discriminatory bills in Sacramento to de-
prive the Japanese of the right to own land and of other such privileges
guaranteed under the Constitution. Since the 1924 immigration laws, agitation of this sort has died down considerably, but there is still a powerful
undercurrent of feeling against the Japanese, which includes Americans who
are native-born children of Japanese. The California Joint Immigration Committee, now under a man named James Fisk, is still active; some of the newspapers continue to delight in spreading fictions about the Japanese fishing
and spy menaces. (If they exist, I am sure our government can handle them
without trouble.) Thus the Japanese element in California—which, after
all, consists of less than 150,000 people, of whom more than half are the
American-born second generation—has an exaggerated position in the public
eye, currently even further exaggerated by the tension between Japan and
the United States. Surely, I say to myself, this group can't be such a threat
to the economic and political life of this State! Yet people insist on regarding
us an integral part of the Japanese Empire. I know a great deal is made of
the fact that we who are American-born hold dual citizenship, but it so
happens that this dual citizenship is not our wish and that in the past few
years over 25,000 of us have dropped the Japanese citizenship—a considerable
number when one bears in mind that the average age of the second generation is only nineteen.

I argue with myself:

We *are* Americans; how could we be anything else? Take me: what am

I if not an American? I am soaked in the lore of this country. Almost my entire experience so far, including all my education, has been American, democratic. I think in terms of the democratic process, the Occident. My favorite writers are Americans: Emerson, Whitman, Mark Twain, Van Wyck Brooks. I follow American standards. I have never been anywhere else. I like it here (in spite of my current doldrums) and I intend to stay, preferably in California, my native State. This is true of nearly all of my fellow Japanese Americans. When some go to Japan, to study at the Tokio University in accordance with the wishes of their parents, they are not accepted or welcomed there, as I have suggested, but are watched by secret police because even with their limited democratic experience, they are considered as corrupt and dangerous by the standards of Japan! . . .

III

Early last January, in a mood of near-desperation, I called up my ex-boss. He asked me to have lunch with him and took me to the beautifully panelled dining-room in the Clift Hotel. I told him my experiences the past several weeks: no job. I remarked, too, that I had not wanted to bother him before this because he and his wife already had done so much for me. He said I was foolish to talk like that, and was deeply sympathetic. Then I asked: could he do anything? I suggested he might try to help me get a job. He winced and said he would try.

He went home and talked to his wife, who also was all for helping me. They called many of their friends, some of whom knew me. Then she asked me to come to see them, and I went. They had a new houseboy, a kibei, who was embarrassed by my coming. We sat down and talked, my two ex-bosses and I. They were uneasy. They could not get any of their friends to take me on in a commercial or office capacity, but two had expressed interest in me as a houseboy. This stung me, and I shook my head rather sharply, which caused an awkward pause in our conversation.

I thought it had never occurred to them I might be interested in working in his business, and I said something to that effect and learned I was mistaken. They had thought of that, said he, very uncomfortable; but there were reasons why he could not take me on. Business was not as good as it had been in '38 and through most of '39; they had been obliged to lay off a number of employees, including two who had been in the firm for years. It would not look right if he took me on now. Besides, his partner (whom his wife did not like personally, and whom I never saw because they did not meet him socially) was "funny," that is, he "had it in for the Japanese." My ex-boss said, "Of course I could shove you down his throat, but that would be unwise in the long run; he could make things damned unpleasant for you, no matter in which department I put you; and it would not help to improve the strained relations between him and me. . . ."

Of course the problem *is* racial. But it *is* also economic. If there was more work, the racial problem would in time, perhaps, ease off by itself. The danger is that many Oriental Americans will fail to realize this. They are apt to hug the idea of the racial problem, and thus damage themselves personally, go sour, and do things which will react unfavorably on the rest of us.

About two years ago I met a young California-born Japanese American who had graduated from the University of Louisiana and spoke with a pronounced Southern drawl. He had a Will Rogers kind of humor when I knew him, except that most of his wisecracks were evidently defensive, issuing from his predicament. He tried to get a job in San Francisco, then went to Los Angeles, his native city. *Nothin' doin'!* My impression of him was that he was able and could develop. He had renounced his Japanese citizenship while still in Louisiana. Yet a few months ago someone whispered to me that this young man had, somehow, been drawn into the Japanese Naval Intelligence Service; nobody knew where he was. Perhaps it is not true, yet conceivably it may be. If it is, God knows what his duties are. His case, of course, is extreme. And I am fairly sure that two years ago he had no idea of entering any service of Japan.

Not that there is danger of any considerable number of Japanese Americans being disloyal to the United States in case of serious trouble with Japan, but I am worried . . . just generally, instinctively worried. The situation in which we find ourselves is not a healthy one. Now and then I feel it is urgent all this be brought out so America can look at it—at me, at us, at herself; we at ourselves, all of us at what we are doing to one another.

What am I trying to say? I am not sure. I am confused, and my long tale probably has no point, unless it is that all of what I have told you is true and that I am confused.

When I received your wire day before yesterday that you would be here today, I tried to work myself into an objective frame of mind. Yesterday and this morning I rode several times in cable cars; I have a notion that riding up that way helps me to attain objectiveness, and that going down tends to push me on the dumps. Riding up, yesterday and today, and getting off on top of the hill—there was the clear, long, wide view of the city, the blue bay, the great new bridge, the ferryboats; the bright cities across the water, including my own home town; Alcatraz, Angel Island, the Golden Gate Exposition—objectivity. But I don't know how well I have succeeded in achieving it. . . . I have had moments of at least near-objectivity in the past, and each time I have felt bewildered contemplating myself. In spite of all the definiteness with which I talk and think at times, I am out of focus and at sea.

If I remember correctly, I began my story with the words "I am an American." I insist I am an American. But am I? What is an American, anyhow? Archibald MacLeish says it's "a strange thing." I'll say it is!

Am I not too insistent on the point of being an American? Now and then

I suspect I have been too hell-bent-for-heaven on finding an "American" job. I may have lost all perspective on the thing. Am I not still trying to get at my problem merely in a surface way? Americanism can't be solely or largely trying to get into an American industry. It is, or should be, a sustaining feeling about America and one's place in America.

Then, too, what is an "American" industry or office? The Matson Steamship Company? Recently I read a statement on the labor question by one of its officials whose Americanism may be doubtful. The Bank of America? Its head is a fellow by the name of Giannini. Someone said that among the most American institutions or establishments in America (in the sense that you don't find them anywhere else, at least) are the Chinese laundry, the Greek restaurant, the Jewish delicatessen store, and the Italian shoeshine stand. Perhaps I should get a job in one of them in order to attain a sustaining feeling about my place in America.

But seriously: in my objective or near-objective moments I realize that, while I may be close to one hundred per cent right on some of the things I have said, I may have been proceeding erroneously, too pugnaciously, even during these past few months. Have I still a chip on my shoulder? Why do I really want to get into an "American" industry? Isn't it mostly to provide myself with some sort of badge or assurance that I belong, that America wants me, even in a humble capacity, and that the color and cast of my face are not a detriment? If so, and I suspect it is so, then, my real purpose is not so much to gain an inside knowledge of the great American business world, nor to find expression or a chance to use my abilities, as it is to bolster and brace up my hurt, uncertain ego.

Usually I consider myself, or want the world to think that I consider myself, rather superior (and I don't doubt that it has crept into my narrative). Now and then I realize that I am a little guy who doesn't really want to be what he is, yet is smug about it, or wants the world to think that everything is fine with him except for a detail here and there. This superiority and smugness throw me pretty much out of kilter. Occasionally I realize I don't want to be only an American or a Japanese American, but that I want to show the other Japanese Americans I can get a job of which they don't even dare dream.

I told you that I was glad when I failed to get a job with a Japanese concern. That probably reveals a weakness in my Americanism. If I were definitely an American, why couldn't I be working for a Japanese boss? Isn't Americanism, perhaps, an attitude of one's mind and feelings that issues out of an inner harmony which is respected by one's environment and should endure anywhere? I haven't that harmony. Nor has most of the second generation of Oriental descent. We are all orphans psychologically, confused; cluttered up with our past, with the past of our immigrant parents; afflicted with our faces—all of which, of course, involves also America, which, cluttered up with *her* own past, thinks she is still the America of a hundred or fifty years ago, when the great majority of people here were Anglo-Saxon Americans.

How to attain that inner harmony? I had a touch of it during my last two years in college, after the student officer stopped me on the campus and I started to get along with my bosses and my family. The climax of that period was the Graduation Dance . . . yet how pathetic that I should mention it again!

I am afraid that I cannot really attain objectivity by myself in any pure form. Nor can the rest of the Oriental second generation by itself. . . . I have mentioned my rides uphill in cable cars. Of course this is ridiculous, but, perhaps, also a bit interesting symbolically. You know how the cable cars groan and grind and jangle and rattle. All those discordant noises cut through any objectiveness I ever experience.—

IV

How do I manage to live? . . . Well, as I have said, I had a little over a hundred dollars when I returned to San Francisco late last summer. Then I put ads in the papers that I had a car and was ready to drive people on any legitimate business almost anywhere. I received a few calls, including two trips to Los Angeles and back, and picked up some money that way. In January, after my last talk with my ex-bosses, I sold the car for a fairly good price. I have been living on that since.

I am determined to stay off relief, although as a last resort I probably will apply to the National Youth Administration, which is not quite relief. I know a number of young Japanese Americans who have been helped by the NYA.

About a month ago, still in the grip of my old idea of wanting to get an "American" job, I thought I would try to enlist in the armed forces of the United States. What could be more "American" than the Army, the Navy or the Marine Corps!

The general recruiting station is in the basement of the Federal Building in the Civic Center. At the entrance is a large poster urging red-blooded Americans to enlist and see the world. I went into the Marine recruiting office first. The sergeant inquired what I wanted, and I told him I would like to enlist. He looked at me and opened his mouth as if to say something, but he did not reply. I emphasized that I was an American, and remarked I wanted to serve my country. Finally he answered: "It has been the general tradition of the Marine Corps not to enlist any members of minority races. We take a few American Indians, that's the only exception. We have no place," he continued, "even for American-born Orientals, because we don't use them for mess duties, cooks, stewards and the like."

I said, "Do you question the loyalty of Oriental Americans?"

"Oriental Americans?" he asked, puzzled. "Oh, I see what you mean; you *are* American. No, we don't question your loyalty." He frowned as if he thought me a wise guy. "It's just the tradition, that's all."

I went to the Navy recruiting office. What did I want? I wanted to enlist. The petty officer looked surprised. Was I a citizen? I was; then he appeared very much embarrassed. He asked me a number of questions: where was I born? how old was I? where did I live? and so on. Then he said he was sorry, he could not give me an application blank. Orientals were accepted only when special calls for their services were issued. "What sort of special calls," I asked. "Well," he said, "we use some Orientals in mess departments. When vacancies occur, a call goes out; sometimes we put ads in the papers. . . . You look intelligent, and you will understand why we have this policy. If we enlisted Orientals generally for all branches, where they would have the right to promotion, a difficult situation might arise. Some of the other men might resent having Orientals in positions over them." I said that seemed to be a poor basis for the policy. If a man proved himself able to hold a superior position or rank, those under him would generally respect him. I pressed him to comment on this, but he just shrugged his shoulders. For a minute I had a good mind to tell him my father had served in the United States Navy and proved himself a hero in the *Bennington* disaster, but then I thought it would be silly, and walked out.

The experience in the Army recruiting office was similar. I would have to get permission to apply for enlistment from the commanding officer of some Army post. I said I was a citizen and asked if every would-be recruit had to get such a permission. The sergeant was annoyed and said the policy regulating Army enlistments did not encourage Orientals to apply. I asked him why. "Listen, young fellow," he said, "I don't want to talk to you. If you want to, come in in the morning and talk to the Colonel, see? Why should I be sticking my neck out? . . ."

After the interviews at the recruiting offices I rode uphill in a cable car. . . . I thought of my brother, of the artistic arrangement of fruits and vegetables in the store where he worked, of the fruits of the earth brought together and arranged in a pattern of beauty, harmony and color. . . . The car groaned and jangled.

LUPE VALDEZ
MET HELEN SMITH

Pleading [in 1926, as a Congressman from Texas] for the defeat of a bill intended to restrict the immigration of seasonal agricultural workers from Mexico, Mr. Garner [Vice President of the United States 1933-41] explained that Texas landowners expected cheap migratory labor and that the Mexicans were satisfied with $25 a season. "They are not troublesome people unless they become Americanized," Mr. Garner continued. "The sheriff can make them do anything."
—HAMILTON BASSO, in *The New Republic*, February 26, 1940.

There are differences that characterize personalities, and that likewise characterize groups, nations and races, that should not be deplored and discouraged. Neither should they be tolerated merely—tolerance being touched with conscious superiority, and therefore less of a virtue than it appears to be. These characterizing differences in individuals and groups are to be sought out, appreciated and fostered as the essential ingredients of a rich common culture. . . . In the most practical sense, everybody needs everybody else, and it becomes more and more evident that we can develop our own potentialities to the fullest only by doing everything in our power, not only to understand, but to bring to active and creative life the highest potentialities in other people. . . .
—BART ANDRESS, executive director The Good Neighbor Committee, in *The Standard* for April, 1938, issued by the American Ethical Union.

A Young Man
from Mexico

GUADALUPE TORO VALDEZ—Lupe, for short—was born on the day after Christmas in 1905 at the Rancho de Las Ajuntas, not far from Hidalgo, in Coahuila, Mexico.

His father, Nemesio Valdez, managed one of the haciendas owned by Lupe's widowed grandmother, Señora Severa Granados de Valdez; he supervised the work, rationed the *peones*, inspected the crops, and bought and sold cattle, horses and sheep. A dashing young *caballero*, he sported picturesque jackets, hats, boots and serapes; rode beautifully on spirited piebald steeds; shot so well he was nicknamed "Buena Vista," which might be translated "Eagle Eye"; and was wont on the most meager, or indeed no, provocation to break into song with a fine tenor. He was twenty when he married; his bride—Paulita Gonzalez, a slim little girl with an eager expression on her small oval face—was only sixteen.

Their second child—a girl, Ziola—came three years after Lupe. And it was a year or so after this that the youthful father was elected to a minor but much-coveted local office. A week later he was deer hunting in the forest near Piedras Negras; a party of hunters, which included his defeated rival, came along; a shot was fired and the fledgling politico fell dead.

Considering herself a glint in the sheen of Mexico's upper crust, his mother had never approved of his marriage, for Paulita Gonzalez came from all but the lowest social level and had a touch of Indian blood in her veins, while the Valdezes and Granadoses were supposed to stem undeviatingly from the *conquistadores*; and now her rancor against her widowed young daughter-in-law began to spurt into the open. The old lady wanted to take the handsome four-year-old Lupe and raise him as befit one who would fall heir to her properties and carry on the Valdez line. But Paulita, just twenty, balked; she would keep her son and her lofty, aristocratic mother-in-law could will her haciendas to someone else!

Four months after the shooting, which was declared a "hunting accident," Lupe's second sister, Amparo Nemesia, was born . . . whereupon, in mid-spring 1910, Paulita Gonzalez viuda de Valdez gathered her little brood and, forfeiting for herself and them the opulence and comfort of the Rancho de Las Ajuntas, followed her own parents, who had emigrated awhile previously, over the border to Texas.

A month later the Revolution broke out below the Rio Grande, and the old Señora Valdez, lifelong supporter of Dictator Diaz, lost everything but her lands; buildings were razed and the crops, sheep and cattle and horses were seized by the revolutionaries. The proud woman died soon afterward of impotent fury and sorrow over what had befallen her and Mexico.

II

Paying a nickel toll, Paulita crossed on foot the International Bridge from Nuevo Laredo, Coahuila, to Laredo, Texas. She carried several bundles and pushed her two little daughters in a squeaky baby carriage, while Lupe, clinging to her colorful satin skirt, toddled by her side. She registered at the United States immigration station, then proceeded to find her people.

Her father, Refugio Gonzalez, was an immigrant tenant farmer; he and his family moved from place to place over the vast stretches of Texas, barely managing to exist, and Paulita and her children became involved in their poverty and roamings. Mamá Juana Gonzalez had several children as young as Paulita's; in fact, three of Lupe's aunts and uncles were younger than he. Together they made a numerous family.

Most of the dwellings in which Paulita and her children lived during their first seven years in the United States were no worse or better than are the average tenant farmer's quarters in Texas nowadays. In summer the shacks were stifling; in winter the interiors had to be plastered with newspapers to keep out the cold northers. The dirt, flies and stench during the hot months were more severe hardships for Lupe and his mother, who had had a taste of life's refinements, than for the others. The water was seldom fit to drink. The diet of frijoles, chile, tortillas, and only rarely some other victual, resulted in the children growing up with lean and lithe little bodies, strong white teeth, and a tendency toward colds, headaches, rashes, and stomach disorders.

Wherever they moved, Paulita, with her knowledge of a better standard of living, strived to improve their condition. They never stayed anywhere longer than ten months, however, and in each new place she faced problems almost overwhelming for one of her limited experience and education. She had received only a few years' schooling in a convent in Coahuila on whose lands (adjoining the Rancho de Las Ajuntas) her parents had worked as farm laborers when she was in her early and middle teens.

Not knowing English was a handicap, for in Texas all the advantages seemed to belong to those who spoke that language. Paulita resented this: English appeared to be an extremely difficult tongue, perhaps quite beyond her powers to learn. During her second year in the United States, in a squalid little sharecropper camp, giving unconscious vent to this resentment, and hoping also to earn a few extra dollars, she started a private school for Mexican children whose parents wanted them to learn good Spanish. But the enterprise met with scant success. Obliged to work in the fields with their parents, the youngsters could not attend regularly.

The ensuing year, when they happened to take up a piece of land near Austin, she obtained work in a local factory in the hope of bettering the family's lot; again, however, she succeeded but slightly; she had to labor sixty hours a week for four dollars. Every once in a while she came near to feeling effort was futile.

When Lupe was nine, his mother, in a confusion of impulses and motives, remarried. The man was Texas-born of Mexican parentage. He spoke fluent English of a kind (which, perhaps, was his chief attribute in Paulita's eyes) and was good-hearted. Lupe and he got along splendidly. But the marriage was a mistake from the start. He had a powerful fixation against schools and education and a curious passion to remain just what he was: an ordinary, illiterate laborer or sharecropper. He objected strenuously to all of Paulita's ideas and efforts to raise the family to a higher level. There were arguments, scenes. To him, education was a superficial acquirement that distracted one from basic, simple values. "We are what we are," he used to say; "you can't change the heart of a tree by flinging ornaments across its boughs." With this Paulita disagreed fervently: education was something to be absorbed from the soil through the roots, and from the atmosphere by the leaves. It was natural enough; was not growth stimulated by fertilizer once in a while? Was not the tree or plant stronger then? Could you not graft superior twigs onto an inferior trunk or bough and cause it to produce superior fruit? . . .

Eventually they separated (or, rather, he simply disappeared one day and was never heard of again). But before that happened Lupe worked in the fields with his stepfather, helping with the plow and harrow, hoeing, weeding, digging, caring for animals. He was small and, like the other youngsters in the family, undernourished, but quick and agile, and possessed considerable endurance. During the cotton season, when the whole family hired out to the big planters, he picked cotton with the rest, and presently scored a good daily average. At night he often slept on a heap of cotton from which he leapt at daybreak when the foreman called.

Until he was eleven, Lupe's education consisted of about three months' annual attendance in dingy, dilapidated one-room country schools between work seasons; and, as is the case of the majority of Mexican tenant farmers' children in Texas even today, his attendance was irregular. When he did go to school, he learned practically nothing. The overworked, underpaid country teachers had enough trouble with the general run of American children, who attended regularly and had no language handicap, without bothering with "these Mexican kids," who were a problem any way one looked at them. Lupe listened without understanding and stayed in the same grade, the first.

When he was eleven, the family chanced to live on a place near Smithville, Texas, and that year, somehow, he managed to get five months of schooling. At the start, still in the first grade, he knew almost no English. During recess time, American children would encircle him, a curiosity, and ply him with questions, to all of which he answered, "I dunno!" This reply provoked howls of laughter, especially when they asked him in what grade he was. But the teacher in this school paid some attention to him. A few months later, when he had picked up a bit of English, he overheard an American boy ask another, "What grade are you in?" The question clicked in his brain and the next instant his smooth olive skin reddened with retroactive embarrassment.

From Smithville the Gonzalez-Valdez clan moved to a place ten miles outside the town of Welder. The nearest school was seven miles away; so Lupe did not attend at all that year. His mother fretted over this, and started another Spanish school, restricting it to her family and the three children of a Mexican neighbor. That winter Lupe learned a good deal of his native tongue and lore, and Paulita's concern for her children's education stiffened into determination.

III

Her second husband had left them by then, and Mamá Paulita—as they all, including her parents and brothers and sisters, had begun to call her—induced the whole family to go to San Antonio. She had heard that workers were needed there. They loaded their belongings on a rickety farm wagon behind a decrepit old mare and an overambitious young mule, and in the small hours of a windy autumn morning in 1917 passed through downtown San Antonio, where a policeman, who knew a little Spanish, directed them to the barrio, the Mexican section. Lupe gaped open-mouthed at the size and magnificence of San Antonio. Passing by the railroad station, they saw a regiment entraining, and recalled hearing six months earlier that the United States was at war with Germany.

The barrio in San Antonio is on the east side, and was—as it still is, largely —a slum district. Housing and sanitary conditions were incredibly primitive, if not hazardous to the health of the entire city.

The newly arrived spent the first few days camping in an empty lot, then rented a shack for five dollars a month, and Papá Gonzalez and his oldest son got jobs in a large packing house. Work there was not pleasant, but wages were higher than at the pecan plants, in which multitudes of Mexicans, male and female, adult and very young, born south and north of the Rio Grande, worked ten hours daily for three dollars a week; and in a couple of months, under Mamá Paulita's management of the exchequer, the two-in-one family forged sufficiently ahead to rent a larger dwelling, which, in fact, rated being called a house.

Education now became a regular part of the routine in Lupe's life. With his sisters and a squad of his aunts and uncles, he attended Public School No. 21 in the barrio. The principal and teachers were all Anglo-Saxon Americans who knew no Spanish, but most of them were aware of the conditions and problems of the community. The entire flock of Gonzalez-Valdez children, ranging in ages from seven to seventeen, started in the first grade. One of the first things they were taught was to clean their teeth: if they could not afford to buy toothbrushes, they should use little mesquite twigs; and if they had no tooth paste, fine wood ashes would serve as a substitute. At any rate, that was how Lupe understood the instructions, and he followed them religiously.

His teacher, a young American woman with a fair complexion and an abundance of tawny hair, liked him and was generally good to all the children. One day after school, just before Christmas, she asked him to help her carry some packages home. When they reached her house, she invited him in to get a handful of her mother's holiday cookies. But, glimpsing a part of the interior as she opened the door, Lupe was awe-stricken. He had never been inside one of these beautiful American homes (although it was really only an average lower-middle-class dwelling). He wanted terribly to accept her invitation, but something—the fear of the outsider, the secret shame of the economic inferior, the hesitancy of the sensitive—made him refuse, and he ran away. Out of sight of the teacher's house, he stopped, weak and trembly all over.

By-and-by Lupe got a job selling newspapers. After school, he called for his quota of papers, then followed the American lads around a while to learn what the big news was to yell about, for his English was still uncertain. It usually was war news; and, reaching his corner, he duplicated the sounds of the other boys as well as he could.

Selling out, Lupe walked the several miles to the barrio. Often he did not get home till nine in the evening, usually famished. On the way he would look hungrily into the restaurants, particularly into a certain Chinese place, in front of which he always slowed down involuntarily, wishing he might eat there some day.

One evening, having disposed of his papers earlier than usual, he paused before this café, fingering the coins in his pockets and dreaming how nice it would be to go in and order one of those dishes whose savory smells reached the sidewalk. Swallowing the overflow of saliva, he hesitated; then, suddenly, a huge workingman from a near-by cotton warehouse lunged in, and Lupe found himself directly behind him, swept in by his desire.

Frightened by his own daring, he raised himself upon the high stool at the counter beside the man. The Chinese waiter put a menu card before him; Lupe knew he would not understand much of it, but before he even had a chance to look at it, the giant next to him bellowed, "Hot fish!" and so Lupe, repeating the words as well as he could, ordered "hot fish," too. It was the most delicious food he had ever tasted. He imitated the workingman by putting on a generous serving of catsup; he ate as the man ate, paid as he paid, and walked out behind him, treading on top of the world.

After this Mamá Paulita was allowed no calm till she let Lupe take her to the Chinese place and treat her to "hot fish"—one of his favorite dishes to this day.

IV

The family was in San Antonio barely a year, when Mamá Paulita, personally unhappy, vaguely unfulfilled, and ever seeking for avenues that might lead to a better future for them all, abruptly fell under the spell of an itinerant evangelist, and soon after decided to turn Protestant—a decision that had a profound effect on the course of Lupe's life.

He and his sisters began to attend the Sunday school of the local Mexican Protestant church, and he enjoyed it. Having inherited his father's tenor, he joined the boy's choir, which sang at the Sunday services, and he liked that, too. Also, the preacher had a powerful, sonorous voice and a talent for rolling, leaping phrases, which fascinated Lupe, giving him pleasant sensations even when he had no idea what was being said.

With the zeal of the new convert, Mamá Paulita herself engaged in church activities. One day she heard of a new denominational school for Mexican boys sponsored by the Presbyterian Church. Somehow, Lupe's name was sent in for enrollment, and in January, 1919, he found himself at the Texas-Mexican Institute, which had begun its career a few years earlier under the guidance of the crusading clergyman and educator, Dr. James W. Skinner, on a three-hundred-acre tract of land near Kingsville, Texas, donated for that purpose by the heirs of the fabulous King Ranch.

About twenty-five boys were enrolled when Lupe arrived. The buildings were temporary frame structures; the school had a meager budget; there were a print shop, a dairy, and about two hundred acres under cultivation. Attending classes in the forenoon and studying evenings, the boys were obliged to work in the afternoons. The teachers were all old-stock Americans; they understood no Spanish, were not interested in the language, and made no attempt to explore the boys' Mexican background. The food and entire routine were "U. S. American." The boys spoke Spanish among themselves, but were required to use English during the class periods.

"To take me from the Mexican environment in which I had been reared and place me in a school of this sort," Lupe Valdez told me years later, "was probably the best thing that could have happened to me at that age. I was thirteen, small and undernourished, and my knowledge of English, even with the year in the San Antonio public school, was scant and rather mechanical. I had learned to read a little by rote; I did not associate words with their meanings, but read pages by memory. Upon entrance, a teacher asked me to read something so she could assign me to the proper grade. By coincidence, she opened her book at the page with Coleridge's poem 'Why the Leaves Come Down,' which—God alone knows why—our San Antonio teacher had made us memorize. I did not let on, of course, but, pretending to read from the book, although I had only the vaguest notion of the poem's meaning, recited with all the fervor and expression I had been taught. The teacher was impressed and delighted, and placed me in the third grade.

"My attendance at Tex-Mex was made possible by the generous contribution of one hundred dollars of a Mr. Sands of Los Angeles, whom I never met and who never communicated with me. Church members scattered throughout the Southwest donated certain amounts to help Mexican boys through school. I learned of Mr. Sands' existence in my second year in Kingsville; later I wanted to thank him in person for what he had done for me, but when I tried to locate him in Los Angeles, I found I had come too late. . . ."

Lupe progressed rapidly. He began to connect English words with their meanings, and after the first half-year he advanced a grade every couple of months. He was obedient and docile, a "good boy," and his teachers thought they had made a find. They fired him with missionary zeal; at fifteen he announced he would become a preacher.

But to describe Lupe during this period as obedient and docile does not give the complete picture. He was capable also of acts which suggest opposite attributes—especially when some unfriendly, careless, or inconsiderate hand hurt his feelings that were enmeshed in his Mexican background and pride.

Once, for instance, he took part in a very undocile incident. It began in the history class, which had been assigned the section on the Texas Revolution in the textbook. The boys—dimly aware of the fact that the United States had taken several states, including Texas, away from Mexico—heard the assignment with tense expressions, for it dealt a bit exuberantly, though factually enough (at least from the North American angle), with the exploits of Sam Houston, who had subdued the Mexicans, albeit the latter far outnumbered the resourceful Anglo-Saxon Americans.

"That evening"—to quote from Lupe Valdez' narrative to me two decades later—"we called a meeting in one of the boys' rooms to talk the matter over. And the more we discussed it, the angrier we became at being assigned a lesson which showed the people of our blood in so unfavorable a light. What to do? First, in all of our copies of the book we defaced Sam Houston's picture beyond recognition. Then we decided the whole story had no place in a textbook from which we were supposed to study. This inspired one of the boys to rip the offending pages from his copy, and the rest of us, in a spirit of exultation, followed suit, telling each other we had paid for the books with the money provided for us, not by our unknown benefactors or the church, but by our parents.

"Next day an abnormally quiet group of boys filed into the classroom. The teacher asked us to turn to page so-and-so. My seatmate was the first to be called upon, and he replied with suppressed excitement, his black eyes dancing, that his book did not have that page. The teacher then called me. My copy, too, lacked the page. She called on the boy behind me, who announced that it was not in his book either. Puzzled, the teacher looked at our texts, then glanced at her own copy. Watching her, the class was so still you could hear the specks of dust dancing on the sheaf of sunbeams that poured in through a window. Finally, red as a beet, she nodded her head and said, 'Let us take the next chapter for tomorrow. Class is dismissed.' . . ."

v

Lupe was going on twenty when he graduated from the Tex-Mex "high school" in 1925. The school was not accredited; he missed much fundamental education, but it was a beginning.

The Mexican Presbytery was anxious to send Lupe to the Presbyterian Seminary in Austin for a short period of training before sending him "into the field." But the idea of preaching with his scant knowledge (except, perhaps, of the Bible) appalled him. He felt deeply the need of more education and experience before he tried to interpret life here and in the hereafter to others. Doctor Skinner was the only person to see his viewpoint, and he encouraged him in his determination to obtain further instruction.

The Mexican Protestant clergy, who were his immediate superiors and advisers, discouraged him: "You know as much as other Mexican preachers, and you speak better English. . . . If you get more education your natural ardor will cool and you won't continue in The Work." Finally it came down to this: if he wanted more training, he would have to get it without their aid; furthermore, if he decided not to become a preacher, he would be obliged to repay, when he could, the several hundred dollars that had been spent on him in his last two years at Tex-Mex on the assumption he would enter the ministry.

His docility got itself unaccountably into reverse, and, in a stubborn mood, he enrolled in the Texas College of Arts and Industries, a State-supported teachers' college (now a regular college), also located in Kingsville.

"How I would manage," he reminisced long afterward, "I had no idea, but I decided to show 'em. For a while I maintained slight, tentative connections with my recent religious background by helping in the Mexican Sunday school in Kingsville, and preaching occasionally before small congregations as a substitute pastor; then, when the minister, a Texas-born half-Mexican, with whom I was boarding, objected to my studying anything but the Bible on Sunday, my held-in insurgence broke forth, and I spoke my mind. In rebuttal, I was called an ingrate, a backslider, and worse. My beginning to smoke just then was regarded a scandal and a logical development of my deplorable attitude."

Texas A. & I. accepted Lupe on the condition that he make good grades the first year; otherwise his unaccredited secondary education would not be recognized. He worked hard, and did well. He had obtained work cleaning business offices before and after school hours, and eventually began to earn enough to pay for his room and to feed and clothe himself.

After two years at A. & I., he was offered a teaching position in the little

town of McFaddin, near Victoria, in southeastern Texas. He accepted it
with alacrity. It was a six-month elementary school for Mexican children;
the pay, $540 the year, which to Lupe appeared a tremendous amount.

He had a total of twenty-five pupils in all the grades, most of them, however, in first and second; all in one room. He boarded in the home of a
better-to-do Mexican family, and became the chum of their Texas-born son,
Gabriel Jiminez, who was also college educated. For the first time since leaving the Rancho de Las Ajuntas, Lupe had all the milk he wanted, and
plenty of sleep. The first three months in McFaddin he gained fifteen pounds.

Associating almost exclusively with the Mexican element, he and Gabriel
attended fiestas in McFaddin, in Victoria and other neighboring towns. The
people liked Lupe, and he liked them. Teaching appealed to him, and he
imagined he might like to stay there permanently and marry one of the attractive local girls.

But there were vaguely disquieting experiences. . . . One evening, driving through Victoria at suppertime, Lupe and Gabriel stopped and entered
an eating place on the main street. They were shown to a table and given
the menu, which they proceeded to discuss in Spanish, the language they
were in the habit of speaking interchangeably with English. The owner was
suddenly embarrassed, then told them in an apologetic manner he could not
serve Mexicans in the restaurant; if they wished to eat, would they mind
stepping into the kitchen in the rear and be served there? "No, thank you,"
snapped Lupe with the icy definiteness of which only the hot-tempered and
often indecisive Latins are capable; "we shall eat elsewhere."

VI

Meantime, of course, things had happened to the rest of the family. Lupe's
elder sister Ziola had "Americanized" her first name to Sally, had learned
typing, and—by the mid-1920's—was working in an insurance company's office
in San Antonio. The younger sister Amparo Nemesia (who later called
herself Gladys) finished her schooling at Pres-Mex, a sister school of Tex-
Mex. And one of their uncles had gone to Los Angeles, where he earned
eighteen dollars weekly in a cafeteria. He sent back such glowing accounts
of Southern California that Mamá Paulita got the idea they should all go
there. But it was Sally who decided matters. Her boss had suggested she come
with him to Los Angeles where he was to open a branch office, and she said
she would.

Early in 1928 Mamá Paulita and her daughters went to California. Lupe
decided to keep his job in McFaddin another year as an economic backlog
for all of them, since they were uncertain how the female part of the family
would fare in Los Angeles, while the Gonzalezes' income in San Antonio was
also subject to unpredictable ups and downs.

But the girls got off to a good start. Sally's boss gave her a raise two months
after opening the new office; Gladys worked here and there, sporadically;

and Mamá Paulita got a steady job as janitress in a downtown office building. Evenings, to improve what English she had picked up in Texas, she attended the Adult Educational Center, which had—still has—special, intelligently conducted classes for the foreign-born.

Arriving in Los Angeles in the summer of 1929, Lupe found his mother full of self-confidence and ambition for his future. He must, she insisted, resume his studies, for she had learned Texas A. & I. was not the best college in the world. Here in California were great universities, where he could learn much that would help him become an effective man. She did not blink an eye when informed he would be subject to a $75-a-semester non-resident fee at the University of California at Los Angeles.

They lived in a tiny apartment in a worm-eaten old house on Figueroa Street, with few conveniences, and daily Lupe rode an hour each way between the city and the new U.C.L.A. at Westwood. Mamá Paulita continued her own education in night school, for the former terror of her life, the English language, now fascinated her. She was a happy woman. Her children would be part of this great North American land yet. She sent small amounts of money to her parents in San Antonio, who were having a hard time as the Depression sank its hooks into the country.

Lupe, however, was anything but happy through most of his first year in Los Angeles. He was in his mid-twenties, and all his life had lived and mingled almost exclusively with Mexicans. Even at Texas A. & I. he had stayed in the Latin-American group. Somehow, in Texas the implication was that Americans were superior to Mexicans (this had been true even at Tex-Mex); Lupe had heard his people called "greasers" and "spicks." And here in California the idea of associating freely with American students did not seem quite right to him. He felt lost and inferior on the campus and uncomfortable at home with the family.

Mamá Paulita's brother, although his junior, talked to him uncle-like, repeatedly trying to convince him that at his age he ought not let his mother continue to support him and pay for his education; education was "mostly the bunk, anyhow"; he ought to go to work. The youthful uncle was sure he could get him a job at eighteen a week in the cafeteria, where he himself was now getting $21.50.

His sisters, too, were not over-enthusiastic that he should continue his studies; and now and then, while recognizing the wisdom of his mother's insistence to the contrary, Lupe tended almost to agree with them. He studied hard, even harder than he had studied at Texas A. & I., but could make only "C's." The teachers impressed him as remote, indifferent.

Then he struck up an acquaintance with Juan Estaban Tablada, a young Californian of Mexican parentage, who also attended U.C.L.A. and who did much to pull Lupe out of the doldrums. Well-oriented, brilliant, a lively conversationalist and a good mixer, Johnny (as Juan was commonly called) had many "U. S. American" friends, and from him Lupe learned that it was perfectly all right for him, or any Mexican, to mingle with them on terms of equality. "Hell, they're no better 'n we are," said Johnny, although his home environment was typically Mexican and he himself was pure Mexican in many respects. Unable to digest American food, he lived on a Mexican diet. His mother spoke almost no English, though his sisters and nieces and nephews knew it as well as their Spanish.

Through his new associations, Lupe learned that a private school conducted for Americans who wanted to learn Spanish needed a part-time teacher for evening classes. He applied, and the job he got, though not much in point of pay, brought him in close touch with "U.S. Americans" of an entirely different type than he had encountered theretofore. The director of the school featured a get-together of the students and teachers every two weeks at some Mexican restaurant, where everyone conversed in Spanish, sang Spanish and Mexican songs, and ate Mexican food.

It was at one of these suppers that Lupe Valdez became acquainted with Helen Smith, one of his pupils.

A Young Woman
in the United States

FRED SMITH—Helen's father-to-be—was not yet eighteen when he ran away from the Missouri corn farm he called home and joined the United States Army. This was in the mid-nineties. . . . A sturdy young fellow, he liked the Army, and soon was a non-com. During the Spanish-American War, or, more accurately, the Philippine Insurrection, he went up for a commission and got it. He served also in the Boxer Rebellion.

While on leave in San Francisco, he met Maude Brinley, a zealous young missionary combatting sin on the old Barbary Coast. She was California-born of New England stock that had reached the Coast by way of Ohio and Minnesota. They married in 1901 and spent the next two years at a garrison in Hawaii, where Helen's oldest sister was born. Fred Smith became a first lieutenant and during the next few years was stationed here and there around the Golden Gate.

Helen was born in 1907 at Fort Baker, California.

Fanatically loyal to her faith, Maude Smith hated Army life, and made no effort to conceal her abhorrence of "hops," bridge, drinking and smoking. The wives of other officers took to calling her Mrs. "Blue-nosey." Finally, three years after Helen's birth, she won her point, and Fred Smith resigned his commission.

First he tried his hand at running a grocery store in San Ubaldo. The work was hard. Two more children came, and Maude was in poor health. Fred gave up the store and leased a vegetable farm near town. Then he bought a dairy ranch, which he traded after four years for a twenty-acre prune orchard.

Here Helen spent most of her girlhood. She attended a small country school about a mile from the ranch. Her mother and teachers regarded her a "model child." "As a baby," she speculated at the age of thirty-three for my benefit, "I must have been terribly frightened by someone, for my fear of people amounted practically to a phobia. At eight or nine I was shy and diffident; I blushed without provocation and was afraid to do anything which might cause me to be noticed."

Much of this time Mrs. Smith was a semi-invalid, while Mr. Smith was so much concerned over the mortgage on his ranch and the paying of his wife's hospital and doctor bills that he gave scant attention to his growing children.

When Helen finished the fourth grade, at the age of eleven, her teacher arranged to have her skip the fifth grade, which meant that the following school year she would be in "the big room," where the three upper grades were. She was quietly elated over this—until she overheard a classmate whom she admired remark disparagingly to another girl, "Helen is the teacher's pet, that's why she's skipping." This comment precipitated a revolution in her life. She suffered the agonies of self-consciousness that only an extremely shy person, already ill at ease in the world, can suffer. She hid around and wept for days, then decided to become the school devil and thus prove definitely she was not teacher's pet.

II

The rest of Helen's school life was Rebellion with a capital *R*. Her teachers were unable to understand what had "come into her"; her parents worried, without understanding what made her "act so," or knowing how to cope with the situation. An *A* student in the classroom, she was a hellion outside it. She smoked before finishing grammar school and started drinking the second year in high school. She led a small gang of rebels, and could get them into, and out of, more trouble than the average child dreamed existed. Because of the bald-faced lies she could tell without a tremor, the gang nicknamed her Angel Face. And the principal ranted, raved and threatened expulsion. She was saved from dismissal only because, when in a tight place, she managed to squirm out by evading definite proof of anything serious enough to merit it.

Helen carried Rebellion into her home. Dissatisfied with the drab, ill-fitting homemade clothes she wore during grammar school, she surprised her father at the age of thirteen by offering to pick prunes in the summertime if he would pay her as any other worker. She said she would bank her money and buy her school clothes with it, provided she be permitted to select her own things. Delighted by this show of industry and thrift, both for themselves and as a possible sign of general reformation, Mr. Smith agreed readily.

Helen worked so hard she became one of the best prune-pickers on the place, if not in the valley, and amazed herself with the money she earned. Her father felt obliged to limit her to an eight-hour day. For the first time she tasted independence in selecting her clothes—over the protests of her mother and elder sister, but with her father's sanction. It was wonderful to resume school in the fall dressed as the other girls were.

Mrs. Smith continued to object to dancing, card playing, and merriment of any sort. Her daughters were not allowed to go to any parties or movies, to do anything socially but attend church, Sunday school, and Young People's affairs. Mr. Smith acquiesced in these things, to please his wife and encourage her to get well. Besides, he was principal of the Sunday school and a member of the church board of trustees: two functions which satisfied his urge for leadership.

As the initial attack against this situation, Helen started using cosmetics, and the more opposition her make-up aroused in the family, the more lavishly she applied it. Then came the King Tut Era (about 1922, when Helen was fifteen), and, in the face of her mother's declaration that she looked like a streetwalker, Helen took to wearing long, dangling earrings. One morning on the way to school a girl whom she admired dared her to have her hair cut; at noon she walked into a barbershop and came out with a King Tut bob. Her father gasped on seeing her; her mother did not speak to her for weeks. But in less than a year her older sister had her hair cut, and two years later Mr. Smith told his wife she would look better if hers were short too.

Besides the regular Sunday and Wednesday-evening church attendance which her parents, particularly her mother, required, Helen was forced to go to various evangelistic revivals, including Aimee Semple McPherson's tent meetings and healing shows. Worse yet were the scenes after the revival meetings in the homes where converts rolled on the floor, jabbering unintelligibly. She decided this was embarrassing and humiliating, and laid careful plans for extending her Rebellion against churchgoing.

First she started arguing with the dogmatic Sunday-school teacher. How could all those animals, even if but two of a kind, get into Noah's Ark? How big, exactly, was the Ark? Was it as big as the ships that came into San Francisco Harbor? . . . Then she giggled at anything that struck her as being the least bit ridiculous, and was generally boisterous in church, until church folk began to report her conduct to her parents.

One Sunday morning Helen came down in her house dress, and announced she was not going to church any more. She would stay home, do the housework, and have dinner ready for them when they returned. Mrs. Smith turned wan and, speechless, dropped in a rocker as if to forestall a faint. Mr. Smith's mouth popped open. The eldest daughter exclaimed, "Well, I declare!" Then Mr. Smith closed his mouth, swallowed hard, and said, "If that's the way you feel about it, Helen, I think you should remain at home."

Mrs. Smith sulked a long time; the rest of the family, however, soon accustomed themselves to Helen's Sunday morning arrangement.

III

Helen loved to read. Lacking guidance of any kind, she read everything she got her hands on. Her studies came so easily she did not need to do any homework. Thus, she would read library books at home while the other children studied. Mrs. Smith had no idea what her daughter was reading, but not having read much in her life, she thought nearly all books harmful, and objected strenuously. Helen would then bring home her school books and read library books during study periods at school. When the teachers complained, she reversed the process. Usually she had books secreted in her room, and read by an old oil lamp far into the night, with clothes draped over the keyhole and under the door to frustrate the telltale crack of light.

She wanted to go to movies and parties and on rides as the other girls did; but this was the tallest hurdle of all—especially now that she had stopped going to church. Before, she would pretend to go to a Young People's party and see a Rudolf Valentino or Charlie Chaplin movie, instead; or enter the church in her parents' full view and slip out the side door to go riding.

One day when she was sixteen Helen quarreled violently with her oldest sister over something trivial (later she could not remember what), and her mother took sides with her sister. This led to a serious clash between Helen and her mother. When her father returned home, he met his problem child in the doorway carrying a suitcase. To his question she replied she was leaving. He said she could not go and led her back to her room upstairs.

Mr. Smith had suspected for some time that the girl was not just a wayward child, but an individual tangled in a problem that needed an answer. Now he talked to her as to an equal, which quickly broke down the antagonism his peremptory ordering and prohibiting had always raised in her. He asked her why she was so unhappy at home. Helen told him that her mother's attitude toward dancing, the movies, and general going out was impossible; that she wanted the privileges enjoyed by other girls in town. "From now on, Helen," said her father, "you'll be responsible only to me; when you want to go out, ask me. If the crowd you want to go out with is all right, I'll let you go. . . . Now I suggest you unpack and that we forget all about this rumpus."

This was the beginning of Helen's respect for her father, which grew with the years.

IV

The early 1920's were hectic years in America, revealing all the weaknesses of the country's culture . . . "and," to quote Helen's words to me in 1940, "we rural youth felt the national restlessness perhaps more than the young people in the cities. We had less outlet for it. Suddenly rebellious against our puritanic parents, steeped in petty prejudices, and suspicious of everything outside our orbit, we found ourselves wading in cynicism and the abrupt iconoclasm of the more adult America. We were unable to adjust ourselves or devise techniques for this new kind of living, and many a rural 'flapper' who made a beeline for the city 'went under.'

"In the country we took up every fad that came along with all the intensity of those who ape. When skirts were short, ours were shorter; when long, ours were longer. We tried all the advertised brands of make-up. We broke the law as often as we could, and community rules all the time. We bragged of driving seventy-five in the hills when we had been drinking; of walking a straight line for a cop; of sneaking past a parent after a spree. Our little town of five hundred had two families who were neither bootleggers nor the customers of bootleggers—my family was one. Under assumed names, we high-school kids visited the cellars of bootleggers, drank new wines, smoked Violet Milo cigarettes, and used long holders, with the quip, 'My mother told me to keep away from cigarettes, and I am!' We were such consummate liars that, on the whole, our parents never found out enough to reprimand us severely, though the whole countryside buzzed with gossip. . . .

"In the summer I plunged into prune picking. I hated the work, but I loved to spend the money I earned. I associated with the ranch all the things I resented—the endless work, poverty, prejudice, stupidity, the lack of facilities, the feeling of inferiority. Most of all I hated the unfair odds in struggling against the elements. Ranch people never got anywhere.

"Toward harvest time there was always the fear of rain, the fear of cracked prunes; then the fear of poor prices. For years after I left the ranch I could close my eyes and visualize an oft-repeated occurrence: My father's heavy voice booming at the foot of the stairs at three or four o'clock in the morning: 'It's raining—everybody out and stack!'—then the springing out of bed, jumping into overalls and pulling on a sweater while still half asleep, flying downstairs, my long hair streaming; running the short distance to the drier, joining the men with lanterns as they worked feverishly to stack the hundreds of trays of drying fruit before the rain had spoiled it; working at top speed under pouring rain, lifting, straining, stacking, placing two empty trays on top of the stack in the shape of a roof to allow the water to run off; racing to the next group of trays spread out on the ground. . . . (Once we had fifteen hundred trays of fruit drying when a rain blew up, and two neighbors, my father, and I stacked them all.) . . . Several hours of this feverish work, then a mad dash around the twenty-acre orchard to cover the stacked boxes of picked fruit which were waiting to be hauled to the dipper. Finally the drag back to the house . . . a hot bath and food. . . .

"One year we had a very fine crop, and it was just ready to be harvested early in September when it started to rain. It rained, and rained. The cultivated ground in the orchard became so soft you couldn't walk on it; the fruit cracked and fell to the ground. And all this time, my father stood at the window watching the downpour, watching his whole year's labor go to waste without being able to do anything about it. The set look on his face impressed me as nothing he could have said would have done. That was, I believe, in 1918, for the government sent soldiers from a near-by training camp to help the farmers retrieve the cracked fruit.

"Summer meant also an endless amount of canning, jelly-making, berry-picking, and preserving to be done, and I usually helped early in the season, before the prunes were ripe. I did not object to this as much as I did to some of the other work, for it gave me a sense of accomplishment to view the jars and glasses in the cellar. But we were all so overworked from May to September that I held this, too, against ranch life.

"At the end of my second year in high school, I decided to work in the cannery in a near-by town instead of picking prunes. My father was reluctant to let me do this, but I won out. I was sorry afterward, but too proud to admit it. . . . I lied about my age to be allowed to work twelve hours a day, but because they realized I was a minor, I was paid no overtime. I left home at four in the morning, walked a mile to a neighbor's, and rode to the cannery with a carful of other people, worked from six in the morning until six at night, and earned less than I did picking prunes for eight hours. And I hated it. I hated the ignorance and squalor of the people (mostly 'foreigners': Mexicans, Filipinos, Japanese and Yugoslavs) with whom I worked; I hated the mess and smell of the fruit cannery. But I stuck it out all summer.

"One thing I remember vividly in this cannery, owned by Italians and employing many women, mostly foreign-born, was the number of small children helping their parents. I used to marvel at those tiny kids working such long hours. When tired, they curled up for a nap at their mother's feet, then returned to work.

"Once the woman in charge came in quickly and hurried down the aisles, stopping for a second to whisper something to every other woman. When she left the room, a peculiar tenseness prevailed. Everyone worked feverishly. Suddenly I did not see any children around. I looked up and down: not a child in sight! The next minute some visitors entered the cannery, walked about a little, talked with the forelady, and left. After a while children seemed to appear from every conceivable hiding place—from under skirts, aprons, boxes, and tables. From the conversation around me I learned that the visitors were 'inspectors from the government.' . . .

"The summer following my junior year in high school I did not know what to do. I dreaded going back to the cannery; yet I hated to confess my mistake by going back to work in the prune orchard. My problem was solved by my father, who asked me whether I would like an office job for a couple of months. I had studied typing and shorthand at high school, and he could, he said, get me a temporary position in the California Prune and Apricot Growers Association office in San Ubaldo. He had some influence in the organization.

"I was delighted. At last I saw freedom from ranch and cannery, and all they stood for. . . . I went to work as a typist at seventy a month.

"I tackled the typewriter as I had the prunes in the orchard; I worked so hard and so fast that my immediate superior had to tell me to take time out once in a while. I was the 'kid' of the whole office force of some fifty people, and, once over my initial natural fright, I enjoyed the job immensely. Some difference from prune picking and cannery work! And more money! I resolved then and there to stick to white-collar jobs and be a lady.

V

"I returned home at the beginning of September with more money in the bank than ever before, with better ideas for clothes, and fired with a real determination. My superior had talked to me before I left: in another year I would graduate from high school, and she said I should learn all I could in the meantime, for it would be my last chance; then I should come back—there would be a job waiting for me.

"School that last year seemed different to me. The old gang did not appeal to me any more. I realized that they had been considerably 'wilder' than even I had believed. They all knew that although I was a 'good sport,' keen for fun, able to drink as much and hold it as well as any one; that although I could get them out of trouble and propose new deviltry—still, I had kept to a strict code: not too much 'petting,' and no free love. (A leftover from my puritan upbringing.) My wishes had been respected while I was in the party, but now I found out that I was not always in the party, and after the immediate resentment, that was all right with me. I commenced to see them less and less, to study harder, and be a chum to a little sophomore who was of California Spanish origin.

"Presentacion Ortiz was a tiny little thing, with dark eyes, heavy eyebrows, white skin, two huge, long, black pigtails, and indifferent clothes, which she bought with the little money she earned working in the summertime in onions and fruit. She was always reading, and we had exchanged favorite books the year before. Now we sought each other's company more than ever, and I had a different kind of fun. I was soon calling her 'Chic' (short for Chiquita—little one), and on several occasions I went to her home. She lived in a shack several miles from school. Her father worked in the local quarry most of the time, and drank more wine than was good for him, but was a delightful man. He made you laugh just by looking at you. He sang, told tales, and played the harmonica. Chic and her mother laughed with and at him all the time. He would grab one or the other at any moment, and they would dance.

"Chic was taking a heavy course and planned to finish her high-school curriculum in three years instead of four. She thought boys were silly, yet she was no prig. She lived in a world of fancy through her reading and an occasional movie, and she was usually merry. Her throaty voice was her greatest charm. . . .

"So, as a senior, I took a heavy course, too, made all *A*'s, and was elected class president and valedictorian. Upon graduation I was presented with a gold pin from the school for high grades, fifty dollars from my father, and a scholarship to a business college. The principal, whose hair had turned almost white during my four-year stay, joined the others in wishing me godspeed —perhaps with more warmth than the occasion demanded.

"I returned to the 'prunery' for six months, saved my money, then went to business college. I was seventeen and entirely self-supporting with a carefully planned budget. I did not want to devote the entire six months to business college to which my scholarship entitled me. Instead, I decided to attend both day and night schools and finish in less time. The school authorities told me it could not be done; in three and one-half months, however, I had earned my secretarial diploma with a good record, and the school found me a better position than the one I had held at the 'prunery.'

"I worked at this but a short time when I heard of a job vacancy in a building and loan association that paid a little higher salary than I was receiving, and the hours and location were better. I applied and obtained the position. Within a year I was earning a hundred dollars a month, holding a fairly responsible position for one of my age.

"When I first came to the city I lived at the Y. W., and my roommate was a lovely, gay young girl, who wore spike heels and a fur coat, and who had her hair paper-curled. She encouraged me to take an apartment with her to avoid the Y restrictions, and we lived happily in a small private place for several months. She was always going out—to parties, to San Francisco, with friends whom I never met. I seldom had dates. Weekends I went home, and enjoyed them; I was treated as a visitor now, not too intimately. But I was lonely. My job took only eight hours a day, with half a day off on Saturdays, and my leisure time became a problem.

"Then my roommate was snatched up by her parents, who had learned she was running around with a married man . . . and I became rather close friends with Sybil, whom I had met at the 'Prunery.'

VI

"Sybil was not pretty, but always dressed in excellent taste, and had a background that interested and impressed me. She had been to college, belonged to a sorority, and was full of pep, independence and fun. Her mother was a pal to her, and encouraged her to have a good time ('you're young only once') —something new in my experience.

"Sybil moved in with me when the other girl left . . . and both she and I had frequent feelings of dislike for San Ubaldo socially. We did not care for public dance halls, and found it difficult to get acquainted with the 'right kind of people,' though we had no clear idea what we meant by that.

"In one of these dissatisfied moods, as a joke on ourselves, we consulted a fortuneteller, who told us we would take a successful trip together. On the way home, we decided to play along with the Fates, and in no time our plans were laid and hatched. We would save every cent we could for six weeks, bringing our capital to $125 apiece, then take a train trip somewhere, work a while and return, or remain there, if we liked it. We saw the railroad agent and announced to our parents that we were leaving for Denver. Sybil had a former college chum in Denver, and I recalled that my father's brother, Uncle Charlie, whom I had never seen, also lived there.

"Sybil's mother was all for our idea. Not so my family. My father dashed up the following Sunday to talk us out of it. We refused to speak about the trip until he finished the good chicken dinner we had prepared, and was presented with a twenty-five-cent cigar. By that time his opposition had melted, and he—the pioneer, adventurer and soldier in him—promised us his co-operation.

"Never since have I enjoyed a train trip so much. I had a portable Victrola and a few of the latest records. We met some nice people, played cards, listened to the Vic, talked, read, and danced the Charleston in the aisles. Finally we were in Denver, with my uncle's family.

"But, after the first thrill of being in a new city, Denver turned out to be no better socially than San Ubaldo, while our jobs were not as good as those we had left. Laughing at our dilemma, we consulted another fortune-teller. This one was a psychologist, and, business being slow that Sunday afternoon, she talked with us for two or three hours. She was a large motherly person, and gained our confidence. I told her my whole story, and to her I am indebted for another change in my ideas. She told me that I had a Master Mind (with capital *M*'s) and could do anything, simply *anything*, I determined to do. It was a splendid thing to tell a young person, and it made a tremendous impression on me, as did her analysis of my faults and weaknesses. She said I was so busy imitating other people, trying to be like everyone else, that I did not give my own personality a chance. I should express my own likes instead of doing always as others did. She went on to the effect that I was given to fits of depression and self-distrust which were harmful, and which I should overcome; that we should leave Denver, since it held nothing for us, and return to California; and, again, that I could do *anything* I made up my mind to do.

"Sybil and I returned to California by way of the Grand Canyon, whose grandeur deprived me of some of the sense of confidence and omnipotence with which the fortuneteller had infused me. Home again, and broke, I decided to borrow fifty dollars from the local bank and go to San Francisco.

VII

"I had lived and traveled, and was practically a woman of the world at nineteen, but here I was still working as a stenographer . . . at the moment for the Publix Theatres in San Francisco. Traveling I had met a diversity of people; now I was thrown in with the class of office workers found in most large cities—those interested in true-story and movie-fan magazines, public dances, dates, 'making' the boss, and the current shows. I lived with Sybil in a downtown apartment, and used my passes to shows. But life was pretty much a bore.

"Chic—Presentacion Ortiz—was attending the University in Berkeley, and got in touch with me. She had finished high school in three years, worked as a governess for a year, and was now 'hashing' her way through the U. She was so alive and natural, yet beautifully restrained; the sort of person one always wants to touch. I loved to pass my hand over her shiny hair. Her eyes seemed to know me as I was, and accept me.

"Through her I met Carlotta, whom Chic called Sholly: a half-Italian and half-Mexican girl; and together we took in some Spanish Club dances and football games at the University. Sholly was a pretty girl of overflowing exuberance, with a merry, expressive mouth, a carelessness about routine and money (similar to Chic's), and a gypsy taste in clothes.

"Chic and Sholly began to tell me that I would become more and more bored with stenography, that it was easy to work one's way through college, and that I should continue my education. They talked me into quitting my job, and I entered the U. in January of 1927.

"I got a part-time job in Oakland, and registered (late) as a regular student. Accustomed to the easy curriculum of a small-town high school, college work got me down. For the first time in my life I had to study, and there was no time to study as thoroughly as I wanted. I rushed from class to class, to cafeteria, to streetcar, to my job in Oakland, to my room (which I shared with Sholly) to get a few hours' sleep, to the library to study—and for what? For four years of grind to obtain an education that I did not need to earn a living. Considering my schedule, I did fairly well in my classes, but I was accustomed to straight *A*'s, and to slave for a *B* or *C* seemed senseless.

"After mid-terms I quit and went back to stenography. I found a $115-a-month job in San Francisco, and it was all right as jobs went, but I was depressed and unhappy. I had failed at something I tried to do, and my self-assurance was down. Besides, I had had a peep at another kind of life which, in spite of everything, looked attractive. I realized there were things in life which as a stenographer I could not touch with a pole a mile long. So after three months of brooding I left San Francisco and went home to the ranch, to think things over.

"The ranch had received many improvements by now—electricity, plumbing, a tractor; and, regarded somewhat as a visitor, I was not called upon to work as I had been when I was younger. I paid for my board, helped around the house a bit, and read everything from *Main Street* and *Babbitt* to *Divine Comedy*. But my money was dwindling, and I knew I could never accept any from my parents, or live on the ranch without paying.

"I got in touch with Sybil, who meantime had found a good job as stenographer in the Del Monte Hotel in Monterey. She lived at home with her mother, and was happy and wisely unwilling to dash with me to parts unknown. So I procured another loan from the bank and was off in a bus for Portland, Oregon. Why Portland, I don't recall, unless it was that I wanted to travel again and get a good distance away from places I knew. Restlessness ——

"The bus arrived in Portland at 5:00 a.m., a most disheartening hour to enter a city. At the Y. W. I was referred to a boardinghouse for working girls, and before lunch I was established in an attractive room. Through a girl, who was interested in a person crazy enough to come to a strange city without a letter of introduction, I obtained employment in a bonding company by three-thirty that afternoon, and once more all seemed well.

"Portland somehow helped me to get hold of myself. Thrown entirely upon my own resources in a strange city, with new friends, new problems, I had to work out my own salvation. The people here were different from people I knew. Working girls in Portland took work as something incidental, and had real fun on the outside. Hiking clubs, parties, and other recreations took up their leisure time. I enjoyed myself and liked the people I met.

"Then I went down with scarlet fever and almost died. My oldest sister came and took me home to recuperate. I was uncomfortable at home. I was broke, and my family had paid even part of my hospital bill in Portland.

"Sybil came to see me. She was getting restless on her fine job at Del Monte, and so when I recovered the two of us returned to San Francisco. We both got jobs with the Standard Oil at $125 a month, and before long I paid all my debts. But I was bored to death. The work was routine and mechanical. Sybil and I "kidded" (I don't know whom) saying 'Good morning, sister!' to our typewriters. . . .

"Then Sybil, her mother and I saw a play by Elmer Rice called *The Adding Machine*—a study of the psychology inside a modern office—which caused us, Sybil and me, to quit our jobs, and in November 1928, the three of us went to Phoenix, Arizona, for the winter.

"I found work in a lawyer's office, Sybil in a hotel; her mother kept house for us, and we spent a delightful winter. We took up horseback riding, and I started studying Spanish at night school because the sound of the language appealed to me. I had picked up a few words before from Chic.

VIII

"In March the heat induced us to leave Phoenix. Sybil and her mother went home. I thought I would try Los Angeles.

"On the train I figured out my record: In eight years I had had more than a dozen positions, and never lost one through dismissal. As soon as the routine was well learned, I became sick and tired of the job, and had to move on. I was like a tumbleweed. I was dissatisfied with my life and what I was doing with it, but unable to find my way out of the stenographic rut into which I had stumbled.

"In Los Angeles I began to work for the Southern California Gas Company, and the third week I was holding down a $140-a-month secretarial job. I took an extension course, did some reading of modern literature (Dreiser, Sherwood Anderson, Knut Hamsun, Eugene O'Neill, Dos Passos, Wassermann and Thomas Mann), got into a so-called lively young crowd, played tennis, went to shows and restaurants, and, on the surface, led a pleasant life. In the back of my mind, however, was always a sense of homelessness, of dissatisfaction, of being empty; which brought on frequent fits of depression that usually dissolved themselves in cynicism.

"The people with whom I came in contact and the things I observed had a lot to do with this. The boys in the offices, the clerks and assistants, seldom had the money to give the girls the gay time they wanted in those days; the bosses generally made dates with the secretaries to get away from nagging wives. I learned a lot from my girl friends. Several had made the mistake of taking their bosses seriously. So early in my business career I decided never to go out with a boss.

"I received a few proposals of marriage, but considered none seriously. In all my rolling around, I knew of no happy marriage, but of many unhappy ones.

"Immediately on starting to work for the Gas Company in Los Angeles I met Pat—a beautiful, half-Italian, half-French girl, with huge black eyes and a creamy skin. She was twenty-six and had been married ten years; pleasant company—but at times something dark seemed to underlie her words and manner. Then I discovered her husband had her terrified. He had married her when she was fresh from a convent in Louisiana. They had gone through the Florida boom and made money there, only to lose it again. He had an ungovernable temper and frequently abused her, and she had twice run away—only to have him find her again.

"At this time he had a selling job which took him on frequent trips. Pat hated to be alone and thought she would like to have me live in their spare room, but she was afraid to ask her husband. Hesitantly she took me to their apartment one evening; Bill, to our surprise, approved of me . . . and I moved in.

"For a while we had a nice time, and I thought she had grossly exaggerated Bill's temper, jealousy, and cruelty. But soon I noticed that he called her long distance in the middle of the night to see if we were in, and employed detectives to watch us. We couldn't even go to a show without fear of a misunderstanding.

"When he returned home one weekend, a male acquaintance called me. Bill answered the phone, and when I had hung up, he accused me and Pat of going out while he was gone, and made such stupid, senseless accusations that, in spite of the fact that his face was distorted with rage, I laughed at him. Pat had never done that. He bellowed that I must leave the apartment immediately, and stormed out, banging the door as he left.

"At the boardinghouse to which I moved my roommate was an attractive girl named Madge who was madly in love with her boss and continued to go out with him even after he married a girl of his own social level. Many a night she cried herself to sleep, while, listening to her, I thought how silly it was to let any man hurt you.

"The person who finally captured my interest at the boardinghouse was Johnny, a pale boy, younger than I, with dark, deep-set eyes, a shock of yellow hair that was generally disheveled; a reporter on the *Times* and an omnivorous reader. I think James Branch Cabell was his favorite author at the moment. He read *The American Mercury* every month, and loaned it to me. His cynicism and taste for good music and books attracted me.

"One evening Johnny did not appear for dinner, and someone said he was on one of his drunks. The following night I came home from a show about eleven-thirty, and there he was sitting up against the door of my room, pale, red-eyed, and so stiff from the effects of bad bootleg he could barely get up. He said he wanted to talk to me. . . . The gist of what he told me was that he was 'finished'; life was not worth living. It was 'empty.' He cursed 'this goddamn country,' which had no culture, and where life was 'just fuss and fury and waste.'

"I hardly knew what to say to him. I urged him to brace up, and felt silly saying that to him; then suggested he go to sleep. He said good night and left. Next morning he was not in his room; nobody I knew ever saw him again. He left all his belongings. . . .

"Other things came to my notice in that boardinghouse, and I decided to try living alone. I took a little furnished apartment. Then who turned up but my old college friend Sholly—only such a Sholly! Dirty, disheveled, and dead-tired, she had run away from home and hitchhiked down from Berkeley. Knowing I was somewhere in Los Angeles, she had stopped enroute in my home town and called my father to ask where I lived.

"I heard her story—pure sordidness. She had changed terribly. Her whole personality seemed warped and diseased. She talked intimately of a type of people of whom I had never heard.

"I couldn't tell her to go, so she stayed. She got a night job in an eating place, and made the most of the opportunity to bring home people she met. I blew up, and Sholly left—with all the loose change and slight valuables in the apartment. Two years later I recognized her picture on the front page of the Los Angeles *Examiner*, where she was described as a gangster's moll.

"I suspected that things like this had their meanings, but I could make neither head nor tail of them; and I, myself, felt like a squirrel going 'round and 'round in a cage and getting nowhere. Unlike my acquaintances at the office, I could pretty well see what lay before me: a ceaseless busyness, a pressing urge to become so physically tired I could not think; an ever-increasing amount of bootleg liquor, so thought would be impossible. I would become encased with the same veneer of metallic brittleness and superficiality that 'protected' my contemporaries. Ten years from now I would probably still be working in an office, with this difference: I'd be afraid to quit then, lest I be unable to get another job on account of my age. But, however firmly attached to some job, I would still be a tumbleweed, homeless, wandering, spiritually barren, searching for stimuli in an effort to keep from seeing myself as I was.

"Marriage, of course, was not entirely out of question, for here and there I caught glimpses of men who seemed all right (you never could be sure); but even with the best of them life might, essentially, not be anything better

than it was in the marriages I saw around me, with husband and wife continuing—because, apparently, needing—the hectic round of outside stimulation they had had before marriage: drinking, dancing, flirting, having affairs. Divorce; then I, the ex-wife, would go back to work if anyone would
have me. . . . I decided to keep to myself rather than go through anything
like that.

"But that decision didn't help; I seemed so deep in the dumps I could not
get out. Evenings, after setting the alarm clock for seven-thirty in the morning, I took half a tumbler of whisky to put myself to sleep. Sometimes I
walked till twelve or one o'clock, till I was ready to drop.

"During one of these nocturnal hikes about town, I happened to step into
an all-Spanish Mexican movie house on Main Street off Plaza. It was late,
the house was full, and I had to go up to the balcony, which buzzed with
subdued talk. The picture was a silent one, and did not impress me; I
scarcely saw it. I sat through it as one in a dream, listening to the delighted
ejaculation, the voices—the melodious, expressive Spanish that had charmed
me before. People all about me were enjoying themselves with the spontaneity of children. Their low laughter was not nervous release from strain
or tension, but came free and easy. They were Mexicans, 'greasers,' as Americans called them; most of them poor as could be, but they were doing naturally what we Americans, oh, so superior to them, were trying vainly to
achieve with our bootleg liquor, cars, and the whole immense, booming
apparatus of entertainment.

"Leaving that ten-cent movie house, I discovered that my depression had
lifted, and I felt for all the world as though blood again coursed in my
veins.

"The feeling of exhilaration continued even after I got to my apartment.
I lay awake long that night. Now I remembered some charming moments
in the past when I had felt, subconsciously, the same elation that had so
'got' me tonight. There were the times Chic had taken me to the shack she
called home, and, with a simple gesture of hospitality and no apology, given
me the best there was to be offered . . . Sholly had once taken me to her
home in San Francisco, where her Italian father charmed me with his
gracious air, his easy conversation, and afterwards almost hypnotized me by
singing arias from Pagliacci. . . .

"About two in the morning I suddenly sat up and turned on the light.
I recalled Johnny's harsh words about the United States, and agreed with
him. By God, life *wasn't* worth the candle here! Not for me, at least, the way
I was now. I understood what he had meant by his statement that it was
'empty.' That was just what it was—empty. Now I understood all the people
of my acquaintance. And all at once I knew what I would do. My decision
was to get out of here, get a new slant on everything—on people, on things,
on ideas, on life in general.

"I would go to Mexico.

"I turned off the light and fell into a sound sleep, from which the alarm clock barely managed to rouse me.

"Next day I started to plan. I felt so alive I tingled. Now I had an aim, a purpose. I was going somewhere. To Mexico! I had a few hundred dollars; I should have a thousand, but in six or seven months I could easily save enough to bring my capital to that amount. Meantime I would learn to speak and write Spanish.

"I consulted the business directory, and found the advertisement of a private Spanish school, daytime and night, where teachers were all natives of Mexico. Besides, it offered a course in Spanish shorthand. That gave me an idea. I would take Spanish stenography and get a job in some office in Mexico City. I called the director, Angel A. Layo, and soon after I had my first lesson.

"During the next four months I read two or three dozen books on Mexico, in English and Spanish, including Flandrau's almost too delightful *Viva Mexico!* and Wallace Thompson's *The Mexican Mind*. During that time I also came to know everybody in the school, and felt almost normal mentally and otherwise, although I suppose I still had more than a suggestion of the hangover of my artificial sophistication and the brisk, cynical manner that went with it.

"Among the best features of the school were the periodic supper parties which Layo sponsored. At one of these, toward the end of my fourth month in the school, he announced that we were about to get a new teacher. Layo winked at us girls, and said he was very handsome; which caused an outburst of giggles."

Intermarriage

THE attention Helen Smith gave Lupe Valdez was at first purely flirtatious, a thing of good-humored competition with the other girls in the school. Soon, however, he caught her interest as an individual. In the first place, he was all sincerity—"something to notice in this world." In a quiet, unobtrusive way, he was such an idealist. His idealism was the sort that glows underneath, and somehow reveals itself without ever flashing to the surface in any obvious form, but working within him nonetheless, propelling his character. Very naturally, matter-of-factly, he believed in life, in love, in people, in the simple everyday things, although he never said so. It was all implicit in his expression, manner, talk.

Helen thought about Lupe. He liked her bright chatter; when she got serious, he liked that, too. He liked her friends. He took up tennis when she offered to teach him. She realized he was falling in love with her, and imagined he might take love very seriously. She thought the best thing she could do for him was to disappear, even if that meant leaving this school: for, after all, she was going to Mexico in a couple of months, and she had no desire to hurt anyone the way she had seen other people hurt—least of all a young man like this Lupe Valdez. It was up to her to "scram," and she tried hard to make up her mind to do so.

Lupe was no help. He invited her to meet his family. They had all heard about the American girl who had caught his fancy, and they waited for her with as much interest as she herself approached the visit. With a gesture like Chic's, years before, Lupe showed her up the rickety steps of the worm-eaten Figueroa Street tenement building to their flat. Mamá Paulita received her at the door with the familiar Spanish welcome, *"Esta es su casa,"* meaning, literally, "This is your house," which contained so much warmth that the physical scene became unimportant before the friendliness of the people themselves. Sally and Gladys obviously adored their brother, and made Helen feel at home immediately.

While she was there on that first visit, a few of Lupe's friends, including Johnny Tablada, came over; it was a Sunday afternoon. Someone produced a guitar, and soon they were all singing. Some of the songs were the loveliest Helen had ever heard. And Johnny Tablada, with his jokes, hearty laugh, mimicry, and narration of incidents in his school career, stimulated Lupe to recount some of his own educational experiences, with which Helen was still unfamiliar.

On subsequent visits she met more friends of Lupe's and Johnny's: Earl Agniar, a handsome Hawaiian with a fine voice and a ukulele, which he played with amazing skill; Joe Albanese, who loved to mimic his Italian father's talk and gestures and Mussolini's bombast as he observed it in the newsreels ——

After the second or third week of their acquaintance, Lupe asked Helen to marry him every time he saw her. He spoke Spanish, which she discovered was an amazing medium for expressions of love. And he argued, logically enough: what was the point of her going to Mexico in order to live among Mexicans when she could marry a Mexican right here in the United States?

By-and-by Helen realized that she could not "scram," and that, in all probability, she was "sunk." She did not give up the idea of going to Mexico and tried to be very reasonable and deliberate. Marrying Lupe would involve all sorts of developments and problems. Her family would object, although that did not matter. She did not care greatly what they might think; her father, she was sure, would eventually come around. Important, however, was the general theory she recalled hearing, and to which her reason subscribed, that intermarriage was even more difficult a business than marriage between people of the same background.

Tossing the problem about in her mind, she reviewed her career anew and contemplated the possibility of her future even in Mexico remaining but a continuance of her past. She might not marry even there. Most of the Mexicans she met in the school probably were no better husband material than the Americans. Also, in her reading about life in Mexico she had noted the inferior status of the woman among Latin Americans. Then, too, a girl alone and unchaperoned in Mexico might be looked at askance. She might be misunderstood; and it was problematical if she could obtain a job in Mexico City, no matter how perfect her Spanish or how efficient her shorthand.

But the more she pondered all this, the clearer stood out the fact that here, for the first time in her life, was a young man really in love with her; one on whose devotion she could always count. This was the sort of thing most girls in her class—the Kitty Foyles—dreamed about and realized only vicariously in the movies. She had seen enough of the Latin Americans in Layo's group to know the difference between the loving and the amorous kind, and she knew that Lupe's beautiful Spanish words were more than words. Throwing away this chance to belong to someone would be a decision to live a future essentially like her past.

But what decided matters was not her reasoning. She just could not "scram"; she was in love herself.

The Smith family raised strenuous objections, then, in resignation, decided it was just like Helen to want to marry a Mexican. There would be no use talking to her. But after a while Mr. Smith came around, as Helen had expected he would. He visited her in Los Angeles, and met and liked Lupe, whose only fault, in his businesslike eyes, was that—unlike Helen, a practical American—he was completely untroubled by the economic problems of marriage. So he took Lupe aside and impressed upon him the importance of making a living and supporting his wife.

Lupe and Helen promised they would wait a year, until he got his A.B. degree, which might open the way to a job, and he knuckled down to a year of hard study.

They were married in June, 1931.

Helen held on to her job at the Gas Company while Lupe tried vainly to get a teaching appointment in California. He did not have the "secondary certificate" required of all high school teachers in the State; besides, both in the high- and the elementary-school field, the Depression and being a "foreigner," a Mexican, worked against him.

Lupe wrote his friend Gabriel Jiminez in Texas, who told someone connected with A. & I. of his predicament . . . and one day Lupe received an offer of a teaching position in the Mexican elementary school in Coleman, near the Panhandle in central Texas, for seven months of the year at eighty-five a month. To his astonishment, Helen at once urged him to accept it. They might have to scrimp a little, she said, to live on $595 a year, but teaching again in any school would give him additional experience in responsibility and a feeling of security. She recognized that deep in him he was still an uncertain foreigner, tentative in many of his attitudes.

She quit her higher-paying position in Los Angeles and they went to Texas.

II

A cotton, sheep and cattle town of six thousand, Coleman was hit by the Depression and was also suffering from the economic hangover of an oil boom experienced a few years before; but its educational system was still fairly well financed—except the Mexican school, which stood fathoms below the rest in standards.

Lupe was dismayed when he first saw the poorly painted, lopsided little one-room frame building, which had recently been washed away from its lowland site by the river and now perched uncertainly on the hillside in the center of the Mexican barrio about a mile from the town proper. The desks were old, inky, disfigured and worm-eaten, discarded by the American schools; the books the same—most of them dirty, without bindings and with pages missing, domiciles of wriggly gray little creatures.

There was no inside lavatory nor even piped-in drinking water. The water was brought in a bucket from the cistern of a near-by resident of the barrio, and a common tin dipper served pupils, whether well or ill, indiscriminately; and, although he tried repeatedly during his three years in Coleman, Lupe could not interest the school board or the superintendent to spend a few dollars to get it piped in and provide the children with a drinking fountain—this in spite of the facts that the State of Texas paid sixteen dollars a year for the education of each Texas child, white or colored alike, and that the census takers were careful to register each Mexican child of school age, whether he ever entered a school building or not. The city claimed the appropriation, nearly all of which was then allotted to schools attended by white "U.S. American" youngsters, giving all other—Mexican and Negro—schools hand-me-downs.

At first only a few children came to Lupe's school, but as cotton picking ended, more turned up. He had some intelligent, avid-minded boys and girls whom he tried his best to encourage, but their environment outside the school conspired against any real progress. When he thought he had definitely taught them something vital, he found his teachings contradicted in their homes, and with irregular attendance prevalent among the children of migratory workers, the home influence was the more potent. He did not know how to cope with this, and had miserable moments about it.

Nor could Helen help him. She was a little uncomfortable in Coleman from the start. The "U.S. American" people there were pious in a straight-laced way, reminding her of home, and school teachers and their wives were expected to be so correct, so exemplary, that she sometimes felt herself the victim of a reversion. Knowing, however, that they were there only temporarily made the situation bearable.

Confessing that, like most Mexicans, he was deficient in the matter of economic planning, Lupe turned his first pay check over to Helen. When later he protested that they should see more movies and have more fun, and maybe even get a secondhand flivver, Helen—with her long fiscal background—introduced him to the Budget, which she had worked out, and reminded him that, while pay checks came in seven months of the year, there were five months without them. They must look ahead to that period. He consented to her full management of the exchequer without understanding the principles and practice of the Budget, and during the next half-year did not bother to ask how it was working out.

One day he found himself looking at the University of Texas summer catalog, for which Helen had sent and slyly put where he would see it. He noticed the fees were unbelievably low compared with those of California, and involuntarily exclaimed, "I wish we could go to Austin this summer!" Helen replied she saw no reason why they should not; they had to live anyhow—why not in Austin? Besides, she might get work in Austin, while a job was out of the question in Coleman.

To show his wife he was not an utter slouch when it came to practical matters, Lupe coolly reminded her it cost something to get to Austin. She asked if he knew how much they had in Postal Savings, and he was astounded when Helen produced her Budget, which showed they would have exactly $280 for the summer.

That this amount was all theirs was difficult to believe. Of course he knew that, thanks to the deflated oil boom, the rent they were paying in Coleman was low (they had a furnished apartment for fifteen dollars a month, while the best ones in town rented for twenty); but he began to realize that even so she must have done some tall scrimping, going without new clothes, and utilizing every scrap of food.

"This lesson in American thrift, preciseness and 'managing,'" to quote Lupe directly, "made me do a lot of thinking. With a system like Helen's, why, anything was possible! . . . We left Coleman the moment school was out, reached Austin six hours later, and found a nice big room in a boardinghouse off the campus.

"I began my graduate work that summer. I majored in Spanish, since I had finally realized I wanted to teach in that field; and minored in English and pedagogy.

"We arrived about ten days before the opening of Summer Session, and Helen canvassed Austin for work, but could not find anything. The Depression. She was quite disheartened. I persuaded her to register at the University with me.

"Because of her failure as a college student in Berkeley five years before, Helen—like my mother—overrated the benefits of a college education, and she plunged into acquiring an education with great eagerness. She brought home the first *A*, and my male ego was touched. She read rapidly, whereas my reading was slow, and she grasped essential points with lightning rapidity. I can't remember ever studying so hard as I did that blistering hot summer in Austin; I did not let her get ahead of me—we both had straight *A* records, and for the first time I began to regard myself as an *A* student. Formerly I had been satisfied with a passing grade; now marks meant something. Teachers took notice of me; my classmates respected my opinions. I began to notice myself. This was the first time that I really competed in the 'U.S. American' sense. It was fun, a new kind of fun; Helen and I laughed as we caught ourselves vying with each other. And something more: it seemed to rouse me out of my Mexican fatalism, the after-effects of old immigrant hurts, and my general reluctance to expose myself to further injury. The *A* was not only a reward for effort, but a symbol of what effort meant. I had let myself be absorbed by something. . . .

"Helen, meanwhile, had obtained spare-time work typing theses and doing other odd jobs around the University; she was even called on a rush job to the Governor's office in the State Capitol, where a lot of clerks were on vacation. But this did not seem to interfere with her school studies. . . . We were able to finish the summer on our meager capital, though we had to borrow from Helen's father to return to Coleman."

III

Coleman looked drab after Austin, but Helen and Lupe Valdez did not mind very much. Only the conditions in the barrio continued to trouble Lupe, whose position as teacher began to develop various ramifications. The Mexican people had confidence in him and brought their troubles to him, with the result that every other day or so he found himself spending his spare time explaining a wrongdoer's side of the argument to some lawyer or the judge, helping to retrieve a runaway daughter, explaining an erring wife's action to the local police, interpreting a woman's ailments to an American doctor, or even officiating at a funeral in the absence of the itinerant priest who generally attended to the spiritual needs and vital events of their lives. Lupe also visited the homes when children failed to come to school and on more social occasions, and talked with and listened to the folks, sang their songs to the accompaniment of the guitar, and sampled their bootleg.

Increasingly he found himself contemplating them and their ways—at the same time that he loved them and regarded himself as one of them—with critical eyes, which now saw partly from Helen's point of view. Poverty and fatalism were poor soil to nurture any urges beyond the immediate instincts to live for a while and to reproduce. Like his erstwhile stepfather, most of the people in the barrio did not, or would not, let themselves hunger for more. A concept and habit of living, centuries old, was at the bottom of it: to be born, to live, to die, was all, was enough. That was the simple program of life, familiar and comfortable. To live and strive was another concept and way. And sometimes, emotionally convinced, Lupe thought whichever way or concept gave most satisfaction was the one to be followed. But he did not think this through at the time. He made his choice gradually, as he was subconsciously impelled to make it and as circumstances fortuitously arranged.

Once this occurred to him: The Mexican people in the United States could better their condition if they were but educated to *seeing* and accepting the necessity of sending their children to school, to high school and college; if only they could be made to see the value, even in a practical earthly sense, of being thrifty, more self-reliant and purposeful. But he had no idea how they might do something in that direction, and a wave of futility engulfed him. One day he wrote the thought down and realized that "there was nothing to it"; it was just words, of which one of the shortest—*if*—was the most important, destroying the sense of all the others.

The problem was too big for one person to tackle, or even think about. Behind it were the post-Conquest centuries below the Rio Grande. Also this: much of the population of the barrio in Coleman, as of scores of other barrios, was of the floating kind; whatever he might try to do here this year would not be developed or followed through wherever they would be next year. The State of Texas and the leading people of communities like Coleman, along with the entire setup in the Southwest and in the United States generally, were partly responsible for the situation. He was impatient with those influential people in town who professed a lively interest in the life and ways and problems of the Mexicans in Mexico, but did not respond positively to anything he mentioned that had to do with the Mexicans in Coleman.

But he saw, too, that the Mexican people were themselves, and in a most immediate sense, greatly to blame for their situation—though, on second thought, he made a footnote to this observation that he did not really mean "blame." They kept to themselves (many did not speak a word of English after living in the United States for ten years), reared their children to do as they were doing, and believed it was God's will they stay poor and ignorant all their lives, not in any resigned manner, but with the positive strength of tradition. When they did get a check for a season's sheepshearing, cotton picking or pecan shelling, they had a gay time while the money lasted, with little thought of the morrow . . . and so it went.

Lupe's impotence in the face of the overwhelming problem had, on the one hand, a depressing effect on him; on the other hand, being called upon by his people to help them in their immediate and intimate perplexities and entanglements gave him a sense of doing something and thus played a subtle role in the strengthening of his character. This many-sided, thought-provoking experience developed in him an objectivity, giving a new awareness to his mind and a fresh tone to his personality. His consciousness of himself was enhanced and sharpened by it. And it released springs of ambition, a drive to learn and teach, which was not Mamá Paulita's aspiration for him, or part of the Tex-Mex teachers' missionary zeal, or an extension of Helen's passion to advance on one's own power, or competition with her, but something peculiarly his own.

IV

To Helen, the Mexican people in Coleman were not like the Mexican people she had known in Los Angeles. Their poverty and squalid condition shocked her. But even in their extreme poverty she found in them many of the delightful traits she had come to associate with Mexico and its people. Their hospitality, devotion to a guest, spontaneity, and singing continued to fascinate her. Her and Lupe's best friends were Mexicans. In fact, it was only in their company that they could be themselves. After doing their best all day to be correct according to the lights of the dominant element in Coleman, it was fun to have over Calisto and Josefa, to pull down the shades, drink a little home-brew, smoke, dance, and sing (even if only in a low tone, so as not to be heard in the street). Calisto and Josefa and their four children lived in a shack on the edge of the barrio, close to the main town, and their economic level was so low that sometimes Helen suspected they had no food—but she could never be sure; they were always at one with life, ready to affirm it, if in no other way, by singing and laughing.

Josefa's father, Don Juan, rented a farm a few miles out of Coleman. He took an instant liking to Lupe and Helen, and they spent many Sundays at his ranch. His wife, Doña Eulalia, always greeted their arrival with shrieks of delight. They had five daughters still on the ranch who had never been to school, and no sons, and no other income; and work was hard for all of them through the entire week, but one would never guess on Sunday that anything was amiss in their existence. Two of the girls had guitars, which they played well; there was also a Victrola, and they danced. Or they ran races up and down the dusty road, or rode a bony old horse which, also an immigrant from Mexico, had been in the family for over a decade. Doña Eulalia had a repertoire of songs which neither Lupe nor Helen had heard before, and Lupe began to write them down. Subsequently this led to his starting a collection of Mexican songs.

In Los Angeles, and before, Helen had never sung. She had never felt like it—"with a radio or an orchestra blaring in one's ears all the time you just don't want to sing." And she had always felt her voice was "nothing at all," too low for accompaniment; she could sing only in one key. Now, on Don Juan's and Doña Eulalia's farm, she began to join in the singing. They all encouraged her, especially Lupe, who could harmonize with anyone ("even me!"); her voice developed so she could be accompanied by a guitar, and she found that singing gave her an immense satisfaction. . . . ("Perhaps Americans would be less tense, nervous, and frozen-faced if they were to break out into song once in a while, for you can't take a lost order, or any other disappointment, too seriously if you can sing about it.") . . . She liked particularly the plaintive Mexican country and ranch songs, the simple *corridos* or ballads, that tell a story.

v

In Lupe's second year in Coleman, partly in consequence of his occasional remarks to the superintendent the previous year concerning the barrio's education inadequacies, the school board authorized a nine months' term for the Mexican children. This was a source of much satisfaction to the young teacher, and meant two more pay checks.

So the young Valdezes invited Mamá Paulita to come to live with them. The invitation was subtly linked to Lupe's newly stirring ambition, which included a determination to help his mother, who he believed worked too hard on her job as janitress in Los Angeles. And Mamá Paulita came, and liked being with her son and his American wife, who spoke such perfect Spanish. After a while, however, she got lonely for her daughters, for the big-city noises and neighborhood excitements in Los Angeles, for the Adult Education Center, and for her economic independence; and—informing her son and daughter-in-law that she had not quit her employment, as they imagined, but had only taken a vacation—she returned to California.

This added to Lupe's, as well as to Helen's, already deep regard for his tiny mother, who at forty-three looked like a girl of twenty-five. They were amused by the extent of her "Americanization."

Before Mamá Paulita left them, the young couple realized they would not go to summer school in Austin that year, but would, instead, have a baby; and so they took a University correspondence course, which they completed during the pregnancy period.

Toni—Antonio or Anthony—was born in July, 1933, and instantly became the central interest in Helen's and Lupe's life.

Mapping out a big future for their son, they became increasingly aware of the inadequacies of Coleman as a community. But their dissatisfaction with the place—or, rather, Helen's—did not come to any point until the occurrence of the following little incident when Toni was six months old:

With their natural and very real love for children, the Mexican people of Coleman were greatly interested in their teacher's little boy and in the young Señora Valdez' "American" methods of taking care of him, which, in the eyes of the Mexican mothers, were so singularly elaborate and unremittingly painstaking that they were downright amusing. Why, the young woman fussed over the child all day long, keeping him ridiculously clean, boiling his milk and tomato-juice bottles, warming his food to a specific temperature and feeding him innumerable times a day by the clock, changing his diapers every time he did the least thing, sunning him, and doing only dear God knew what else with, for, and to him. To catch a glimpse of the infant and his mother was to get material for a full day's conversation with one's neighbors. . . . One day while Helen was wheeling him in his buggy in the street, an old Mexican woman stopped her to view the boy; and, exclaiming at his beauty and glowing health, she quickly, impulsively leaned down and touched his mouth with a bony forefinger that had not recently had contact with soap and water, and then left.

Helen returned home in rare ill humor. She spent her mornings sterilizing everything and preparing germless formulas; now this woman with her dirty finger ——!

Lupe was touched to the quick. The old woman had meant no harm, he said. She had admired the baby and her touching his mouth was, in Mexican superstition, merely a bit of magic to ward off the Evil Eye. The dirt on her fingers was probably harmless "clean dirt."

There was tense quiet between Helen and Lupe for awhile.

Then Helen admitted she probably had been a little hasty and silly, a little too germophobic. She went on to say, however, that she would have felt the same way if a "U.S. American" woman had touched the baby's mouth with a dirty finger. Her reaction did not mean to imply that all Mexicans were dirty and all "U.S. Americans" clean. It signified only that to her cleanliness was a virtue, that she did not believe in the Evil Eye and other such superstitions, and that she was not disposed to take chances with "clean dirt."

Whereupon Lupe admitted he had been foolish to take the matter so personally. He did not approve of unclean fingers touching Toni's lips, either. But how could he help feeling appreciative of the old woman's interest in his child?

They laughed.

But for Helen the incident put the finishing touch on her conditioning against Coleman, including the barrio. The dirty finger had reached beneath her rational make-up. She realized she still was a good deal of an Anglo-Saxon, and always would be. She regretted her sharp reaction to the episode, but after it happened she could find little good to say about the town and favored their leaving it.

Lupe, too, had no objection to making a change . . . but the incident, as he inevitably kept thinking of it, raised his self-consciousness and made him vaguely miserable for a time. By-and-by, however, the hurt wore off; then he and Helen often discussed "our first crisis," seriously and with amusement.

VI

When Toni was a year old, they went to Austin for the summer. Helen obtained part-time employment in an oil operator's office, while Lupe's contract for the following year carried a slight raise; so that economically things were looking up for them. Lupe finished several academic requirements that summer, but Helen did not go to school. To augment their exchequer, she typed theses and term papers at home.

They returned to Coleman for another year. Then Helen prevailed on her husband not to sign another contract; Depression or no Depression, they would go elsewhere and make out somehow. To preclude the possibility of their weakening under any economic pressure, Helen mentioned their decision to the superintendent of schools long before the question of contract renewal came up.

Toni's severe illness early that year made it difficult for Helen to save anything; and after settling in Austin for their third summer, when Lupe had registered and they had paid for the boy's nursery school, they had only sixty-five dollars left. For a while things looked bleak. Helen seemed unable to find employment. Finally, the University offered her temporary work. And two months later, when he got his Master's, Lupe was appointed to an assistantship.

"For the first time," quoting him several years later, "I realized the pleasure of enjoying my work fully. Instead of trying to teach English to Mexican children I taught elementary Spanish to responsive college students, and I felt I had found my work at last. That year I began to study French, to make myself better qualified as a language teacher."

Early the ensuing winter Helen, who had taken a civil service examination and passed it with a high mark, was appointed to a well-paid position as secretary to the head of the State Employment Service, which shortly developed into that of executive secretary . . . and the next two years in Austin gave the young Valdezes more financial leeway than they had yet known. They paid the several hundred dollars Lupe owed the church organizations sponsoring the Tex-Mex school because he did not become a preacher. They bought a secondhand car. They were able to send gifts to Mamá Paulita and the other relatives. They lived in a nice apartment. Toni was doing excellently in kindergarten. Lupe became a member of Sigma Delta Pi, the honorary Spanish society, and was made first its treasurer and then president. He was also secretary of the Austin chapter of the American Association of Teachers of Spanish, and sponsor for the Latin American Club.

Helen liked Austin. Compared to Coleman, it was a big city in more ways than one. It did not require her to watch her every word and gesture. She could light a cigarette without pulling down the shades or going into a closet. She was not obliged to answer the religious census or explain to anyone who cared to interrogate her why she had not gone to church last Sunday. Here they could be themselves.

One of their earliest friends in Austin was Patricio, one of Lupe's former schoolmates at Tex-Mex. He was attending the University, and he, Helen and Lupe had many conversations about economic and social problems, which stimulated them all to read and discuss matters further.

Patricio knew other Latin Americans in town, and Lupe and Helen themselves, by the time they had come there for their third term, had a circle of friends and acquaintances. There were Luis and Magdalena, a young Venezuelan couple who belonged to the upper class in their country. They were in Texas because their government had sent Luis to take a special course of study at the University. From them Helen and Lupe learned something about Latin-American life.

"At first I thought"—quoting Helen—"that their being wealthy and our being poor would be a factor in our relationship, but we soon saw their values were as purely human as were those of the poor Mexicans we knew in Coleman. When we visited them, they received us with the same charming hospitality and warmth. . . . My 'U.S. American' upbringing shrank from having them call on us in our poorly furnished duplex, but when they came I forgot all about that; they were as oblivious of the surroundings, apparently, as I was at their place. They had two little children and a servant they had brought with them from Venezuela, and could easily arrange to come to see us, while it was harder for us to get away; and so, after we became close friends, they would drop in on us two or three times a week, without invitation or warning. Luis always brought his guitar, which he played beautifully, and the four of us would sing. Luis and Magdalena knew Chilean, Venezuelan, Cuban and Bolivian songs; Lupe contributed Mexican and Spanish ones.

"One Christmas Eve, at their place, with the children in bed, we got together about ten o'clock; it was just daylight when we parted. What did we do? Sang, mostly; and talked; and Magdalena danced the Venezuelan *joropo*, Lupe the Mexican *chiapanecas*, and I the Charleston; and we ate and drank.

"Like most Latin Americans, these Venezuelan friends drank moderately and slowly—not, like most 'U.S. Americans,' to get the stuff down; not holding their noses, as I had seen people drink vile bootleg in Los Angeles and elsewhere, but with relish, because they enjoyed it—and they never got drunk.

"Luis and Magdalena knew we did not have much money, but they never referred to it. 'U.S. Americans' would have talked about it, or hinted at the economic situation, and offered apologies. Among us money was never mentioned. When they came unexpectedly, as they usually did, their arms were loaded with bottles of beer and plenty of cigarettes to last the night. After a few hours, when we wanted something to eat, Magdalena and I would send the boys out to buy sandwiches, or I would make some. When we went out, Lupe and Luis would vie with each other to see who could snatch the bill. Never did we go 'Dutch' anywhere, with the inevitable wrangling afterward over the expense of the evening. Nor did we talk about the cost of this and that—not even of living. I never knew how much rent Magdalena was paying, or where she bought the children's toys; and I can't imagine knowing an American woman as intimately as I knew Magdalena without knowing all about her budget!

"Magdalena, like Mamá Paulita and Sally and Gladys, cared little about money as such. One night Magdalena brought me a lovely purse for my new spring outfit. I was surprised. It was neither my birthday nor Christmas. Magdalena saw my bewilderment, and asked quickly if I did not like the purse. I replied that it was lovely, and just what I needed, but that I was surprised. Apparently, she had been shopping, had seen the purse she knew was what I had been wanting, and bought it just because she wanted to. . . . Mamá Paulita is the same way. The other day, in her presence at the Fair, I admired a pair of hand-carved Mexican book ends. A day or so later they were mine. Latin Americans give because they want to, not because they think the other person is planning to give them a Christmas gift that costs so much, and so a gift must be selected of the same price. . . .

"Other friends of ours in Austin were Dr. and Mrs. Castañeda, the librarian of the García Library of the University, and his wife; an assistant in the English Department and his wife (both Americans, from the North); a young American woman, with an M.A., who was a secretary. Toni and her little daughter liked to play together. . . .

"Some of these friends jerked us up every now and then with their 'kidding' as to how much more Mexican Lupe was than I was 'U.S. American,' and whether Toni would be a Mexican or 'U.S. American.' We laughed whenever this came up, but we knew, too, it was a serious question. Lupe and I discussed it every once in a while, and our ideas and instincts tended in the direction of a selective mingling of 'U.S. American' and Mexican ways and values. We realized that materially an American standard of living, including American diet, was necessary for Toni and us two; and thought that culturally, spiritually, we should veer strongly toward the Mexicans, but that we should not forget the United States was an English-speaking country which did have good things hidden here and there even culturally and spiritually. We determined that Toni would know both English and Spanish, and we hoped he would be seized by such curiosity about both the North and Latin Americas that he would have good use for both languages.

"Lupe was of the opinion that, with all its faults as it worked out in practice, the United States political system was preferable to Mexico's or almost any other country's in the world—here defeated candidates did not shoot their successful rivals! He held with Thomas Jefferson, in fact, that the United States form of government was one of the hopes of the world. I agreed with that. And I continued partial to the American budget for the fixed salary the family had to live on, but as we began to have a little more money than we had during the Coleman period, I closed my eyes to extra or unexpected expenditures. I think once upon a time money had seemed awfully important, I mean money for itself; now it was important to me only as a means. The budget became more and more elastic, and less specific.

"Our outward mode of living in Austin was quite 'U.S. American'; on the other hand, we both preferred our Latin-American recreations and friends. Perhaps the chief reason for this was singing. I was wild about *Cuarto Milpas* and *Qué Bonita Chaparrita*, a ranch love song, and *Herminia*, which Lupe's grandfather, Refugio Gonzales, had taught him. I corresponded with Chic who married Eric Davis, the now famous artist, and lived in San Francisco and was very happy. . . . We also kept up with Latin-American novels and magazines to which we had access at the University library, and we hoped Toni would seek his cultural life more or less in the same direction.

"Now and then all this made me rather self-conscious, especially on top of the dirty-finger incident. My Anglo-Saxon or Puritan background, or whatever one wishes to call it, was all a-tingle, reproaching me, calling me a traitor —or at least to that general effect. In these moods I remonstrated with myself, saying that before I knew Lupe I had not liked myself. I had been neurotic, 'empty,' along with almost everybody else I knew; Chic being about the only exception. Like nearly all the people of my acquaintance I had been subjective, uneasy, unrealistic, and in need of all sorts of diversions and compensations for the lacks and shortcomings within and about me. I had lived in a world which was superstructure erected upon superstructure, and in which I could not have felt anything but uneasy. Deep-down in me, I had sensed the instability and superficiality of it all, as had everybody else. . . . To think back to the 1920's, was terribly confusing at first; in time, however, it occurred to me that the period was a sort of climax in the mass subjectivity of the American people, which was an intolerable condition and required many masks and diversions and vents—speed, jazz, gin, sophistication and all the rest of what Johnny called fuss and waste and culturelessness. . . . I argued with myself in this way, and realized that everything I had disapproved of was not to be blamed on the old Anglo-Saxon Puritan tradition. The fault, in all probability, could not be fixed, unless we said that it lay in the tempo and the subjectivity of 'U.S. America.' We were all too much in a hurry. There was no leisure and objectivity—the two things from which culture could come. There was too much 'progress.' 'U.S. America' had started a culture once; then the Civil War came, and the Machine, and then there was no time for anything basic or enduring, and by the 1920's, with the help of the First World War, things went pretty well haywire.

"Now, in turning to Mexico, I liked myself. I felt normal (except now and then when this self-consciousness seized me and I felt unnatural because I felt natural!). And, I asked myself *why* had I turned to Mexico? Although placed in the New World, Mexico is really an old country; in some ways, because of the Indian influence, older than Europe. As in Europe, where the seeds of culture had been laid long ago, before the Machine, Mexico—in spite, or because, of its material backwardness—had a culture, or something that I needed, that the U.S.A. as a whole needs; and so I turned there . . . I slowed down to see myself. . . . I relaxed . . . and I saw that machinery and material 'progress' by themselves, and speed and jazz, were delusions and not real expressions of humanity. This turning toward Mexico, toward the Old World, I explained to the Anglo-Saxon American in me, had begun with Chic, in that Mexican movie house on Main Street in Los Angeles, in Angel Layo's Spanish school. . . . The point was that now I liked myself, that I was relaxed and quiet, that I saw myself and the world in which I lived, that I had what I wanted.

"Thinking thus, I did not mean, of course, that Mexico and the old culture had all the answers for me. As I say, the answers, perhaps, are both here and there. . . . Maybe Toni someday will see them."

VII

"One week end"—continuing Helen Smith de Valdez' narrative to me—"we left Toni with Luis and Magdalena, and went to San Antonio to visit Lupe's grandparents. When we entered the barrio, I was shocked, even though Coleman had conditioned me somewhat to the Mexicans' squalor and poverty in Texas. The numerous Gonzales family lived in a tiny shack without an indoor bathroom, and water had to be brought into the house by bucket from the faucet in the yard. But their hospitality was the kind I had learned to expect, even in the most tumbled-down hut. They were so undeniably glad to see us nothing else mattered.

"Mamá Juanita allowed me to watch her prepare supper, but would not permit me to lift a finger to help. I think we had *huevos rancheros* that night ('ranch-style eggs'—eggs cooked in tomato or chile sauce), for I remember watching with fascination as she pounded the slices of tomato, onions, and green pepper in the *molcajete*, or hollowed-out stone which sat upon the table on its three short legs, by means of another stone, shaped to fit into the hand. Then she quickly made tortillas (those of *maza*, or corn dough), deftly cutting off a portion, then taking it up in her hands, patting it until it was paper-thin and round, and frying it on top of the scrubbed-off part of an old wood stove.

"That evening I met all the *parentala*, or relatives, most of whom lived within a few blocks. There were so many I could not keep them all straight in my mind, and there were tribes of children; yet everyone greeted me with the same warmth. One of Lupe's uncles brought a tub filled with ice and bottles of bootleg beer. It was stifling in the shack on this August night, so we all moved out into the yard, gathering around in chairs; and drank, smoked, talked and visited, till the boys started singing.

"It must have been near midnight when someone remembered that a girl living across the street had a birthday the next day. So, of course, we had to serenade her. We waited until a few minutes after twelve, then Lupe, one of his young uncles, and I sang *Mi Viejo Amor* under her window. My first experience, and I enjoyed it to the utmost! Before the second verse had ended a lamp was lighted inside (no electric lights in that part of the barrio), there was a sound of movement, then the girl's father appeared. With disheveled hair and hastily donned clothes, he stood in the open doorway, smiling warmly, inviting us to come in. *'Esta es su casa.'* . . . We trooped in, and were served hot Mexican chocolate and *pan dulce* (a sort of coffee cake), and everyone congratulated the young lady—an unimpressive, dark-skinned, sleepy girl of about sixteen. . . ."

VIII

Lupe's assistantship appointment expired in 1938; now what and whither?

Toni was five. Were they going to send him to public school? In Austin? His surname was Mexican or Spanish; and Helen feared that on that account he might have to endure a lot of merciless gibing from children whose names happened to be Anglo-Saxon, and whose attitudes were reflections of their parents' prejudices against Mexicans and "foreigners" generally. This did not happen in nursery schools among little children, but it did among older boys and girls; and might not that affect him unfavorably? Both Helen and Lupe—he from personal experience and close observation—knew how acutely that kind of gibing affected the vital inner make-up of many Mexican children attending American schools. They decided not to risk it with Toni. California was considerably better in this respect; the thing to do was to return there.

An equally important, and more immediate, consideration was Lupe's professional future. To attain eventually his full effectiveness in teaching, he would have to get a Ph.D. The University of California at Berkeley had a renowned Romance Languages Department. . . .

And so it was there—at the home of Professor Rudolph Altrocchi, one of his teachers, whom I happened to be visiting late in the autumn of 1939—that I met Guadalupe Toro Valdez, a slight, rather quiet, young man of thirty-four, dark-haired, handsome, with a smooth olive complexion and a pleasant tenor voice. Later I met Helen Smith de Valdez and little Toni.

Listening to Lupe, I sensed that, while crystallized in many important respects as an individual, he was still in the process of adjusting himself to the setup and life in the United States. His old background and his new circumstances are still being fused. There exist difficulties, both within him and on the side of his environment in the United States.

For instance: a prevailing idea among middle-class "U.S. Americans" is that it is insulting to call a Mexican who is light-complexioned and well-educated a Mexican; he should be called a Spaniard. This has been causing Lupe—and Helen—no end of trouble, and their Mexican friends have the same problem. Lupe resents being called a Spaniard. He is proud of his native nationality, and associates the name Spaniard with the *gachupines* of his early childhood. The contemporary Mexicans cannot forget that the *gachupines* were responsible for the virtual slavery of most of the population of Mexico for over three hundred years. "U.S. Americans," on the other hand, have the notion that only the mestizos and Indians should be called Mexicans. Lupe is well liked by his wife's old-stock American friends, by her father and even her mother, and other relatives, but his in-laws, particularly his mother-in-law—to his annoyance, which is being slowly weakened, as time goes on, by a tendency toward amusement—still refer to his being "Spanish" behind his and Helen's backs.

Helen Smith de Valdez is a young woman with the concise and, at the same time, easy manner of one who knows what she wants. A few months after arriving in Berkeley in 1938 she got the position of secretary to an executive of the University of California, which she still holds. For the time being, she earns most of the little family's living. Last summer Lupe taught in Summer Session at Berkeley, and has also been making a little money tutoring. His Ph.D. is not far off.

Helen's regard for Mexico and Mexicans now is deeper, if more critical, than it was when she first met her husband. She feels the Mexican immigrants in the United States have it in them to make other important contributions to the sum-total of American life besides manual labor, for which they are now chiefly known (and not respected) in the Southwest and elsewhere. "They have," she said to me, "an eye for form and color, and have already contributed definitely to our art. Look at Miguel Covarrubias' work; his beautiful maps of the Pacific Basin Area at the Golden Gate Exposition have gained him international recognition. . . . Mexican popular music has a beauty not to be found in American jazz and other popular music. . . . Their language is melodious, expressive. We Anglo-Saxons ordinarily speak in monotone; they speak with inflections and emphases that are beautiful. . . . But principally, I think, the Mexicans can teach us how to live, rather than how to utilize time as we dash from this busyness to that nervous occupation. They seem to have a grasp of the fundamentals and essentials for living that we lack, or refuse to recognize. They care less about time, money, or how much they do; and more about friendship, hospitality, pride in the creation of something colorful, dramatic and beautiful. . . ."

But, as her intense reaction to the superstitious old woman's dirty finger in Coleman indicates, Helen does not accept all of Mexico and all the ways of its people. She believes with Lupe that the Mexicans' virtue as to time and money is all too often carried too far, just as are such "U.S. American" virtues as thrift and individualism. She has no sympathy with the Mexican fatalism.

At seven, Toni is a charming, bright little lad, with a delightful sly humor that pokes fun at things, at people, at oneself, and makes everyday troubles seem trivial. It is definitely Mexican humor, including a pronounced, although restrained, talent for mimicry and caricature. Sometimes he sends everybody into gales of laughter with a gesture or slight twitch of his face.

He came home one day with holes in the knees of his new whipcord pants after only a few days' wear. Helen discovered this, and called him over, exclaiming in shocked tones. Toni looked at his knees speculatively, then met her stormy eyes, smiled disarmingly, and said airily, "Well, Mother, boys will be boys, you know—specially in marble-time." While she was trying to think of a comeback, and was at the same time searching her memory to recall when she might have used the phrase "boys will be boys" before him, he walked off.

One evening he came in from playing hot, dirt-streaked, and with his shoes muddy. Helen opened her mouth to remonstrate with him, but before she could do so, he said dramatically, "Boy, I'm so tired I think I'll faint." "If you do that, Toni," said Helen, "I'll have to throw some water on you." A chuckle, then: "If you do, Mom, I guess there'll be a mud puddle under me, I'm so dirty." A pause, whereupon the chuckle broke out into a giggle. "Or a pud-muddle, as Mrs. Katzenjammer would say."

I asked him if he was mechanical. He replied, "No, but I'm pretty readable," meaning that he read considerably. He is subscribed to two boys' magazines, one "U.S. American," the other Mexican.

In many respects, Toni is very "U.S. American." He loves American games and sports, funnies, and ice cream, ice water and Popeye the Sailorman, apple pie and his scooter, orange juice and all-day suckers. He does not like Mexican food. He has a ten-cent-a-week allowance, and is so careful (almost miserly) with it that his mother must urge him to spend it. "An American trait?" she asks. *"Quien sabe?"*

In the fall of 1939, Toni was found too advanced for the low-first grade and was placed in the high-first. He speaks English and Spanish, and was rated high in Stanford-Binet intelligence tests. He has a fine tenor voice, and is very social. Mamá Paulita, whom he sees every once in a while, calls him Tonio, enjoys his humor more than anyone else, and collects his funny sayings and wisecracks.

At fifty, Mamá Paulita persists in being a pretty woman. Her still-black hair is waved, and her clothes, like her manners, are always in good taste. She is still the janitress of the same building in downtown Los Angeles she took over in 1928. Her work is not easy, but it does not seem to affect her. She loves to sing and go to dances. She lives in a little apartment of her own. She speaks good English with an accent, but continues to attend the evening adult-education classes for the foreign-born: education has become a habit with her. Sending little gifts to her children, grandchildren, relatives and friends is her favorite indulgence.

Her first daughter, Sally, married in the early thirties, but the marriage did not turn out well. Her former husband is an old-stock American; she retains his name and is known as Sally Jones. She has a son, Robert, who at the age of nine, is at the Culver City Military Academy. Working irregularly in recent years, Sally lives with Mamá Paulita, who helps her also to keep the boy in school.

Gladys, the one-time Amparo Nemesia, is married to Bill Howes, also an old-stock American, now of Detroit, who met her in Los Angeles in 1930. Bill is a mechanic working for General Motors. They have a five-year-old daughter, Gladys June.

When Mamá Paulita entered the United States at Laredo in 1910, she registered at the immigration office as "Paulita Gonzalez viuda de Valdez and three children." This caused Lupe, Sally and Gladys some trouble when they started to take steps to become citizens of the United States. But now they are all naturalized.

IX

Lupe and Helen Valdez work very hard—he studying, coaching, translating, grading papers; she in the office during the day and typing theses many an evening. But they do manage to take some advantage of the social facilities of the International House, the Spanish Club, the Italian Club, and the honorary Spanish society, Sigma Delta Pi.

Their close friends are a mixed lot. There are Chic and Eric Davis whom they see about once a month. There is a young lady who is an immigrant from England, who has lived in France and now teaches French at the University. There are a German-born professor and his Latin-American wife who have four children born in the United States; two Italian American students; a young lady of Dalmatian parentage from Fresno; and so on.

Playing the guitar and singing are their recreational mainstays. They read a great deal. They subscribe to a few "U.S. American," and about an equal number of Latin-American, magazines and reviews; among the latter, the excellent Buenos Aires literary journal *Nosotros*. They get the better Mexican novels from a bookstore in Mexico City.

Lupe's and Helen's most powerful dream is to have enough money in the near future to go to Mexico for a few months; then, later, perhaps to Guatemala, Ecuador, Bolivia, and some of the other Latin-American countries.

If everything turns out as Lupe and Helen plan, someday he will be a regular teacher or professor of Spanish somewhere. He is purposely preparing himself to teach not only grammar, but also the history, mores, and cultural heritage of the people of Latin-American countries. He thinks it is important that "U.S. Americans" begin really to know and understand the nations to the south. Helen shares this thought with him. They are receiving the publications of the Middle America Institute at Tulane University in New Orleans, which is delving into the cultural resources of Mexico, Guatemala, and other Central American lands; and follow with interest the efforts of the United

States Department of State to establish cultural contacts and exchange with Latin America.

When I first met them, Lupe and Helen were deeply interested in the news from San Antonio, where Mayor Maury Maverick and some of the city's educators obtained a grant from one of the Eastern foundations for the purpose of preserving some of the cultural values and materials of the Mexican people in that city, and finding ways and means of making them a more vital and accepted part of the city's life than they are now.

They have noticed that similar things are occurring elsewhere. In Oakland, California, the supervisor of the board of education, Dr. E. W. Jacobsen, who is a son of Swedish immigrants, is interested in the same idea and is trying to work it out, with scores of teachers in his system who are sympathetic to it. Two or three high-school principals in Los Angeles and some of the professors in the state teachers' colleges in San Jose, Fresno and Santa Barbara are beginning to turn in the same direction. There seems to be an entire movement growing out of an extremely fertile situation.

As a teacher and generally as an individual, Lupe means to have a hand— somehow—in work such as this which will improve the relations between the various elements of the "U.S. American" population, and charge with new dynamics the cultural life of the United States and in time, perhaps, react favorably on the problems of the entire Western Hemisphere.

I last saw the Valdezes in April, 1940. They had invited a few of their close friends to their little dwelling in Berkeley. Among them were Eric and Chic Davis: both extremely charming (seeing Chic, I had no trouble understanding her subtle influence on the course of Helen's life). Part of the talk was, inevitably, of the war in Europe. Hitler had just taken Denmark and invaded Norway; were the Low Countries next? Then war in earnest? Then what? Would France and Britain be able to hold the Nazis? Would the United States get in? Should we take Greenland? And how about the Nazi agents in Mexico, Guatemala, Brazil, Bolivia, Chile, and elsewhere? . . .

But as the evening wore on I noticed that our talk was more and more of the Americas, North, Central and South. The implication was that Europe probably was done for, at least for a long while. The future was here, in the United States and to the south and north of it, in our inner resources, in some of the things we brought over and developed here in the last few centuries, in some of the things that flourished in Mexico, Guatemala and Peru ten or two thousand years ago and more recently.

At one point of the conversation little Toni dominated the party for a few minutes. He wanted everybody to look at the picture of a Mexican boy in the latest number of the juvenile magazine he had received from Mexico that afternoon. The boy's trousers were torn in the knees. "You see, Mother," said Toni, "boys will be boys—in Mexico, too," with a mischievous glance at Helen, which, more than his words, set everybody to laughing.

IN CONCLUSION: A LETTER

Py Gott, poys, ve got a democracy and ve gotta make it vork. Dat means ve all gotta pitch in and do somethin'. Ve oughta know vere ve is goin' and how ve is goin' to git dere. . . . Ve gotta see dat goot men gets into offis. Maybe ve ain't so vise. I dunno. But, py Gott, poys, in dis country ve kin speak out and do somethin'. Ve is men. Ve . . . gotta cohoperate.—OLE PETERSON, a Scandinavian immigrant and a farmer in northern Wisconsin, speaking at a public meeting in 1939, as reported by Boyd Carlisle Shafer, of Stout Institute, in *The Social Frontier*.

America with her unique experience of multiform contacts of races and peoples is in a position to invest the concept of democracy with a broader and richer meaning than any nation has done so far. . . . She can, if she will, encourage the search for the unique and the distinctive in social life, side by side, with a strong emphasis on the basic human interests.
      —JULIAN DRACHSLER, in *Democracy and Assimilation*.

It will be a bad day when the various races of our miscellaneous nation forget in one dull clamorous Americanism the deep idiosyncrasies of their origin.
      —CHRISTOPHER MORLEY, in *The Saturday Review of Literature*.

"All of Us Came
from Somewhere"

Baltimore,
March 15, 1940

Dear Mr. Adamic: When a man chews food with his lower jaw flapping; when a man spits in the street; when a man who doesn't take enough baths gets to my windward, or when a man is deliberately rude without provocation, then I resent his very existence without regard to whether he came to this continent on the Mayflower, first-class or steerage. Aside from things of this nature, I do not care how, when or whence anyone came here.

This was not always my attitude. I am still young: just thirty.

A few years ago, when I worked in a shop in Buffalo, a city with a vast population born in or stemming from Poland, in spite of the fact that every man in the place knew more about the work than I did and could do a better job, from the very first morning there I felt a sense of superiority to the men with the peculiar "foreign" names. This feeling continued and did not diminish during the two years I spent in that shop; it was not directed sharply at specific persons except in cases where such persons were guilty of the above-mentioned offenses. Rather it was a general, blanketing thing that immediately indicted everyone with x's, y's and z's in his name.

I recall quite clearly, however, that when I got to know any of those individuals who did not specifically offend me as persons I came to like them quickly. They laughed at the same jokes which struck me funny; they were just as hungry at noon and just as tired at night, and all of us together grumbled about the foreman. Only a few I disliked individually—for causes enumerated, except that I think I disliked them just a little more because in addition to their bad habits they were "foreigners."

The trouble was that I never bothered to analyze and understand this attitude of mine. These men used to go home at night to Buffalo's east side. I went home to a nice house, my father's, in a restricted middle-class "American" section. My workmates from the east side were never seen in our immediate neighborhood.

This all took place just prior to the first New Deal administration. Perhaps due to the time, or perhaps my new associations at work, something stirred curiosity in me which prompted my going to night school to study economics. In retrospect, I think it had shocked me to find how worried these men were over how long their jobs would last. That men could support families on the wages we were getting seemed impossible and why this great country of unimaginable natural wealth was crumbling away beneath their feet, I could not understand. So I set out to see what could be found out.

The professor under whom I studied was from Harvard, quite "pink" and a clever rascal; week by week he would plot the course which the New Deal would most likely follow the next week or the next month. In most cases he called his shots with wondrous skill. He made it all very exciting, as Giant America stirred and tried to lift herself up once more. But this man was above all very human, and he burned into all of us the supreme right of men and women to live like human beings.

By the time I left that shop and moved into the office, although I still felt superior toward the bulk of the men in the shop, a new feeling had attached itself. I felt they were not getting a square deal in life. How could they be expected to know enough not to chew with their mouths hanging open, not to spit in the street, etcetera? What kind of education had they gotten out of this system? And more important, what kind of education were their children getting? . . . The amazing thing was that living where they lived many of them were such swell fellows.

About this time two clever young chaps born in Buffalo of Polish immigrant parents, Kull and Marcynski, were added to my list of good friends. I liked and admired them. Sometimes I would go with them into their world, where I was treated most courteously; then I would take them into my world, where, to my shame and indignation, they were frequently slighted.

Now, when I speak "of my world," I do not mean Heaven or Park Avenue, but just plain middle-class America. So that you may understand, my father's people came from Ireland four generations ago. My mother's people came from France and England about ten generations back from me. These latter have fought with honor in all the wars in which this country has become embroiled. In the early days they prospered and grew wealthy; they owned huge tracts of land; one of them, Arthur Cooke, was the first Chief Justice of the Colony of Pennsylvania under William Penn, who at one time also owned a third of New Jersey (prior to this, however, he had been thrown out of Rhode Island for going to sleep in church); another was his successor, John Symcock; another fed the whole Army of the Northwest in the War of 1812 because Congress would not appropriate money for it, supplying in round numbers 800,000 rations at forty-five cents per ration, and so he collapsed financially and died in jail for debt—his name was John H. Piatt. Of course there isn't much in the family records which deals with the horse thieves, pirates, misers, and witches; things like that don't get into the records. . . .

But, New American or Old American, we all have a certain function here. Let me put it this way: a person has either a positive or negative influence on the society of which he is a part. There can be no zero value, for a person who fails to contribute something positive and for one reason or another does not bother to do anything negative, must necessarily have his score added up to show a negative result, as he has made of himself a drain on the whole. . . . So, among other things, the job that devolves on this country is one of education, to be made readily available to all Americans. Not education merely as it is today, when there is so much talk of free schools, and I find in the streets of Baltimore, where I now live, youngsters playing hooky from school to get downtown to polish shoes so they can take home a few nickels for bread. That is a disgrace to this country, and any man who can see such things and talk of equal opportunity is lightheaded. If I were a Negro and had grown up in a Baltimore row house, with filth and vermin, little heat in winter and little air in summer, and only a smattering of food winter or summer, I am very sure that now I would be a *Native Son*-like criminal. The same applies to many of the "Little Italys," etcetera. So I cannot help but admire these many people in such places, and by many I mean the vast majority of them, that grow up and continue to be law-abiding members of the community. Their *solid courage* alone makes of them a definite asset to America. And when a brighter day comes for them, as they well deserve, America will feed much on their strength.

Then too, they, all of these groups, are rich in their own traditions and cultures, about which I know a little, but too little. And in this regard, it behooves America to move with speed, for each day some of this is lost forever.

In line with this, I think it is urgent that in each major community in this country some light be found to show the way to interesting immigrants from Italy, Bohemia, Poland, Greece and other countries to band themselves together with second-generation people of their respective backgrounds and with us old-stock or partly old-stock Americans—with this purpose: that we would get out of their minds and feelings what is left in them and remains worth while for us today. Start clubs. Dozens, scores, or even hundreds of them in cities, say, like Buffalo, Baltimore, Chicago, Cleveland, Pittsburgh, New York, etcetera. Decorate and furnish the clubrooms with originals or skillful replicas of objects in the typical rooms which the immigrants once knew as home. Endeavor to get numerous pieces of native handwork and folkcraft. Collect the literature where possible, classic and modern, in the original and in translation, which was and is available from the mother countries. Produce old country plays and pageants. Don't suppress the immigrants' mother tongues; start classes in them. Conduct contests in every form of writing, without neglecting the other special arts and crafts which carry over from there. Bring all this out of the attic, dust it off, make it interesting, and let the young second generation see just why they have every cause to take delight and pride in their descent and in their names, regardless of the consonant content of them. And show us old-stock Americans that we have something in our "foreign sections" which is not to be deplored, which may, in fact, be part of the hope of this country.

Set this sort of thing moving in such a way that the leaders of the several old-stock and new-immigrant units in a city would co-operate, producing joint festivals and musicales and dances. Let all the units shuttle around amongst one another . . . which would certainly tend to raise the level of each group's respect for itself and for others.

All of us came from somewhere, Iraq or Ireland; such a program could be made to appeal to any and all of us, and out of it we would all get on a common footing, while retaining for America all the wealth of tradition and folklore. It excites me just to think of how much we would all gain from it . . . how much downright fun it would be to see all that is hidden and locked up in the hearts of our friends Aristidines, Pucelli, Goldberger, Mioduszewski, Kull and Marcynski!   J. N. K.

The End

THE PROJECT

"I am an ex-alien who became an American citizen while in the United States Army during the [First] World War, and the views expressed here are only my own. I represent no one and nothing except, I hope, a certain emotion for this land of my adoption which is an amalgam of love and hope, and on which I have no monopoly. . . .

". . . I am deeply mindful of the fact that [over] one-third of our population is of recent, largely non-Anglo-Saxon immigrant stock, the beginning of whose background in this country is Ellis Island rather than [Jamestown or] Plymouth Rock. I belong to this numerous new element, but I am not for it as *it* is, as against the old American stock as *it* is, nor the other way about. I am for the whole of present-day America, not as something that is finished and satisfactory . . . but as material out of which the future has to be wrought, as something in the process of becoming. . . .

"America is only beginning, and every beginning is somewhat of a mess. As I have tried to show in my novel *Grandsons*, human America is chopped up into numerous racial, class, and cultural islands surrounded by vague seas, with scant connection and communication among them. The old Melting Pot idea has not been carried out any too well. Human America is poorly integrated, and I am for integration and homogeneity, for the disappearance of the now sharply defined, island-like groups, and the general, organic merging of all the groups into a nation that culturally and spiritually will be a fusion of all the races and nations now in the United States on the general politico-cultural pattern laid out by the earliest immigrants on this continent and their descendants . . ."

From *My America*, page 207.

Plymouth Rock and
Ellis Island

Summary of a lecture delivered before about one hundred audiences all over the United States between early October, 1939, and early May, 1940.

EIGHTY-FIVE years ago, Walt Whitman said of the United States: "This is not a nation but a teeming nation of nations." The United States has been that from the start. It was recognized as such by the Founding Fathers. John Adams, Benjamin Franklin, and Thomas Jefferson, who were a committee created for the purpose, recommended to Congress that the new national emblem of the country should contain, besides the emblems of the Original Thirteen States, also the national emblems of England, Scotland, Ireland, France, Germany and Holland, as representing "the countries from which these States have been peopled." . . . This has always been a country of many strains.

There is no doubt, however, that once upon a time, early in its career, the United States was a much simpler place in its human make-up than it is today. Even, say, a hundred years ago the people of this country were largely derived from Britain: Anglo-Saxons, who—along with the other elements of the population at the time—were mostly Protestants. There were few Catholics and few Jews. There were, to be sure, great numbers of Negroes, but they were nearly all in the South, and slavery created the illusion that they were outside the processes of American culture. Upon a different basis, the same was true of the Indians.

As the dominant element, the Anglo-Saxon Americans in the East began to create a cultural pattern which was then stretched across the country as the people began to move West. The threads being woven into this pattern were the English heritage, the English language, the Colonial experience, the Revolution and its ideas, the sense of the frontier, and, to no slight extent, particularly in the Northeast, the attitude to life called Puritanism. In connection with these cultural beginnings, there appeared a system of national hopes or aspirations that came to be called the American Dream—a matter mostly of faith in the human individual and the concepts of liberty, fraternity and equality, of general welfare and democracy which were stated or embodied in the Declaration of Independence and the Constitution. This Dream was the flowering of the idealistic, socially creative urges of the early immigrants here and their descendants, whom I now like to call the old-stock Americans.

At the beginning of their story as a group in this New World were Jamestown and Plymouth Rock.

After the Revolution, which had occurred in part because England did not permit free immigration into the Colonies, new people came over right along; but

for a good while they were chiefly Anglo-Saxons with some Germans and Hollanders
—Protestants nearly all of them.

We have no immigration figures prior to 1820. In that year about 8,000 immigrants
entered; in 1830 the number was 23,000; in 1840 approximately 84,000 came in.
There were many Catholic Irish among the immigrants during these decades, but
most of them still were Anglo-Saxons and Protestants of the German and Dutch
strains.

Then the Machine roared its way onto the national scene, bringing on the
Industrial Revolution and the passion to develop the country in a hurry and to get
rich quick; and came, too, the Civil War or the War Between the States, which was
a great drain on the man power; and there began the New Immigration.

In the last hundred years 38,000,000 immigrants came over; 24,000,000 in the
last fifty years. And the majority of them were non-Anglo-Saxons and non-
Protestants, and were not very closely attached to the attitude to life called Puritanism.

Some of these new people came in a spirit of adventure or with chiefly materialistic
motives, or because they were lured over by American industrialists. Most of them,
however, were escaping from oppression, terrorism, even massacres; from army
service and militarism generally; from life in ghettos and from economic or personal
frustration or fear of frustration. It was as if they came in response to the lines
struck—in 1886—on the pedestal of the Statue of Liberty:

> *Give me your tired, your poor,*
> *Your huddled masses yearning to breathe free,*
> *The wretched refuse of your teeming shore,*
> *Send these, the homeless, the tempest-tost, to me:*
> *I lift my lamp beside the golden door.*

To most of them, as it had been to most of the earliest immigrants, the Pilgrims,
America was a refuge, a chance for a better life. . . . They came and spilled themselves over America, 38,000,000 of them, in what was a mere moment in history;
representing over fifty different national backgrounds, speaking as many languages
and several hundred dialects, owing allegiance to over twoscore rulers and governments, and adhering to about a dozen different religions.

The majority of these new people went into the cities, to work in factories and
mills, in small shops and stockyards, on the new bridges, roads, and skyscrapers; or
into the small mining towns and camps. But many, too, went on the land as pioneers.
Or they went into fishing along the various coasts of America and on the Great
Lakes; or to the woods as timber workers. . . . And everybody worked and built
and dug and grubbed and carried burdens, and as America stands today, there is
hardly a building here, hardly a bridge or mile of railway or highway, hardly a
vehicle, hardly anything that is not, in part, a result of immigrant labor.

This is one of the greatest stories under the sun, the story of the coming and
the meeting of all these peoples, in so brief a period, on this vast and beautiful
continent. It is, as yet, a story little known and perhaps never to be written fully.
. . . Personally, I am trying to get at it, just now, in a project which I began early

in 1939 with the aid of a grant of the Carnegie Corporation of New York. It is a study of the various and complex developments in our American life which revolve around, or issue from, this fact of the 38,000,000 immigrants coming here in the last hundred years. It will eventually result in a series of books.

I undertook this job because the New Immigration seems to me one of the most important of the more neglected facts in American history; important from the viewpoint of our future in the United States. . . .

So far I have sent out about 150,000 copies of what I call my broadside (some of you may have seen it)—a questionnaire in which I ask for information on the subject: and I have received (by May, 1940) about 9,500 replies, letters ranging from a few lines to more than a hundred pages, and masses of other material: clippings and scrapbooks, manuscripts and obscure books and pamphlets. This material came to me, and is still coming, from all manner of people, old-stock Americans and immigrants and their children, from men and women in all walks of life, from about 1,500 cities and towns all over the country. Also, since the beginning of my project my assistants and I have traveled about fifty thousand miles, talking with people individually, in twos and threes and in small groups; and have written an endless stream of letters. And through this work now in process I am getting a sort of closeup of America. The variety of the place! And the possibilities here, good and bad, because of this variety!

Most of us, old-stock and new Americans, are not aware of the human resources we have here, and of the opportunity before us to create a great culture on this continent; a culture which could approach being universal or pan-human and more satisfying to the human make-up than any culture that has yet appeared under the sun. *Nor are we aware of the dangers ahead of us if we fail to take advantage of this opportunity.* . . . Most of us need to become conscious of this situation, of this new America; need to become naturalized to it. As a country, we need to look into the resources of genius and talent, character and cultural values in the new groups; if for no other reason, because it is almost certain that, with the rest of the world, we are facing difficult times ahead, and the probability is that we will need everything we've got to keep on even keel during the next few decades.

We have something over 300,000 Indians, who are mostly in reservations, a problem somewhat special and apart; and about 13,000,000 Negroes, also a rather special and uniquely acute problem, possibly destined to be the ultimate and most severe test of our forming culture, of our pretensions to democracy—a test which the country will be able to meet, I feel, only if the white elements soon begin to solve the problems among themselves.

The whites number about 115,000,000. Slightly over half of them are Anglo-Saxons, or think they are, or pass as such, partly, largely, or wholly. They are Protestants or of Protestant background. There are about 20,000,000 other people here who are not Anglo-Saxons but are Protestants, or of Protestant background. About 10,000,000 are Irish Catholic, or of that background; between 15 and 20 millions of the German, about 5,000,000 of the Italian, about 4,000,000 of the Scandinavian, about 2,000,000 of the French, and between 8 and 10 millions of the various Slavic backgrounds. Half a million each will cover those of the Finnish, Lithuanian, and Greek backgrounds. Also, we have several hundred thousand Orientals, and there are not inconsiderable Mexican and Filipino elements. And we have 4,500,000 Jews, about 22,000,000 Catholics, and 5 or 6 million people of the Eastern Orthodox faiths. . . . These are estimates, but I believe fairly close.

We have here now 12,000,000 immigrants and between 30 and 35 million American-born children of immigrants who are designated in the Census as "native of foreign white stock." And we have, perhaps, 10 or 15 million grandchildren of immigrants who are not distinguished in the Census. This constitutes about half of the white population. Most of this half is non-Anglo-Saxon and non-Protestant.

Most of the new people are in cities. In 1930, at the last Census, New York City had a population of 7,000,000 of which 73% was foreign-born or of immigrant parentage. Chicago was 64% "foreign"; Philadelphia 50%; Cleveland 65%; Boston, of all places, 71%; Detroit, San Francisco, Minneapolis, and St. Paul 57% each; etc. Most of the large cities north of the Mason-Dixon Line and east of the Mississippi are over 50% "foreign," so-called; which is true also of many small communities.

English, of course, continues to be the prevalent tongue of the country, and there is no least desire anywhere to have it supplanted; but we do have over 1,000 newspapers and magazines published in about forty foreign languages, and about 1,000 radio programs daily in other languages than English, and hundreds of parochial and "national" schools in which a great number of American-born children are taught more than a score of foreign languages.

These facts and estimates, I think, are charged with dynamic possibilities, good and bad, but I believe mostly good if we are careful and intelligent. Involved in these facts is much of the future of the United States.

Each of the new-immigrant groups has a number of successful, prominent or famous individuals. There are over 2,500 immigrants in *Who's Who in America*—scientists, artists, musicians, educators, etc. The great majority, however, are humble folk, workers and farmers who skate on the thin ice along the margins of our erratic economy. Some are or were on relief, though not nearly as many as generally imagined. . . . There is no doubt, though, that most of them are economically better off here than they would have been in the old countries. They generally realize this and are glad to be here; their devotion to this country, in many cases personally known to me, is almost beyond adequate statement.

But while this is generally true, many, perhaps most, are not quite at ease, not quite at home, spiritually or culturally. They are more or less different from the old-stock Americans, and are regarded as different, and they feel prejudice in various forms directed against them from various sides, from the dominant group, because they are different. Of late years, the Depression has had a hand in this. In many places the foreign-born and those of their American-born children whose names had a so-called foreign sound were laid off first, before the old-stock workers, sometimes even before the Negroes. This caused a vague, often unconscious sense of panic among immigrants and their families, and the tendency became for various groups to stay together and hold onto their "foreign" sections, which in better times had begun to show signs of disintegration. . . . In recent years, too, there has been a powerful backwash of group feelings or national emotions from the drastic events in Europe; some of it natural and inevitable, and some of it purposefully stimulated by agents of Old World governments. [The power of this backwash has increased enormously since May, 1940.]

At the risk of oversimplification, this backwash and the Depression have been effective in increasing prejudice and intolerance, and in driving—more or less—the various elements back upon their own resources as groups.

Anti-Semitism has increased; we all know that—with the result that the tendency among the Jews in many parts of the country is to suppress their talents and ambitions, and to draw apart from the main streams of American life. . . . To a lesser extent, in milder forms, the same is true of many other new groups.

My impression is that, in this game of prejudice, *the most consequential* are the attitudes of the old-stock people because they are the dominant group, the leaders, and whatever they do is more important, it seems, than what is done by the newer people. . . . Such words as "alien" and "foreigner" are flung about all too carelessly, with all too much derision. Many people, when they say "alien," mean not only the alien, but also the naturalized immigrant; and often not only him, but also his American-born son or daughter if his or her name happens to sound "foreign."

This thing is spreading. It is noticeable in the halls of Congress. It creeps into the speeches of professional patriots. It is being organized: we are said to have about eight hundred societies and movements whose purpose is to spread prejudice. It is being taken up by Americans who are not old-stock but of the more favored, earlier new-immigrant groups.

As I say, the old-stock Americans' prejudice is the most serious in its effect; but, in fairness, I hasten to add that, by and large, the old-stock people who are hooked to the best traditions of America are rather less apt to be prejudiced than some of the new groups, which—as a hangover from the Old World nationalism—maintain, here and there, active unfriendliness toward one another.

Together, old-stock and new-stock elements manage to produce a stream of prejudice that runs through our cultural atmosphere and touches most phases of the country's life; and, in turn, produces much inner chaos, which plays havoc with individual character, which makes people insecure and puts them on the defensive, which inhibits and kills ambition, talent, initiative, and the inclination to participate in things.

In fairness again, let me say that amidst all the snobberies and related attitudes there is also much friendliness, or would-be friendliness, on the part of the old-stock and new Americans, one toward the other. On a rough estimate, I should say, from what I am able to discern from my current study, that 60 or even 70 per cent of old-stock Americans incline to be friendly on the whole, although much of that friendliness, unhappily, is spoiled in part by the tendency to be condescending and patronizing. And, also on a rough estimate, I should say that about half of the people in the newer groups are not actively prejudiced. . . . I might say, too, that much of the prejudice is a superficial business, not personal, just general, careless and stupid.

I am not blaming or excusing anyone here; the villains in this game of prejudice are also its victims. I find, for instance, that prejudice, essentially, is worse on the prejudiced than on their targets; it turns the former into objectionable people, robbing them of humanity and spiritual health.

My point is that we have entirely too much prejudice, that it is growing, and that that is bad for America.

The cleavages among the various groups are deepening; groups are pulling apart, into various corners, away from one another. This is true of the old-stock element as well as the new group. . . . I know personally, or I correspond with, hundreds of old-stock people, particularly in the East, but also elsewhere, who may be representative of millions, and who are uneasy because their cities, as they say, are full of "these foreigners"; and who feel the country is going to the dogs, in part, because of that. A feeling is creeping up on them that this is no longer their country, no longer America, Anglo-Saxon America; and they confess they are beginning to feel like aliens here. So they are withdrawing; their attitudes are getting rigid . . . and they hold onto their money if they have any, and they blame "these foreigners" if they haven't any. They are becoming unhooked from the country's expansive and creative impulses, from the American Dream; and are being drawn into the fear- and confusion-made trends to contract, to narrow down, to grow anemic, neurotic, and reactionary.

And this, by and large, is true, too, of the new groups. As I say, they are withdrawing into themselves, into ethnocentric sections, into national or group pride and egoism. This is true of immigrants and, increasingly, also of their American-born sons and daughters. . . . There are, of course, numerous exceptions; generally, however, the new groups (especially those of the east- and south-European and Near Eastern backgrounds, and of the Jewish and German backgrounds just now) have no firm sense of what psychiatrists call belongingness, which is considered necessary for a full, balanced development of character and personality, and for one's effectiveness in a creative way within a culture.

To repeat, this is true of immigrants and of their American-born children; of many, perhaps most, of them: and remember their number runs into tens of millions. . . . They *are* different from the old-stock Americans. Their Old World heritage, in most cases, is not England, but Poland or Italy or Bohemia or Armenia or the Balkans, etc. And the beginning of their vital American background as groups is not the glorified Mayflower, but the as yet unglorified immigrant steerage; not Plymouth Rock or Jamestown, but Castle Garden or Ellis Island or Angel Island or the International Bridge or the Mexican or Canadian border; not the wilderness of New England, but the social-economic jungle of the city slums and the factory system; not the Revolution of 1776, but the Industrial Revolution of the last seventy-five years; not the peals of the Liberty Bell, but the first glimpse of the Statue of Liberty.

The majority of the new Americans are not subjectively identified with America as a state, a culture, and an idea, although most of them want to be, even desperately so; but the stream of prejudice that runs through our national atmosphere makes it hard for them to achieve that identification. I find that most of the new people, when they say "we," don't mean "we Americans" or "we the people in this town," but "we who live in this section and are of Polish or Armenian, etc., origin or background." When they say "Americans," they don't mean themselves.

The majority are on the defensive, are oppressed by feelings of inferiority, tens of millions of them; and, in consequence, they hang back and tend to be what Mencken used to call "assistant Americans" and to suppress their ambitions and keep away from the main streams of American life. They are "marginal" people, economically, socially and culturally, and are geared not to the expansive and creative impulses of America, but to the fear- and confusion-prompted trends to contract and narrow down.

What is the answer? A great many people say tolerance. But I don't know about that. Tolerance, I am afraid, is not enough. By and large, I suppose, I prefer tolerance to intolerance, and I am aware of Webster's definition of tolerance; but all too often, as I study this problem, I find that tolerance is something very different from what a good many people think it is. Usually, tolerance, as it works out in practice is nothing more than inactive intolerance; at best a negative virtue. Channing Pollock called it "a smug sense of infallibility." It implies a superiority complex. One is tolerant when one endures, or stands for, something one doesn't like. Tolerance is mostly intolerance grown subtle, polite, and beyond reach, where you can't deal with it. It is mostly veneer for intolerance, which cracks easily; which has been cracking in recent years in this country under the impact of the Depression and the backwash of the events abroad. Something more is needed: we will have to begin to accept one another.

"This is not a nation but a teeming nation of nations," a country in process of becoming a nation; it always has been that, and, to my mind, it will be no tragedy should it remain that for some time to come, even forever. It always has been a heterogeneous country, a mixture of strains and religions; which has been, and is, the basis of much of its uniqueness in the world and the source of much of its power. It may be no accident that many of the most dynamic cities and regions in this country have been and are those which include the greatest variety of national and cultural backgrounds.

On its sound, positive side, America always has welcomed diversity, variety, differences. The Revolution, as I say, was fought, in part, because England did not permit free immigration into the Colonies.

The Founding Fathers were mostly Anglo-Saxons, but eighteen of the signers of the Declaration of Independence were of non-English origin or descent. The springs of this country's central ideas and ideals have various sources. The Declaration of Independence, one of the greatest pieces ever written, *is* an Anglo-Saxon document, written by Jefferson in the English language; its contents, however, are not the exclusive patent of any one strain. In fact, there is good basis for believing that an early, if not the first, draft of the Declaration was written by an Italian, Mazei, who was a close friend and associate of Jefferson. No one strain has a monopoly on the ideas of liberty, equality, fraternity, democracy. . . . Before the Revolution, the sermons of the anti-British preachers in New England were based on passages dealing with liberty in the Old Testament, a Jewish book. . . . Government based on the consent of the governed is an all-important concept. The Founding Fathers got it, as it has been shown by historians, from the thirteenth-century Scholastic philosophers, who were Spaniards, Italians and Frenchmen.

At its best, Americanism is nobody's monopoly, but a happy concentrate of some of the highest aspirations and tendencies of humanity at its best nearly everywhere at one time or another. As it seems to me, it is the highest body of idealism in the world today. It is, among other things, a movement away from primitive racism, fear and nationalism, and herd instincts and mentality; a movement toward freedom, creativeness, a universal or pan-human culture.

In the course of my project, I have been repeatedly impressed by immigrants telling me or writing to me how they felt when they first glimpsed the Statue of Liberty: how tears filled their eyes, how they wanted to fall on their knees, how they lifted their children to see the goddess. These immigrants were Americans before they landed. They were part of the same movement, the same surge toward freedom, that brought over the Pilgrims. Their stories seem to me intensely exciting literary material and a source of inspiration for freedom and democracy. The inscription on the Statue of Liberty remains significant.

Americanism welcomes differences, and if we can stand another motto, I suggest: Let's make America safe for differences. Let us work for unity within diversity. My guess is that if we try this, much of the diversity to which some of us possibly more or less object will cease to be important or objectionable. Let us begin to accept one another as we are. I don't mean, of course, that one should like everybody, I mean that one's decision to like or dislike or be indifferent to a man should be made on the basis of his essential qualities as a person, not on the basis of the fact that he was born an Albanian or Yankee, or that he came over in steerage or that he can sport a Mayflower blossom on his family tree. . . .

We need to be trained, or train ourselves, in the direction of becoming creatively, positively, interested in a man partly *because* he is different; *because,* being different, he is apt to have something out-of-the-ordinary to offer to us personally and contribute to the evolving culture and civilization. Emerson said, "It is the 'not-me' in my friend that charms me."

Inviting diversity, being interested in it, will tend to produce unity in a democratic country; will tend to make it dynamic; will operate against the concentration-camp-like foreign sections and ghettos and restricted residential districts, and will encourage movement and dispersal, at the same time that it will work for harmony and fusion. . . . Inviting diversity brings out the basic sameness of people, just as the opposite results only in more and sharper differences. It breaks down both the superiorities and inferiorities, which are equally bad—two ends of the same stick.

Inviting diversity builds individual character and thereby helps to endow the country with ability to tackle problems as they come up. We in this country, of late, are not dealing with our problems successfully; in great part, it seems to me, because millions of us are involved in a complexity of group bickerings and prejudices, name-calling, and ignorant racist arguments and attitudes, which are chewing up and burning up our characters and personalities, our initiative and will. . . .

What to do? . . . In New York and elsewhere a group of us—we call ourselves the Common Council for American Unity—are working on plans to project some of these ideas into a long-range, statesmanlike movement, which will enlist education, literature, the movies, radio, and other cultural forces. [See page 347.]

Personally, in the project which I mentioned and which is to result in a series of books, I am trying to work toward an intellectual-emotional synthesis of old and new America; of the Mayflower and the steerage; of the New England wilderness and the social-economic jungle of the city slums and the factory system; of the Liberty Bell and the Statue of Liberty. The old American Dream needs to be interlaced with the immigrants' emotions as they saw the Statue of Liberty. The two must be made into one story.

There are many things that I want to do. I want to stress what I have tried to bring out in *My America*, namely, that the United States is not anything finished and perfect, but a process in numerous ways and respects; that the road ahead is long, and that we have to be patient. There is need of emphasizing the necessity of our curbing our individual and group egoisms and beginning to realize that, whatever our background or religion, we probably are not nearly as perfect as we like to think; of stressing that our present value is not as something finished, but mostly as material for the future. There is need of saying that what is needed is less humiliation and lacerating of one another and more humility on the part of all of us. And, to end the list, there is need of stating Americanism so that it will include all of us, regardless whether our name is Hamilton, Starzinski, Jurgelionis, Brown, Kikuchi, Rodriguez, Schmidt, Krismancich, Coolidge or Steinberger; and so that within it we will all be able to achieve a subjective identification with the country and face its problems, not in a mood of mutual fear, defensiveness, indecision, fretting and withdrawal, but with affirmative intelligence, passion, and will.

This—roughly—is my task as a writer just now, and I hope that it soon will become the task of other writers and of educators and historians. But in various ways we can all work at the problem. It is a job of education, self-education, self-control.

Perhaps you can help me in my project or study. You may know something I ought to know. I suggest you get a copy of my broadside. It may be had free by writing for it. Address: Louis Adamic, Milford, New Jersey. [See page 302.]

There are many things one can do, or avoid doing, in order to help in this problem. . . . If one is a newspaper editor, one can do much by running an occasional series of articles on the new-immigrant groups and their problems, and generally report their activities, as is being done by some of the papers, notably the Cleveland *Press*.

If one is a librarian or bookseller, one can "push" such books as *Giants in the Earth* by O. E. Rölvaag, *My Antoniá* by Willa Cather, or the recent biography of O. E. Rölvaag by Theodore Jorgensen and Mary Solum, or *We Who Built America: The Saga of the Immigrant* by Prof. Carl Wittke. And one can urge people to read such books dealing with old America and its values as Van Wyck Brooks' *Flowering of New England*, Carl Van Doren's *Benjamin Franklin*, Carl Sandburg's *Lincoln*, Freeman's *Robert E. Lee*, Elizabeth Page's *Tree of Liberty*, or *The Heritage of America*, the Commanger-Nevins anthology of American material from the beginning till now. There are hundreds of good books that should be read by old and new Americans, in order to help keep themselves geared, emotionally and intellectually, to the motives and propulsions of this country.*

Schools should begin to exploit the backgrounds of their students and teachers for educational purposes. There should be displays of background materials and symbols. Schools with large numbers of so-called "foreign" youngsters should have periodic talks and lectures dealing with their backgrounds. Teachers should watch out for manifestations of prejudice among the youngsters and devise ways to deal with them. . . .

One can do, or avoid doing, many things. One can keep an eye on politicians, including those in Washington, who tend to cry "alien" every chance they get in order to accent their "patriotism" or disguise their own intellectual barrenness. . . . One can stop avoiding people because they are of another background and one can even go out of his way to meet and mingle with them. There is altogether too much clannishness and apartness in most groups. Some of the groups, too, are afflicted with entirely too much sensitiveness. I know the reasons for this oversensitiveness, but there is need of conscious effort away from it. I urge formation of small groups in communities which will develop ways and means for people of various backgrounds to meet and get to know what they have to offer one another. [See page 285.]

Whatever one's background, one should not be ashamed of it, regardless of any prejudice against it. Shame of that sort is damaging to character and inner make-up, and it tends to turn one into a negative person outwardly. One should seek all the good elements out of one's background and then (without being too sensitive about the elements which are not so good) hang onto them insofar as they are valid in his life here and now, and this not out of any personal or group egoism or pride. Hanging onto them will benefit one personally, help to make one a more effective person and citizen; and, thereby, in numerous indirect, often indiscernible ways

---

* Some day I hope to prepare, or help to prepare, an extensive list of books the reading of which may become a factor in the purpose that interests me here. I fear I am not aware of many of them, and I shall be grateful for suggestions and other aid toward making this list as complete as possible.—L. A.

probably add something to the sum-total of the evolving culture, to the tone and color of life in general in this New World. . . . In the past there has been entirely too much giving up, too much melting away and shattering of the various cultural values of the new groups. There still is too much of that, to the detriment of individuals and of America.

One can be careful with words. Perhaps the worst that can be said for such words and expressions as Hunky, Polack, Kike, Goy, Jap, Chink, Nigger, Greaser, and Wop is that they are ill-mannered. . . . The word *race* should be used sparingly. There really is no Slavic, Italian, Jewish or Scandinavian race. Such differences as exist among people are due, in the main, to different environment, history and experience; when we meet in the same environment and have a common life we tend to become alike. . . . *Minority* is a bad word, a European word, a symbol of an important phase of the tragedy over there. *Melting Pot* is a poor phrase and concept. It means that everybody is to be turned into something else with heat.

Our period is a difficult one. I don't know how the current world crisis is going to develop or what this country is going to do in the long run in connection with it. Whatever happens, I hope that a good many of us will be careful and intelligent. . . . As I've said, we have here between 15 and 20 million people of the German background. The thing to do is to remember that they are one thing and the German Bund is another thing; that Hitler is over there and Thomas Mann is here. [The same goes for the Italian group.]

It may be that the worst is yet to come in the Old World, that we are witnessing the beginning of a cultural blackout over there, and that it is going to to be our job here to save some of the good phases of Western culture and make them elements of the American culture. We have abundant materials for such a job.

When this country was formed, there were people, Jefferson included, who believed that the hope of the world was here. They probably were right. But we must be careful. There is need of exerting our individual and collective intelligence. We have serious economic and social problems; as we proceed to try to solve them, we should watch out that prejudice and intolerance don't turn the American Dream into a Nightmare.

The future, ours as the world's, is in unity within diversity. Our various backgrounds are important and valuable, but, in the long run, not in themselves, not as something perfect and final. They are important and valuable only as material for our future American culture. As I say, we have a chance to create a universal, a pan-human culture, more satisfying than anything humanity has as yet devised or experienced.

The American Dream is a lovely thing, but to keep it alive, to keep it from turning into a Nightmare, every once in a while we've got to wake up.

The
Broadside

An abbreviation of this questionnaire *appeared initially in several hundred immigrant or foreign-language newspapers during the winter of 1938-39. There were numerous revised editions of the broadside; the following is the latest before the script of this book is given to the printer.*

UNUSUAL motives and circumstances, more or less explained below, prompt this *questionnaire* broadside. I have tried other, more familiar ways to get at what I want to do, and found them unsatisfactory. . . .

In the part entitled "Plymouth Rock and Ellis Island" of my last book, *My America,* published in May, 1938, I try to point out the following facts and ideas:

(1) That, in point of the composition of the population of the United States, Ellis Island is rapidly becoming as important as are Plymouth Rock and Jamestown.

(2) That the United States as it stands today is—racially, socially, culturally, religiously, spiritually: in short, humanly—an extension not alone of the British Isles and The Netherlands but, more or less, of all Europe and, to an extent, of parts of Asia and Africa.

(3) That present-day America, with its great industries, skyscrapers, endless railways and power lines, is perhaps as much the result of the labor and genius of immigrants who came over in the last sixty or seventy years as of old-stock Americans, who are mostly, or think they are, of the Anglo-Saxon strain.

(4) That in the upbuilding of the country in the last century more immigrants from various European countries have perished in industrial accidents than early American colonists were killed in subduing the wilderness and in the War for Independence; and that it is urgent for America that this fact—which is the most important part of the American background of tens of millions of our citizens—be realized and appreciated by the country as a whole.

(5) That very rapidly the United States is ceasing to be a preponderantly Anglo-Saxon country, for our population now includes tens of millions of non-Anglo-Saxons; and that, for that reason, a new conception of America (along the lines dimly suggested above) is necessary.

(6) That the presence in the United States of this vast new-immigrant element is an unprecedented opportunity for creating on this continent an extraordinarily rich culture and civilization, at the same time that it immensely complicates American social, economic, political, cultural, and spiritual forces and problems; that inherent in our present population are certain dangers to America, to her liberty and unity, democracy and trend to equality, as well as to the various old-stock and new-immigrant groups as such; that alien-baiting, anti-Semitism and kindred attitudes

and ideas are spreading . . . and, lest these dangers to America and the various groups increase and intensify, all of us—new and old-stock Americans—must begin to become intelligently, patriotically, actively, *critically* interested in this entire situation, now generally wrapped in darkness and shot through with fear and sentimentality.

This is the gist of what I am driving at in *My America*. But what I say in that book is tentative, incomplete. I plan to write a group of *independent* books which will deal, as exhaustively as possible, with the immigrants who have come here in the last hundred years, and with their children and grandchildren who are native Americans but different from, say, Americans of Yankee stock, and with their problems as such in relation to America as a whole, with America's problems in relation to them, with the problem of Americanization or assimilation, with the faltering idea of the "Melting Pot," and with the future of the United States from the viewpoint of the fact that the composition of its population is rapidly changing. I don't like the phrase "Melting Pot" [see page 301] but since it is popularly used, let me say that I want to dig into the "Pot." I suspect that some of the stuff in it is rather cold and some so hot it is burning holes in it, at the same time that it probably holds great spiritual and cultural resources now largely neglected and wasted but still available to be developed into enhancements of a positive democracy in the United States.

The collective title of this group of independent books will be The Nation of Nations Series, using a phrase by Walt Whitman: "Here is not a nation, but a teeming nation of nations." The first book, *From Many Lands,* is scheduled for publication late in 1940, to be followed sometime in 1941 by *Plymouth Rock and Ellis Island* and later by others at about eight-month intervals.

My subject is scattered the country over; its most important facts and phases are hidden in the least likely places . . . and my project will most probably strain all my resources. I shall need and seek all the help I can get, and this prospectus is addressed to almost anybody in the United States who happens to read it.

Please read and study *all* the numerous questions I ask, then write me a letter— one page or fifty pages—answering in your own way as many of them as you can or wish to answer. Feel free to write to me about anything else connected with this subject that is not covered by my questions. *I ask for utter candor.* If you wish, mark your letter "confidential"; I shall respect it as such. If nothing else, tell me if you approve of this project, or the contrary; tell me, especially, if you disapprove of it, giving your reasons.

Please do not assume that someone else will write to me, or that I already know, the facts and ideas that occur to you as you read my questionnaire.

I am seeking information, I want to be instructed. I have certain ideas, but my mind is fluid; the ideas I have are not dogma, but open to revision. The fixed factors in my viewpoint are concern for the United States, its culture, its traditional democracy and the future development of the human type here, and the conviction that the story of the successive waves of immigration into this country contains a great promise for the future which will turn into a great danger, especially now in connection with the new world war, if we do not get busy to help realize it.

Please let me hear from you as soon as convenient. If you cannot write to me at once or in the immediate future, put this questionnaire where it may arrest your attention later. My present tentative plan is to continue the survey part of my project till the end of 1941. This may possibly be extended into 1942. . . . If you write to me about something that will especially interest me, I shall try to come to your city or town and study or investigate the thing further. [Nearly all the material in *From Many Lands* was procured in this manner. I shall continue to be interested in personal, family, group and community stories, especially in those quite unlike the tales and studies in the present volume.]

I hope to distribute hundreds of thousands of copies of my broadside (to be revised from time to time). I hope to get some of them posted on the bulletin boards of clubs and organizations and social and educational institutions, and to receive their aid in distributing them. I shall be grateful for addresses to which one or more copies should be sent. If you yourself want more copies, please let me know, stating the number desired. No charge.

Social science departments of several colleges and high schools have found the broadside useful as an aid in studying immigration and population problems.

QUESTIONS FOR IMMIGRANTS AND THEIR AMERICAN-BORN DESCENDANTS

What is the history of your racial or national group in the United States? In your community, or where you lived in the past? Is there any written material? Where and how could I obtain it?

When, why and whence did people of your stock first come to America? When and why did they first come where you now live? What did the majority engage in at first? What do they engage in now? What did they have to go through to gain a foothold? (I think that the stories of the earliest immigrants of the various new-immigrant groups are quite as interesting and significant as are those of the earliest Anglo-Saxon or Dutch colonists. The wilderness of American city slums or mining towns of sixty or seventy years ago was perhaps worse than that of the virgin region of New England with its Indians in the seventeenth century.)

Which towns in America were started by your people? When, how, and why? Are these towns still inhabited mostly by your people? Who could tell me the stories of these towns?

How does America look now to people of your racial or national stock? How did the Depression affect them? What are they thinking, saying? Are the old-timers glad to be here or sorry they ever came over? Why? Are some of them planning or dreaming to "go back to the old country to die"? Are most of your immigrants naturalized? If not, why not?

Do they mingle with persons of other new-immigrant backgrounds? With old-stock Americans? To what extent? Are they going into local, state, national politics: to what extent?

Are they encountering prejudice or discrimination because they are "foreigners"? How do they cope with it? Does this prejudice include the immigrants' American-born children? What are they doing about it? Are there any organized efforts in your community to cope with open and hidden intolerance?

What are some of the other problems facing your people in your city or town today? In America at large?

Do many change their names: why and how?

Do members of your group tend to be prejudiced against other groups? If so, against which groups? How does their prejudice manifest itself?

All immigrant groups have contributed vastly to the upbuilding of America as it now stands. Who were or are some of the outstanding people of your national group in the United States? In professions? Sports? The arts? Industry and business? Education and religion? In special fields? In the labor movement? In politics? Are their life stories interesting, dramatic, illustrative of the life of your people in America as a whole? I am especially eager to hear of immigrants or second-generation workers who are not widely known but who have invented gadgets and new production methods which are now a part of American industrial operations, or have made other important but not generally recognized social, economic and cultural contributions.

I should like to hear of old couples of your race or nationality who have been in America a long time and whose children, grandchildren, and possibly great-grandchildren are by now scattered all over America, performing various functions, facing different problems, living interesting or average American lives. What are their names, where do they live? Who knows the entire stories of such specific families?

To what extent are your "national" or "racial" colonies in the various cities breaking up? How are they breaking up? What does that mean in terms of living to the old immigrants and their American-born children? Is it good these colonies are breaking up? Why or why not?

What are some of the characteristics, good and bad, of your people in America? Which characteristics are being destroyed or enhanced by American forces? Which would benefit America if they were preserved and developed here? What have your people brought over in them that, if it became part of American life in general, would add to the color and tone of the culture of the United States and would enhance American democracy and devotion to liberty? Your people brought to America certain cultural gifts and talents. Which of them were destroyed, perverted, or damaged by conditions in this country? Which were enhanced? Which have any value for the future of America? Why? What can be done to restore those that were damaged?

What role does organized religion play among your people? In your own life?

How has the Depression affected your people? Their attitude toward the United States? How has it affected you personally, and your attitude?

How do you, personally, swing politically—say, in reference to the New Deal? Are you typical of your group? Who, to your mind, are the great men and women of America? Would you vote for a President for third term? How important in Al Smith's defeat in 1928 were the facts that he is a Catholic and the son of immigrants? Will the fact that Wendell Willkie is a grandson of German immigrants play a role in the 1940 campaign? [Those reading this question after November, 1940, will please put it in the past tense.]

The immigrants' children and grandchildren interest me. (In this connection, if possible, please see the chapter, "Thirty Million New Americans" in the book, *My America,* available in most libraries.) My observation is that many of these New Americans, as I call them, are oppressed by feelings of inferiority in relation to old-stock Americans, to America as a whole. Is that your observation, too? How do those feelings of inferiority manifest themselves? Are American-born children uneasy or unhappy because their names are "foreign"? Are some of them ashamed of their "foreign" parents? Do many leave home? Why? What happens in such cases? How have some of them overcome their feelings of inferiority?

Are people of your strain marrying persons of other backgrounds? Are such unions successful? What are the problems of children born to such couples? I'd like to get case histories.

Do critical developments in the Old World and the backwash they send here tend to enhance the consciousness of your people in America of their old-country beginnings and backgrounds. Do they affect their American-born children? How?

What do you, personally, think of your people as a part of the forming American nation? Of other new-immigrant groups with which you are familiar? What proportion of Italians and Germans here are pro-fascist or pro-Nazi? I shall welcome answers to this question especially from persons of Italian and German origin.

How do your people speak among themselves of old-stock Americans—bitterly, enviously, with admiration or respect, or otherwise?

Your opinion of the old-stock Americans you know well? Of the old-stock Americans generally as the dominant group in the United States? Do you feel that old-stock Americans are "dying out," "slipping," that is, not reproducing themselves as numerously as the new-immigrant groups; and that, as a writer hints in the November, 1938 *Harpers,* the future in America "belongs to the Bohunks," meaning people of new-immigrant stocks? If so, are the latter fit, or becoming fit, to run the country as well as, or better than, it is being run now? Will they be disposed and able to continue America on the basis of the principles and ideas which motivated the Founding Fathers?

QUESTIONS FOR OLD-STOCK AMERICANS

What do you think or feel about all "these foreigners" being here? By and large, are they an asset to your town or city: to the country at large? Or ought they to be "sent back where they came from"? In either case, why do you think so? When you speak or think of the "foreigners" in your town, do you mean—consciously or unconsciously—to include the immigrants' American-born children, or even their grandchildren, if their names are something like Stankovich, Zlamal, Zamblaoskas, or Mioduszewski? Do their names make them so very "different" from you? Or is there something else? Are you, as an old-stock American, occasionally uneasy—deeply or just a little—as you glance about and see the "foreigners" more or less making their way into American life? If so, why? What is your reaction to these facts—that La Guardia is Mayor of New York; that Lehmann is Governor of the State of New York; that Knudsen and Hillman, immigrants from Denmark and Russia, respectively, are two of the seven members of the Council of National Defense? I know old-stock Americans who confess they feel like aliens in their own country. What with all "these foreigners" around, this is no longer their kind of America! What is there to be done about *that*?

If you are an employer, a factory superintendent, an office manager, or a foreman, will you give me your opinion of the new-immigrant groups represented in your shop, mine, or office?

What were some of your thoughts as you read my questions addressed to the immigrants and their American-born children?

I hope to hear from many social workers, teachers, librarians and other persons, whether of old or recent-immigrant stock, whose work touches on, or deals with, this problem.

GENERAL QUESTIONS

Calvin Coolidge once said: "Whether one traces his Americanism back three centuries to the Mayflower, or three years to the steerage, is not half so important as whether his Americanism of today is real and genuine. No matter on what various crafts we came here, we are all now in the same boat." More recently Franklin D. Roosevelt said that "we are all immigrants here." Do you agree? Please give the reasons for your agreement or disagreement.

I want to hear from Americans who are of many backgrounds—say, English, German, Czech, Jewish, and Armenian; or any other combination.

President William Green of the American Federation of Labor once said: "Our republican institutions are the outgrowth of ten centuries of the same people in England and America. They can only be preserved if the country contains at all times a great preponderance of those of British descent." In view of the fact that those of British descent are no longer in "great preponderance" and their number is not increasing in proportion to those of non-British descent, do you think that our republican institutions are doomed because of this change in our population? Personally, I don't think so, but your thoughts may be different on this point. I believe because of this there are serious dangers ahead for America, for her entire culture and setup, but we can act to avoid catastrophe. If you share this thought with me, *what* can and should we do? Adult education? What kind?

What about the Negro? . . . I hope to hear from many colored people: what is their opinion of, and attitude toward, the "foreigners" of various nationalities? The "foreigners'" attitude to them? [See next chapter.]

And what about "Americanization"? . . . As I see it, the old "Americanization" idea, often fear-motivated, aimed to purge the immigrant of his old-country background (of which the "Americanizers" had no clear notion except that it was bad because "foreign") and thus turn him neatly into an Anglo-Saxon American, or an imitation of one, and in a few nightschool lessons endow him with the background of America from the Colonial days on. Assimilation was supposed to work one way: from the immigrant's natural old-country background to Americanism as conceived by patriotic old-stock Americans. Millions of aliens were naturalized and learned more or less English, which gave the "Americanizers" the illusion that their idea was headed success-ward; actually, the average immigrant remained a good deal of the national he was in the old country. Implicit in the old "Americanization" idea, which scorned his natural background, was an insult to him, and he resented it. Also he was a little scared. In many cases, as he inevitably and silently compared his adopted country with his native land, he became more conscious of his old-country background than he was before he came over, and he frequently followed his natural inclination as a foreigner and drew aside, away from the main streams of American life, into his semi-defensive "national colony" or "foreign section," where, to a great extent, he is to this day, and where his children were born.

The result is now that many American-born sons and daughters of immigrants, when they say "we," mean their group in the "foreign section" where they live and the "old country." In their own minds and feelings, they are imperfectly identified with America.

To my mind, what is now needed is a new consciousness of America, of ourselves as a people made up of over fifty races and nationalities. What is needed is a new Americanization idea which will recognize and *accept*, not merely tolerate, the various national and racial groups as such; which will see the desirability of diversity in our population; which will take a firm stand against alien-baiting and insist that the immigrant citizens and their American-born children belong here as much as the old-stock Americans because this is their America as much as anybody's; which will help all the citizens to identify themselves with the United States; and which will, thus, work toward national unity—against fear in our national life—toward gradual assimilation or cultural fusion that will operate naturally, not one way, but in many directions. By that I mean that Anglo-Saxons will have to become partly assimilated or fused into the various new-immigrant groups just as the latter will have to become partly assimilated into the Anglo-Saxon group and into one another.

Am I right or wrong about this? How can desirable assimilation be encouraged, helped? I feel that every American, old or new stock, ought to have a thought on this matter. What is yours? It may be important. Please let me have it.

Louis Adamic
Milford, New Jersey.

Special Questionnaire
on the Negro

Extract from an article originally published in the Fall, 1939, North Georgia Review, *Clayton, Georgia, and later reprinted in numerous Southern newspapers.*

I AM disturbed by the fact that so few people are seriously troubled by the Negro Problem. I refer to it as the Negro Problem, but of course it is not a problem that involves or concerns only the Negro. It is, I feel, a section of the American Problem which involves all of us, white and black, old-stock white folk and people of recent-immigrant stocks. In fact, I think it is one of the things in our country's life that ought to engage our national intelligence most seriously and continuously. The ultimate test of the American civilization probably will come with the success or failure of efforts to solve the Negro question. I may be wrong about what I have just said, but I throw out the observation for what it may be worth as stimulus to people from whom I hope to hear.

My sympathy for the Negro, both in the South and in the North, is rather deep, but I think it is not sentimental and personal. It is objective. But greater than this sympathy for the Negro is my concern, in connection with it, for America as a whole, for white and black America; in fact, for white almost more than the black. I shall explain this in a moment.

I have not written much about the South, but I have spent a good deal of time below the Mason-Dixon Line, looking at various conditions, including the Negro Problem, to refer to it again by that imperfect title; and my opinion is that it is as bad for the whites as it is for the Negroes, or much worse for the whites than it is for the Negroes.

Few will disagree with me if I say that the Negro is generally considered inferior to the white man, and that his social-economic-political position, both in the South and in the North, but especially in the South, is predicated on that belief. If pressed for an expression of my own view on this point, I might be disposed to grant that a great many Negroes are inferior in certain respects to some whites; then I would hasten to add, *"But what part of that inferiority is actual and how much of it is due to the white-imposed, white-approved situation in which the Negro finds himself?"* I do not believe that, let me say, the Negro contralto, Marian Anderson; the Negro scientist, Dr. Carver; the Negro economist, Dr. Abram Harris, and the Negro actor, Rex Ingram, whom I happen to know personally, are inferior as all-around human beings to any white person. Dr. Carver probably is the most important man in the South; yet I know whites in the South (and in the North) who hold him to be an inferior being, not fit to be received as a social equal in their homes or sit with them at the same table or wait for a train in the same waiting-room.

Not that I am critical of the whites for this attitude. I understand it. Or, at least,

I think I do. I know that it is not a deliberate individual attitude. Nor is it merely a deliberate official policy. It is an organic thing, which goes deep, deep into the white human make-up. But what does it all mean to America's future? *How long can we afford it?* This white attitude toward the Negro, emphasized every once in a while by rope and fagot, undoubtedly helps to keep the Negro actually inferior, if he actually is inferior; it certainly helps to make him inferior if he is not actually so already. But I feel, too, that it is helping to degrade the whites who have this attitude. For one thing, this attitude is shot through with fear, and fear, especially fear that goes through generations, has a corrosive, ruinous effect on character and personality. And there is another thing: the human organism, the human spirit, mind, ability, etc., develop and grow best amid excellent or superior persons who are willing to admit anyone to equality with them if he proves himself. In such an atmosphere the individual must strive to improve himself; and striving, he grows and develops; he is a positive man or woman, involved in a positive, creative, re-creative process. In the South, it seems to me, where a vast section of the population is popularly, collectively, officially branded inferior, the process has had the tendency to be just the opposite. To feel superior, all that a white person has to do is look in the mirror: he is white—*ergo* superior: there is no need for him to excel or improve himself. The effect of this is evil. I believe it was a factor in the creation of the vast "pore white trash" element. If this process continues, it is apt to be disastrous both for Negroes and whites—for the South—for America. This, as I say, is my belief: *am I right or wrong?* Tell me.

I find that many southerners insist that the Negro Question is a southern problem, a concern of the South alone; and they resent it if a non-Southerner interests himself in it. If you who read this happen to be one of these Southerners, I should like to hear from you and learn why you think I, or any non-Southerner, should respect your position. In this connection, I wish you would consider what I say in the paragraph immediately preceding this one; and, also, that we have large Negro populations in New York, Philadelphia, Chicago, Detroit, and other cities. Can the Negro question in the North be dealt with apart from the Negro question in the South? Can you isolate the so-called Negro Problem from the entire racial-cultural problem in America? Isn't it part of the same vast complexity which involves us all and is a matter of general prejudice and intolerance, of ignorance and fear? If so, how to get at the situation?

As I say, I know that the Negro Problem is something organic and frightfully difficult; I don't blame anyone very drastically for any phase of it. I do think, however, that, in view of the all-around seriousness of the problem, all of us, white and black, but perhaps especially the white South, are exerting our individual and collective intelligence far too little to get at the beginning of some solution. I may not be aware of efforts to solve or touch the problem; I should like to hear of them.

I should like to hear from you who read this on any phase of the problem, including those which I do not even suggest in the above remarks and questions. I should like to hear from both whites and Negroes.

Louis Adamic
Milford, New Jersey.

In Reply
to the Broadside

Most of the letters from which I extract below reached me during the writing of
From Many Lands. In some cases hastily written, and in none originally intended
for publication either by the writers or by me, they are samples of the better, more
interesting replies to my broadside. Where the correspondents' names are given, they
are used with their permission. My publishing them is not to be construed as imply-
ing agreement with every word in them.

AN IMMIGRANT FROM LONDON

I AM a Londoner, brought up in that city and its suburbs, educated in the common schools and later at Culford in Suffolk. I was the son of Canadian parents
whose ancestors were Irish on my father's side and Scottish and Yorkshire on my
mother's side. My father built and sailed ships out of New Brunswick, having a
shipyard at Courtney Bay, near Saint John. My mother was born on the Petitcodiac
River above Moncton in that Province. My father retired from the sea and settled
in London in the shipping business in 1881, when I was born. He apprenticed me
to an old London engineering firm.

I was in a consulting engineer's office for nearly five years after apprenticeship,
and in 1906 I went to sea in tramp steamers. I served as fourth, third, second and
chief engineer up to 1911, when I came to the United States and wrote books for a
year. I went to sea again in American-owned ships of British registry and served
until 1914, when I returned to serve the British forces. I served on war transports
and in the Royal Naval Reserve until 1919, when I was demobilized and returned
to my job in the American ships. In 1922 I stayed ashore to write, and am still at it.

I am the first of my family to come to the United States. My brother had gone to
Canada and was later killed in war. I came here because I had always been interested
in this country. Some of my forebears moved into New Brunswick after the
Revolution. I knew the history of America. I had friends here. There were no quota
or passport barriers then. You just came in. If there had been the restrictions imposed now I might not have come. I might have tried South Africa instead.

I find it difficult to answer questions involving attitudes to the United States of
other people of my own stock. There is no such thing, so far as I know, as a British
bloc, a British "racial" group, in America. I mean politically. In my town [Westport,
Connecticut] the Italians from Sicily and Southern Italy are a compact group. Once
a year or so they disrupt all New York-Boston traffic for hours with a half-mile long
religious procession. If British residents in America combined in this manner there
would be loud cries of disapproval, and rightly so. We come from a small, densely
populated island; we value privacy and seclusion, and, as I understand my country-

men, we feel that being American does not consist of interfering with other people's comfort. I have had so warm a welcome from America that I have no desire to wear it out.

We feel that what we are and where we have come from is of no special importance. There is no cohesion, in the religious, "racial" or political sense, among us. There is a barber in my town, an Englishman. I believe our boy goes there; but I have patronized an Italian barber for eighteen years and shall continue to do so regardless of Mussolini's activities. I see no reason why I should change merely because I am an Englishman. I occasionally consort with Irish Catholics (very aggressive), Germans who love Hitler, and other Catholics who hate Jews. I consort also with liberals like my neighbor Van Wyck Brooks. On one occasion, when I sailed to Glasgow from New York, I sat beside a Negro student at the table and enjoyed his company. Many phobias popular in American strike me as silly; but I can exist without hiring a hall. I never have to tell anybody what I am or to emphasize my origin. As one Creole lady remarked bitterly, when I was a resident of New Orleans, "It sticks out all over!" In England they accused me of having become American! So the balance is redressed. Arnold Bennett, in his *Journal*, describes me as being "a bit changed by residence in the U.S.A."

It has always been my view that for good or ill I brought as much to America as America has given to me. I was unable to get excited over "liberty" because I had always had it, but I recognize that others from Central Europe are less happily situated. I have sometimes wished they did not interpret liberty to mean the unrestricted scattering of empty containers and newspapers on the streets, and for the activities of Italian, Polish, German, Jewish (etc.) political groups I have only a cold and increasingly dangerous dislike. I can see the time coming when I shall become active in advocating the abolition of private uniforms, private armies and in limiting the scope of foreign propaganda in America.

If the above view seems arrogant let me disavow arrogance. I would credit the arrogance to Mr. William Green, with his declaration: "Our republican institutions are the outgrowth of ten centuries of the same people in England and America. They can only be preserved if the country contains at all times a great preponderance of those of British descent." I see no reason for such talk. It is equally unwise to use loose phrases like "Anglo-Saxon" or "Nordic." Knowing the history of England, I hesitate to insist on anybody having "purity of race." Illiterate fanatics like Hitler can roar and rant about "Aryan blood." I have a sense of humor as well as some knowledge of history. Let us hope Hitler some day discovers a Jewish or French ancestor. I myself would enjoy finding that I had racial connections with men like Disraeli, Marx, Einstein, Freud, Steinmetz and Israel Zangwill. I would be perturbed if by some genealogical cantrip I found a Goebbels growing on my family tree.

I think the chief defect of Britishers as a class in America is that there are not enough of the "immigrant type" among them. Of course, as President Roosevelt said, "We are all immigrants here." But what I mean is that the tendency has been for the British arrivals to be less proletarian. The reason for that, of course, was that Britain had her colonies, where the underprivileged of all classes have been welcome. There has been a noticeable gap in immigration from England between the professional servant class, butlers, gardeners, chauffeurs and maids, brought in by wealthy Americans who have need of them, and people like myself, who were under no imperious economic or political necessity to come to America, but who have had no objection to, as we seafaring men used to say, "giving the natives a treat."

I have always felt a certain timidity about being too vociferously political in America. Not having much talent that way, I walk with delicacy among the pitfalls and swampy places in the political field. My personal conviction is that Roosevelt is doing a good job and would be doing a far better one if the rich would let him. I have not forgotten those days when the banks were closed! I am more or less repelled by the Union League Club brand of Americanism, for I feel instinctively that the people who support such institutions as the D.A.R. and the Social Register would have been unequivocally on the side of George III if they had lived in 1776.

The phrase, that the future of America "belongs to the Bohunks" is to me fraught with peril. It is too easy. It takes far too little notice of a very remarkable tendency in American life since the turn of the century. It disregards the teachings of history and ignores that part of racialism which, like the bulk of the iceberg, is out of sight.

In the first place, if we are to get anywhere we have to rid our minds of non-sensically looselipped phrases like "Bohunk" and "Anglo-Saxon." It was an American bad habit a few years ago to label whole sections of the earth's population by such names. It remains even today one of the average American's unfortunate legacies from his semi-frontier, nickelodeon past. To him foreigners were Limejuicers, Dagos, Spigs, Wops, Frogs, Yids, Squareheads, Hunkies, Heinies, Chinks, and so forth. It pandered to his own vanity, to regard with benign intolerance those to whom he, with almost imbecile generosity, was extending the hospitality of his native shores. To listen to some old-stock Americans, and others of suspiciously recent stock too, one would imagine that every immigrant, on being admitted, was placed in full possession of all the kindly fruits of the earth, free, gratis, and for nothing; that he did nothing for America at all in return, and all the gratitude was to be on his side, forever and ever. That cock won't fight!

It was this confusion in thinking which lay behind the above broad, coarse classifications. America may in future "belong to the Bohunks," but the Bohunks of the future will no more resemble the immigrant generation than President Roosevelt resembles his Dutch and Finnish ancestors.

I have spoken of that part of racialism that is out of sight. By this I mean the tendency of "Bohunks," "Wops" and so forth (without the slightest disrespect for them as persons) to divest themselves of their native customs, clothes and religion, and become merged in the general mass. That this is only superficial may be granted. We have to remember the political and economic background of our immi-grant. The Central European comes from a region where civil and religious wars persisted long after the English system had begun to solidify and crystallize into what we now describe as democracy, representative government, or what you will.

I am not arguing with those wild-eyed enthusiasts who slap the Fascist or Fifth Column label on everything they lack the knowledge to understand, nor do I have the patience to tarry with old-stock Americans who snarl at President Roosevelt because he refuses to execute all liberals as "reds." What the "Bohunk" has to accept is a system of political living evolved from British precedents. Neither he nor the Italian, Russian or German immigrant has anything *politically* to offer. The Irish, with their genius for a certain type of politics, have contributed the Tammany Hall system. Like their Central-European contemporaries, they come from a country torn by strife and retarded by centuries of injustice. Like them, their conception of a community is largely tribal, and the lineal descendant of the tribal Celtic and Balkan chief is the Tammany sachem and the district leader. Most of America's internal political problems today concern the evolution of this antiquated tribalism into a more modern system. I see very little possibility of it happening in our time if the "Bohunks" monopolize the future. I see no chance of America becoming a homogeneous civilization unless Bohunks and other blocs lose their native self-consciousness and cultivate a realistic attitude toward political abstractions. Fish who are aware of water will drown. Human beings who brag about being able to breathe are in danger of suffocation.

Are American-born children uneasy or unhappy because their names are foreign? I wish I could answer that question. What do you mean by "foreign"? It has interested me keenly ever since I came to America. To illustrate, in 1913 I was doing some copy writing in New York for an advertisement. The firm's name was Bamberger. I knew this was a variant of Vambery, a Hungarian name as common as Smith in America. I thought this an interesting point, much as I would if the firm's name had been Burns (Scottish) or Goethe (German). Arminius Vambery was one of my enthusiasms. But those in charge were horrified at the notion of even mentioning the racial or national origin of the firm. "Bohunk, Wop and Yid names are out," was the word given me. I could be as sentimental as I liked over a name like Cholmondely or Hastings or Baltimore, but anything from Central Europe would be better forgotten, old chap.

Now why is this? Why do Americans invariably brag of or mention the most distant Scottish and English relative, while remaining extraordinarily reticent concerning a Slovakian or German grandparent? Why do those with German, Italian, Slavonic or other names anglicize them? And why do people with similar names in England preserve them unaltered from one generation to another? . . . I personally have nothing but contempt for a man who changes his name because he is ashamed of his origin, but I am aware that those who seek to alter awkward cognomens have a case. In the first place many of their names are unpronounceable by us because we are unfamiliar with their languages and alphabets. Czech and Polish names become unmanageable in America and would be changed by custom if not by desire.

Again, we have to face the fact that the traditions of a Central European who has come to America as an immigrant are useless to him here. They do not have to be repugnant to him. They do not have to be dishonorable or uninteresting. As most of such immigrants are of peasant stock, in a country without any such peasant class, all the politico-cultural background of such people has to be left on Ellis Island. An Englishman who has left Magna Carta and the Bill of Rights finds them here. The descendant of the peasants who went through the Thirty Years' War, the Napoleonic Wars and the Balkan Wars, finds liberty of conscience and freedom from tyranny. He finds a tradition and an official acceptance of tolerance. But he didn't bring them with him, and from what we see and know of Europe there is precious little chance that, if America had been settled in the first place from Central Europe, if semi-oriental absolutist institutions had taken root in North America, as in South and Central America, there would not have been any "Land of Opportunity" here. It would have been, much more probably, a hellish and enlarged replica of present-day Europe.

June, 1940   WILLIAM McFEE

FATHER WAS AN ENGLISHMAN

My father was the oldest son of a good family; asthma forced him to leave England in his early twenties. He came to California, bought a ranch, and lived there the rest of his life. He died at the age of sixty-seven, and in all those years he returned to his native land but once, and then only for a short visit.

His wife, my mother, was American, her ancestors dating back to the founding of Jamestown, and including in the line colonial governors, "Mayflowerers," and officers in the Revolutionary Army. All his friends and close associates during those long years were old-stock Americans. He took an active part in the life of the American community where he lived, and was liked and respected by his neighbors. But he never ceased to be as English as the day he left the shores of England!

What was true of him is, I believe, true of most Englishmen in America, despite the fact that the country was founded by men of the Anglo-Saxon strain. The fact that they speak a common language sets them, to outward appearance, less apart from the natives of their adopted country than are the Spanish, or Portuguese, or Italians; many do not carry their loyalty to the same extent as did my father, who refused to "betray" his country by becoming a citizen of the United States, but, naturalized or not, each one, to the day of his death, remains at heart a British subject.

I am reminded of "Uncle Johnnie Price," living many years before my day, who left England in his teens, settled in California, which was then a Spanish province, and became a prosperous *ranchero*. Said one who knew him in his old age, "He was called Don Juan; he married a Spanish wife; he spoke only Spanish; he even *looked* like a Spaniard—but in spite of all this he was as English as John Bull himself."

This attitude, I believe, extends to the second generation. I must become personal, for only so can I illustrate what I mean (but please do not print my name).

I was born in America; I played with American children, went to American schools. The only member of the English family whom I knew personally was my father himself; to counterbalance his influence, I was in close contact with my

American grandparents and aunts and, of course, my mother—all of them proud of a long descent of "pure American" stock. Nevertheless, so strong was the English influence in our home that I was sixteen years old before I realized that I was an American and not an English girl. I was away from home at the time, attending boarding school, and it was a fellow pupil who instructed me in my true nationality, and backed it up with arguments which were irrefutable. I cannot forget the surprise I felt as the truth dawned upon me: not shock or indignation, for I had no objection to being an American, but astonishment. It had never entered my childish head that I was not as British as Victoria herself—an individual, by the way, for whom I felt far more respect than I did for the President of the United States.

Now, here is a curious thing. Since that day, thirty-two years ago, I have accepted my American nationality. I am an American, and a proud one. I am abominably conceited over my long line of American ancestors. When others brag of Mayflower descent I make polite noises, and reflect that *my* forebears antedated the passengers of that historic ship by almost twenty years. I correspond with my English relatives, but think of them as belonging to a race apart. When I recall that I once sang *God Save the Queen* to the tune to which I now sing other words, I laugh and wonder where children get their notions. But—when Edward VIII abdicated and married Wally Simpson; and again, in the dark days before Munich, I realized with a shock which I cannot describe that I am still English. The abdication speech brought lakefuls of tears from sentimental Americans. I shed none; my emotion lay deeper than tears. It was shame—bitter, personal shame—for scandal which had tarnished the luster of the British Crown, shame for a king who had failed *my* people. When the threat of German bombs hovered over England, it was not only the danger to my aunts and cousins which caused me anxious, wakeful nights; concern for them was submerged in overwhelming concern for the danger which threatened *my* country.

Do not misunderstand. *I am American.* I cannot emphasize that too strongly. I do not like English ways. I certainly have no desire to live in England. Should there ever be a war between the two countries, my loyalty would lie wholeheartedly with my mother's, and not my father's people. Be that as it may, explain it as you can, it is a fact that when David of Windsor threw away his Crown; and again, during the Munich nightmare, the years rolled back, and I, a mature American school teacher, became as thoroughly, utterly British, as was the little girl of the nineties who sang *God Save the Queen* to the cattle on a California ranch. . . .
May, 1939

THEY CAME FROM SCOTLAND

Mother McLeod is eighty-six now and slightly deaf, so she does not always hear the questions I put to her; but, upon being urged, she will relate the common little family tales which have to do with the McLeod clan back in Scotland and here in America. She rocks slowly in her rocking chair; then she tells about herself, about her husband, their reasons for coming to the United States, their early life in Kansas, and these other little recollections which I have gathered together.

Mary Whiteford's father was a farmer in Scotland who owned his own farm. When she was a young girl, her mother died, and the family moved to Glasgow, to live with an elder sister. It was there she met John McLeod, who was born in Torans of Campsey, in 1853, the eighth of a family of nine children. His father was a coal miner. The mother died when the boy was two. He had very little formal education and started going to the mines with his father and working regularly while still a mere lad. At sixteen he became what is known in Scotland as a stationary engineer.

Mary and John were married in 1872, when both were nineteen. They lived in Edinburgh, near where he worked. In five years they had four children.

Scotland at that time was flooded with advertisements about the wonderful new coal fields opened in America. Although they were happy, near their friends and relatives, John McLeod decided that America held for him and his family a better chance of advancement and a stronger promise of happiness.

A tall, broad-shouldered, husky coal miner of twenty-eight, John went first to the anthracite fields in Pennsylvania; but, not liking it there, moved on to Kansas. Shortly he forwarded passage money to his family, directing them to Osage City, Kansas.

Mary was a rather shy, tiny person, never weighing more than ninety-five pounds, with soft red-blond hair and brown eyes. She was expecting her fifth child soon. But, anxious to re-unite her family, she took passage at once, despite the protests of friends and relatives who feared for her owing to her pregnancy. It was a stormy trip; for nineteen days they were tossed and rolled about on the Atlantic, and, in the midst of this, far from husband, home, country, friends, her baby was born. Despite all this, her faith and courage did not falter; after landing, she made the long difficult trip to Kansas.

When she and the children arrived in Osage City, a blizzard was raging, snow was deep, and the children did not know their father in his wide Stetson and high boots. He had become quite an American by then; had applied for his citizen papers.

In Scotland they had had comfortable stone houses in which to live; in Kansas at that time there were only cold and drafty wooden miners' shacks. Work was not at all plentiful, and at times they had very little to eat. Now and then Mary was a little afraid, and longed for Scotland.

Surrounding Osage City were large cattle ranches, with waving grass in every direction. On the Dragoon River, near by, were camped a tribe of Indians. The ranchers on their horses, the large herds of cattle, and the Indians in their bright blankets were an odd sight to Mary McLeod. Accustomed to the mountains of Scotland and homes by the sea, the prairies seemed to her to stretch endlessly, and it took untold faith, love and courage to make a happy home. She laughs now about one thing she did in that first year. To each caller she served afternoon tea, as had been her wont in the old country. To the people of the various nationalities comprising the town, this seemed a peculiar courtesy for a coal miner's wife, so she packed it away with other memories, and now gleefully talks of her "tea parties."

John's father, Daniel McLeod, came the following year to make his home with them. Seeing how meager their fare was at times, and feeling that the children should have more, he traded his old-fashioned gold watch chain for a cow. He made his home with them until he died, many years later, at the age of eighty-six.

In their third year in America John and Mary experienced their first great sorrow. Their only daughter, a child of five, became ill and died. . . . They buried her in the small cemetery and resumed their daily life. That same year another baby girl was born to them.

As the children entered school, John McLeod, worn and weary with the long hours in the mine, took time from his few hours of sleep to devour all that was printed in their textbooks. He worked their arithmetic problems and read their histories and geographies, attempting to learn all that was possible about his adopted country.

Four more children were born to them. The older boys began dropping out of school to work in the mines.

Again a feeling of dissatisfaction filled John McLeod. His and his older boys' life was a matter of midnight at noon. They had no real family life. They left the house in the morning when the younger children were still in bed, and often returned evenings when they already had retired. And John McLeod realized that, in a way, they were doing in this country just what he and his ancestors had done in the old country. With all the glorious sunshine, the soft green prairies, the shaded denseness of trees, the small creeks and the two rivers not many miles away, here they were, spending their waking hours lying on their sides, picking away at the never-ending coal vein, working in darkness deep in the earth, lit only by tiny miner's lamps.

So, in 1896, when his youngest child was two, John McLeod made another momentous decision; he left the mines and moved his family to a rented farm. He lived there two years, then went into partnership with another man on a cattle ranch; and now the ex-coal miner and his sons were herding Texas steers on Kansas prairies. Besides these half-wild steers, they kept cows. But learning to milk the cows was one thing that John attempted and failed to do; the hands that had held a pickax for so long just could not seem to get the knack of it. He would not admit defeat, however, but insisted that he was "too busy"; the children could do it. He worked there six years, then bought five hundred acres of his own, having saved enough money to make a substantial down payment.

Now he who had lived most of his days burrowing in the ground spent them in the intense sunshine of a Kansas farm. A man who knew nothing of cattle, horses, hogs or crops made a success of this new venture. And he continued to read and study: history, law, science—anything to satisfy his hunger for knowledge.

One hot summer day, the McLeods received word that some cousins from Scotland were coming to visit them. The men were in the hayfields. Heat or no heat, the women folks were baking cakes, pies, bread, scones, everything good that could be made ready to welcome the relatives they had not seen for so long. It was a proud moment to show these Old World cousins that they had made no mistake in their choice of Kansas; and to people who lived in a country where they had no relatives it was a very happy moment, too, for simply social reasons.

In the haste to finish everything before the arrival of their visitors, one of the daughters picked up the kerosene can intending to hurry the fire. In an instant the can exploded, throwing flaming oil over the girl and about the kitchen. Mother McLeod grabbed for a large quilt and succeeded in beating out the flames from the girl's clothing. The house burned with most of its contents. The girl lay near death for months, but with indomitable Scotch spirit tiny Mother McLeod made her fight back to health. They rebuilt the house and started again, but before they did this they lived in the granary that had been made livable with what they had saved from the fire.

The strength and courage of that little wisp of a woman! I wish I had words to really describe her. . . . Once, while they were still living in town, one of the older boys was playing on the coal cars. When two cars ran together, he was sitting in such a way that the fleshy part of his hip was cut off. The doctor fixed it as best he could and said the boy would never walk straight again. But with infinite patience and faith, Mother McLeod massaged and worked on that leg so that today he stands and walks as straight as any man.

A few years after the fire, her son Robert, who became my husband, fell from the horse he was riding while they were binding wheat and was run over by the binder. His leg was broken and cut almost in shreds. With the help of the doctor and Mother McLeod, who never left his bedside, he recovered without the loss of his leg.

Bearing and raising ten children never overcrowded the McLeods' hearts or home. Two homeless orphans, a boy and a girl, were taken into the family and made part of it. Of the ten children, seven are living; one is a miner, one a baker, another a mechanic, two work in banks; the girls are married.

After the children were grown and scattered, John McLeod was elected probate judge of his county, served two terms, then took up the insurance business, living in Osage City until his death in 1934.

He and Mary made one visit to Scotland, but returned with a deep feeling of thankfulness that their home was in the United States.

These are the physical facts of their lives, but one who has not known them cannot understand the kindliness and understanding of their natures, the little niche that John and Mary McLeod have carved for themselves in the country of their adoption.

July, 1939   Mrs. R. W. McLeod
                                                    Smith Center, Kansas

A HARVARD PROFESSOR LOOKS AT HIS FELLOW GERMAN AMERICANS

I was born in the Middle West near Kansas City, Missouri. My father, who was a clergyman originally trained for the missionary service, came to America in 1851, charged with the task of organizing into congregations the German settlers of various sections of the Middle West. He spent more than fifty years of his life organizing churches in various sections of Wisconsin, Illinois, Kentucky, Kansas and Missouri. As soon as one church was on a sure foundation he moved further into the wilds and began work on another group.

My mother's father, also a clergyman, began his work in Canada in 1856. After coming to the United States he served congregations in Illinois and finally in Baltimore.

So I have through my ancestry come in contact with various German groups in different parts of the country. I was bilingual in my childhood, as German was used entirely in the home, and have never had occasion to discontinue the use of the language for any length of time. My education, however, was in the public schools of Kansas City before I came East to college, and I thus had opportunity to develop a measure of objectivity about the group of which I am a part and its relationship to the rest of the population of the United States. . . .

The reasons for the immigration of Germans to this country have been manifold. Very few came in a spirit of adventure, before the last decades of the nineteenth century at least, although there were some early German colonies at a number of points from Maine to Georgia. The best-known large group were, of course, the Pennsylvania Germans, who were largely political and religious refugees. There was also a considerable immigration in the eighteenth century, likewise partly political, partly religious. Some of the Hessian soldiers imported by the British stayed here. In the nineteenth century the immigration of '48 and the following years brought the largest number of cultured Germans. Of the several hundred German authors, who wrote in this country in German during that period a very considerable proportion belonged to the *Achtundvierziger*. Something like forty or fifty of these German American authors are of sufficient importance to be listed in Wilhelm Kosch's *Literatur-Lexikon*.

After the middle of the nineteenth century the German immigration was largely caused by economic conditions. This was particularly true in the eighties, when the depression following the *Gründerjahre* sent literally millions to North America. After that, until the postwar years, the immigration dwindled to an insignificant number. . . .

The settlers were from so many different regions of Germany and of so many different classes that it is not possible to generalize satisfactorily. But I think we can say that at first the vast majority engaged in farming. This, especially in Pennsylvania and New York, in Wisconsin, Illinois, Minnesota, Iowa, Kansas, Nebraska, and the Dakotas. However, every imaginable trade and profession was represented and with the growth of the cities some centers of the population showed a very large proportion of Germans—Milwaukee, St. Louis, Chicago, Cincinnati, Cleveland, New York, Philadelphia and Baltimore. In these cities they kept up their religious and educational traditions to such an extent that in some of them German was long recognized as a language of instruction along with English. In Cincinnati and Baltimore, and I think also in Milwaukee and St. Louis, there were a certain number of public schools, known as German schools, in which all the instruction was in German, as least as far as the fifth grade. The First World War, of course put an end to this.

The number of German publishing houses, printing newspapers and periodicals as well as books, was at one time very great. I believe that bibliographies of these publications have been collected though not published. As far as Pennsylvania is concerned, the Pennsylvania German Society has a great deal of material, the various scholars scattered throughout the country also have partial or complete bibliographies. The main centers for such publications were New York, Philadelphia, Chicago, Milwaukee, Cincinnati and St. Louis. There was even a *German-American Encyclopedia*, published about the time of the Civil War or shortly after.

In other fields of cultural activity theatrical groups and choral societies were the principal ones. The number of German theaters and stock companies in New York, St. Louis, Milwaukee and Chicago that gave regular performances was at one time very great. These activities also have almost entirely disappeared since 1917.

The church groups are of considerable importance. They represent a number of different denominations, all of which had well-developed headquarters, seminaries, publishing houses and in some instances well-organized school systems.

Numerous towns in the United States were started by the Germans. . . . I should like, however, to mention particularly Middletown, Maryland, built after the manner of a German *Strassendorf*. The houses are substantial two-storey brick structures, the fields extend behind the houses in very long, comparatively narrow strips. The population in Middletown, as nearly as I could make out on a visit some twenty-five years ago, was still made up of the descendants of the original Germans. Other towns near by were settled by Germans. They are Shakers, and the women, when I was there, still wore the characteristic costumes of the Shakers and spoke German.

Through the Middle West, but particularly in Wisconsin, are a large number of German-founded towns and villages. . . . In the neighborhood of Davenport, Iowa, there were so many Germans of Low-German stock that the church services were until about 1914 held in *Plattdeutsch*, and employees in shops in Davenport were required to know that dialect. . . . In Missouri there was a purely German village or town, Hermann. I never saw it, but I understand that it looked exactly like any one of the wine-growing villages along the Rhine: red-tiled roofs, and all the rest of it. . . . In Texas there was and is a very large group of Germans in the neighborhood of Brownsville. This was recently made the subject of a historical novel published in Germany: *Weiter Weg,* by Heinrich Meyer, a German-language author, who is an instructor at Rice Institute in Houston. . . . In Louisiana there was a considerable settlement of German mystics. . . .

These are only a few of the settlements that occur to me. I think one statement would practically apply to all of them: The use of the German language, though it was not entirely discarded, has declined very much since 1914. The war helped, but this was by no means the only reason for the encroachment of English upon German. The automobile, the radio, the moving pictures have all done their part to level these German settlements with their English surroundings. There probably has been a great deal of intermarriage of the children of German immigrants with children of other groups. How this went I had an opportunity to observe in the case of the Middle Western German churches about 1900. The German churches in the cities (Kansas City, Missouri, was my home at that time) had only German church services. The members of the congregation were in very large measure German-born or children of Germans. Now I cannot think of a single instance of Germans in the third generation in this country belonging to a German-speaking church. Within a few years after the turn of the century it became necessary to have English Sunday evening services because the children of the older members knew too little German or wished to go to churches attended by their friends at school. The next step was to introduce English confirmation classes, and then English Sunday school; and before 1920 not a few of these churches had abandoned German entirely, although still belonging to the Deutsch-Evangelische Synode von Nordamerika. Very much the same thing happened with the college conducted by this Synod at Elmhurst, Illinois. That was originally organized on the plan of a German Gymnasium, and when I was a boy all instruction was in German. Now it is just one of many denominational colleges in the Middle West in which not only is the instruction in English, but many of the faculty know no German at all. I think the other German synods, such as the Missouri Lutheran Synod, Iowa Lutheran Synod, and the Synods of Wisconsin and Ohio have gone through a similar development.

On the whole the German immigrants adapted themselves relatively quickly to their Anglo-Saxon surroundings. Except in those regions where the population was solidly German or in cities where there were good German newspapers, societies, churches and theaters, the use of German was ordinarily not kept up in the second generation. Not only that, the immigrants themselves switched to English as soon as they could. The results, needless to say, were sometimes grotesque. Many immigrants had very little formal education, did not speak a good literary German when they came over, associated with Anglo-Americans who spoke bad English, and consequently developed a vernacular which was neither English nor German and in many cases all but illiterate. Kurt Stein in his book *Die schönste Lengevitsch* has adequately portrayed this type. It is therefore not surprising that the children of these immigrants, when they went to school, very soon realized the shortcomings of their parents' speech, attributed it quite incorrectly to their origin and lost as little time as possible in copying in every respect speech, manners and ways of the Anglo-American associates. They did not want to be Germans, but Anglo-Americans. As for the older generation and their reaction under these conditions, some regretted the attitude of the younger generation, but I think on the whole they approved of it. Most of them were definitely glad that they came to America. The answer in every case would be that their economic well-being was definitely improved by the change. There were some, of course, who did not do so well and thought they might have done better in Germany. Some of these went back. There were also some successful ones who returned to Germany after they retired. I know specific instances of this. This latter group included also some who had become naturalized but felt that the persecution during 1916-20 had made it impossible for them to continue here happily. . . .

In my observation the German immigrants mingled more readily and to a much greater extent with other nationals and where it was possible with the old-stock Americans than any other group. They have not entered politics to any very considerable extent and never as a group. I believe that statement will hold in all parts of the country for most periods.

I remember in my youth in the Middle West, nearly forty years ago, all groups who were not Anglo-Saxon in origin were looked upon as curiosities. In the schools the children of such foreign-born parents were often ridiculed and usually kept at arm's length. This was particularly true in Kansas City and the surrounding country where the percentage of foreign-born did not exceed two per cent. The prejudice included the American-born children of immigrants. The immigrants themselves did not take any organized steps as far as I can recall to overcome it. They went their way and if necessary kept to themselves. The children, however, reacted in a very large number of instances by attempting to adapt themselves to their American surroundings and discarding as quickly as possible speech, customs, and manners of their parents. These statements do not apply, I should like to say, to the professional classes.

Do many change their names? Yes. They do not wish to be set apart from the great mass of their fellow citizens. Sometimes, however, a change in name is not made with the purpose of disguise, but merely to make it easier for their fellow citizens to pronounce and remember it. I recall an Austrian German a few years ago whose name was Kotlechner. He was not at all ashamed of his Austrian origin nor desirous of discarding his name, but he dropped the middle syllable and made the name Kotchner, simply to make it more easily pronounceable. The most frequent method of changing the names is by translation. Gutjahr becomes Seasongood or Goodyear. Sometimes there is a mere adaptation to English sounds, as in Willcke to Willkie. In many instances such adaptation and translation leads to absurd results. . . .

On the matter of prejudice, my recollection of the German group in the Middle West is that they scorned the Anglo-American even more than the Anglo-American scorned them. One reason for this feeling of superiority was the broader knowledge of the Germans even when that did not go beyond the natural breadth which would result from knowing two continents, two languages, and two civilizations. But I recall, too, an inclination on the part of the Germans to despise the relative shiftlessness of the Anglo-Americans, for you must not forget that earlier settlers in the Middle West did not necessarily everywhere represent the best elements from the East. The "sturdy pioneer" was not always a choice specimen. He was in many instances a representative of those groups who were not able to make both ends meet in the East and were looking for an easier living not a harder one. To be sure, many of these statements apply to immigrants as well.

The characteristics of the German group as generally recognized are diligence, frugality, loyalty, honesty, orderliness, a law-abiding nature. They are generally musical, normally more artistic than Anglo-Americans whose ancestry goes back to

North English and Scottish immigrants. They are usually religious and, as a rule, unpolitical. As far as my observation goes, these characteristics have persisted more or less in the descendants of the original German immigrants. To be sure we find all imaginable gradations, as one would expect to find in any such large group. I do not think that any of the qualities above enumerated have been destroyed. It is especially curious that the unpolitical nature of the Germans seems to persist even after many generations in this country. If we review in our mind the names of American statesmen and politicians, it is astonishing how few German names we find. Hoover and Willkie are the outstanding exceptions in recent times, and both are unusual or irregular as politicians. On the other hand, a casual survey of any college catalogue or the *Who's Who* will reveal a very large percentage of German names. Once I amused myself by checking the names of the Harvard faculty that were German or whose bearers I knew to have some German blood; the percentage was extremely high.

I think what good qualities were in the German element have acted as a leaven in the past and will do so in the future. But I do not think that the German element as such will ever play a considerable role in the government of the United States.

Politically the German element is pretty well divided among all the parties. In the middle of the nineteenth century there was a decided drift to the Republican party; whether this was because of a sympathy on the part of the Germans with the cause of the North in the Civil War or whether, as I am inclined to believe, it was a more or less accidental association, it is hard to say. Certainly a very large number of the poorly educated immigrant Germans associated the name "Republican" with the idea of a *Republik* and felt that by joining the Republican party they were devoting themselves to the principles for which they had in many instances suffered abroad. . . . But at the present time there are certainly just as many Democratic Germans as Republican. As you know, Wisconsin and other strong municipal centers of German immigration were heavily socialistic about the turn of the century. In the course of the following ten or fifteen years immigrants of the tradesman class continued to be largely socialistic in sentiment. I don't know how many were inclined toward communism. As for those Germans who are not closely associated with any organized German groups, the determination of their political affiliation certainly has nothing whatever to do with their origin. My own sentiments are very strongly anti-New Deal. I am in no sense typical of the German group, but typical, I think, of a profession and a geographical division, by which I do not mean, of course, that New England and Harvard University as a whole are anti-New Deal, but I do mean that in my own particular group here the sentiment seems to be preponderantly against the New Deal.

It has been my observation that many of the New Americans of the German as well as other backgrounds are oppressed by feelings of inferiority in relation to old-stock Americans, to America as a whole, and it is because of these feelings that the New Americans gave up their language and adopted the ways and manners of the old-stock Americans as soon as possible. . . . In a town in New England lives a Greek family. Father and mother both came from the educated class in Greece; he is a professional man. All the children went to college. Unfortunately, the great majority of Greeks in New England come from the laboring and small-shopkeeper class, and the children felt they were looked down upon by their classmates in college. A boy almost developed an abnormality. He kept to himself, associated very little with other students. In spite of the fact that their name was highly respectable and distinguished in Greece, the children, to the great distress of their parents, agreed to give it up for an Anglo-Saxon name. . . . With the anti-Hitler wave rolling over the country, similar cases now are occurring in the German American element.

On the subject of intermarriage, I think the descendants of German immigrants have intermarried with other nationalities to a very great extent, perhaps to a greater extent than other new strains. That, I believe, is more or less natural. The cultural and linguistic difference between a German and an Anglo-American is much less than between the descendants of Mediterranean and Eastern European groups. This is what makes it so difficult to determine the percentage of population represented in the German stock. I think the figures ordinarily given, even by the Census Bureau, are far too low. The Census figures do not go back far enough. I am inclined to believe from my observation that the percentage of the American population that has some German blood is rapidly approaching fifty. It is increasing from year to year because intermarriage is going on steadily. As far as the success of such mixed unions goes, there is only one observation and that has been made before: A German husband and an Irish wife ordinarily get along very badly, especially if she leans toward the Shanty Irish type. The German husband becomes irritated with her slatternly ways. On the other hand, an Irish husband and a German wife get along very well. I have observed cases to support this old contention. Other unions, if they were unsuccessful, were so because of conditions that had nothing or very little to do with origins and backgrounds. The only exception to that is the question of political and national sympathies, which became so acute in 1914. I know of many instances of marriages between a German man and an English or Anglo-American wife that have either gone on the rocks or had a very stormy time because of the divergent sympathies of man and wife.

From about 1925 to early in 1940 these difficulties were not so sharp as during the First World War. Since the invasion of Holland and Belgium, however, there has been a recrudescence of the frictions characteristic of 1916-20. But the situation is by no means identical. The German Americans whose sympathies are with Germany as a nation are hesitating as they never did in the period of the previous war, and they would throw themselves in a body and very vigorously on the side of American defense at the first sign of danger. I am sure the exceptions are negligible.

I am convinced the proportion of pro-Nazi Germans and German Americans in this country is very small. It goes without saying that the *émigrés* are violently opposed to the Nazis, though bitterly unhappy over the prospect of a dismemberment of Germany in case of an Allied victory. German Americans who had no direct knowledge of life under National Socialism have been, I think, more inclined to make excuses and to be optimistic for the future than recent arrivals from Germany. As the Hitler campaign unfolded these have become ever more uneasy. But I am sure that only an extremely small number, certainly not more than five per cent, ever felt enough in sympathy with the Nazi movement to join the Bund. I know that was the case in the Boston area where the old German societies would not even rent their halls to the Bund. I think the Bund membership in Boston never exceeded twenty-five.

The problem of the immediate future will therefore not be that of an ethnic group. German Americans will be just as divided, and just in the same proportion, on matters of foreign and domestic policies as any other group. Those who have had some experience of Germany since 1918 can be trusted to vote more intelligently than most Americans who have not set foot out of the country, since they have learned to recognize the forces hostile to democracy, no matter how successfully they may be disguised. America will be glad of their assistance in adapting our government to the requirements of the era without surrendering all of our privileges.

June, 1940 TAYLOR STARCK
Harvard University

FROM GERMANY *VIA* LONDON

As a youngster, I had the desire to join the young Imperial German Navy, but a kindly fate kept me away from that by an uninterrupted collection of *D*-minuses in mathematics. My good father, realizing my inability to adjust myself to official life, pomp and circumstance (he, himself, was a privy counselor of the government and a reserve officer, as were practically the rest of my family), had the immense fine judgment to send me to England for the purpose of learning the one important language not included in my humanistic training and observe the way of other nations.

My stay in London, in 1890, had a tremendous effect upon me. . . . Up to that time, my reasoning, certainly not induced by my high-minded and decidedly common-sense parent, but through exposure to the *milieu* ran somewhat like this: I have to be thankful to fate that I am a German and not a degenerate Frenchman, shop-keeping English, etc., etc. Secondly, I am to be grateful that among the Germans I am not an uncouth Bavarian, sloppy Suebian, etc., etc., but a Prussian, although not one in the strictest sense, for I came to life in the Saar Valley. Thirdly, it is something to be proud of that among the Prussians I was the son of an Imperial officer and not the hapless offspring of a banker, manufacturer, or shopkeeper. Lastly, it is a happy fact that I am a Protestant and not a (epithets to be applied *ad lib.*) Catholic or Jew.

Being liberally supplied with money which I did not have to earn, I considered London a right pleasant place, asking mostly "How much." Then, suddenly, came the awakening. Here was a wonderful empire. Here was an aristocratic government running the country in a democratic way. And here, on top of all, was a language of unlimited possibilities to set into motion plans of illustrious scope.

From England I turned to America. I had the great advantage of being invited into the family circle of my Uncle Herman, who, in 1850, had departed from the post-revolutionary Germany. There my new outlook was shaped . . . then enhanced by my American father-in-law, Philip Rappaport. . . .

The rest is a simple story. After engaging in journalism and business I became absorbed in the Theodore Roosevelt Conservation cause. Looking backward it seems that my life could not possibly have run any differently nor, to me, more satisfactorily. That includes, in particular, an appreciation of all things that belong to me, notably wife, children and grandchildren. I married when I was twenty-three and she eighteen. We had our three children before I was thirty. In consequence of an affliction engendered in the war I suffered the one hard blow of my life, losing my eldest boy. . . .

During the war in 1917-18 I served as military secretary which, at the time, was the liaison officer between the State of Indiana and the War Department. . . . In 1915 began my life's work, creating state parks, and subsequently I became director of the newly established Department of Conservation. For fourteen years, the happiest of my life, I worked at that task. Today, like an old pensioned fire department horse, I am still at it [as consultant to the National Park Service and a member of its Advisory Board], grateful that the government lets me. I have not gathered any riches that "thieves dig after or the rust eats" nor did I ever care to. No one of the millions who enjoy our state parks or have benefited from better practices in conservation owes me anything, not even thanks. On the contrary, I am in their debt that they have permitted me—a chance immigrant—to do what he wanted to do. Only in these United States could a thing like that have happened.

This, my insistence on the debit balance, is no maudlin sentimentality (generally cashed in on by way of political preferment) nor snooty humility but the honest truth of my feelings, so help me God.

June, 1940.   RICHARD LIEBER,
                                                                        Indianapolis, Indiana

THE *PLATTDEUTSCHE* IMMIGRANTS

My mother's brother, twenty-two years her senior, had left Germany for America in '45 as a young boy in a sailboat which took more than three months to arrive. As he prospered, he would return home every two or three years and tell of the wonders of the United States. Each time he came he took back one of his sisters to keep house for him. But they married so fast in America that he soon had to come back for another one. On these visits to his home place, a farm not far from Bremen, he would bring as gifts machine-made pitchforks by the dozen, factory-made brooms, barrels of white flour, razors and washboards, all of which the people of the community considered wonderful. They caused much talk about the New World beyond the Atlantic.

My father came from a very rich section located a few miles from the Holland border. Being still single when their parents died, he and his brother emigrated to America, about the time of the Civil War. Father came to Missouri, lived with a cousin, and went to school for a few years. When he came of age, receiving his share of his parents' estate, he bought a farm. But fate apparently wanted to make a city man of him. The locusts cleaned him out completely that first year. . . . Working his way East, he reached Pennsylvania and went to work in a mill. But his first week there, he broke several fingers, so he went on to New York, where after a few years he became a contractor-builder. Eventually he met my mother, whom her brother had recently brought over to keep house for him.

We always lived in communities with a large percentage of old-stock Americans. They were very good to us as neighbors and friends. The only thing we envied them were their pretty names. . . . Those who went to boarding school always brought their friends to visit us when they came back to town, and we all felt at home together. Indeed, we were always quite puffed up about our Sunday suppers. Everybody wanted to come to them. Abundance and generosity were always the chief aspects of our family table.

One of the things that impressed me greatly as a child was that our neighbors, most of whom were better situated economically than we, seemed to live so meagerly. In our pantries and cellar we had barrels of apples, potatoes, sugar, flour, and wine. Any youngster coming to call for us on the way to school could help himself to anything he saw on the table or on the shelves. There was always a bowl of cookies, and if the child hesitated, my mother said to him, "Take a handful; put some in your pocket." This never happened when we called for the neighbors' kids. Their parents bought things by the pound and by the dozen. If they had unexpected guests, it was our family that always supplied them with linens and bedding, eggs, or potatoes, or even meats. I recall my uncle describing a neighborhood going to seed by saying, "The sort of people who buy five cents' worth of potatoes are moving in."

My people were Low-Germans, and practically all Low-Germans are Lutherans. Like the Dutch, their religion is a sort of moral training. They are not fanatics. As children we went to an Episcopal Sunday school. We were taken out because the teacher told of fire and brimstone. My father could not understand anyone in his right mind telling children of such a terrifying hell.

All Low-German immigrants I have ever known were naturalized citizens. They all seemed to feel that America was a dream come true. How it started I don't know, but there was an unwritten law among them that a man had to have his own business. So they became grocers, butchers, confectioners; some started restaurants and saloons (before the Irish politicians forced them out), and others had milk routes. Many became wholesalers in the various lines. None had engaged in such businesses in the old country. As a youngster I heard my father and uncle say that only a lazy, unambitious fellow ever became a fireman or a policeman; it was unmanly to get one of these "sure thing" jobs, and even today a Dutch or Low-German name is rarely found in the list of either group.

All the early immigrants I knew could read and write. For their times they were quite well educated. They compared favorably with the majority of the American-born here at the period. On the whole, they did not live in colonies; their businesses made it necessary for them to spread out, but they had sectional or group benevolent and cultural societies, many of which are still going strong.

The Low-Germans whom I know feel that Hitler isn't any better than Bismarck, and the latter wasn't popular with them. Of course those who came to the United States during the last twenty years feel differently. To be frank, they are as unlike the old-timers as possible. Their whole idea of living seems to be colored by their experiences in Germany during the deflation era. Thrift is unknown to them and the stalwart old-timers view them as people from a world they never knew.

The second generation of the Low-German immigrants also falls short of the old-timers' standards. The thrift and foresight of their parents gave the youngsters a feeling of security, so they didn't bother to take full advantage of their opportunities. Many went to college; the majority, however, were satisfied to take a job after elementary or high school, figuring the old folks had money enough so they themselves didn't have to make a fortune. However, with the exception of a few who became church sextons and the like because of limited intelligence or some physical handicap, I don't know any who ever became laborers or performed menial tasks. Those who were not professionals became bank clerks, accountants, salesmen, or real-estate operators. The second generation did not stick to the stores in which their fathers prospered. Some Anglicized their names. Some became too "Americanized" the wrong way, in that they brag about the size of America, rather than feel and speak of what this country stands for—democracy, liberty, and progress toward general welfare. Some of these don't care what happens to the next fellow, not realizing that in such an attitude lies a great danger to the United States. But in this they are no worse than, it seems to me, all too many younger people of older American strains. . . .

The Low-German immigrants have definite ideas about material values. They can't understand people buying cars and not owning their houses and probably other property besides. I do know that nearly every family I was acquainted with was putting something aside for a little place in the country where they would go to when they were older. I also seem to remember that it was taken for granted among my father's friends that they should retire when they got to be fifty. The idea was "Give the young people a chance."

The old-timers believe in taking care of the unfortunate and disabled among them. It is accepted as a phase of life that there always are persons for whom things go wrong, in spite of the fact that they are thrifty, have lived right, and worked hard. In Brooklyn, New York, the *Plattdeutsches Volkesfest* worked for a Home for the Aged, of which I have heard all my life, and they now have large grounds near Garden City. The various German American benevolent groups hold their picnics there, and the old folks still are the life of these festivities.

I like to watch them, and the play of expression across their strong bony faces. Weak and trembly with old age, they still stand up as characters, as individuals. I am proud of them.

Take my father. He is very old now. He speaks fluent and expressive English with a strong Low-German accent, but often—especially of late—he breaks into his old-country dialect. Mentally and emotionally he is nearly all here, an American, but part of him harks back to Germany; not to the Third Reich, but the country he knew. He refers to "that fellow," meaning Hitler, unfavorably. . . . Occasionally I watch his face as we sit at the dinner table or in the parlor. Something is written in

those deep lines America ought to read and understand: a rough poem about the glory of this country.
February, 1940

GRANDFATHER WAS A LOMBARD REBEL

My grandfather, Domenico Altrocchi, came to America a little over a century ago, in 1835, as a political exile. He was from Lodi, near Milan. As a Lombard and a rebel, he could not countenance Austrian tyranny over Lombardy, and had to escape in order not to be imprisoned or possibly shot without trial, which was then the Austrian method.

He was a musician, a pupil of the famous Donizetti. He established an excellent school of music in New York City, in competition with more than a thousand music teachers (even at that time). He married a young pupil of his, Pauline Hemenway, a resident of New York, of straight New England stock going back to about 1635. In fact one of her ancestresses was Mary Dunster, sister or cousin, I am not sure which, of Henry Dunster, first President of Harvard College.

Their youngest child and second son became my father; he was born in New York City. He married Pauline Zamvòs, partly Greek and partly German. My parents were living in Florence, Italy, when I was born in 1882; they at once registered me in Washington as an American citizen. I am, therefore, American-born, although not born in America.

We lived in Italy during the first eighteen years of my life, as members of the American colony in Florence, and with home traditions and customs partly American and partly Italian. I had, as far back as I can remember, the dream of coming to the United States; I always considered myself an American. When I finally came, in 1900, and especially when I visited several relatives in New England, I had the immediate sensation of being completely at home.

Like most people in this country, and elsewhere, I can count many different so-called strains of blood in my ancestry, fractions of English, Greek, French and German, besides Italian and New England. Although I may sometimes detect a conflict of tendencies within my own personality, and while I have an intimate understanding, through experience and literature, of Italian temperament and points of view, I feel a preponderant kinship with Anglo-Saxon concepts and ways of life. When in Italy, I feel as if I were a foreign cousin of Italians; in America I am always at home.

Concerning allegiance, I have an altogether too idealistic point of view. My conviction is that American citizenship should never be acquired for financial, utilitarian, convenient reasons, no matter how expedient; only real loyalty should govern free choice of citizenship—an unpractical point of view, to be sure. Of course *I* never had to make the choice, for, I repeat, I never was or felt anything but American. But my idea applies to the millions of Americanized immigrants, many of whom, consciously or unconsciously are sitting perpetually on the fence. They love the relief of living in a free land and the possibility offered of exploiting it in order to better their conditions and rise in the social scale; they have a grateful affection for the country of refuge and rescue and a great admiration for it, but mingled with a constant nostalgia for the old country which, in retrospect, looks far more desirable than it was when they eagerly abandoned it for something better. Such people are ever pumping up an *Italia bella* complex and, in times of crisis, might swing back to their first love. Of course sentimental associations can hardly be eliminated; it is difficult to differentiate them from allegiance, which is also to a great extent a matter of sentiment and tradition; this problem, however, concerns only the immigrant generation, not—generally, at least—its children if born or raised under our American standards.

This question of split loyalty is important enough, especially in this period of the *Blitzkrieg* and the Fifth Column. Obvious though the following facts are, they must be repeated. A clear distinction should be made between the cultural values of the old country, which values are, to be sure, the direct results of the developments and accomplishments of those people through the centuries, and any country's temporary government. It would be just as irrational to hate Goethe and Beethoven because we hate Hitler as it would be to despise Dante and Michelangelo because we despise Mussolini. Unfortunately this distinction is often canceled by war passions. A broadly cultured spirit believes that the arts and sciences transcend limitations of nationality. A real American, who feels, thinks and speaks American, simply cannot approve of nazism or fascism, which are antipodal to all his ideas and must, therefore, be repugnant to him. But here too arguments may be set up. Some men will say: Of course I would not approve of fascism for this country, but in Italy it seems to work; it may be the best form of government for Italians. After all, their government is none of my business; I love Italy and cheer whatever form of government it may choose to have.

Such an argument overlooks a very important fact and is an unintentional insult to Italians. It is equivalent to saying that they are not sufficiently evolved, politically, on account of their short experience (only about fifty years) in free government, to use liberty. Similarly the Germans and Russians seem unable to use it. But, to put the matter personally, my liberal grandfather, his close friend in New York, Garibaldi, Italy's "Great Liberator," and countless other heroes of the Italian *Risorgimento* who strove and fought for the freedom of Italy in the nineteenth century would writhe in their graves if they knew that modern Italians are not only considered unfit by Italian Americans for freedom and self-government, but quite capable of submitting abjectly for seventeen years to one of the worst forms of tyrannical, unscrupulous dictatorship the world has ever seen.

From this point of view, Americans who are proud of their Italian ancestry must, at the same time, be unproud, indeed ashamed of the Mussolini phenomenon. Nor can the Italians themselves avoid blame, for they should not have tolerated the imposition of dictatorship. The Italian King, their symbol, betrayed the constitution which he had sworn to uphold; Italians permitted a one-man tyranny which must be intolerable to any freedom-loving people. And if some of them tolerated it in silence and inaction (perhaps a majority did) while hating it in secret, then too they should be ashamed of having been turned by the arrogance of a cheap boss into a herd of inarticulate, spineless sheep.

There is here an incongruous, and therefore funny, though grim, aspect of the situation. Mussolini constantly bellows his heroic bombast about "living dangerously," saying that "it is better to live one day as a lion than a hundred years as a sheep." The latter epigram is not at all his invention; it is purported to have been scratched on the side of a barn on the 1918 Italian front by a captain; it was probably old stuff then. But the joke, and a tragical joke, is that what Mussolini has actually done is to give the lie to that heroic phrase: he has forced forty-five millions of Italians to act quite *un*dangerously, like sheep, blindly, mindlessly following a self-imposed shepherd who, judging from the unanimity of American verdict, has nothing in common with the fabular lion. The fact that hero Mussolini waited until France was prostrated before he made his assault brands it as wanton and him more like a buzzard than a lion.

One pernicious influence on Americans of Italian descent in this country, as Westbrook Pegler pointed out, is in the Italian-language newspapers, many of them blatantly pro-fascist, largely because bought and paid for by Italian government propaganda. Another is the subtle work of at least some of the Italian consuls. Inconspicuously but with steadfast hammering they have worked on ignorant immigrants, taking advantage of old patriotism and latent nostalgia, ever exalting fascism, even forming black-shirted units, training them to wear Fascist badges, to use the Fascist salute and to sing the Fascist hymn. Both of these influences, working directly against the normal and desirable process of Americanization, should be promptly attacked by our all too lenient government, and stopped.

In spite of these negative facts, however, Americans must be cautious and not brand as a hyphenated citizen any man who does not happen to have an Anglo-Saxon name. Such branding would be manifestly unfair. Let us remember this: a surname now means but little. Because our country was first settled by Englishmen, some people take it for granted that anybody with an Anglo-Saxon name is *ipso facto* a good American and vice versa. And since some of our earlier waves of immigration were from Ireland, Holland, old Germany, France, Scandinavia, we are apt to consider names from those lands as indigenous, while names from lands most of whose people emigrated later, such as Italian names, are *ipso facto* considered foreign. All this is natural, but is becoming more and more incorrect every year. Why assume that Carnegie, Ford, Lindbergh, Morgenthau, Du Pont, Vandenberg, Stettinius, Pershing, Knudsen, Lippmann, Willkie, Kaltenborn, etcetera, are thoroughly American names and call La Guardia an Italian, who is as true an American as any of them?

It is a direct and beneficent result of our new immigration and our democracy that many of our most loyal and distinguished fellow citizens have un-Anglo-Saxon names. It is conversely true that many with Anglo-Saxon names are opposed to our democracy, e.g. Browder, Bridges, etcetera. "What's in a name?" said prophetic Shakespeare. And let us not even for a moment or even by inference appear to subscribe to that most absurd of notions: The "pure race," the "Nordic superiority" and similar nonsense. There is no such thing as a "pure" race; "races" have been mingling from times prehistorical; the only difference is that in America in the last century the process has been much more rapid and on a larger scale. I have been told that when it comes to counting blood corpuscles, there probably is not an Englishman living who has not French, Germanic or Latin blood in his entirely British arteries. Thus with all "races."

Notions die hard and snap judgments are unavoidable. If I may become personal again, since I can say that my Italian-surnamed family has been American for three generations, that is for more than a century, does not that fact outbalance the "foreignness" of that surname? And since I am waxing autobiographical, let me add more Americana. As early as 1902 I was an American soldier as a member of the National Guard of Missouri (Third Regiment, Company D, Kanas City). I attended the oldest of American colleges, Harvard (Class of 1908). During the First World War I was a lieutenant in the A.E.F., assigned to liaison service in France. Before I enlisted, I was sent to Italy as an agent of President Wilson's administration, with a diplomatic passport, to direct all oral propaganda from the Roman office of the American Bureau of Information (La Guardia, by the way, was my very best speaker). I was given such assignments because of my professional command of the French and Italian languages.

I shall end this statement by mentioning one of my experiences as American propagandist in Italy at the time when her morale was at its lowest, just after the defeat at Caporetto. This little episode has a bearing on my Americanism.

I made many speeches in theaters, squares, open fields, academic halls, to laborers, professors, assorted throngs. My data were furnished by Washington; the oratorical form, calculated to impress and to stimulate final resistance against the Germans, was left to me. I vividly remember rehearsing, in my hotel room in Rome, my speech. Conscious that I was not gesticulating as Italians might expect, I stood before a mirror to see if I could add to my verbal appeals appropriate hand waving. Alas, how awkward, how ridiculously unspontaneous my gestures were! I decided to omit them altogether; I must be myself, ungesticulatory. And thus, as one of my local managers told me, although, judging from my Tuscan accent, my audiences might well have taken me for an Italian, the structure and the delivery of my talks were quite foreign to Italians, that is, they were American. And one of the reasons why, in all modesty, I "got away" with that job, which was antipodal to my scholarly training, was that my performance appeared to Italians as exotic, so different from the windmill vociferations with which they had been deluged.

And they still are being deluged. Although in matters of political oratory we Americans are hardly in a position to throw stones, least of all at a time of Presidential conventions and elections, we may well say that we have never been so destructively, indeed criminally misled by words as the Italians of Fascist Italy. By autocracy and venomous propaganda Mussolini forced his people to join forces with their traditional enemies the Germans, whom they have hated and fought for more than a thousand years, and basely to betray their sister nation, France, and their old friend, England. To me the infamous axis is anathema. As a hundred per cent American of mixed Italian and New England descent, though ever loving the beauty of Italy, its extraordinary contributions to civilization, and the many fine characteristics of its people, I am unequivocally opposed to fascism and wholeheartedly for the Allies.

RUDOLPH ALTROCCHI
Professor of Italian Literature
University of California, Berkeley

June, 1940

LITTLE ITALY, NEW YORK, ON JUNE 10, 1940

Outdoors in our block the reaction to the news, yesterday, of Mussolini's declaration of war on England and France was a curious, but only seeming, calm, as I [American-born son of Italian immigrant parents, a graduate of Columbia University] returned home from work early in the evening. Everybody was unusually quiet. I missed the shouting and laughter of children on the sidewalks, the cries of boys playing stick ball in the street. The neighborhood iceman sat on the shoe repairer's doorstep, but they were not arguing as is their custom. Men and women in front of stores and tenements looked about almost furtively, as though they were suddenly being watched. Down the street a group of men stood in front of the grocer's. Their discussion was subdued. Their gesticulations were slow, devoid of the usual drama and animation. Some of them looked far off. They tried not to think and talk, or could not. I know most of them; nearly all are immigrants who came over shortly before or after the First World War. A small proportion of them are pro-Fascist, but they really express themselves only in the privacy of their homes. . . .

After supper I dropped in on the people next door, a family of three: a man, his wife, and her niece. Forty-six years old, he holds a city civil service job. His wife is the same age. They have been in America since 1920. Her niece is twenty-five, here only six years. The women listen to Italian radio programs all day, read *Il Progresso*, and swallow propaganda hook, line and sinker. The man has two brothers in Paris, both on the dole there. A brother of the wife, father of the girl, was killed in the war in 1918. One of the girl's brothers now is a soldier in Libya. The man is completely dominated by his wife, who makes him support her niece when she is not working.

I said, "What was the idea of Italy going to war?"

The man answered, "She gave France and England an ultimatum: turn over to us Corsica and Malta, let us use Suez, get off Gibraltar—or else! They refused; Italy went to war."

I said, "But did you hear what Roosevelt said on the radio—that Mussolini stabbed France in the back?"

"It isn't true!" the three of them cried in unison.

The girl went on: "Why do we Italians have to emigrate and go begging to other countries? Why does Italy have to pay at Suez? . . . Sanctions! So they wanted forty-five millions of us to starve! They want to keep us bottled up in the Mediterranean, between Suez and Gibraltar, and even there we can't do what we want. England and France have everything. They took everything before we awoke. Now we are awake, and we want——"

Her aunt interrupted her, "Who gives England the right to stop our ships at Gibraltar? Gibraltar belongs to Spain; England stole it from Spain."

"But," I said, "this is not a war merely to get this or that. It's a war for world domination. It's a revolution. . . . If Hitler is not stopped, the whole world may be enslaved."

The man: "What are you talking about!"

His wife: "Hitler is ruled by Mussolini; I heard it on the radio yesterday."

Her niece: "Italy has been the underdog long enough. Now it's our turn."

"If Germany wins," I said, "Hitler will dominate Italy. He does already."

"So we'll be Germans!" laughed the man, feeling stupid. "So what!"

"But Italians will be slaves," I said.

"Oh, you're crazy!"

The women sat tense, tight-lipped. Behind their tenseness, behind all their words, was really only confusion. . . .

The background of these three people is significant. Ever since they have been in America they have had no contact with the country; not really. Work and home, work and home. The women work in a dress factory a few weeks every three or four months. They are not even in contact with the community of "Little Italy" or of our block or immediate neighborhood. They consider themselves a little better than the general run of Italians and Italian Americans. Isolation. The girl especially has been isolated. When she arrived in the United States at nineteen, she started going to night school, but the instructor antagonized her. She developed the notion he did not like Italians and foreigners generally. She quit. Result: isolation, loneliness. She is not particularly good-looking; who cares about her, or what she thinks? People in the factory, which is Jewish-owned, with Jewish bosses, are pretty much like herself; but, to keep up her ego, she holds herself superior to them. She is very aloof. Underneath, of course, she is insecure, scared. . . .

By a slightly different route her aunt has reached the same mental condition. She doesn't want to associate with the general run of people. She and the girl have locked their senses and minds against all impressions except that of the radio and their favorite newspaper, the exciting Fascist propaganda. When they are at home, the dial of their radio is constantly set on the Italian stations. They get broadcasts from Rome. They seldom go out. I think life in the streets scares them. They are a glaring example of the failure of "Americanization."

The man spent some years in Paris. He has read a few books. He now has a semiclerical job which brings him only superficially in touch with other people. He considers himself an intellectual, also superior to the people of the neighborhood.

I asked him, "Would you shoot a Frenchman?"

"No," he replied without hesitancy.

These seeming pro-Fascists do not know the deeper, hidden meaning of fascism. Once they understand it, they will want to fight it.

This is an extreme case; with variations in form and degree, it represents, on a guess, less than ten per cent of the immigrants in our "Little Italy." But even here there is the contradiction: he would not shoot a Frenchman. When he said, "So we'll be Germans! So What!" he meant he might be a German politically. Beyond that his mind was just confusion.

I spoke to other people last night. They all know me, and were frank. Most of them expressed shame and apprehension. Roosevelt was right; "only maybe he should not have said it for our sake. We all voted for him in '32 and '36. But what can we do?" Their mood affected the children; it changed, at least momentarily, the entire texture of the atmosphere of the neighborhood.

I met an ardent Fascist of a few weeks ago. Now he is outraged by the fury and horror of the Germans' total war.

In some of the families the difficulties between the immigrant parents and their American-born children are considerable. There are arguments, fights. Most of the youngsters don't give a hang about Italy. They play ball in the park, dance the woogi-woogi, shoot dice in the doorways, and—a few—drive around in cheap cars. They appear not to know what is going on in the world. Now and then, however, at the supper table, they suddenly say something about "Musso" and the old man flares up, although, if you examine him, he really hasn't much use for Mussolini. It is just that in recent years "Mussolini" and "Italy" have become synonymous among people incapable of careful thought.

The young Italian Americans, as a rule, are nowhere culturally. Nice kids, some of them; but, really, neither Italians nor Americans. They have little notion of democracy. Many are without jobs, without any perceptible future. They are "wops" and "dagoes" when they get outside the neighborhood. They are up against a vague difficulty in relation to America. Are they part of the country or aren't they? . . . "What the hell! So what!" . . . They try not to think about such things. They succeed in this easily. They follow all available excitements. They do not understand Hitlerism and Mussolini's fascism. They don't give a damn, or so they say if you ask them. But they are carried forward in the grip of something in the air. A force. Something is happening in this world. It is affecting America. Them. Us. In case of a real crisis in this country, I think, the young Italian Americans will respond if the government and the leaders will know how to appeal to them. The crux of the problem is not that they are "Italians," for they are not, but that they are, as I say, nowhere, in a cultural no man's land.

I spent an hour last night in the corner candy store where a bunch of young fellows hang out. I caught phrases: "Ford says he can make a thousand planes a day. . . . La Guardia is a wop, too, ain't he? . . . Did you hear what Roosevelt said about Musso? The sonoffa—" meaning the latter.

There is a boy in our block who spends a lot of his free time in the branch library. He has read up on Italy. A year ago he dreamed of going over some day for a visit. He wanted to see Florence. Now that's out. Last night I met him in front of the library as it closed at ten. I asked him, "How do you feel about all this?"

He said, "Mussolini's action puts me in position where I am obliged to fight my own mother."

A CATHOLIC

Father Coughlin? . . . The Catholic group as a rule does not hold with him. While we respect his calling, we feel that a theological training does not qualify a man to speak on economics. If we were critical of Rev. James Cannon, Bishop of the Methodist Church South, in the Hoover-Smith campaign, we are equally critical of our "radio priest," for the same reasons. We know that the priest speaks with authority in the matter of faith and morals, but we aren't willing to follow him when he talks on political questions.

We don't hold at all with the thought as expressed by our Jewish friends that he is anti-Semitic. Although there is evidence to the contrary, we don't think he is really; at least not primarily. His chosen function as a radio voice and "leader" depends on publicity, on sensational statements, on ready public response; and he knows, as we all know that it is popular at this moment to criticize the Jews. He did publish those foolish "Protocols"; that was unpardonable. He claims to speak against communism, and therefore feels justified in his mind as to his program. He has interpreted liberty as meaning license, as far as his own work goes. He is definitely wrong there. From the attitude of those to whom I [a third-generation American living in St. Paul] have talked regarding him, I don't believe he has the support of the Catholic group. I see boys in front of my church every Sunday selling his paper, *Social Justice;* the sales are very few. I had no idea this paper was so important until I was in New York last summer and observed men and women selling it on many corners. I have never heard the paper or Father Coughlin mentioned by the clergy from the pulpit. . . .

One of the things we thought would happen as a result of Cardinal Pacelli's (the present Pope's) visit to America a few years ago would be the silencing of Father Coughlin. There was a definite statement to this effect in the *Osservatoro Romano,* the Vatican newspaper. The grapevine had it that Cardinal Pacelli was minded to stop him, but it seems that so long as Coughlin had the endorsement of his own bishop there wasn't anything that could be done about it. It was thought that when his former bishop passed on the new bishop wouldn't stand for him; however, along comes the new bishop, and while Coughlin isn't nearly so wild now, and for a few Sundays was off the radio completely, with no explanation for the silence, still he goes on. It must be remembered that the Church is somewhat sensitive to the financial side of the business, and Coughlin is definitely a financial success.

The Catholic group, although large, are a minority in American life, and it is only a short while since there was active opposition to it by the Ku Klux Klan and other organizations like it. The Al Smith affair is recent; just lately Jim Farley has been up for discussion. The Catholic feels that he should make himself as inconspicuous as he is able to, particularly in a political sense. The Gallup straw vote shows the Catholics are not anxious at all to see Jim Farley run for President this fall. They probably would support him all right if he should run, but they would much rather not see him be nominated. It would, in the mind of most of us, bring forth the old hatreds and fights, and that is certainly undesirable.

For this reason, the average Catholic doesn't like Father Coughlin. There are enough things to explain without having to apologize for him. His talks are unquestionably inflammatory; but what has he accomplished? His support of Lemke achieved nothing. The Catholic well knows that no conversions will result from such talks, and that it is putting the priest and the lay Catholic "on the spot" to explain such things. These ideas put forth here, I believe, are pretty generally held by the Catholic group. As we see it, most of the support that he has comes from non-Catholic sources.

The Catholic is proud of his place in American life, and he has arrived there, not by virtue of this sort of thing, but in spite of it. The Catholic is proud of the 182 schools and colleges giving out B.A. or B.S. degrees that are maintained under Catholic management. There are sixty thousand students in these colleges, over three hundred thousand students in Catholic high schools and academies, and probably well over a million in the parochial schools. The Catholic has done this because he believes that religious education must go along with other types of education. He has paid his taxes to support the State, county, and city schools and then pays again to support his own schools; the average cost of education in the grades runs about sixty-eight dollars a year per pupil.

The one thing that those opposed to the Church would like to see come about is the elimination of this educational program. But notice that the first thing a dictator does when he comes into power is to scrap the Catholic schools. This happened in Russia, in Italy, in Germany, and in those nations just taken over by Germany. While the Church itself is somewhat tolerated in those countries, with the exception of Russia, the religious orders and the schools are not. The only real opposition to the totalitarian concept is our Holy Mother, the Church, not with guns and ammunition, but with ideas and ideals. The Church stands for three things: the supremacy of the home, the permanency of the marriage bonds (which is but a corollary of the first), and the right to hold private property. Match these three things against the totalitarian concepts! They are a pretty fair bill of rights; lacking any one of them, there is no liberty of any sort. To keep these three ideas before the people, there must be some sort of an educational program; that is the reason for the Catholic schools.

This present war may wreck civilization in Europe. We hope and pray that we in America will be spared. If the totalitarians win, the Church in Europe certainly won't be spared; it is on the firing line right now. It will be up to the American Catholic to carry the burden, for the benefit of humanity at large and for America as a nation. It will be ideas and education amongst which there will be need of a religious concept, that will rehabilitate civilization. What religion, at the moment, knows where it stands, except the Catholic? Where is there a firm, organized religious program, outside of the Catholic Church? . . .

April, 1940

AN EDUCATOR CONSIDERS THE NEGRO

The Negro is one of the oldest stocks in this land. He has cleared forests, dug mines, tilled the soil, and has always been a vital part of the upbuilding of the country. Today there are twelve million of these people.

They have served in every war; in fact, one of the first men to lose his life in the military service of our country was Cristus Attucks. He gave his life in the opening skirmish of the American Revolution.

Today there are an increasing number of Negroes contributing in the fields of education, art, literature and religion. The record these people have made in our country is one of the most remarkable in the history of any race. I have often said that they have accomplished more in a shorter period of time against greater obstacles than has any other people ever.

ARTHUR HOWE,
President, Hampton Institute in Virginia

May, 1939

A NEGRO TEACHER

I am a Negro teacher in North Carolina.

American democracy is only enjoyed by certain groups. The Negro teacher is expected to teach American democracy just as the white teacher does. But this idealism does not exist. The student soon discovers the fallacy of this lesson. Doors of opportunity are closed in his face. He is crushed in more ways than one. He cannot even join the Army or the Navy and get ready to be able to die for his country.

In a number of places in the South when a Negro is frank enough to speak out he is styled as a radical. There are any number of problems that I would like to relate but for fear this will be published I will refrain from it now.

One question haunts my mind: Can the people of the United States afford to criticize Germany for crushing the Jews when people in America will hang Negroes up trees and cut off parts of their bodies for souvenirs? . . .

The Almighty God is not pleased. I pray that He will open the hearts of Americans so that the Negro will have the opportunity to stand in any hall in this country and sing his heart out to the full capacity of his talent—that he will be given the chance to stand up and be a man and express to the world the God-given instincts and genius that are within him.

April, 1940

FROM LITHUANIA AND POLAND

My father was born in what is now Lithuania; then it was in Russia. The men in the family had been tinsmiths for generations. There was little opportunity for advancement in the old country: they were Jews.

Stories about the wonders of America reached the little village in Lithuania. In 1888 my grandfather set out to verify them. He went to work as a tinsmith in New York. He was employed on one of the earlier skyscrapers. In two years he returned to Lithuania to get his family. My father was then a young man of nineteen, an apprentice in the family trade.

My paternal grandparents are now dead, and the family is four families, living in Brooklyn and the Bronx. My mother is American-born. Her mother came from Poland in the 1870's. When my father met my mother, she was working in a garment factory. He was a tinsmith all his life here. He died two years ago.

Of the four families, only one is what might be called well-to-do. They made some money in real estate. But all four, at one time or another, underwent long spells of poverty. Occasionally, although not within my memory, some of us were close to having nothing to eat. Depressions, Unemployment. This last Depression hit all of us terribly, including the comparatively well-to-do family. But nobody has yet uttered one word of regret for coming to or being born in the United States. All the foreign-born ones are naturalized. We are Americans: and how!

We younger people in these four families find ourselves in all sorts of situations. A few of us are unemployed or work only part-time. About a dozen of us went to college, Hunter and Columbia, Brooklyn College and New York University. I am a substitute teacher in the New York school system. Several of my cousins are lawyers, dentists, office workers. One is an actor, or trying to be. One writes; has published a short story in *Story*. Four of us are teachers. A half-dozen or so are still going to school.

All my friends are of similar origins. All Jews. Sometimes this worries me a little. Why can't we get together with Gentile Americans? Of course I know the superficial answer, but——

We are all Americans, as I say, and we love America. I love my native New York: the place has so much to offer, especially in music and lectures, which I attend once or twice a week at the New School for Social Research and elsewhere, when some worth-while person talks. But we are certainly made conscious of our immigrant beginnings and the fact that we are Jews when we look for work. We are not ashamed of our backgrounds, but now and then in applying for jobs we—those of us who do not "look Jewish"—give different names and religions without compunctions as the only means to a desired end. This phase of American life I regret very much. It has a hidden, undesirable effect on us; we sort of "sneak" through life. Perhaps it will not always be so.

September, 1939

AN INTELLECTUAL FROM RUSSIA

I am of the group of old Russian intellectuals whose number probably does not exceed three hundred in this country—the product of the latter part of the nineteenth century in Czarist Russia.

Born of Jewish parents in the middle seventies, in a provincial city of forty thousand, on the middle course of the River Volga, I grew up in an entirely Russian atmosphere and on terms of social equality with the rest of the Russian population. There were hardly half a dozen Jewish families in the city. There was no ghetto, and while we were acutely aware that there was political anti-Semitism (limitations on the number of Jewish boys that could enter gymnasiums and universities, and other restrictions) there was no actual anti-Semitism. The town is Simbirsk, now renamed Ulianovsk because it happens to be the city in which Ulianov, or Lenin, was born. Lenin, whose family we knew well, was about three years ahead of me in the high school (classical gymnasium). Curiously enough, Kerensky was also born in the same city, and Kerensky's father was the director of our school.

My father was an artisan—piano tuner, repairer of all kinds of instruments, with a flair toward inventions—and impractical. The family environment was nonreligious and liberal. Thus it was almost predestined that I should belong to some of the liberal circles while at high school and later in the University, with the same consequences—arrest for political activities, expulsion from the University, and migration first to Belgium, then England and later to the United States (in 1897).

This is a typical history of a Russian liberal of the latter part of the last century. Some of the Russian intellectuals returned to Russia under assumed names and continued work there. Others remained and entered into the life of the country of their adoption. I stayed on and was one of the first class of four who graduated as forest engineers from Cornell in 1901. Upon graduation I became a member of the United States Forest Service, and for the last thirty-eight years was and still am a Federal "bureaucrat."

I believe the influence in America of this small group of Russian intellectuals, just as the German immigration of '48, was out of proportion to their number. Their broad cultural education, their knowledge of many languages and, therefore, access to the literature of the world, and understanding of world affairs, helped to broaden American scientific and cultural horizons.

As to my own contribution, if it should interest you, I must refer you to several overgenerous papers by some of my colleagues in *The Journal of Forestry*. As an instance of such influence is the recent project of shelterbelt planting in the prairie-plains region, the idea of which was born on the steppes of Russia.

Ideologically, I cannot identify myself with any group, though, by the strange workings of our "Melting Pot," all of us are forced, whether we want it or not, in our own self-defense, to seek identification with some group. "They" won't let you be just plain Americans.

Of course I am a New Dealer—not on account of specific measures advocated by the New Deal, but because of the spirit back of them. In other words, I belong to that amorphous group known as the American liberal, more or less of the *New Republic* and the *Nation* stripe.

It is for the first time that I am giving out such personal information, and I hope you will use it, if you do, with some disguise, certainly omitting my name, perhaps merely as a typical story of my kind of immigrant. I do not desire publicity.

May, 1939

AN ATYPICAL JEWESS

Though a Jew by birth, on both sides, I have been educated since my earliest childhood in complete oblivion of the fact (which I greatly regret). I have never had any contact with the Jewish community of the cities where I lived, I have been educated in schools that are ordinarily closed to Jews. I have participated in social existence in a manner and degree apparently unknown to most Jews, and since habit and propinquity are what decide one's fate, I have been married to two Christians, both of old-stock American lineage, and my first marriage ended for no reasons even remotely associated with race, religion, or color!

So I [a well-known novelist] am not a very typical candidate for information such as you request. In the light of what I am told of prejudice, discrimination, and other dire manifestations arising about us, I feel peculiarly placed in that I may truthfully say I have never in my entire life felt myself to be the victim of such feeling or action. In other words, my mother seemed to see to it that her children should become completely assimilated and I should say that externally she succeeded. I feel like a Jew only in terms of my profound outrage at the Hitler barbarism and in my affection for certain Jewish friends which is perhaps the warmer because they are Jews. I like their warmth, their responsiveness, and their spontaneity of feeling. I am strongly repelled, however, by loud, conspicuous, vulgar Jews, though no less repelled by loud, conspicuous, vulgar people of any other strain. I resent the clannishness of the Jewish community which insists on labeling everything it is proud of as Jewish, though at the same time wishing to participate to the fullest extent in the life and activities of the communal world around it. I hate the way Jewish writers and year books list all Jews of accomplishments *as Jews*, and see no more legitimate reason for that than for the Episcopal or Swedish or Scotch or Unitarian (thoroughly to mix up religion and nationality) community to draw a ring around accomplished people of its persuasion and say, "Look at us!" So long as I am allowed to, I prefer to be identified nationally and politically as an American, "racially" (if necessary for purposes of legitimate inquiry) as of Jewish descent, and in religion as agnostic. This would be the exact truth. I have respect for all religions and philosophies that are tolerant and sincere. I detest untruthfulness and snobbery in regard to ancestry on either side, and give equal credit to all the constructive forces which have contributed to the present status of individuals. There was a period in my life when I was ashamed of being a Jew, but not because that feeling was forced upon me from without. My husband has totally dispelled this and now I take it for granted; I am content with, though not militantly proud of my ancestry as Jewish; my pride where it is great is in the characters and accomplishments of my forebears, not in the mere fact that they were Jews. [Her mother was a very prominent woman a generation ago.]

From all this you may gather that the only solution I can possibly see for the Jewish problem is free and universal intermarriage and assimilation. I practice it myself, with success. My children are not yet old enough for me to know whether they will amount to more than do people of unmixed extraction (if there is such a thing anywhere!) But I hope they will, because of the strong qualities of their divergent ancestry. I realize that intermarriage between everyday typical non-Jewish Americans and Jews, let us say, like either the rich Park Avenue vulgarians or the poor Bronx garment workers, is fantastically unlikely. Yet at least in the public education system, they are all equal as children, where their contacts should begin.

I had innumerable intimate friendships in Vienna in prominent families of all types from mercantile, financial, and intellectual to the nobility, and if I may say so I do not know one such family into which Jews had not successfully married. Yet where are they now! So long as Hitlers, following in the steps of all the historical Jew-persecutors, are able to upheave civilization, so long will it be useless for us to envision a universal Utopia which would consist of general relationships like those between my husband and myself, and between us and the community.

It seems hopeless now. Yet I know that I would no more go to Palestine or any other remote place designated as the Jewish homeland, than I would go to Mars. . . .

I blame the Jews for the large proportion of their own troubles—not for Hitler, but for giving the world at large so much reason to resent them, and for wanting, as a recent magazine article said, to eat their cake and have it, too, in terms of citizens' privileges with which they try to combine their Jewish racial and religious aloofness. Yet, when times are bad, they naturally cling together for comfort and refuge. . . . Actually, in a way, they are not to blame.

I suppose it is a total mess. Anyway I am an ardent American, liberal, freedom-loving democrat. I loathe anything anywhere that subordinates the rights of human individuals to the state. So I do not like the Russian "communist" idea, either. Nor the Italian Fascist one. Nor what they seem to believe in in Japan. I am opposed to all totalitarian ideas and practices. . . .

AMERICA—NATION OR CONFUSION

My people on my father's side came to this country so long ago that I do not know when exactly nor definitely from where, though undoubtedly in the early seventeenth century from England or Wales. On my mother's side, my people came from Ulster, Ireland, about 1750. On my father's side they intermarried for generations in Connecticut with Yankee stock. I think, therefore, that I come under the definition of Barrett Wendell who said an American is a person who has no definite connection with any other country, but has at the most a vague tradition of the country from which his people came.

To say this is in no way a derogation of any immigrants, but simply to say that an American is one who, to my mind, thinks with a native background and not a foreign background; and that an immigrant, no matter how worthy, how idealistic and however brilliant, cannot possibly think with a native background. Certainly I could not go to England or to France and become one with the English or one with the French. I might fight for England or France in a war, and might become a leader of the bar in England and be intensely and entirely devoted to England, but I still would not be an Englishman in the sense of one whose roots had been in that country for many generations. It is not a question of worth of character, but simply a matter of psychology. You can't get a native background by merely being willing to have one.

Now, an individual immigrant, idealistic and with sensitive perceptions, may become imbued with the native habits and traditions of a country, but, clearly, when immigration comes at a million or more a year, as it once came to this country, the vast majority will remain alien in thought for life, particularly when they tend to live in groups.

Moreover, I would say that an ordered politics and law, and even the finest fruits of literature, art and music, can grow only in a people that has common standards, that has gone through common joys and suffering, and has its roots in a common past.

Abraham Lincoln in his Second Inaugural referred to "the mystic chords of memory stretching from every battlefield and patriot grave to every living heart and hearthstone all over this broad land," which, he said, would again swell the chorus of the Union when again touched "by the better angels of our natures." The mystic chords of memory are apt to become jangling and discordant when as in many of our Eastern cities and some of our states, only thirty per cent of the people have native-born parents. It is all lopsided.

The comment has been made frequently that one of the causes of our bad crime record is that the unhomogeneous population causes quarrels, and that even jurors, where they are diverse in their origin, do not understand each other and do not have the common reactions that jurors drawn from a homogeneous community would have.

Certainly, the great literatures have sprung from people who lived a long time together, understood each other, and spoke a common language of hope and longing. The literature of the great Periclean Age in Athens sprang from a people with a deep and happy sense of a great and common past, a people who had lived long together and understood each other. The literature of the Elizabethan era and the Victorian era in England were likewise the overflowing of the thought and feeling of united peoples with common experiences and backgrounds.

The extreme diversity of our population, the fact that in many cities two-thirds of the population is foreign-born and the children of foreign-born, produces grievous disunion in our social life and creates political friction. The political campaigns of William Hale Thompson in Chicago, where he appealed to alien group after alien group on the basis of its ancestral prejudices, is a striking example of the noxious effect of racial groups in our politics. This country has been cursed for ninety years by a German vote and an Irish vote, and recently by an Italian vote and a Jewish vote and a Czech vote and a Polish vote. Our politicians play with the prejudices and feelings of racial groups in their votes on American matters. In Chicago it is customary to see that each of the prominent racial groups is recognized in the county ticket and the judicial ticket. In 1915 and 1916 there was tremendous agitation among racial groups to influence our governmental action in the World War, and after the World War there was great racial activity not only on the World Court question and the League of Nations question, but on the immigration question itself. It has commonly been remarked that Congressmen and Senators will listen more eagerly to a representative of a so-called alien group than to a native-born American. One of my friends wrote to his Senator: "I realize that my opinion and that of my friends is subject to a serious disqualification. We are all the children of native-born Americans." Many of our decisions are influenced more by the prejudices of racial groups, acting in behalf of their countries of origin, than by consideration of the intrinsic merits involved. Our diversity hampers our thought and debate at every turn.

The capacity for self-government is a rare thing. England and the United States are, to my mind, the only large countries that have shown marked and continued capacity for self-government. France, on the whole, has done admirably since 1871, but clearly before that her record was checkered.

The nations from which our recent immigration has come, however worthy they may be individually, have not shown that capacity. Germany has not shown that capacity. Nor has Italy. The Balkan States have not shown that capacity. Russia and Spain have not shown it. We have swamped our big cities with immigrants who are not imbued with the habit of self-government. It would be serious enough if all these immigrants, speaking a different language and having different traditions, came from one country only, but they have come from twenty or twenty-five different countries, old established countries, with different languages, political systems, prejudices and traditions.

I confess that when I go to certain American cities I do feel like an alien in my own land, and it is not a comfortable feeling. I heard a distinguished Harvard professor, of old Massachusetts stock, say that you could go to Fall River and never see a Yankee face. I think that if you lived in Yugoslavia, you would have some feeling of sadness if you went to your chief cities and did not see a single Yugoslavic face. This is not a mere matter of sentiment. It is on the facts and concepts underlying such sentiments that strong nations are built. The extreme diversity of our population is a danger to our democracy. It would be a danger to any democracy.

You will note that I am saying nothing about races, Anglo-Saxon or any other. The argument is not based on a claim of superiority. I base everything on the conviction that a people must live a long time together in a country before it can become in the truest sense a nation, and that if that unity of background is destroyed, the nation is in danger.

It took perhaps a thousand years after the Frankish invasions to make a nation of France, one thousand years before the new races were fused into a new French people, and yet those races were to a great extent all closely allied. It took probably one thousand years after the Anglo-Saxon invasion to make an English people, and yet the Angles, Saxons, Danes and Normans were simply branches of one stock. But we have taken in people from a score of old, long-established nations.

If we had persisted in taking mass immigration, we would in my opinion have destroyed our unity and forced us to wait many hundreds of years for a new fusion. Moreover, I think that no nation in the world would consider permitting the foreign-born and children of the foreign-born to become seventy per cent of the population, as is the case in many of our cities and some states. It is, as I say, all lopsided. Surely, the foreign-born and children of the foreign-born should never exceed, say, twenty per cent of the total population. England would not allow immigration to come in until, say, one-half the population were immigrants or the children of immigrants, and only one-half were the descendants of those who had been in England more than one generation. France would not allow it. Italy would not allow it. Yugoslavia would not allow it. No country in the world would allow it. You will pardon me for saying it, but surely one of the reasons for the lack of political advancement in the Balkans is the jangling of diverse nationalities.

Therefore, I flatly do not agree with President Roosevelt when he says that "We are all immigrants here." If a man, descended from those who came here three hundred years ago, is not an American but still an immigrant, then an Englishman whose people came to Britain with William the Conqueror or Hengist and Horsa is still an immigrant and not an Englishman; and the Frenchman whose ancestors came with Clovis is an immigrant and not a Frenchman.

As to the adjustment of the native-born American to the new foreign stock: Of course, it is inevitable that we are all affected by the language, the customs, and the political ideas of everyone in the country. It is impossible for any of us to avoid being "adjusted" in that sense. But clearly, it is not unfair to say that the immigrant who comes to a well-developed country, with established political institutions and a language and national traditions, should do most of the adjusting. If I went to England, it would be for me to adjust myself to their ways, and not for the English people to adjust themselves to me. It is true that we have taken such masses of immigration that we have made adjustment difficult. But the fact, after all, remains that the immigrant is coming to an established country with established political institutions, a literature, and strong and beautiful traditions, and that while this country can learn from other countries and from people of other countries, after all a country and its institutions cannot be made over to suit the latest immigrant if it expresses the desires of the great mass of those who came before.

I hope you will realize, as I have said time and again in my book,* that I am not obsessed by a superiority complex. I know that it is all a question of numbers. One, ten or a hundred immigrants are lovable and appealing individuals, but millions, when they come from twenty-five different nationalities and when the total of the foreign-born and children of foreign-born equal about one-third of our population and in some of our states two-thirds, are a national problem. The immigrant is as much a victim of the situation as the native-born.

EDWARD R. LEWIS
July, 1940   Winnetka, Illinois

* *America: Nation or Confusion,* published in 1928 by Harper & Brothers, now out of print, but procurable through secondhand booksellers. I do not agree with much that Mr. Lewis has to say, here or in his book, but his point of view and many of his ideas are respectworthy and deserving of serious thought.

Common Council
for American Unity

DURING my project I had a hand in the creation of the Common Council for American Unity, incorporated in the State of New York on November 22, 1939, with the following purposes:

1. To help create among the American people the unity and mutual understanding resulting from a common citizenship, a common belief in democracy and the ideals of liberty, the placing of the common good before the interests of any group, and the acceptance, in fact as well as in law, of all citizens, whatever their national or racial origins, as equal partners in American society.

2. To further an appreciation of what each group has contributed to America, to uphold the freedom to be different, and to encourage the growth of an American culture which will be truly representative of all the elements that make up the American people.

3. To overcome intolerance and discrimination because of foreign birth or descent, race or nationality.

4. To help the foreign born and their children solve their special problems of adjustment, know and value their particular cultural heritage, and share fully and constructively in American life.

As it develops its financial and other energies, the Common Council will aim to achieve its purposes with the following program, as published in tentative outline on June 12, 1940:

1. Assembling as complete information as possible about our different racial and nationality groups, their backgrounds, contributions, problems, and activities and about interracial and intercultural problems in general, including among other things:
   a. Stimulation of theses and research in this field by students in social science departments of our universities and others.
   b. Co-operation with foreign-language groups and especially with foreign-language historical societies.
   c. Establishment of archives for original manuscripts, letters, scrapbooks, newspapers or other records of historical importance.
   d. Field studies.
2. Dissemination of such information and material through such means as:
   a. Magazine devoted to these subjects and problems.
   b. Stimulation of articles in other publications.
   c. Information service to English-language press.
   d. Center of information for answering individual inquiries.

  e. Publication of suitable pamphlets.

  f. Exhibits of what each group has contributed to American life and culture.

  g. Bookshop for distribution of books and materials on these subjects.

3. Speakers' Bureau.

4. Educational work on radio.

5. Work with schools.

  a. Publication of pamphlets, bibliographies and other material suitable for school use.

  b. Working out programs and suggestions for schools and teachers.

6. Work in motion-picture field.

7. Close co-operation with appropriate government departments and officials.

8. Legislative work against unfair and discriminatory proposals and for constructive measures, through appearance at Congressional hearings, education of public opinion, public meetings, etc.

9. Study of interracial intolerance in English and foreign-language press, on platform and radio, and reply thereto by such means as:

  a. Press releases.

  b. Getting people to answer—by way of "instant rejoinder"—attacks and misinformation in local editorials, letters to the editor, etc.

  c. Arranging for radio time to answer attacks on radio.

10. Development of local discussion groups consisting of persons of various backgrounds.

11. Educational releases to foreign-language press.

12. Educational work on foreign-language radio hours.

13. Work with immigrant organizations to promote education, suitable programs for second generation, community contacts, etc., through such means as personal conferences, attending conventions, newsletters, development of discussion programs for local branches, etc.

14. Co-operation with social, educational, patriotic and other agencies, working, or interested in this field.

  a. Technical information on naturalization, immigration, and other questions necessary in advising foreign born.

  b. Program and personnel information.

15. Annual national conference, for common counsel, co-operation and exchange of ideas, of foreign-language editors and organization officials, and all others working in this field or interested in ethnic and interracial problems.

16. Personal service bureau, to advise and assist the foreign born, particularly those not within reach of competent local agencies, in solving their individual immigration, naturalization and adjustment problems.

17. Publication of naturalization pamphlet, handbook for newcomers and other literature designed to facilitate citizenship and adjustment.

18. Encouragement of the folk arts and other potential contributions and the promotion of opportunities for instruction and participation.

19. Essay and other contests, especially for young people of foreign parentage,

designed to stimulate interest in and appreciation of their particular cultural heritage.

20. A further revision of American history textbooks to give adequate recognition and space to the newer strains in our population.

21. An ethnic and racial encyclopedia or handbook of the American people.

As I write, the board of directors of the Common Council includes: Nicholas Kelley, chairman; John Palmer Gavit and Will Irwin, vice-chairmen; Eliot D. Pratt, treasurer; Louis Adamic, Sigurd J. Arnesen, Mrs. George Backer, Edward Fisher Brown, Allen T. Burns, Fred M. Butzel, Mrs. Thomas Capek, Elizabeth Eastman, Sylvan Gotshal, James L. Houghteling, Mrs. James A. Kennedy, Frank J. Lausche, Read Lewis, Mrs. Jacob A. Riis, Josephine Roche, Mrs. DeWitt Stetten, Robert K. Straus, Ida M. Tarbell, Graham R. Taylor, and M. F. Wegrzynek.

In September, 1940, the Common Council began to publish a magazine, *Common Ground*—Louis Adamic, editor; Miss M. Margaret Anderson, managing editor; Frank Mlakar, assistant. The partial contents of the first issue is: "Head and Hands Working Together" by Mary Ellen Chase, dealing with old-stock American traditions; "Lost and Found" by William Reilly, an autobiographical-philosophical essay; "American Immigrants" by Prof. A. M. Schlesinger of Harvard; "Letter to Mother," a poem by John Ciardi; "When America Was the Land of Canaan" by Prof. George M. Stephenson of the University of Minnesota, a study of Swedish "America letters"; "The Story is Yet to be Told" by Michael De Capite, a critical essay on books about immigrants and the second generation; "On Becoming American" by Lola Kinel; an article on Shevchenko, the Ukrainian poet, by Van Wyck Brooks; a study on "race" concepts and superstitions by George S. Schuyler; "On Democracy and Defense" by Robert M. Hutchins; book reviews by Oswald Garrison Villard, Margaret Anderson, B. E. Bettinger, Frank Mlakar, and others; material of interest to organizations working in the racial-cultural field and to school teachers; and a suggestion how to turn the war-created crisis in the United States into an opportunity, including how to organize groups mentioned in the final chapter in this book, just preceding "The Project" section. The first issue is 100 pages, about 62,000 words. Sample copies 50¢; a year's subscription $2.

Those interested in additional information about the Common Council for American Unity may write to its executive director, Read Lewis, 222 Fourth Avenue, New York.

Notes and
Acknowledgments

IN *From Many Lands* I found it impossible to cover every element in the population of the United States. In deciding to use the materials I include in preference to others I was influenced by considerations of timeliness, by whether or not books or magazine articles about a group have appeared in recent years, and by the fact that during the first eighteen months of my project some of the groups were more co-operative in the matter of replying to my broadside than others, thereby making my task pertaining to them easier.

I wish to emphasize that *From Many Lands* is the first of a series of *independent* books. The groups neglected in this initial volume will be covered in those still to come. This does not mean that the groups included in the present book will be omitted entirely in the forthcoming books.

Only to list the names of people who have so far been helpful in my project as a whole would require a dozen or more pages. I am grateful to them all, and hope their active interest in this work-in-progress will continue.

For their special aid in the assembling of material for *From Many Lands* I want to thank the several persons who appear under real or disguised names in the various stories; they gave much of their time to making the respective chapters as accurate and authentic as it was humanly possible to make them.

To Frank Mlakar, Margaret Anderson, and Gertrude Frey I owe my gratitude for their help during the writing and proofreading of the book.

Without the Carnegie grant-in-aid I could not have begun my project and brought it thus far. To Frederick Keppel, president of the Corporation, and Charles Dollard, his assistant in charge of personal grants, I wish to express my deepest appreciation for their consistent interest and encouragement.

L. A.

Set in Linotype Granjon
Format by A. W. Rushmore
Manufactured by the Haddon Craftsmen
Published by HARPER & BROTHERS
New York and London

11113

Adamic

From many lands